15



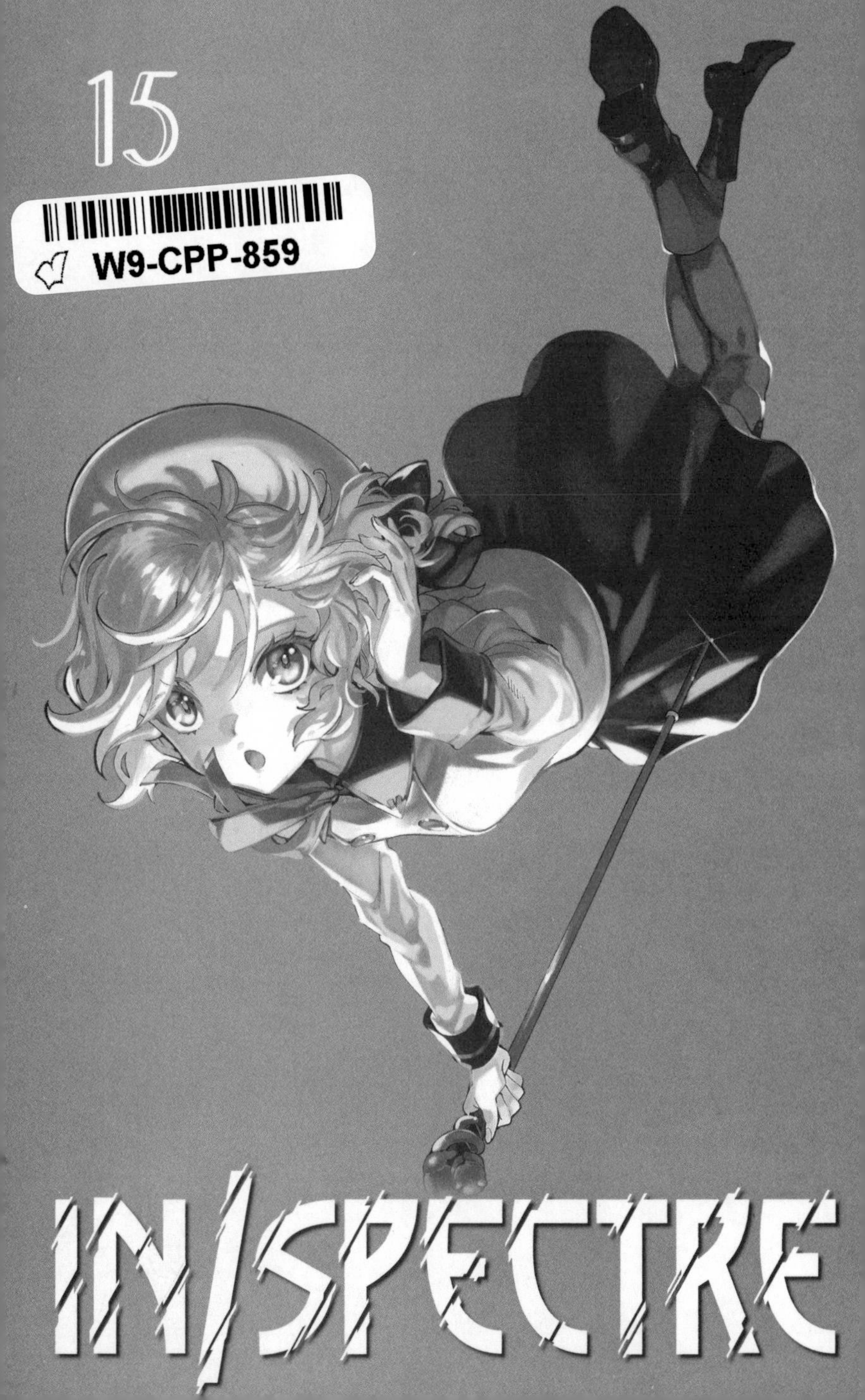

# IN/SPECTRE

## CONTENTS

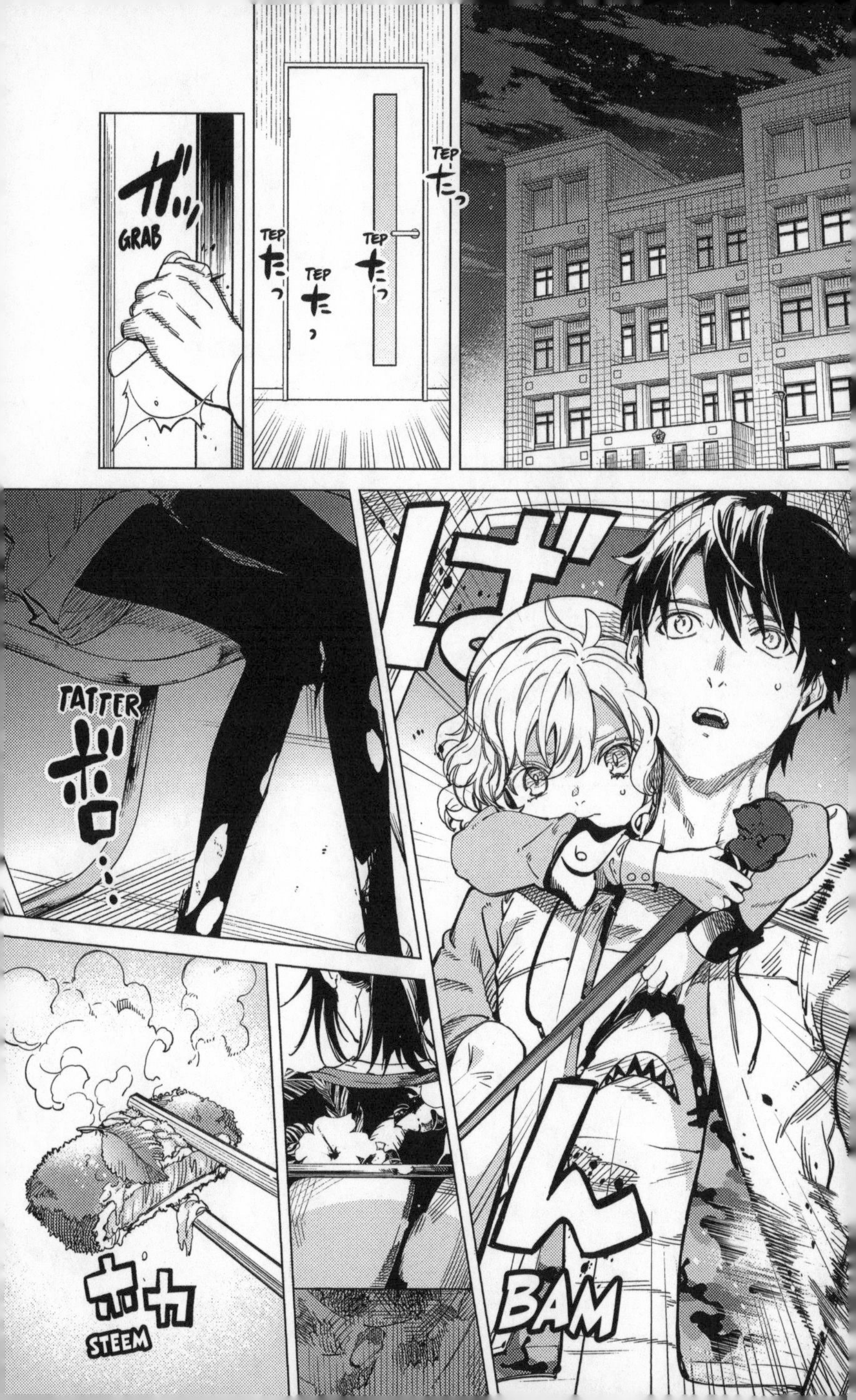
TEP
たっ
TEP
たっ
TEP
たっ
TEP
たっ
ガッ
GRAB
ばん
BAM
TATTER
ボロ…
ホカ
STEEM

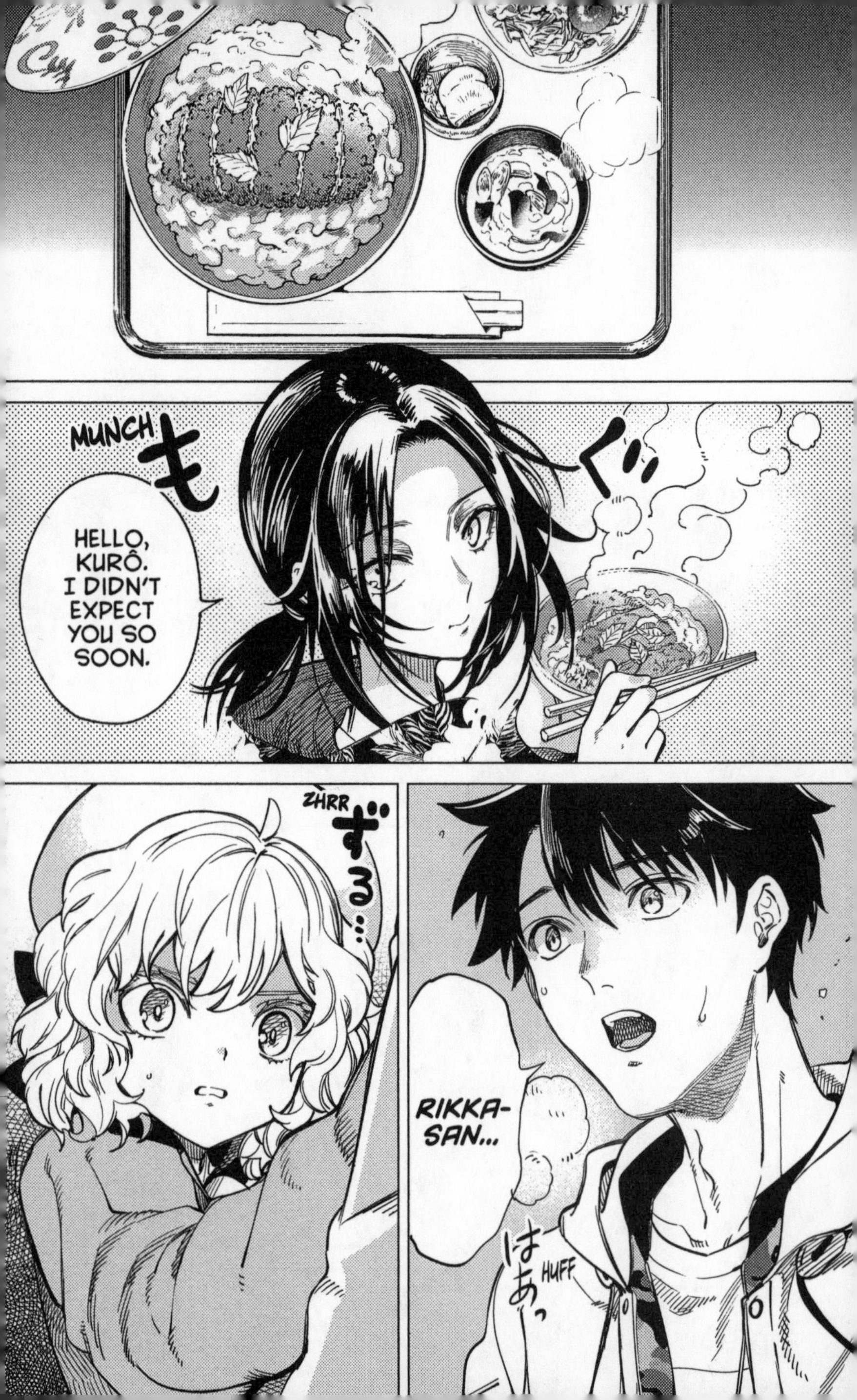
MUNCH
も
ぐ
HELLO, KURÔ. I DIDN'T EXPECT YOU SO SOON.
RIKKA-SAN...
はあっ
HUFF
ZHRR
ずる...

CHAPTER 40: "THE RETALIATION AND DEFEAT OF KOTOKO IWANAGA PART 2"

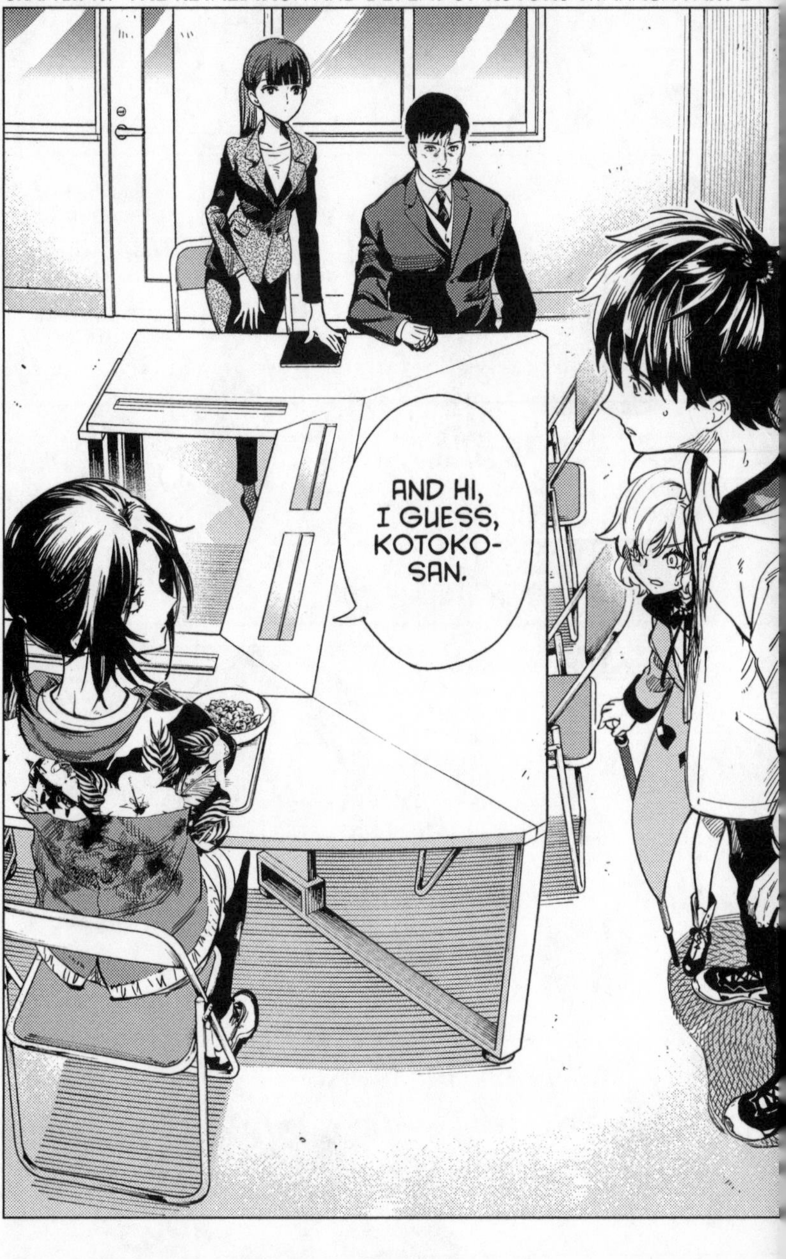
AND HI, I GUESS, KOTOKO-SAN.

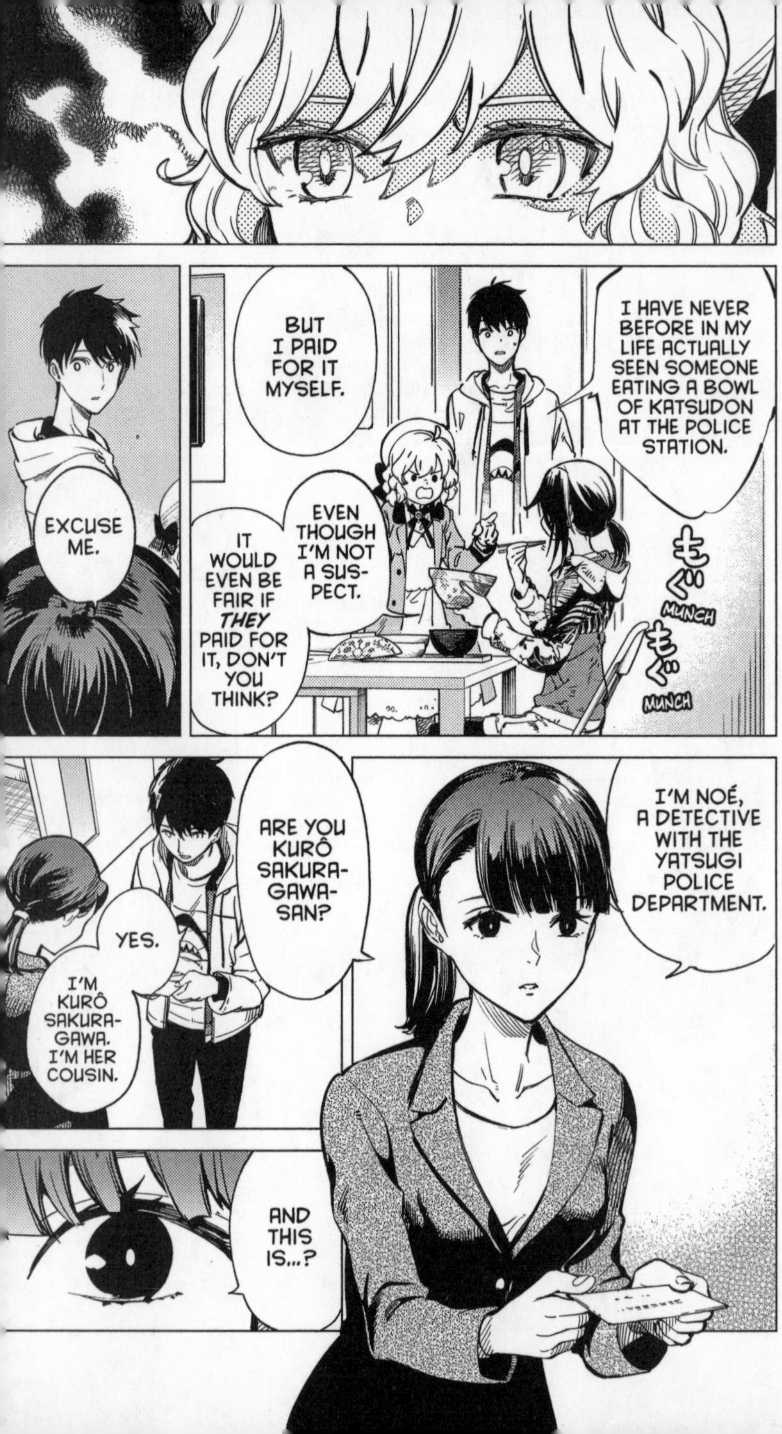
I HAVE NEVER BEFORE IN MY LIFE ACTUALLY SEEN SOMEONE EATING A BOWL OF KATSUDON AT THE POLICE STATION.
BUT I PAID FOR IT MYSELF.
EVEN THOUGH I'M NOT A SUS-PECT.
IT WOULD EVEN BE FAIR IF *THEY* PAID FOR IT, DON'T YOU THINK?
もぐ
MUNCH
もぐ
MUNCH
EXCUSE ME.
I'M NOÉ, A DETECTIVE WITH THE YATSUGI POLICE DEPARTMENT.
ARE YOU KURÔ SAKURA-GAWA-SAN?
YES.
I'M KURÔ SAKURA-GAWA. I'M HER COUSIN.
AND THIS IS...?

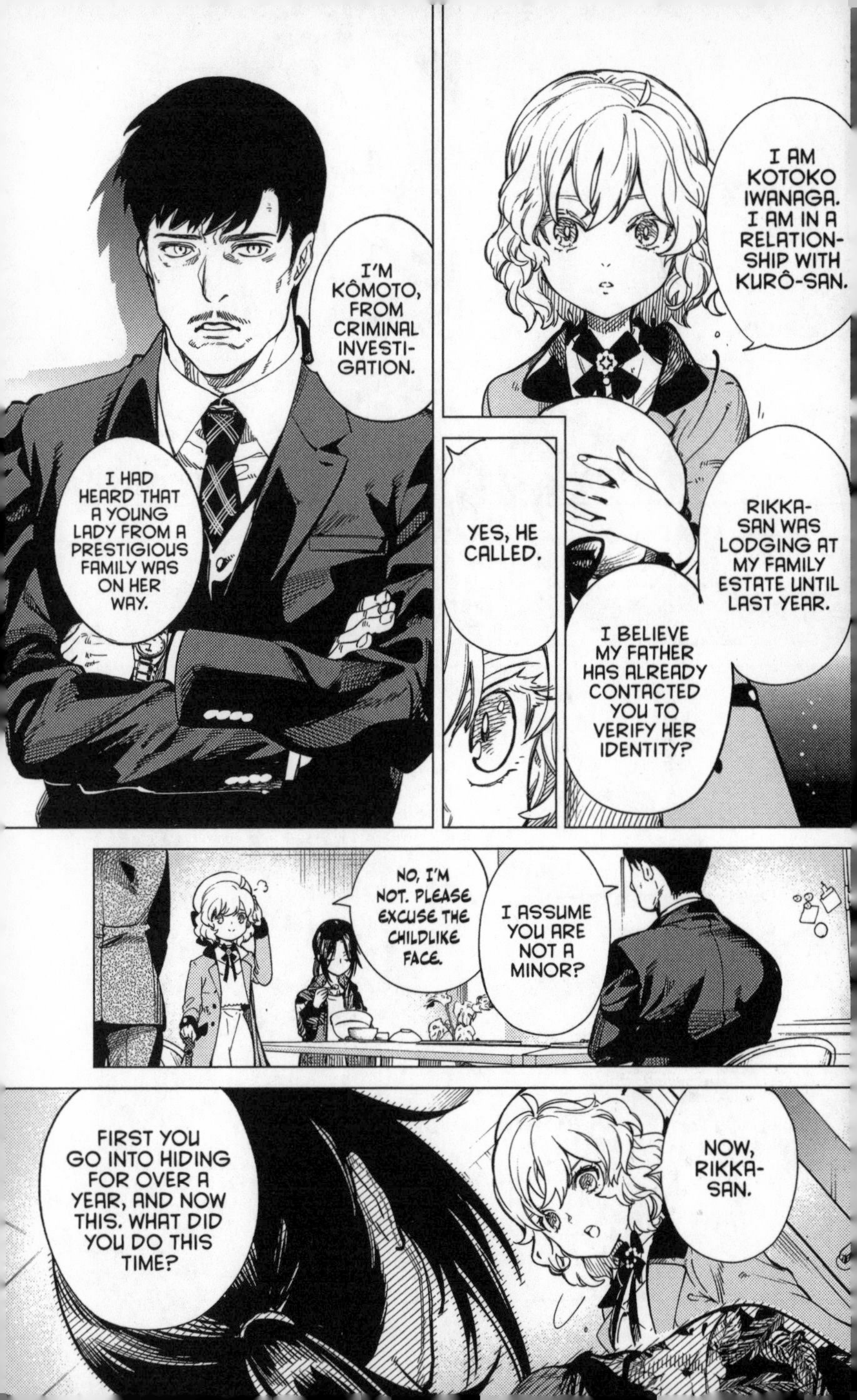
I AM KOTOKO IWANAGA. I AM IN A RELATIONSHIP WITH KURÔ-SAN.
RIKKA-SAN WAS LODGING AT MY FAMILY ESTATE UNTIL LAST YEAR.
I BELIEVE MY FATHER HAS ALREADY CONTACTED YOU TO VERIFY HER IDENTITY?
YES, HE CALLED.
I'M KÔMOTO, FROM CRIMINAL INVESTIGATION.
I HAD HEARD THAT A YOUNG LADY FROM A PRESTIGIOUS FAMILY WAS ON HER WAY.
I ASSUME YOU ARE NOT A MINOR?
NO, I'M NOT. PLEASE EXCUSE THE CHILDLIKE FACE.
NOW, RIKKA-SAN.
FIRST YOU GO INTO HIDING FOR OVER A YEAR, AND NOW THIS. WHAT DID YOU DO THIS TIME?

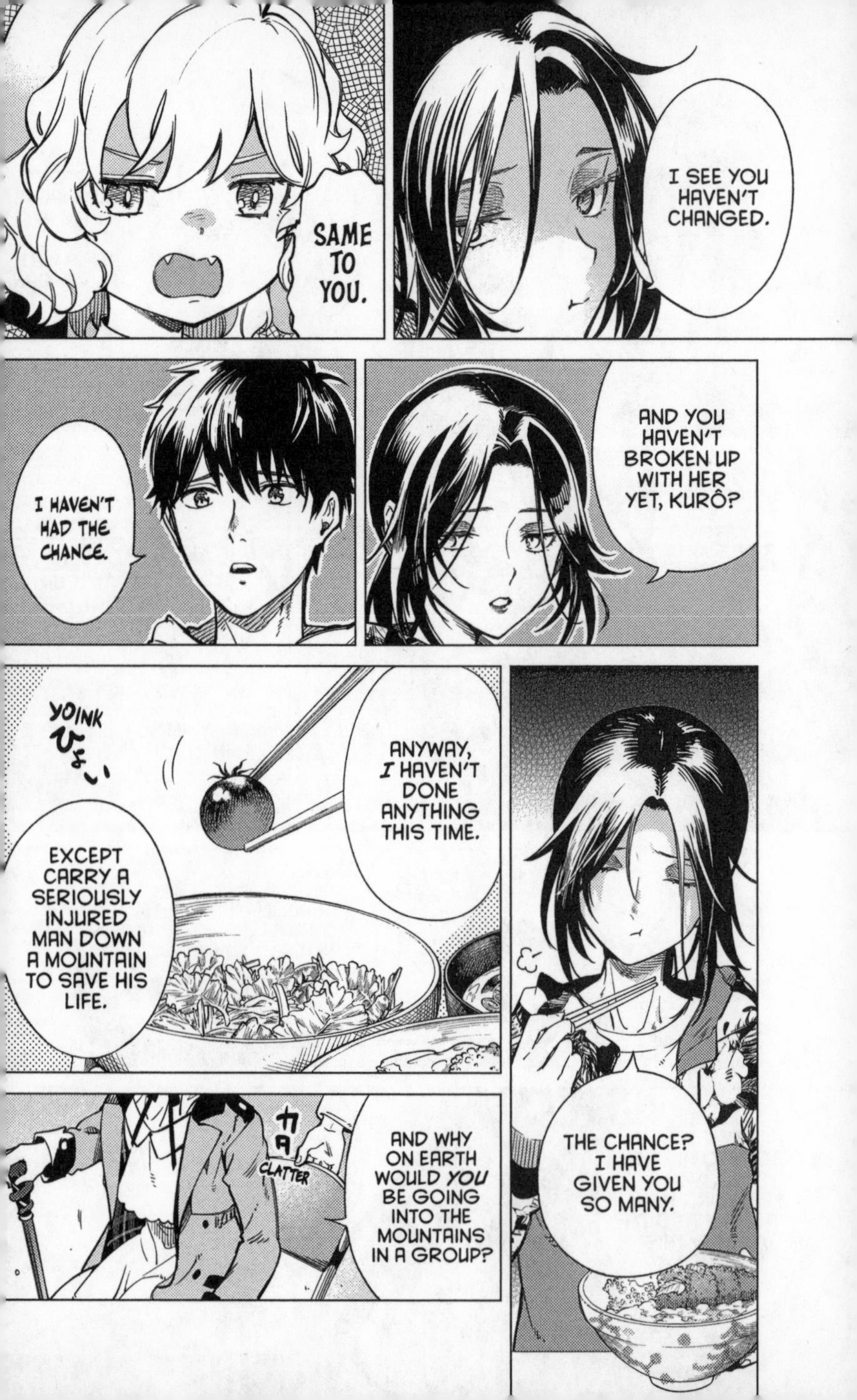
I SEE YOU HAVEN'T CHANGED.
SAME TO YOU.
AND YOU HAVEN'T BROKEN UP WITH HER YET, KURÔ?
I HAVEN'T HAD THE CHANCE.
THE CHANCE? I HAVE GIVEN YOU SO MANY.
ANYWAY, *I* HAVEN'T DONE ANYTHING THIS TIME.
YOINK
ひょい
EXCEPT CARRY A SERIOUSLY INJURED MAN DOWN A MOUNTAIN TO SAVE HIS LIFE.
AND WHY ON EARTH WOULD *YOU* BE GOING INTO THE MOUNTAINS IN A GROUP?
カタ
CLATTER

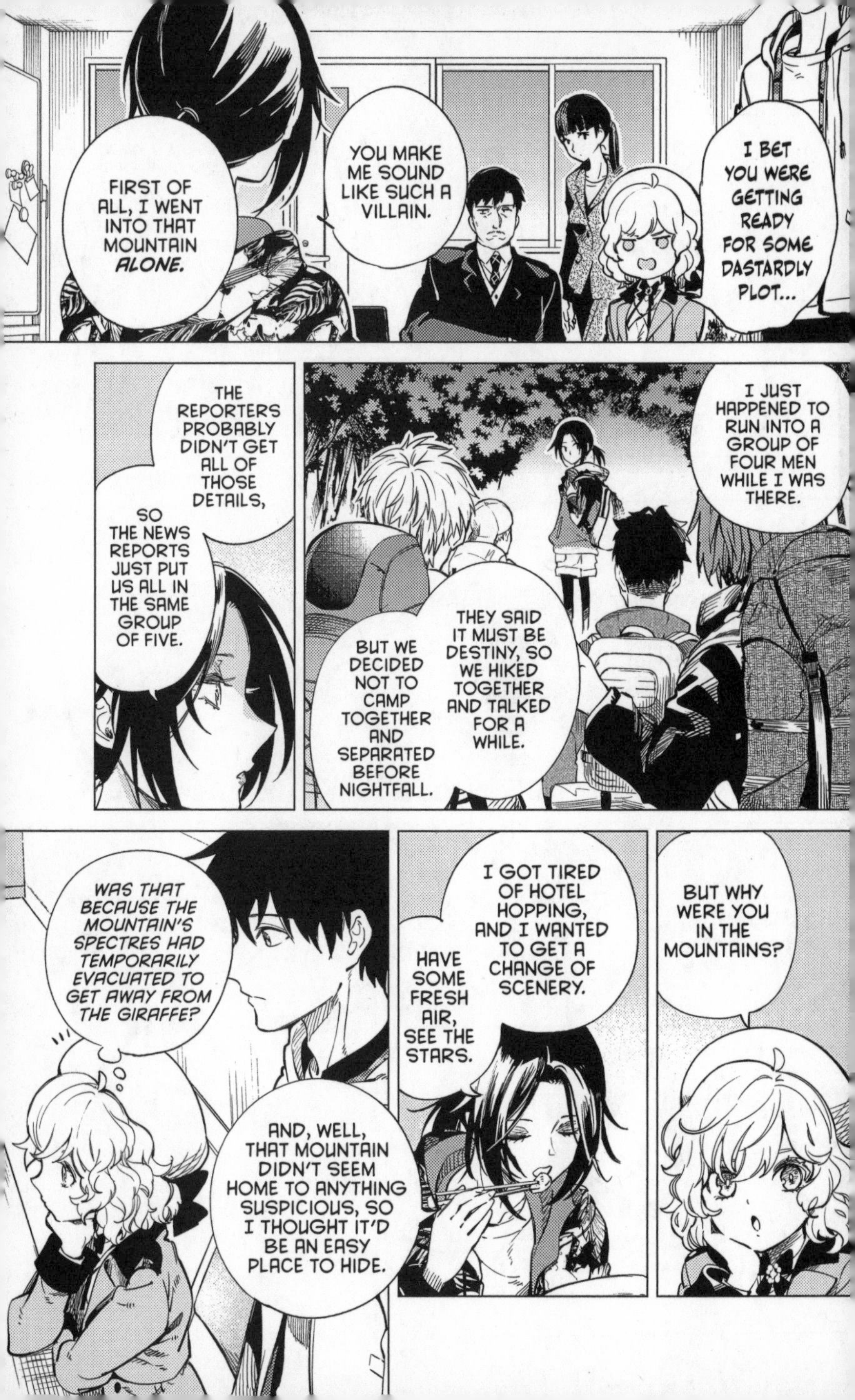
I BET YOU WERE GETTING READY FOR SOME DASTARDLY PLOT...
YOU MAKE ME SOUND LIKE SUCH A VILLAIN.
FIRST OF ALL, I WENT INTO THAT MOUNTAIN *ALONE.*
I JUST HAPPENED TO RUN INTO A GROUP OF FOUR MEN WHILE I WAS THERE.
THEY SAID IT MUST BE DESTINY, SO WE HIKED TOGETHER AND TALKED FOR A WHILE.
BUT WE DECIDED NOT TO CAMP TOGETHER AND SEPARATED BEFORE NIGHTFALL.
THE REPORTERS PROBABLY DIDN'T GET ALL OF THOSE DETAILS,
SO THE NEWS REPORTS JUST PUT US ALL IN THE SAME GROUP OF FIVE.
BUT WHY WERE YOU IN THE MOUNTAINS?
I GOT TIRED OF HOTEL HOPPING, AND I WANTED TO GET A CHANGE OF SCENERY.
HAVE SOME FRESH AIR, SEE THE STARS.
AND, WELL, THAT MOUNTAIN DIDN'T SEEM HOME TO ANYTHING SUSPICIOUS, SO I THOUGHT IT'D BE AN EASY PLACE TO HIDE.
*WAS THAT BECAUSE THE MOUNTAIN'S SPECTRES HAD TEMPORARILY EVACUATED TO GET AWAY FROM THE GIRAFFE?*

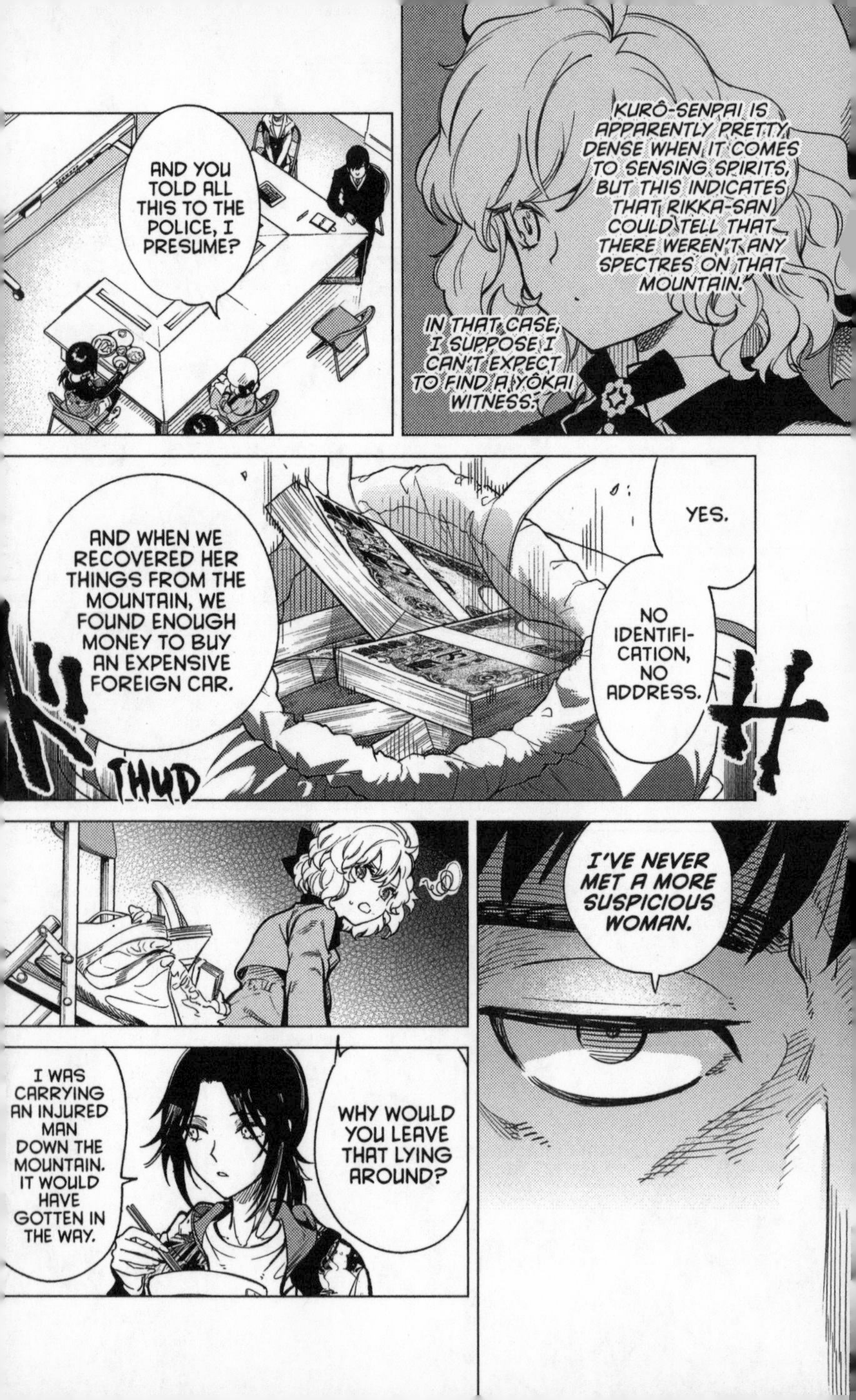

KURÔ-SENPAI IS APPARENTLY PRETTY DENSE WHEN IT COMES TO SENSING SPIRITS, BUT THIS INDICATES THAT RIKKA-SAN COULD TELL THAT THERE WEREN'T ANY SPECTRES ON THAT MOUNTAIN.
IN THAT CASE, I SUPPOSE I CAN'T EXPECT TO FIND A YÔKAI WITNESS.
AND YOU TOLD ALL THIS TO THE POLICE, I PRESUME?
YES.
NO IDENTIFICATION, NO ADDRESS.
AND WHEN WE RECOVERED HER THINGS FROM THE MOUNTAIN, WE FOUND ENOUGH MONEY TO BUY AN EXPENSIVE FOREIGN CAR.
THUD
I'VE NEVER MET A MORE SUSPICIOUS WOMAN.
WHY WOULD YOU LEAVE THAT LYING AROUND?
I WAS CARRYING AN INJURED MAN DOWN THE MOUNTAIN. IT WOULD HAVE GOTTEN IN THE WAY.

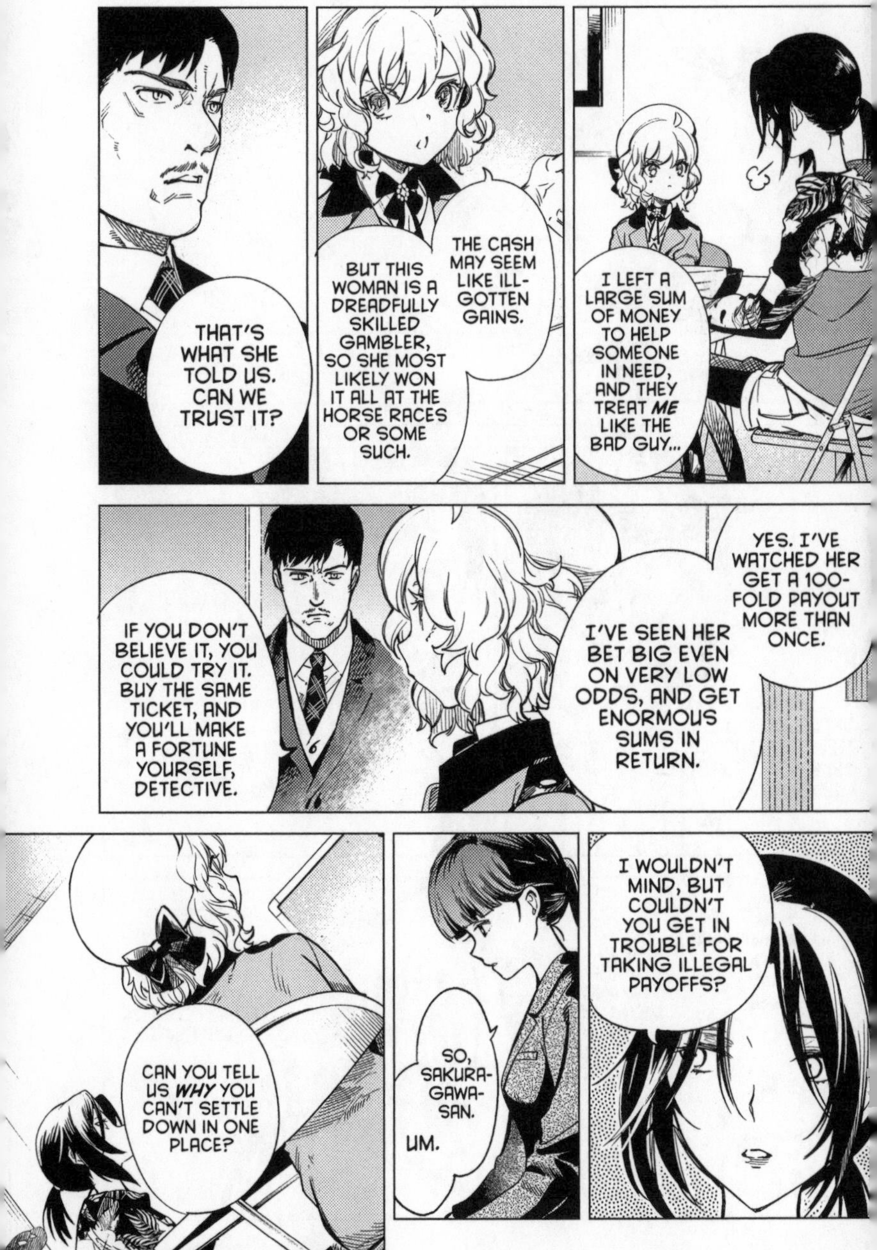
I LEFT A LARGE SUM OF MONEY TO HELP SOMEONE IN NEED, AND THEY TREAT *ME* LIKE THE BAD GUY...
THE CASH MAY SEEM LIKE ILL-GOTTEN GAINS.
BUT THIS WOMAN IS A DREADFULLY SKILLED GAMBLER, SO SHE MOST LIKELY WON IT ALL AT THE HORSE RACES OR SOME SUCH.
THAT'S WHAT SHE TOLD US. CAN WE TRUST IT?
YES. I'VE WATCHED HER GET A 100-FOLD PAYOUT MORE THAN ONCE.
I'VE SEEN HER BET BIG EVEN ON VERY LOW ODDS, AND GET ENORMOUS SUMS IN RETURN.
IF YOU DON'T BELIEVE IT, YOU COULD TRY IT. BUY THE SAME TICKET, AND YOU'LL MAKE A FORTUNE YOURSELF, DETECTIVE.
I WOULDN'T MIND, BUT COULDN'T YOU GET IN TROUBLE FOR TAKING ILLEGAL PAYOFFS?
SO, SAKURA-GAWA-SAN.
UM.
CAN YOU TELL US *WHY* YOU CAN'T SETTLE DOWN IN ONE PLACE?

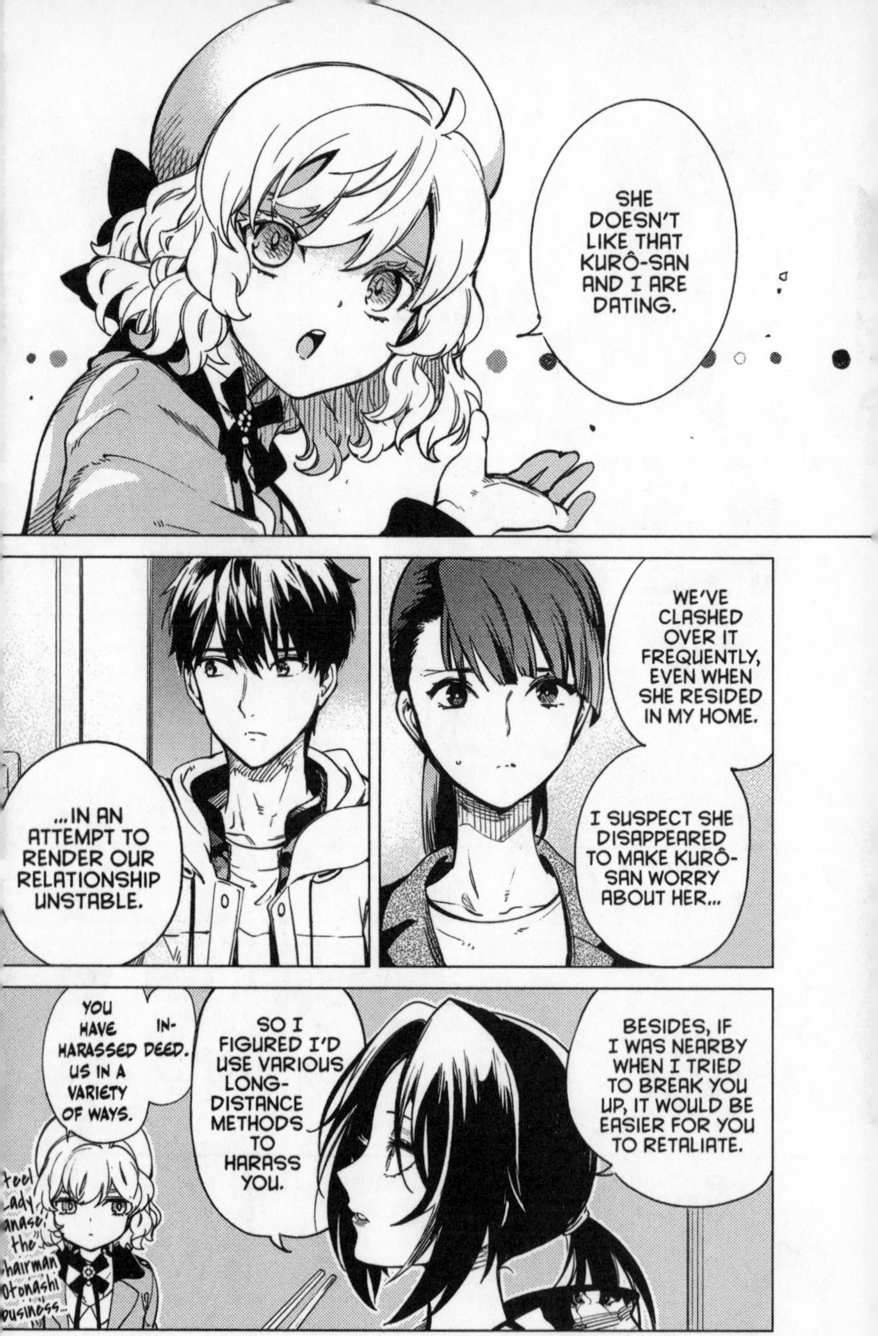
SHE DOESN'T LIKE THAT KURÔ-SAN AND I ARE DATING.
WE'VE CLASHED OVER IT FREQUENTLY, EVEN WHEN SHE RESIDED IN MY HOME.
I SUSPECT SHE DISAPPEARED TO MAKE KURÔ-SAN WORRY ABOUT HER...
...IN AN ATTEMPT TO RENDER OUR RELATIONSHIP UNSTABLE.
BESIDES, IF I WAS NEARBY WHEN I TRIED TO BREAK YOU UP, IT WOULD BE EASIER FOR YOU TO RETALIATE.
SO I FIGURED I'D USE VARIOUS LONG-DISTANCE METHODS TO HARASS YOU.
IN-DEED.
YOU HAVE HARASSED US IN A VARIETY OF WAYS.
teel Lady anase, the" hairman Otonashi usiness...

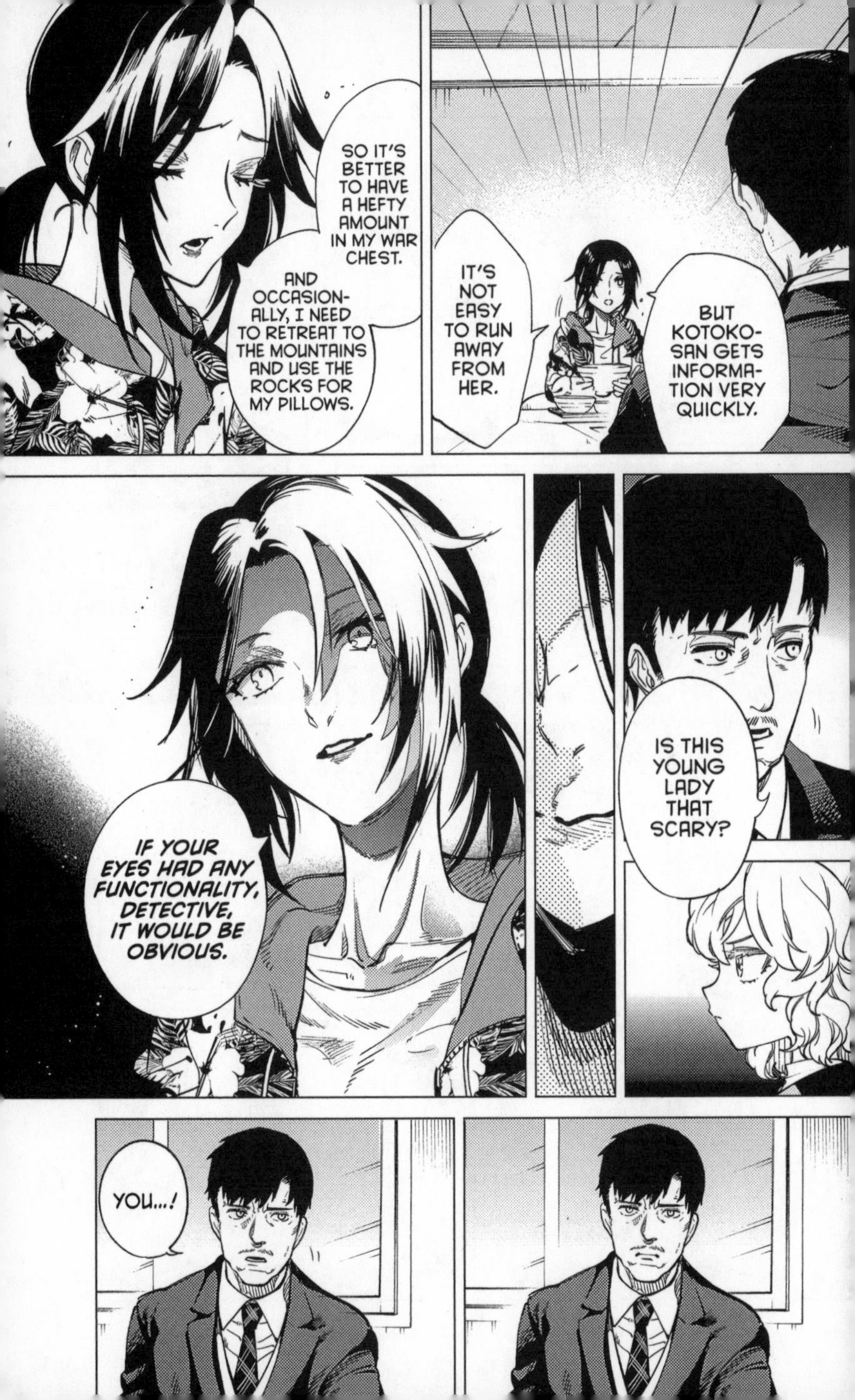
BUT KOTOKO-SAN GETS INFORMATION VERY QUICKLY.
IT'S NOT EASY TO RUN AWAY FROM HER.
SO IT'S BETTER TO HAVE A HEFTY AMOUNT IN MY WAR CHEST.
AND OCCASION-ALLY, I NEED TO RETREAT TO THE MOUNTAINS AND USE THE ROCKS FOR MY PILLOWS.
IS THIS YOUNG LADY THAT SCARY?
IF YOUR EYES HAD ANY FUNCTIONALITY, DETECTIVE, IT WOULD BE OBVIOUS.
YOU...!

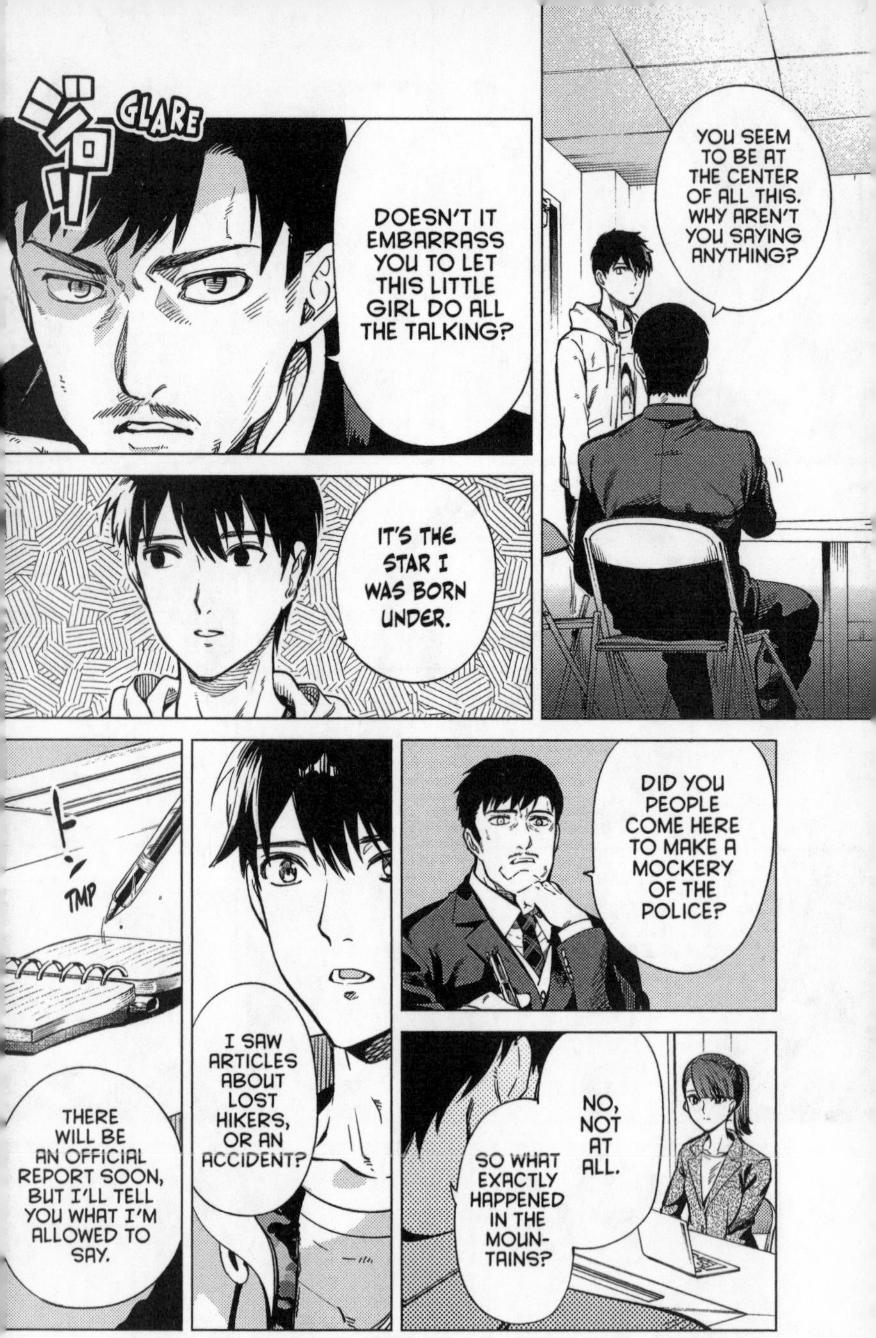
YOU SEEM TO BE AT THE CENTER OF ALL THIS. WHY AREN'T YOU SAYING ANYTHING?
GLARE
DOESN'T IT EMBARRASS YOU TO LET THIS LITTLE GIRL DO ALL THE TALKING?
IT'S THE STAR I WAS BORN UNDER.
DID YOU PEOPLE COME HERE TO MAKE A MOCKERY OF THE POLICE?
NO, NOT AT ALL.
SO WHAT EXACTLY HAPPENED IN THE MOUN-TAINS?
I SAW ARTICLES ABOUT LOST HIKERS, OR AN ACCIDENT?
TMP
THERE WILL BE AN OFFICIAL REPORT SOON, BUT I'LL TELL YOU WHAT I'M ALLOWED TO SAY.

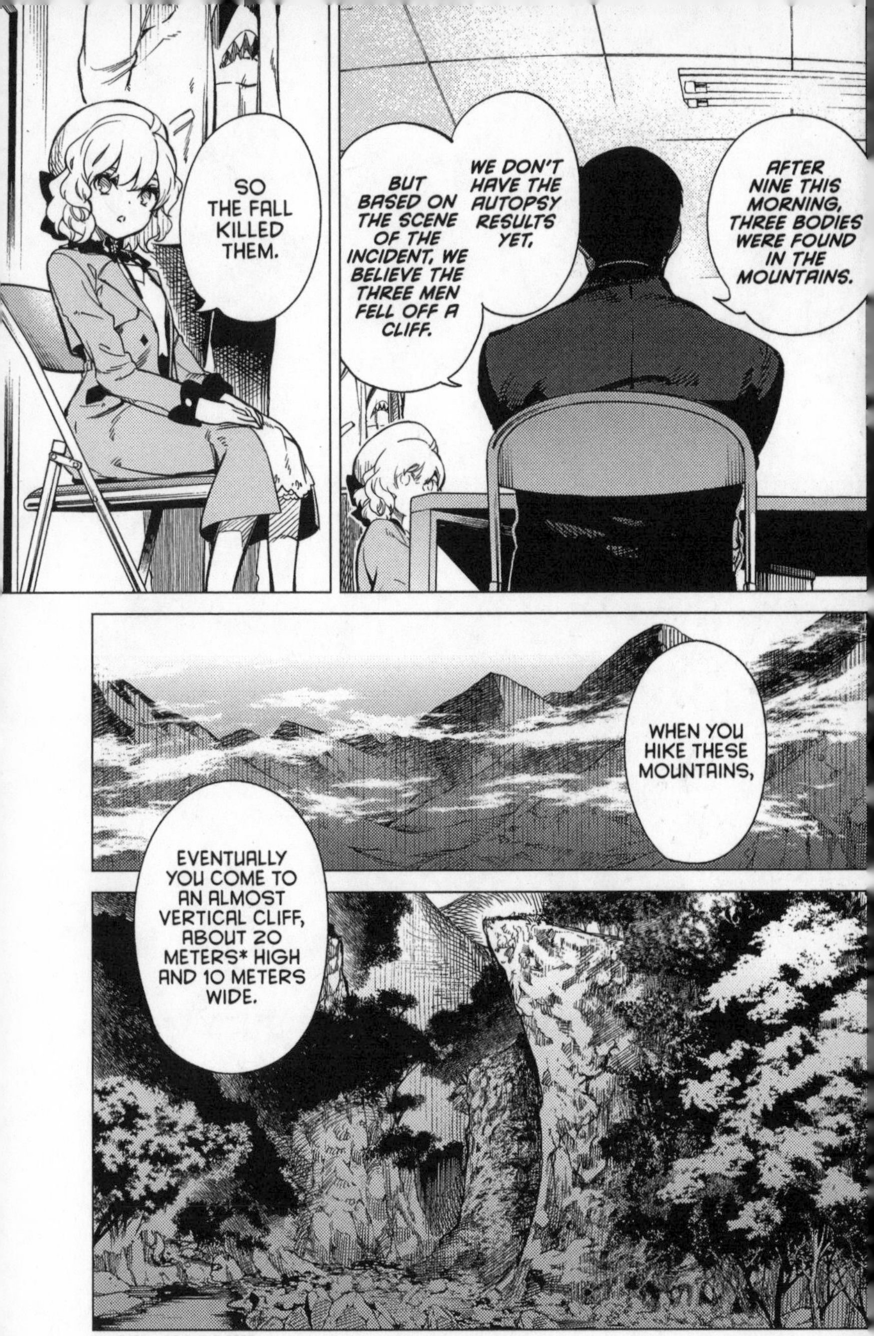
AFTER NINE THIS MORNING, THREE BODIES WERE FOUND IN THE MOUNTAINS.
WE DON'T HAVE THE AUTOPSY RESULTS YET,
BUT BASED ON THE SCENE OF THE INCIDENT, WE BELIEVE THE THREE MEN FELL OFF A CLIFF.
SO THE FALL KILLED THEM.
WHEN YOU HIKE THESE MOUNTAINS,
EVENTUALLY YOU COME TO AN ALMOST VERTICAL CLIFF, ABOUT 20 METERS* HIGH AND 10 METERS WIDE.

*1 METER = ABOUT 3 FEET.

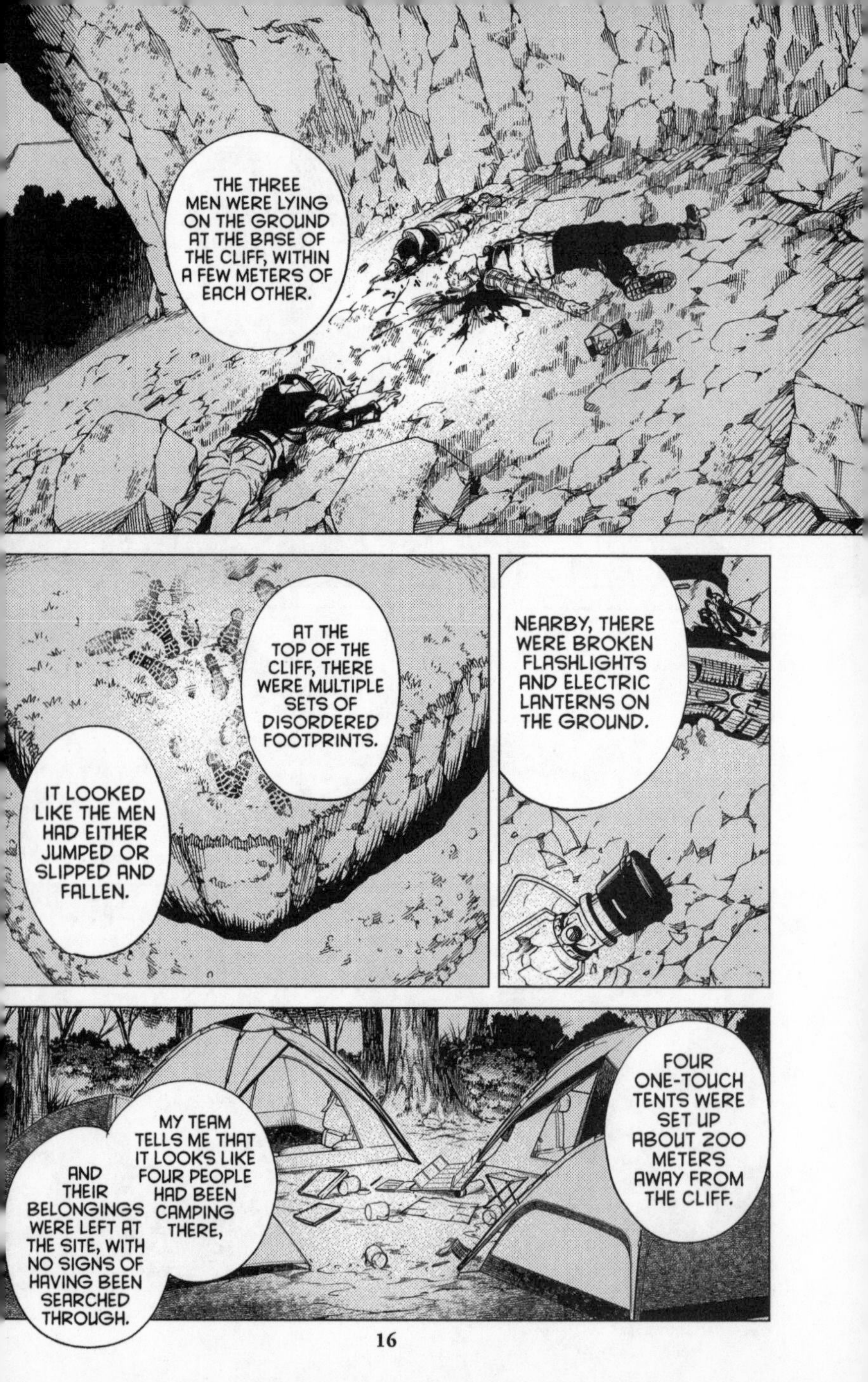
THE THREE MEN WERE LYING ON THE GROUND AT THE BASE OF THE CLIFF, WITHIN A FEW METERS OF EACH OTHER.
NEARBY, THERE WERE BROKEN FLASHLIGHTS AND ELECTRIC LANTERNS ON THE GROUND.
AT THE TOP OF THE CLIFF, THERE WERE MULTIPLE SETS OF DISORDERED FOOTPRINTS.
IT LOOKED LIKE THE MEN HAD EITHER JUMPED OR SLIPPED AND FALLEN.
FOUR ONE-TOUCH TENTS WERE SET UP ABOUT 200 METERS AWAY FROM THE CLIFF.
MY TEAM TELLS ME THAT IT LOOKS LIKE FOUR PEOPLE HAD BEEN CAMPING THERE,
AND THEIR BELONGINGS WERE LEFT AT THE SITE, WITH NO SIGNS OF HAVING BEEN SEARCHED THROUGH.

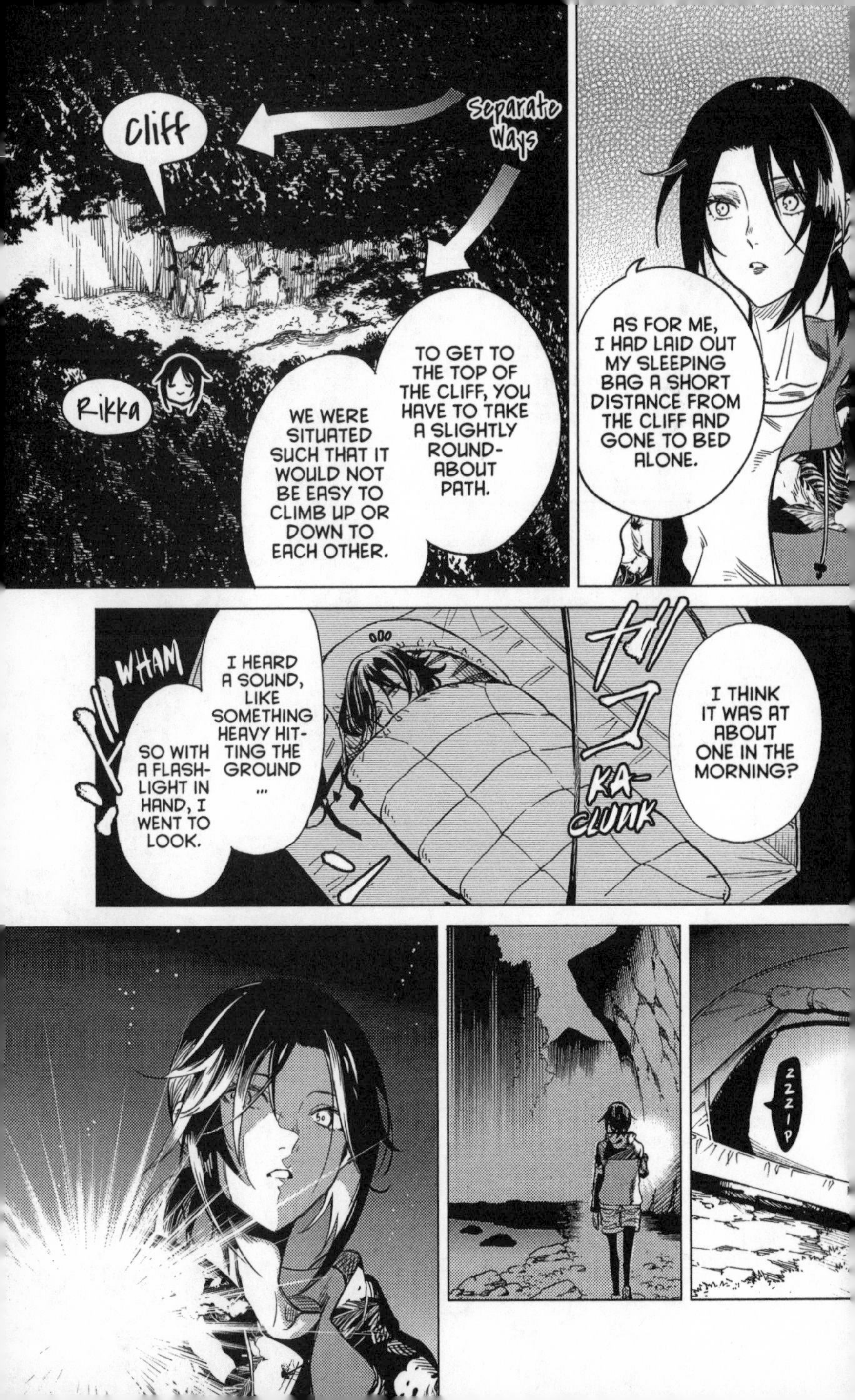
AS FOR ME, I HAD LAID OUT MY SLEEPING BAG A SHORT DISTANCE FROM THE CLIFF AND GONE TO BED ALONE.
Separate Ways
Cliff
TO GET TO THE TOP OF THE CLIFF, YOU HAVE TO TAKE A SLIGHTLY ROUND-ABOUT PATH.
WE WERE SITUATED SUCH THAT IT WOULD NOT BE EASY TO CLIMB UP OR DOWN TO EACH OTHER.
Rikka
I THINK IT WAS AT ABOUT ONE IN THE MORNING?
KA-CLUNK
I HEARD A SOUND, LIKE SOMETHING HEAVY HIT-TING THE GROUND ...
SO WITH A FLASH-LIGHT IN HAND, I WENT TO LOOK.
WHAM
ZZZIP

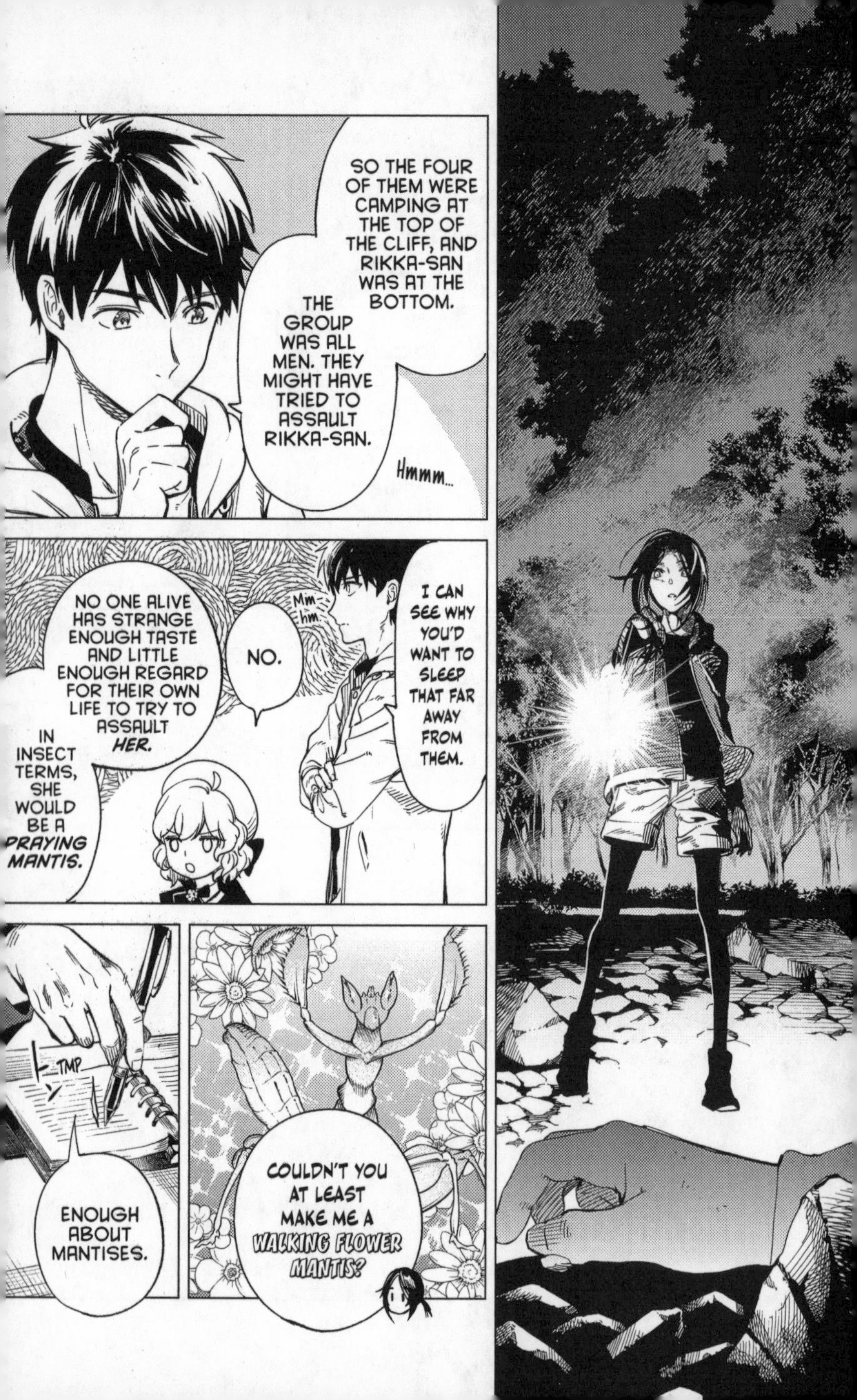
SO THE FOUR OF THEM WERE CAMPING AT THE TOP OF THE CLIFF, AND RIKKA-SAN WAS AT THE BOTTOM.
THE GROUP WAS ALL MEN. THEY MIGHT HAVE TRIED TO ASSAULT RIKKA-SAN.
Hmmm...
I CAN SEE WHY YOU'D WANT TO SLEEP THAT FAR AWAY FROM THEM.
Mm hm
NO.
NO ONE ALIVE HAS STRANGE ENOUGH TASTE AND LITTLE ENOUGH REGARD FOR THEIR OWN LIFE TO TRY TO ASSAULT *HER*.
IN INSECT TERMS, SHE WOULD BE A *PRAYING MANTIS*.
COULDN'T YOU AT LEAST MAKE ME A WALKING FLOWER MANTIS?
TMP
ENOUGH ABOUT MANTISES.

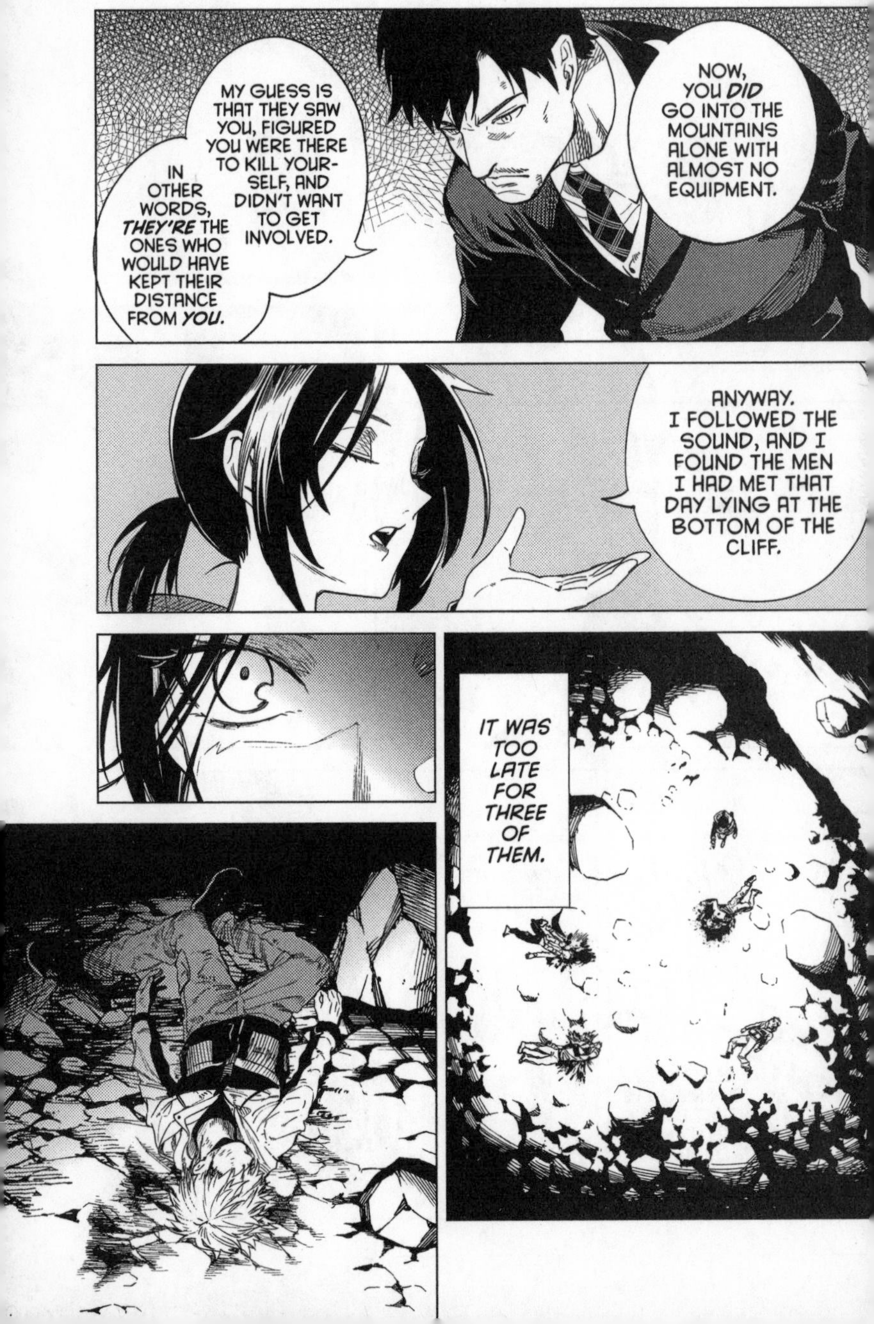
NOW, YOU *DID* GO INTO THE MOUNTAINS ALONE WITH ALMOST NO EQUIPMENT.
MY GUESS IS THAT THEY SAW YOU, FIGURED YOU WERE THERE TO KILL YOUR-SELF, AND DIDN'T WANT TO GET INVOLVED.
IN OTHER WORDS, *THEY'RE* THE ONES WHO WOULD HAVE KEPT THEIR DISTANCE FROM *YOU*.
ANYWAY. I FOLLOWED THE SOUND, AND I FOUND THE MEN I HAD MET THAT DAY LYING AT THE BOTTOM OF THE CLIFF.
IT WAS TOO LATE FOR THREE OF THEM.

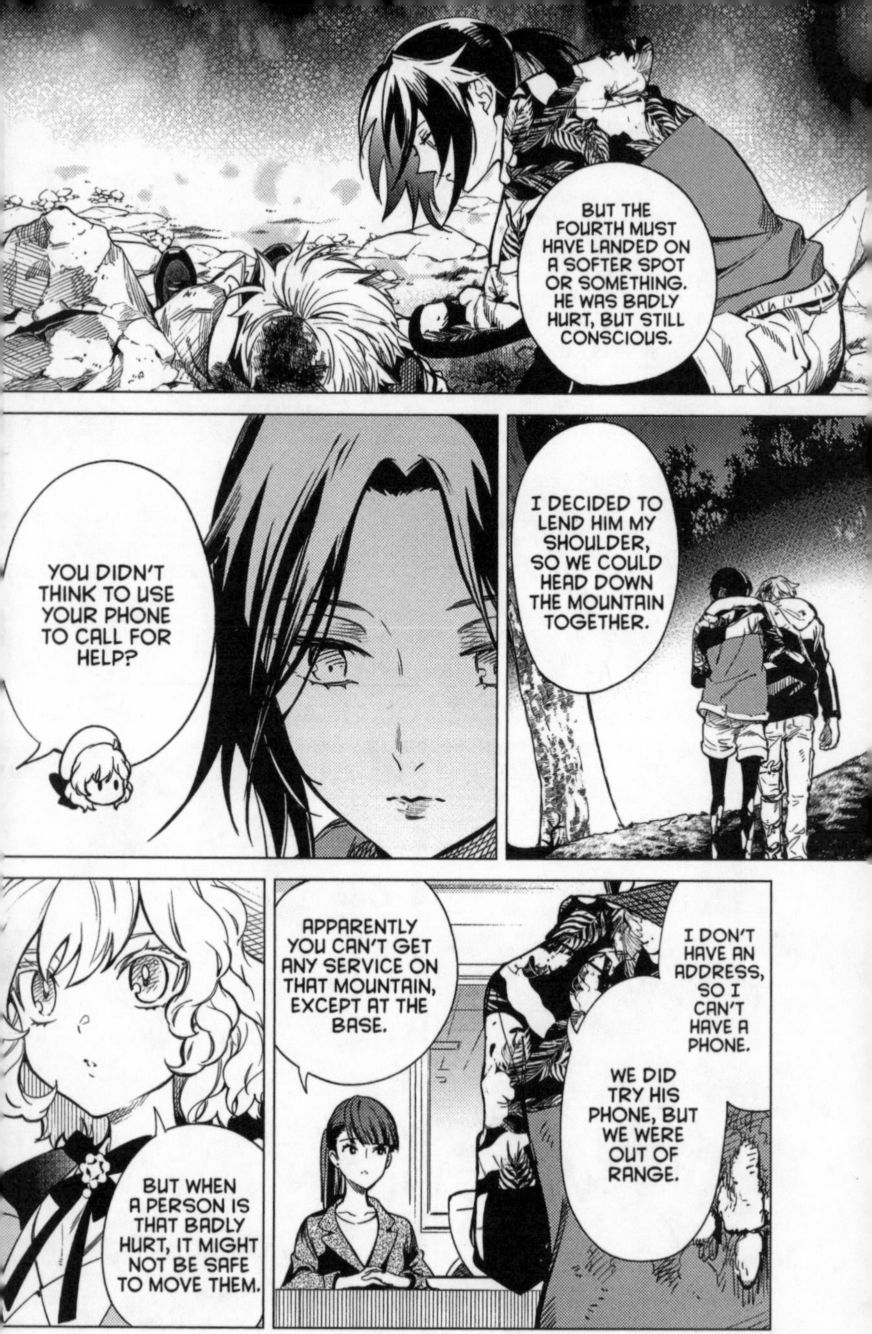
BUT THE FOURTH MUST HAVE LANDED ON A SOFTER SPOT OR SOMETHING. HE WAS BADLY HURT, BUT STILL CONSCIOUS.
I DECIDED TO LEND HIM MY SHOULDER, SO WE COULD HEAD DOWN THE MOUNTAIN TOGETHER.
YOU DIDN'T THINK TO USE YOUR PHONE TO CALL FOR HELP?
I DON'T HAVE AN ADDRESS, SO I CAN'T HAVE A PHONE.
WE DID TRY HIS PHONE, BUT WE WERE OUT OF RANGE.
APPARENTLY YOU CAN'T GET ANY SERVICE ON THAT MOUNTAIN, EXCEPT AT THE BASE.
BUT WHEN A PERSON IS THAT BADLY HURT, IT MIGHT NOT BE SAFE TO MOVE THEM.

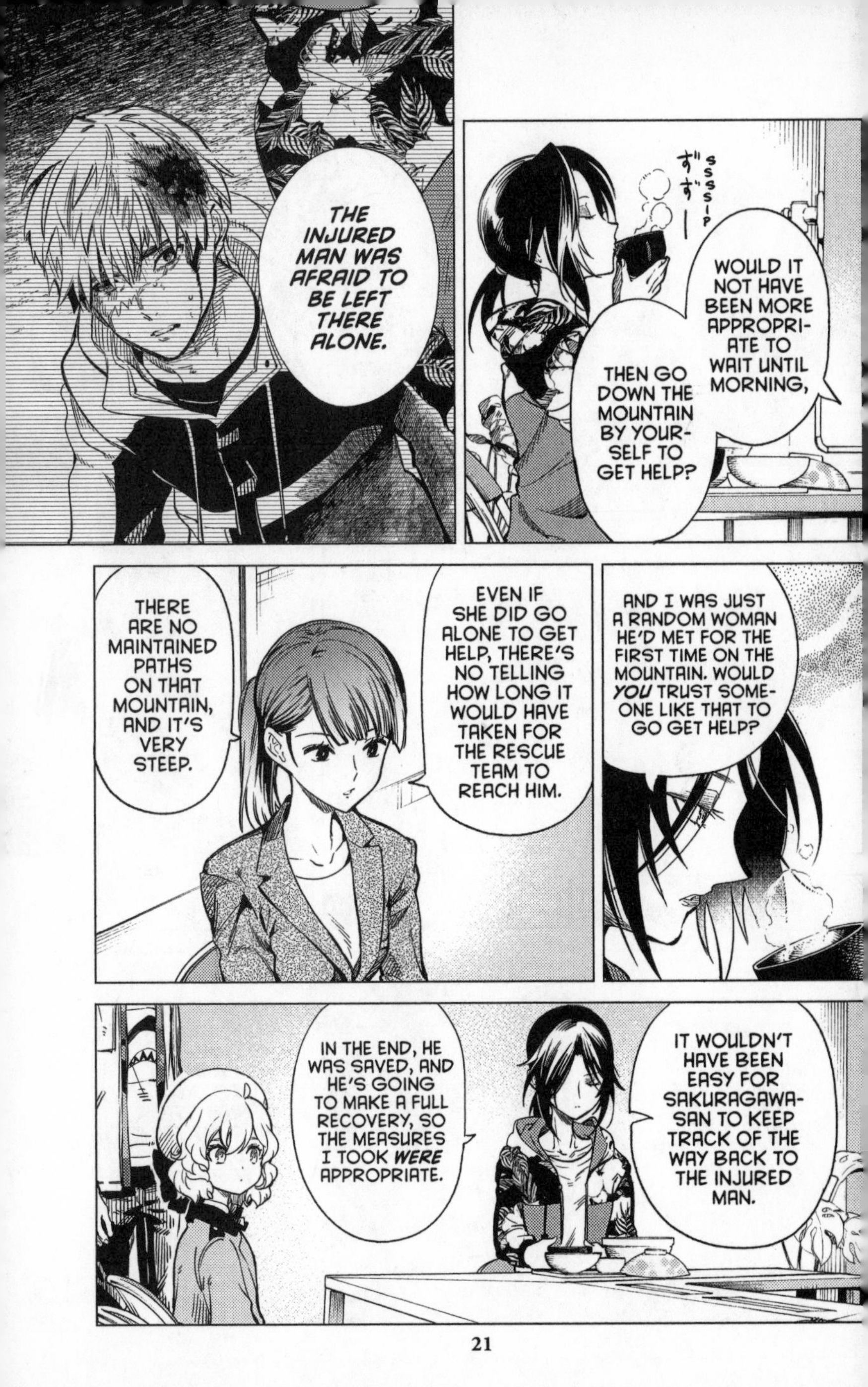
ずずー
SSSIP
WOULD IT NOT HAVE BEEN MORE APPROPRI-ATE TO WAIT UNTIL MORNING,
THEN GO DOWN THE MOUNTAIN BY YOUR-SELF TO GET HELP?
THE INJURED MAN WAS AFRAID TO BE LEFT THERE ALONE.
AND I WAS JUST A RANDOM WOMAN HE'D MET FOR THE FIRST TIME ON THE MOUNTAIN. WOULD *YOU* TRUST SOME-ONE LIKE THAT TO GO GET HELP?
EVEN IF SHE DID GO ALONE TO GET HELP, THERE'S NO TELLING HOW LONG IT WOULD HAVE TAKEN FOR THE RESCUE TEAM TO REACH HIM.
THERE ARE NO MAINTAINED PATHS ON THAT MOUNTAIN, AND IT'S VERY STEEP.
IT WOULDN'T HAVE BEEN EASY FOR SAKURAGAWA-SAN TO KEEP TRACK OF THE WAY BACK TO THE INJURED MAN.
IN THE END, HE WAS SAVED, AND HE'S GOING TO MAKE A FULL RECOVERY, SO THE MEASURES I TOOK *WERE* APPROPRIATE.

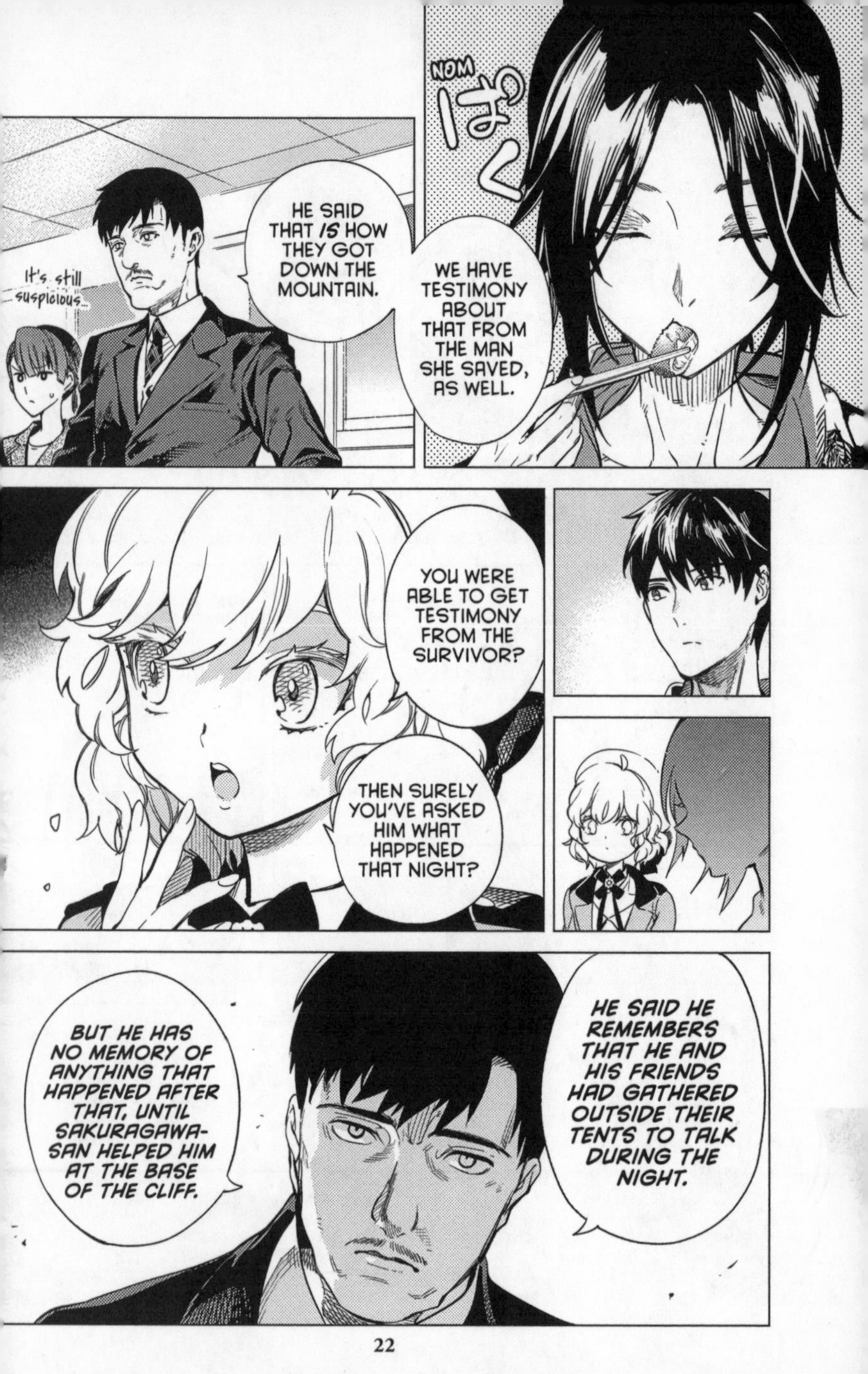
NOM
ぱく
WE HAVE TESTIMONY ABOUT THAT FROM THE MAN SHE SAVED, AS WELL.
HE SAID THAT *IS* HOW THEY GOT DOWN THE MOUNTAIN.
It's still suspicious...
YOU WERE ABLE TO GET TESTIMONY FROM THE SURVIVOR?
THEN SURELY YOU'VE ASKED HIM WHAT HAPPENED THAT NIGHT?
HE SAID HE REMEMBERS THAT HE AND HIS FRIENDS HAD GATHERED OUTSIDE THEIR TENTS TO TALK DURING THE NIGHT.
BUT HE HAS NO MEMORY OF ANYTHING THAT HAPPENED AFTER THAT, UNTIL SAKURAGAWA-SAN HELPED HIM AT THE BASE OF THE CLIFF.

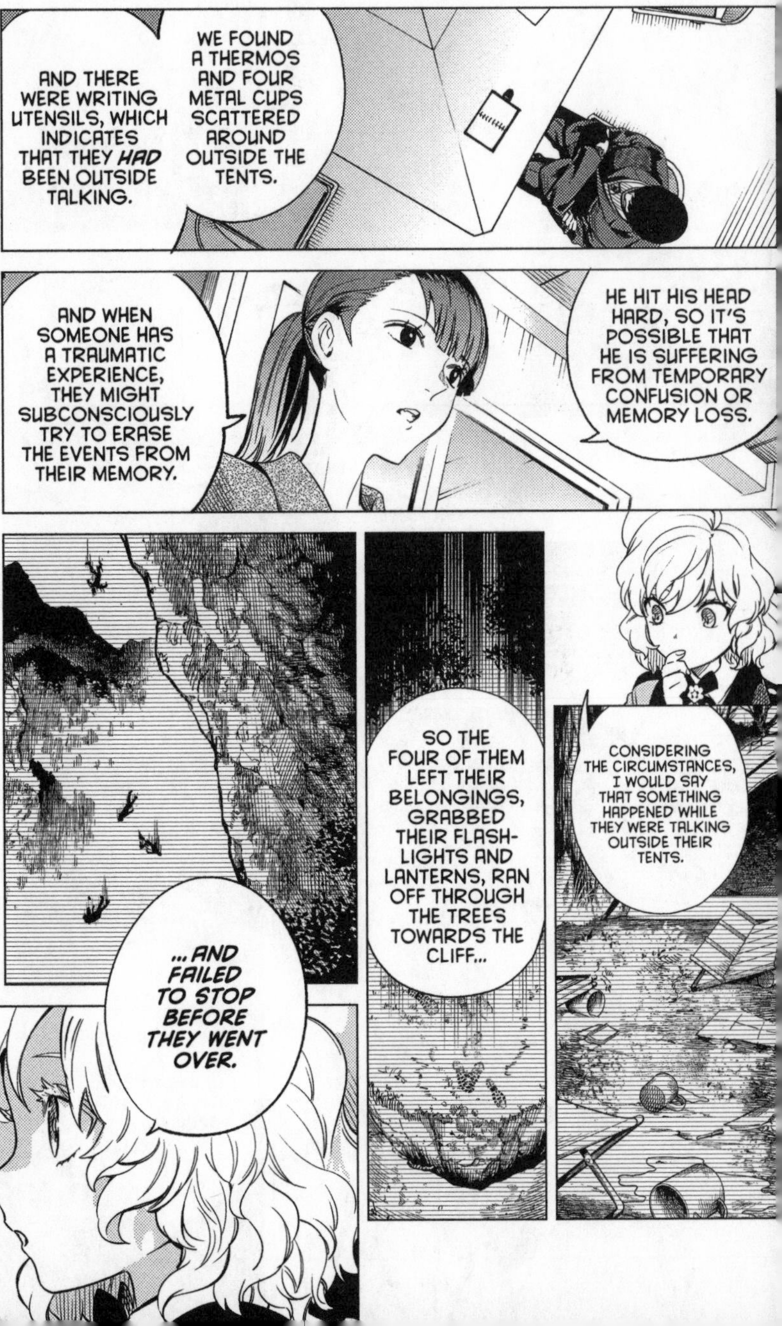
WE FOUND A THERMOS AND FOUR METAL CUPS SCATTERED AROUND OUTSIDE THE TENTS.
AND THERE WERE WRITING UTENSILS, WHICH INDICATES THAT THEY *HAD* BEEN OUTSIDE TALKING.
HE HIT HIS HEAD HARD, SO IT'S POSSIBLE THAT HE IS SUFFERING FROM TEMPORARY CONFUSION OR MEMORY LOSS.
AND WHEN SOMEONE HAS A TRAUMATIC EXPERIENCE, THEY MIGHT SUBCONSCIOUSLY TRY TO ERASE THE EVENTS FROM THEIR MEMORY.
CONSIDERING THE CIRCUMSTANCES, I WOULD SAY THAT SOMETHING HAPPENED WHILE THEY WERE TALKING OUTSIDE THEIR TENTS.
SO THE FOUR OF THEM LEFT THEIR BELONGINGS, GRABBED THEIR FLASH-LIGHTS AND LANTERNS, RAN OFF THROUGH THE TREES TOWARDS THE CLIFF...
*...AND FAILED TO STOP BEFORE THEY WENT OVER.*

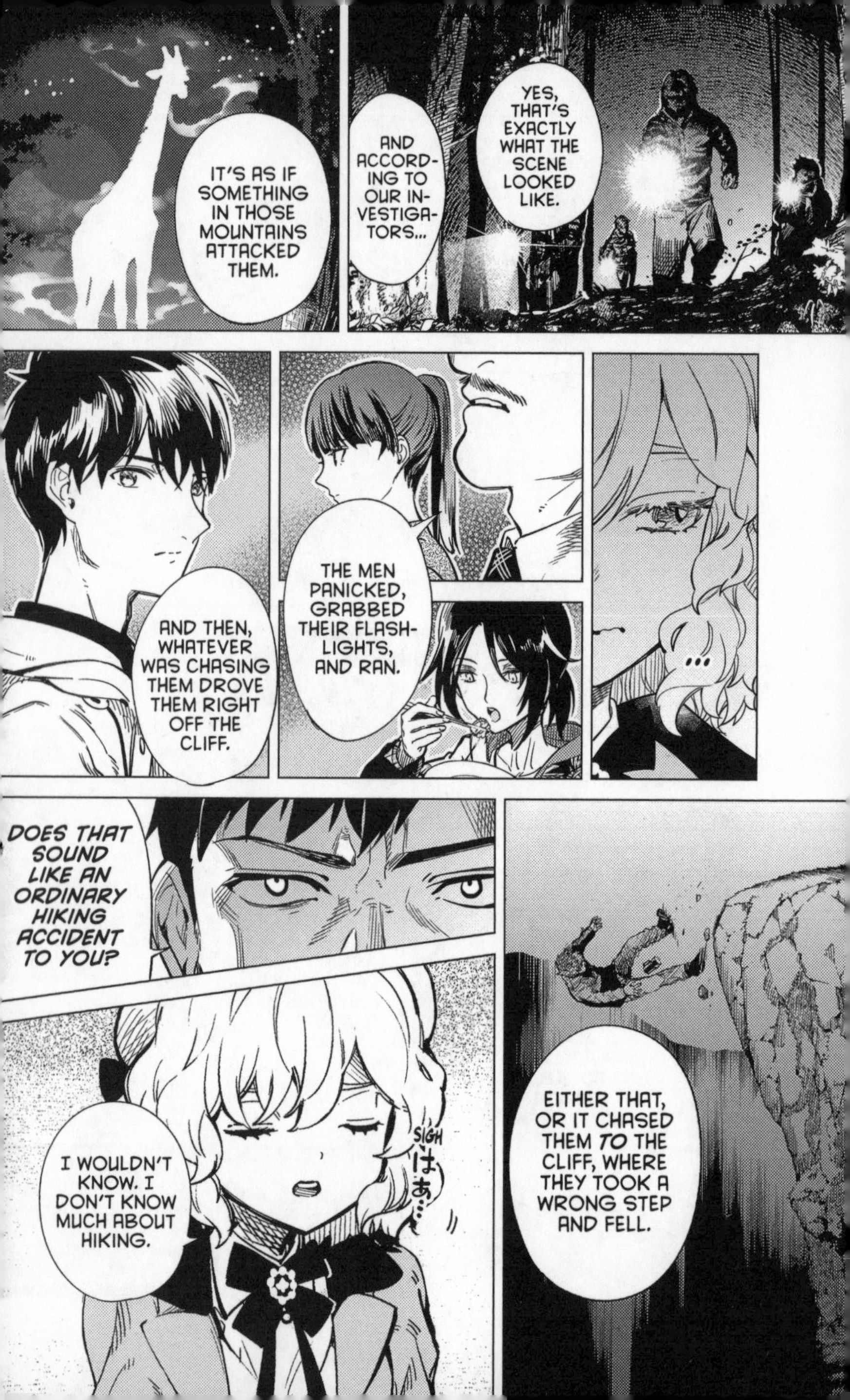

YES, THAT'S EXACTLY WHAT THE SCENE LOOKED LIKE.
AND ACCORDING TO OUR INVESTIGATORS...
IT'S AS IF SOMETHING IN THOSE MOUNTAINS ATTACKED THEM.
...
THE MEN PANICKED, GRABBED THEIR FLASHLIGHTS, AND RAN.
AND THEN, WHATEVER WAS CHASING THEM DROVE THEM RIGHT OFF THE CLIFF.
EITHER THAT, OR IT CHASED THEM *TO* THE CLIFF, WHERE THEY TOOK A WRONG STEP AND FELL.
*DOES THAT SOUND LIKE AN ORDINARY HIKING ACCIDENT TO YOU?*
SIGH はぁ…
I WOULDN'T KNOW. I DON'T KNOW MUCH ABOUT HIKING.

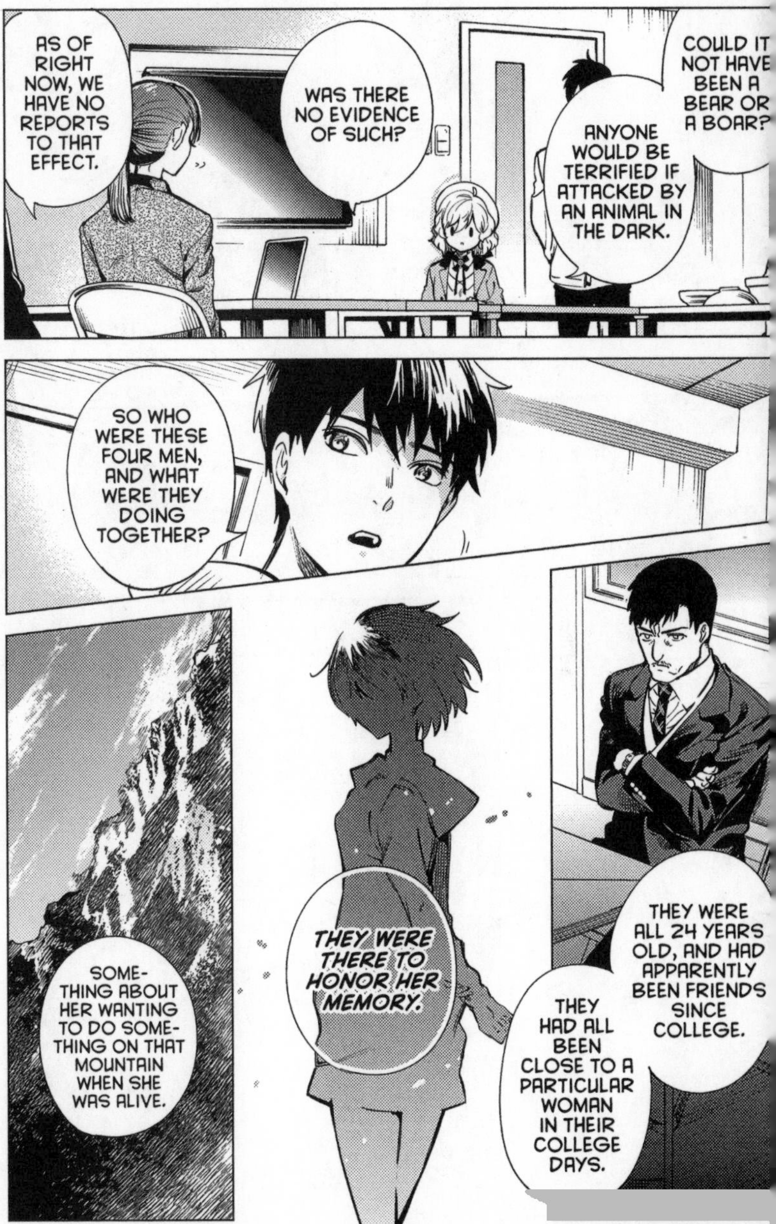
COULD IT NOT HAVE BEEN A BEAR OR A BOAR?
ANYONE WOULD BE TERRIFIED IF ATTACKED BY AN ANIMAL IN THE DARK.
WAS THERE NO EVIDENCE OF SUCH?
AS OF RIGHT NOW, WE HAVE NO REPORTS TO THAT EFFECT.
SO WHO WERE THESE FOUR MEN, AND WHAT WERE THEY DOING TOGETHER?
THEY WERE ALL 24 YEARS OLD, AND HAD APPARENTLY BEEN FRIENDS SINCE COLLEGE.
THEY HAD ALL BEEN CLOSE TO A PARTICULAR WOMAN IN THEIR COLLEGE DAYS.
*THEY WERE THERE TO HONOR HER MEMORY.*
SOME-THING ABOUT HER WANTING TO DO SOME-THING ON THAT MOUNTAIN WHEN SHE WAS ALIVE.

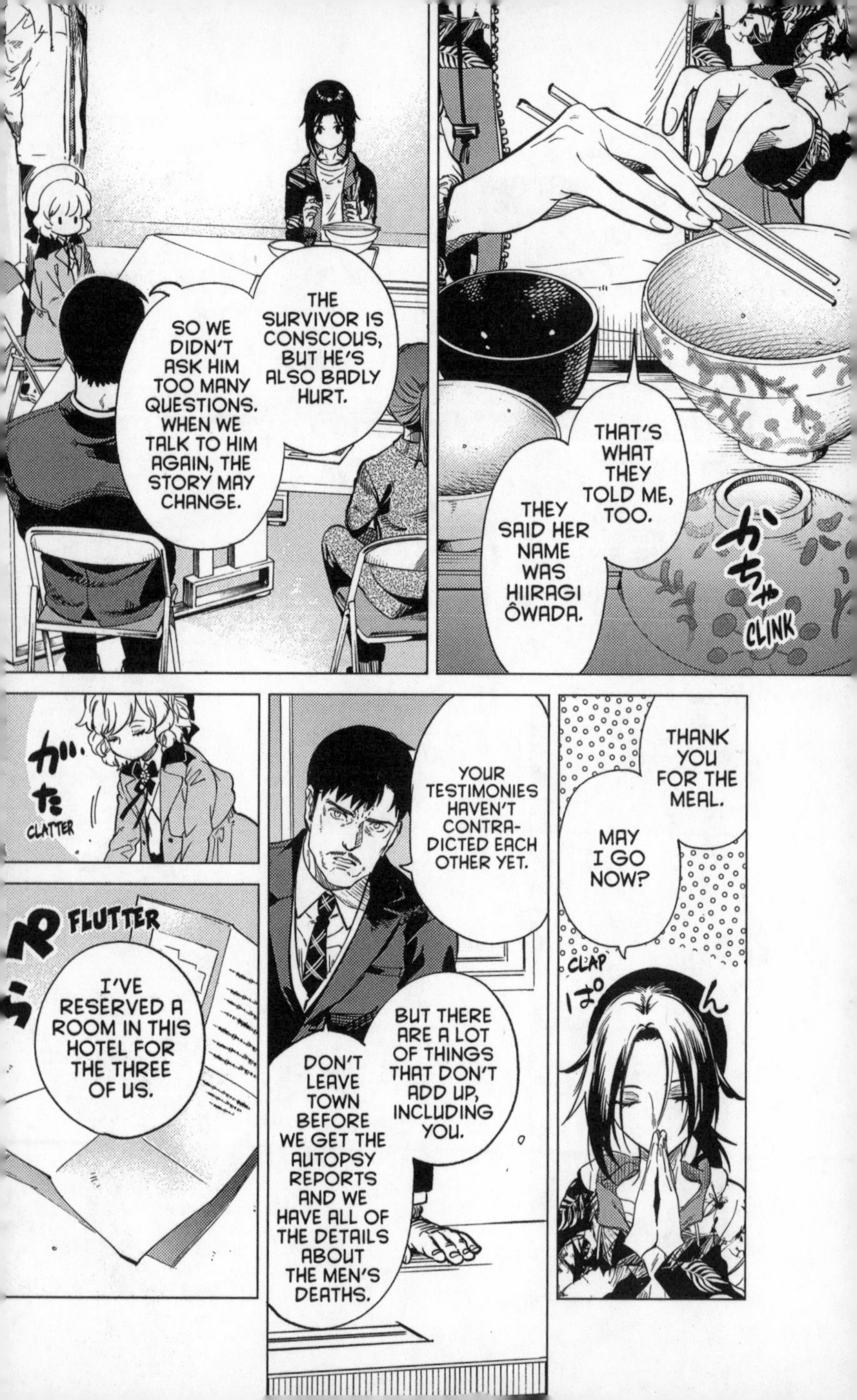
THAT'S WHAT THEY TOLD ME, TOO.
THEY SAID HER NAME WAS HIIRAGI ÔWADA.
かちゃ
CLINK
THE SURVIVOR IS CONSCIOUS, BUT HE'S ALSO BADLY HURT.
SO WE DIDN'T ASK HIM TOO MANY QUESTIONS. WHEN WE TALK TO HIM AGAIN, THE STORY MAY CHANGE.
THANK YOU FOR THE MEAL.
MAY I GO NOW?
CLAP
ぱん
YOUR TESTIMONIES HAVEN'T CONTRA-DICTED EACH OTHER YET.
BUT THERE ARE A LOT OF THINGS THAT DON'T ADD UP, INCLUDING YOU.
DON'T LEAVE TOWN BEFORE WE GET THE AUTOPSY REPORTS AND WE HAVE ALL OF THE DETAILS ABOUT THE MEN'S DEATHS.
がた
CLATTER
FLUTTER
I'VE RESERVED A ROOM IN THIS HOTEL FOR THE THREE OF US.

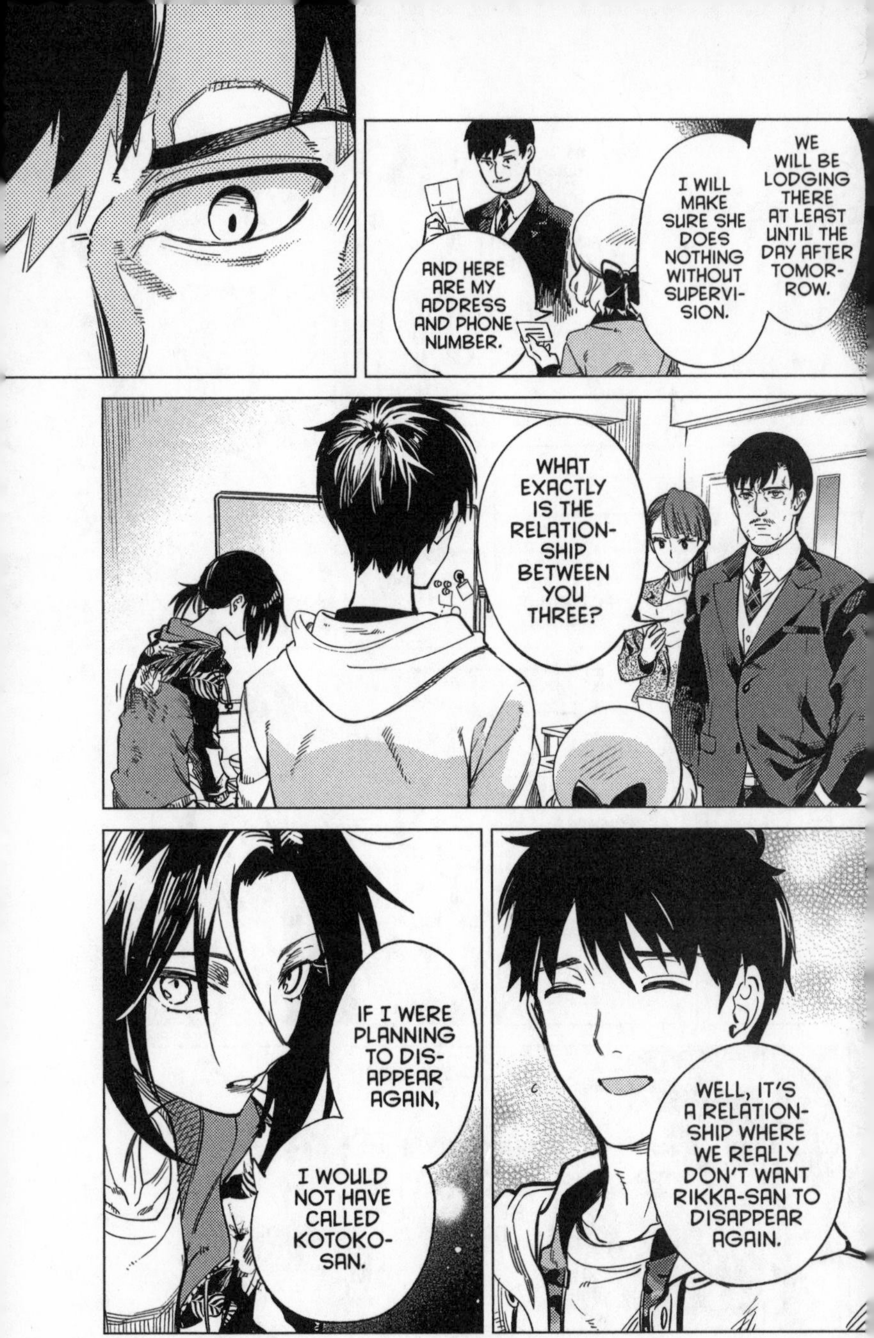
WE WILL BE LODGING THERE AT LEAST UNTIL THE DAY AFTER TOMORROW.
I WILL MAKE SURE SHE DOES NOTHING WITHOUT SUPERVISION.
AND HERE ARE MY ADDRESS AND PHONE NUMBER.
WHAT EXACTLY IS THE RELATIONSHIP BETWEEN YOU THREE?
WELL, IT'S A RELATIONSHIP WHERE WE REALLY DON'T WANT RIKKA-SAN TO DISAPPEAR AGAIN.
IF I WERE PLANNING TO DISAPPEAR AGAIN,
I WOULD NOT HAVE CALLED KOTOKO-SAN.

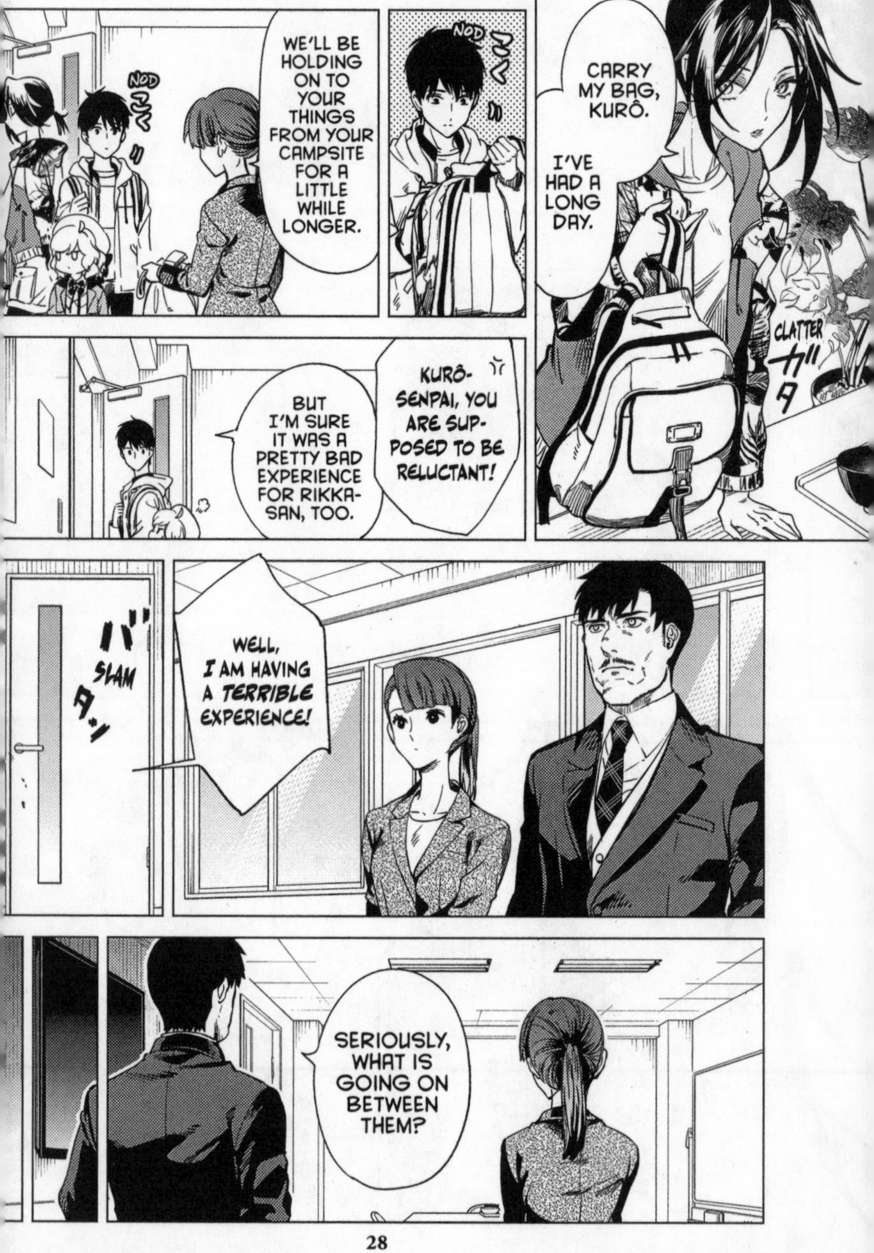
CARRY MY BAG, KURÔ.
I'VE HAD A LONG DAY.
CLATTER
NOD
WE'LL BE HOLDING ON TO YOUR THINGS FROM YOUR CAMPSITE FOR A LITTLE WHILE LONGER.
NOD
KURÔ-SENPAI, YOU ARE SUP-POSED TO BE RELUCTANT!
BUT I'M SURE IT WAS A PRETTY BAD EXPERIENCE FOR RIKKA-SAN, TOO.
WELL, I AM HAVING A *TERRIBLE* EXPERIENCE!
SLAM
SERIOUSLY, WHAT IS GOING ON BETWEEN THEM?

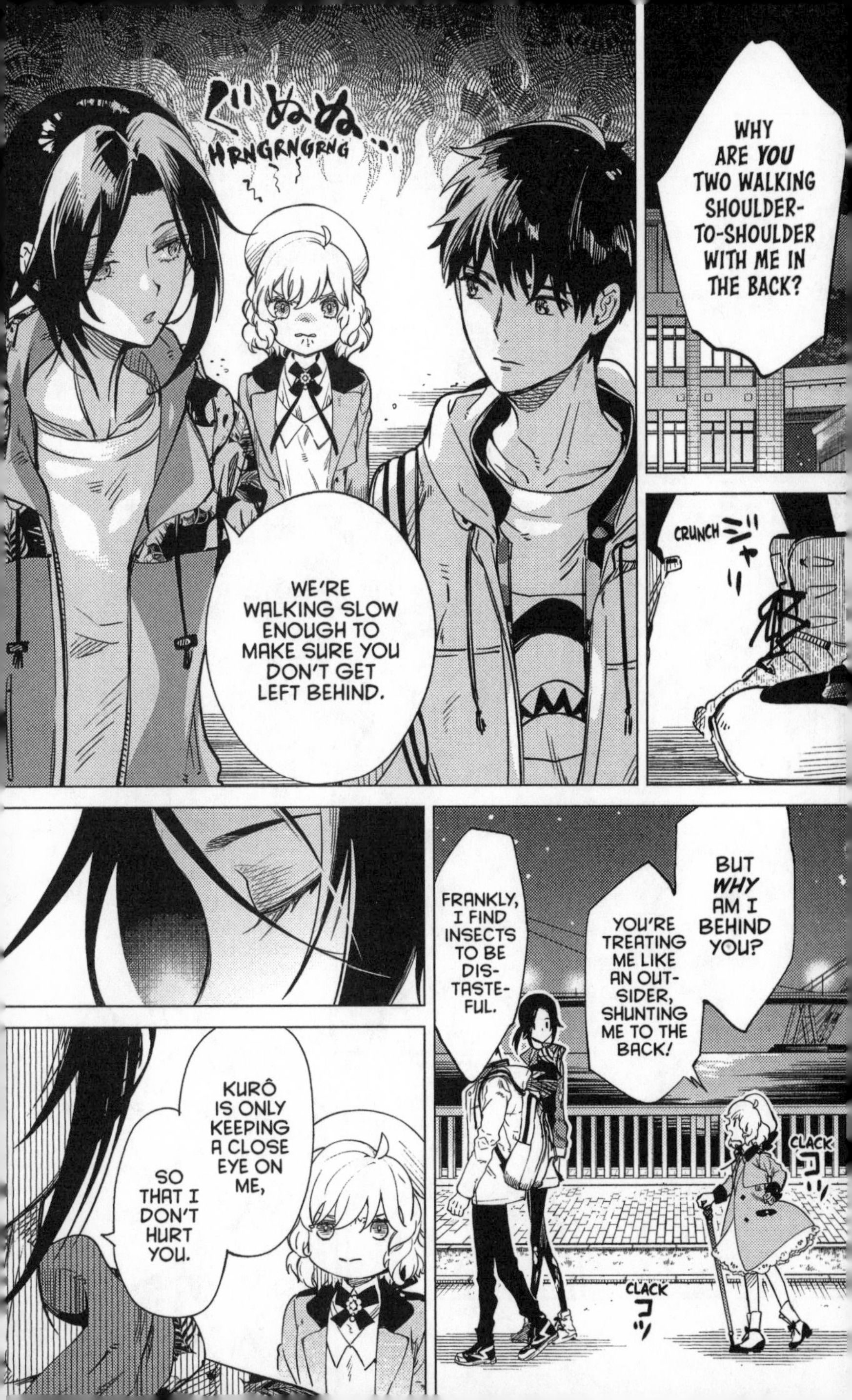

WHY ARE *YOU* TWO WALKING SHOULDER-TO-SHOULDER WITH ME IN THE BACK?
CRUNCH ジャリ
ぐぬぬ
HRNGRNGRNG
WE'RE WALKING SLOW ENOUGH TO MAKE SURE YOU DON'T GET LEFT BEHIND.
BUT *WHY* AM I BEHIND YOU?
YOU'RE TREATING ME LIKE AN OUTSIDER, SHUNTING ME TO THE BACK!
FRANKLY, I FIND INSECTS TO BE DISTASTEFUL.
CLACK コッ
CLACK コッ
KURÔ IS ONLY KEEPING A CLOSE EYE ON ME,
SO THAT I DON'T HURT YOU.

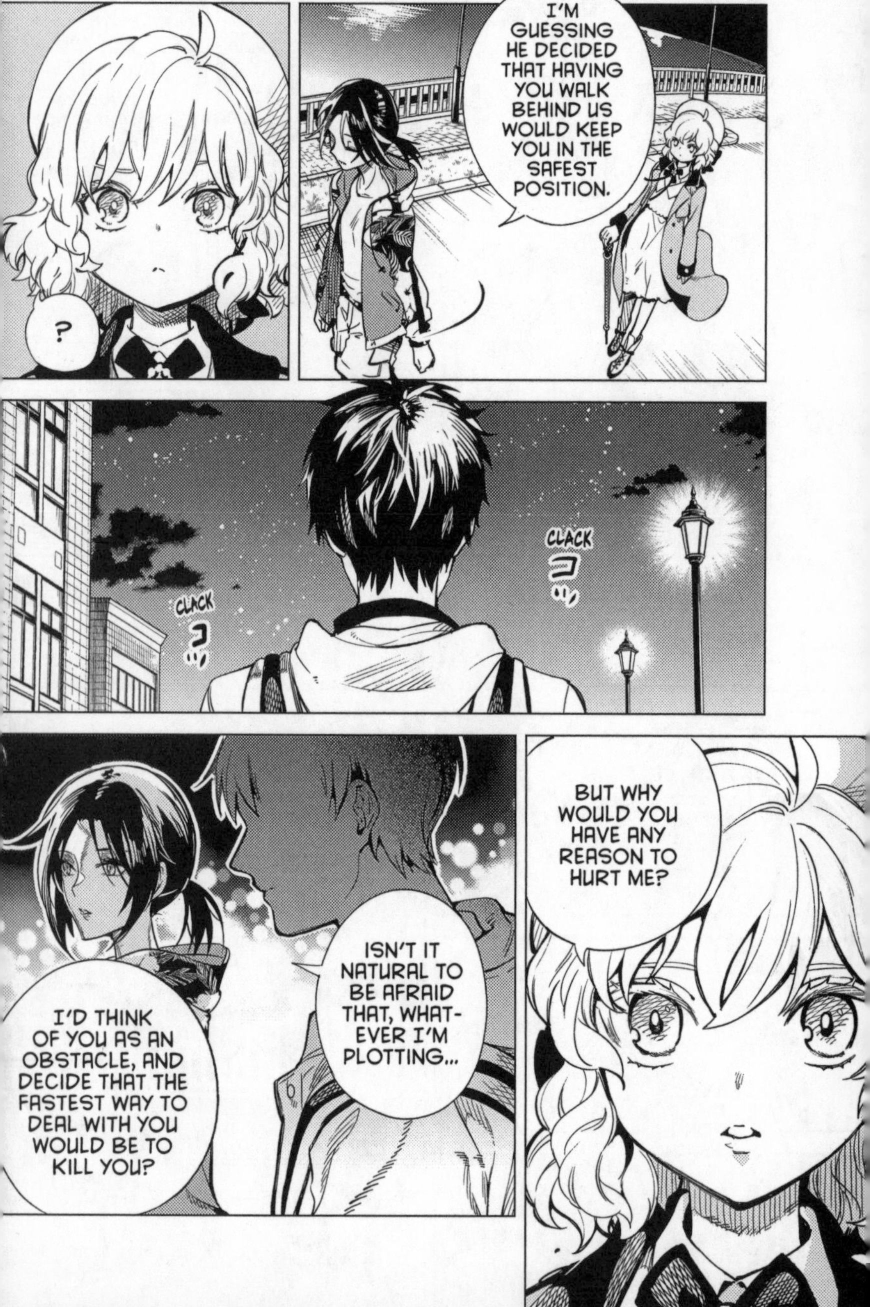
I'M GUESSING HE DECIDED THAT HAVING YOU WALK BEHIND US WOULD KEEP YOU IN THE SAFEST POSITION.
?
CLACK
CLACK
BUT WHY WOULD YOU HAVE ANY REASON TO HURT ME?
ISN'T IT NATURAL TO BE AFRAID THAT, WHAT-EVER I'M PLOTTING...
I'D THINK OF YOU AS AN OBSTACLE, AND DECIDE THAT THE FASTEST WAY TO DEAL WITH YOU WOULD BE TO KILL YOU?

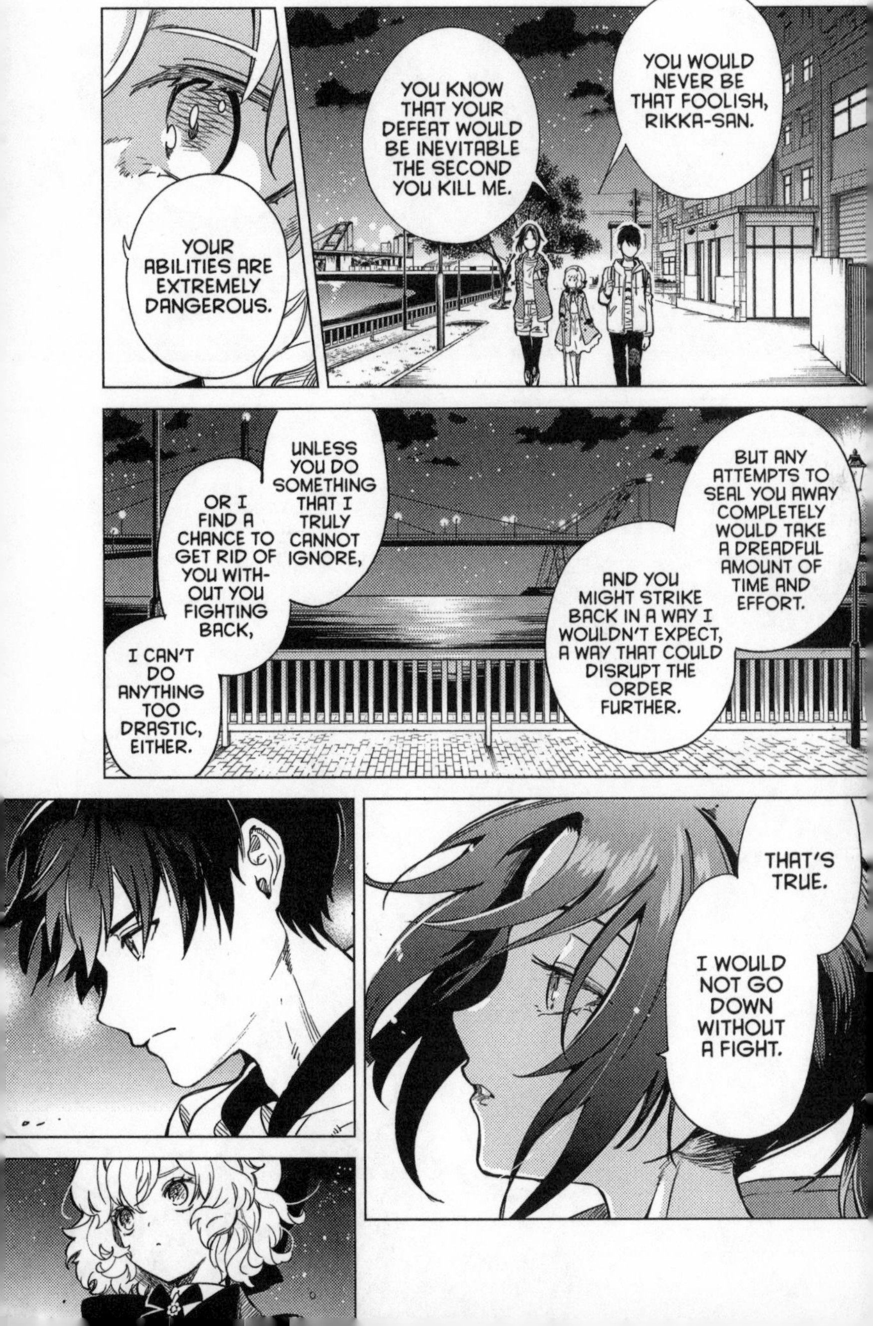
YOU WOULD NEVER BE THAT FOOLISH, RIKKA-SAN.
YOU KNOW THAT YOUR DEFEAT WOULD BE INEVITABLE THE SECOND YOU KILL ME.
YOUR ABILITIES ARE EXTREMELY DANGEROUS.
BUT ANY ATTEMPTS TO SEAL YOU AWAY COMPLETELY WOULD TAKE A DREADFUL AMOUNT OF TIME AND EFFORT.
AND YOU MIGHT STRIKE BACK IN A WAY I WOULDN'T EXPECT, A WAY THAT COULD DISRUPT THE ORDER FURTHER.
UNLESS YOU DO SOMETHING THAT I TRULY CANNOT IGNORE,
OR I FIND A CHANCE TO GET RID OF YOU WITH-OUT YOU FIGHTING BACK,
I CAN'T DO ANYTHING TOO DRASTIC, EITHER.
THAT'S TRUE.
I WOULD NOT GO DOWN WITHOUT A FIGHT.

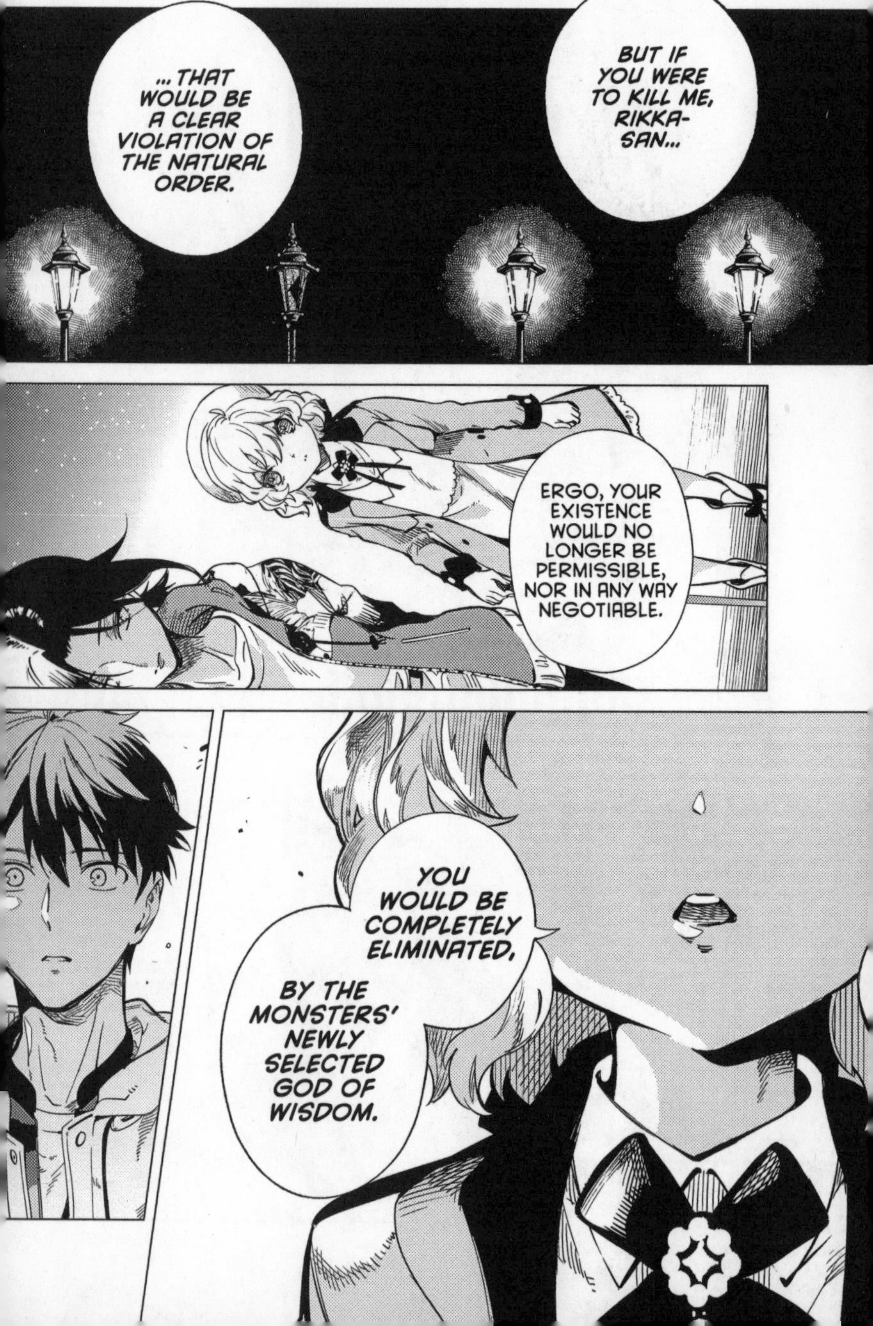
BUT IF YOU WERE TO KILL ME, RIKKA-SAN...
...THAT WOULD BE A CLEAR VIOLATION OF THE NATURAL ORDER.
ERGO, YOUR EXISTENCE WOULD NO LONGER BE PERMISSIBLE, NOR IN ANY WAY NEGOTIABLE.
YOU WOULD BE COMPLETELY ELIMINATED,
BY THE MONSTERS' NEWLY SELECTED GOD OF WISDOM.

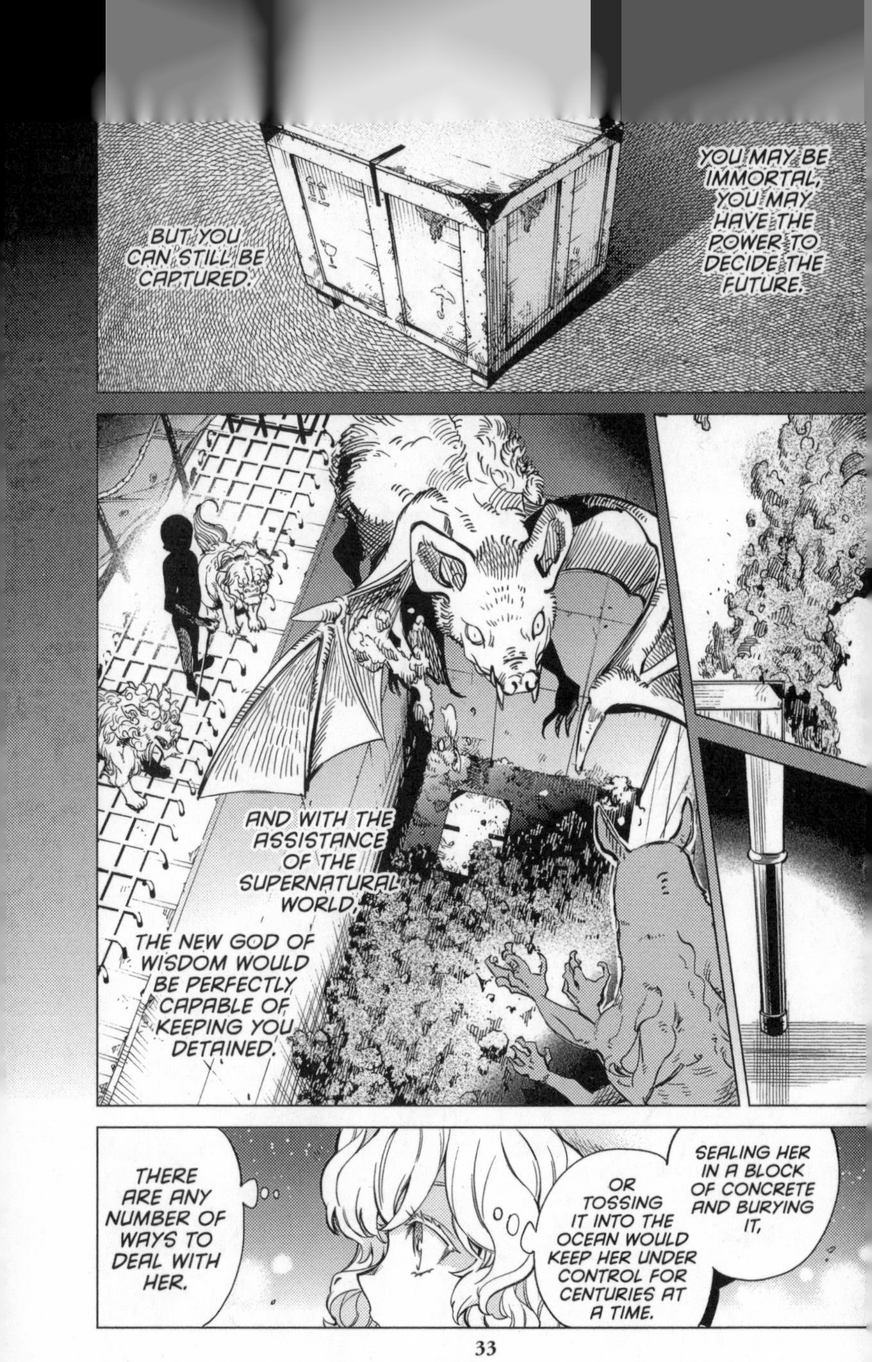
YOU MAY BE IMMORTAL, YOU MAY HAVE THE POWER TO DECIDE THE FUTURE.
BUT YOU CAN STILL BE CAPTURED.
AND WITH THE ASSISTANCE OF THE SUPERNATURAL WORLD,
THE NEW GOD OF WISDOM WOULD BE PERFECTLY CAPABLE OF KEEPING YOU DETAINED.
SEALING HER IN A BLOCK OF CONCRETE AND BURYING IT,
OR TOSSING IT INTO THE OCEAN WOULD KEEP HER UNDER CONTROL FOR CENTURIES AT A TIME.
THERE ARE ANY NUMBER OF WAYS TO DEAL WITH HER.

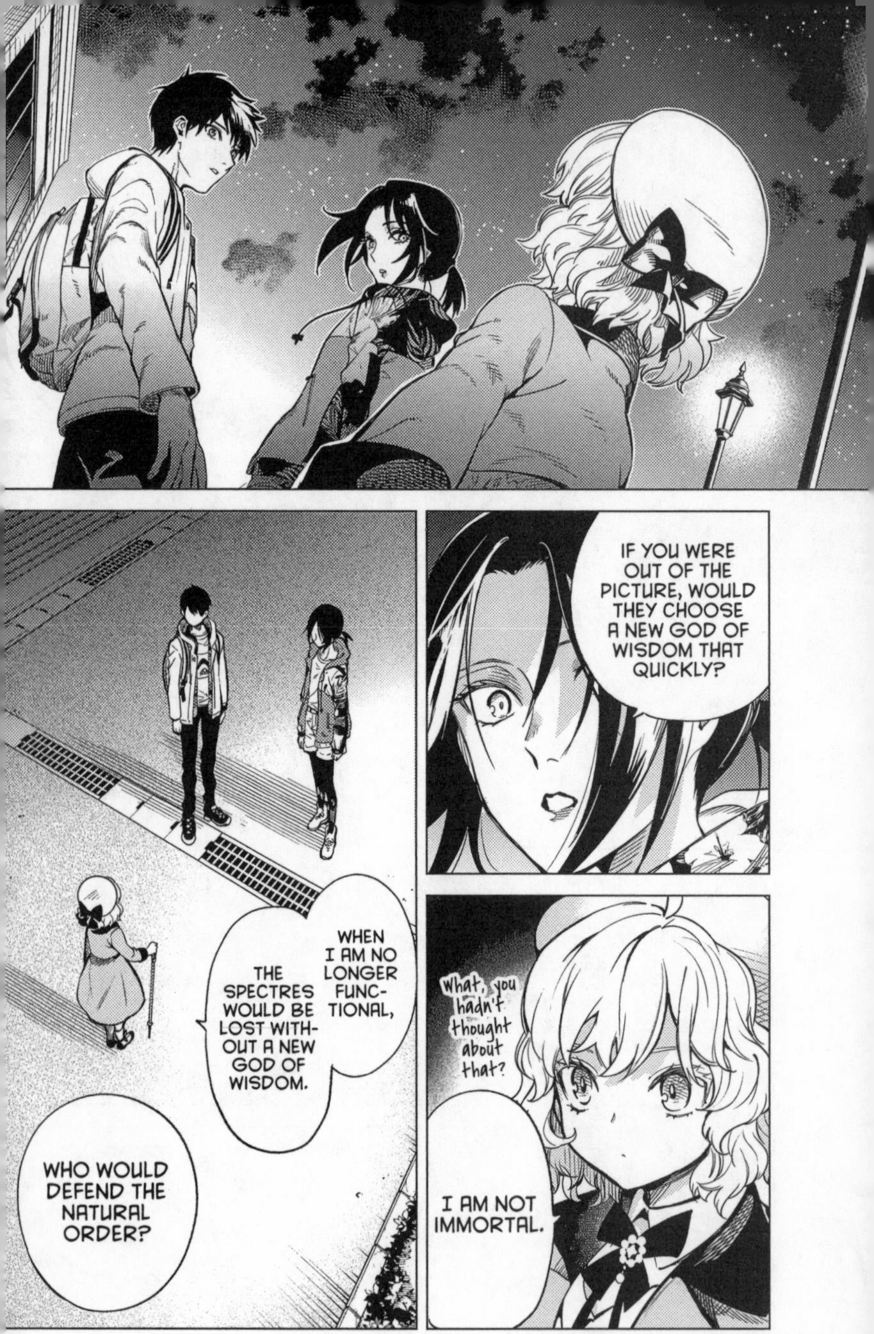
IF YOU WERE OUT OF THE PICTURE, WOULD THEY CHOOSE A NEW GOD OF WISDOM THAT QUICKLY?
What, you hadn't thought about that?
I AM NOT IMMORTAL.
WHEN I AM NO LONGER FUNCTIONAL,
THE SPECTRES WOULD BE LOST WITHOUT A NEW GOD OF WISDOM.
WHO WOULD DEFEND THE NATURAL ORDER?

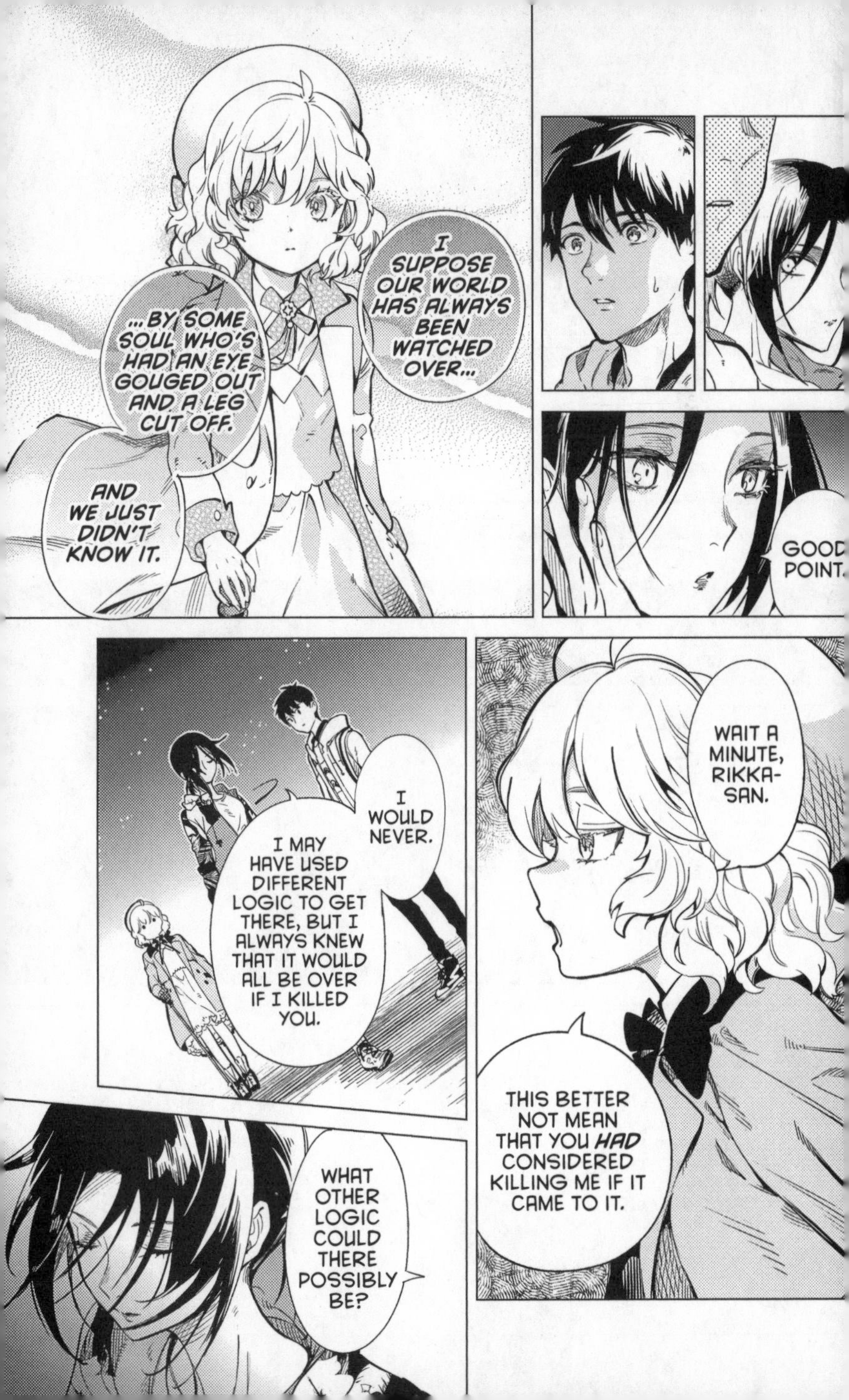
GOOD POINT.
I SUPPOSE OUR WORLD HAS ALWAYS BEEN WATCHED OVER...
...BY SOME SOUL WHO'S HAD AN EYE GOUGED OUT AND A LEG CUT OFF.
AND WE JUST DIDN'T KNOW IT.
WAIT A MINUTE, RIKKA-SAN.
THIS BETTER NOT MEAN THAT YOU *HAD* CONSIDERED KILLING ME IF IT CAME TO IT.
I WOULD NEVER.
I MAY HAVE USED DIFFERENT LOGIC TO GET THERE, BUT I ALWAYS KNEW THAT IT WOULD ALL BE OVER IF I KILLED YOU.
WHAT OTHER LOGIC COULD THERE POSSIBLY BE?

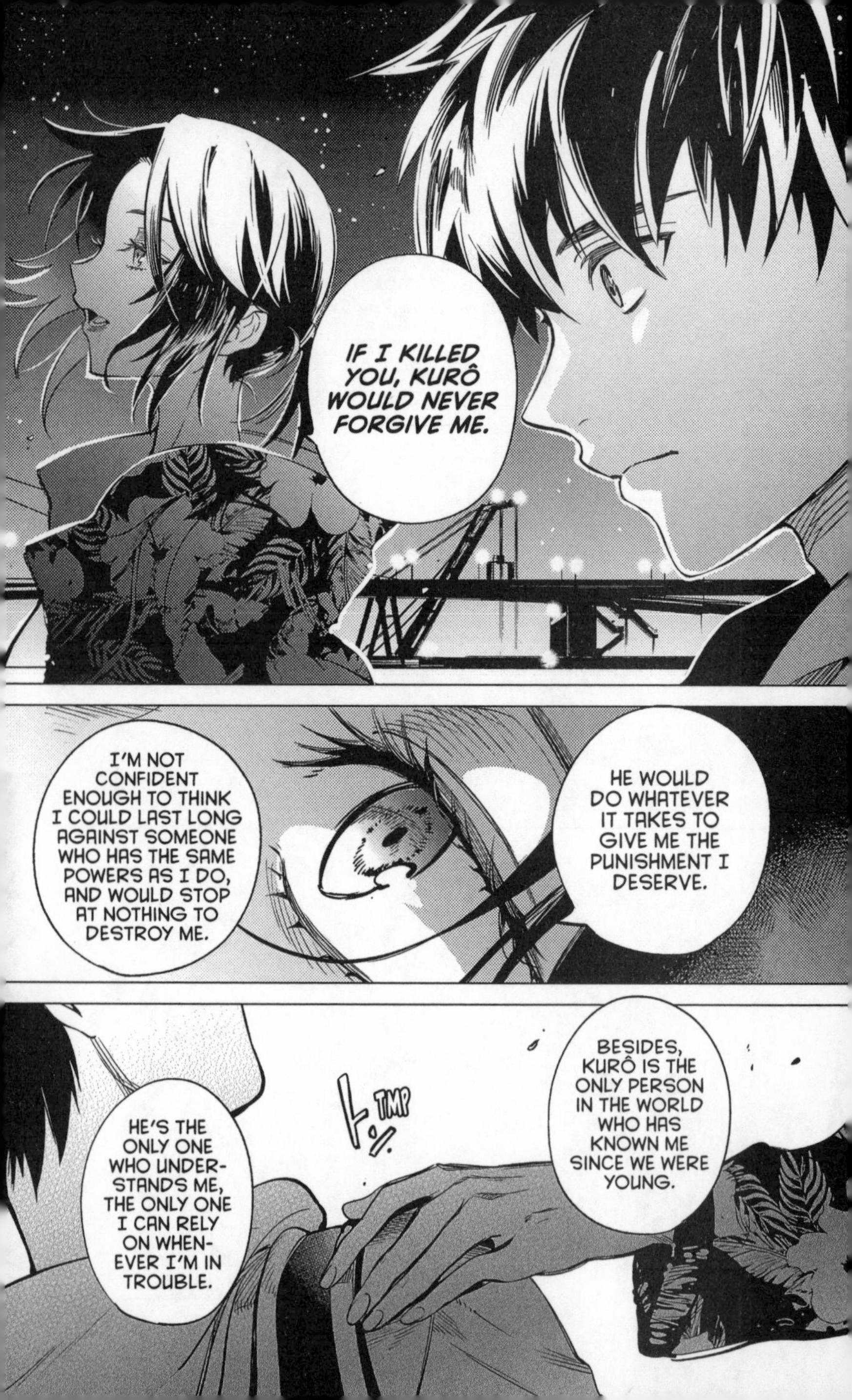
IF I KILLED YOU, KURÔ WOULD NEVER FORGIVE ME.
HE WOULD DO WHATEVER IT TAKES TO GIVE ME THE PUNISHMENT I DESERVE.
I'M NOT CONFIDENT ENOUGH TO THINK I COULD LAST LONG AGAINST SOMEONE WHO HAS THE SAME POWERS AS I DO, AND WOULD STOP AT NOTHING TO DESTROY ME.
BESIDES, KURÔ IS THE ONLY PERSON IN THE WORLD WHO HAS KNOWN ME SINCE WE WERE YOUNG.
TMP
HE'S THE ONLY ONE WHO UNDER-STANDS ME, THE ONLY ONE I CAN RELY ON WHEN-EVER I'M IN TROUBLE.

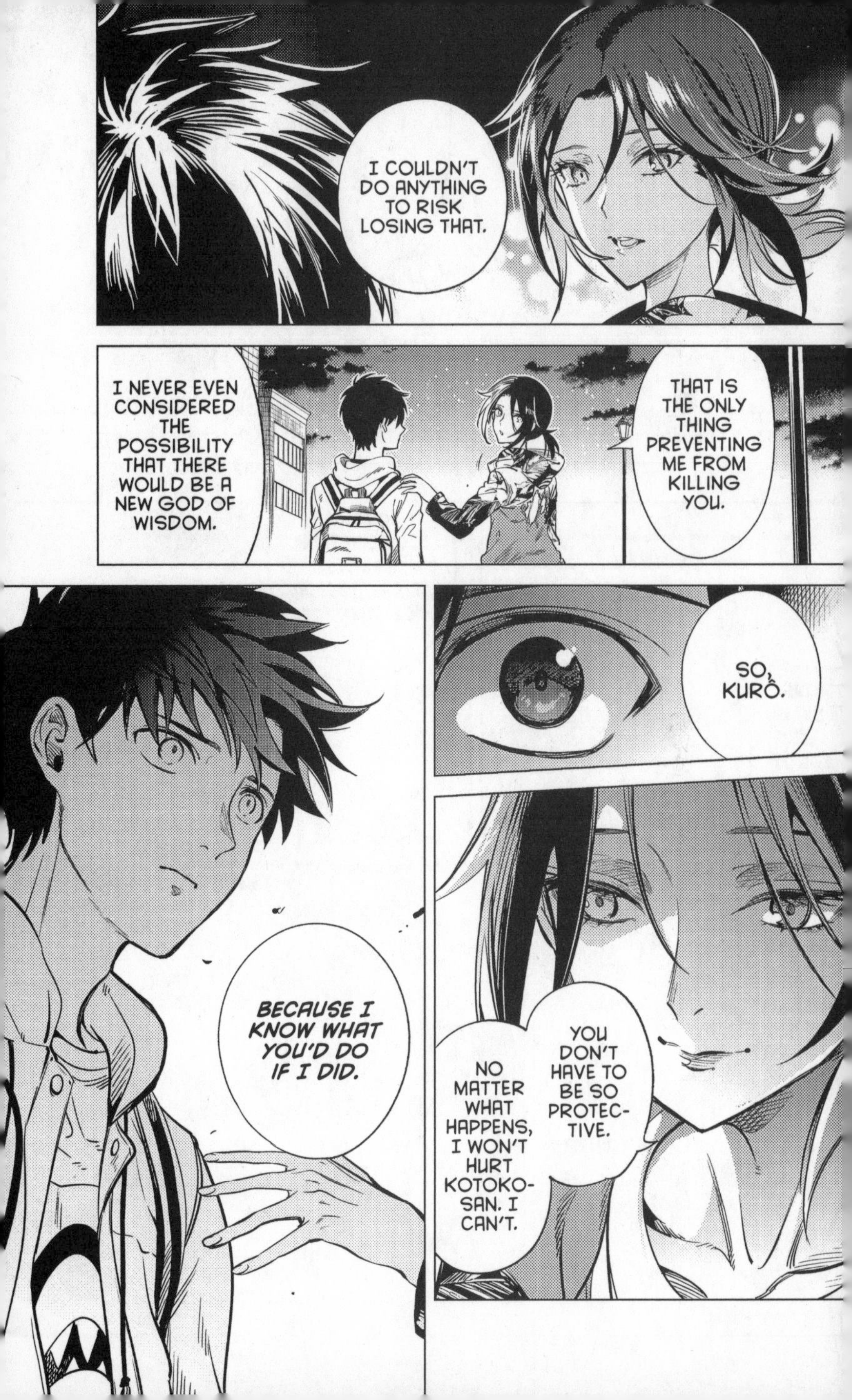
I COULDN'T DO ANYTHING TO RISK LOSING THAT.
THAT IS THE ONLY THING PREVENTING ME FROM KILLING YOU.
I NEVER EVEN CONSIDERED THE POSSIBILITY THAT THERE WOULD BE A NEW GOD OF WISDOM.
SO, KURŌ.
YOU DON'T HAVE TO BE SO PROTECTIVE.
NO MATTER WHAT HAPPENS, I WON'T HURT KOTOKO-SAN. I CAN'T.
*BECAUSE I KNOW WHAT YOU'D DO IF I DID.*

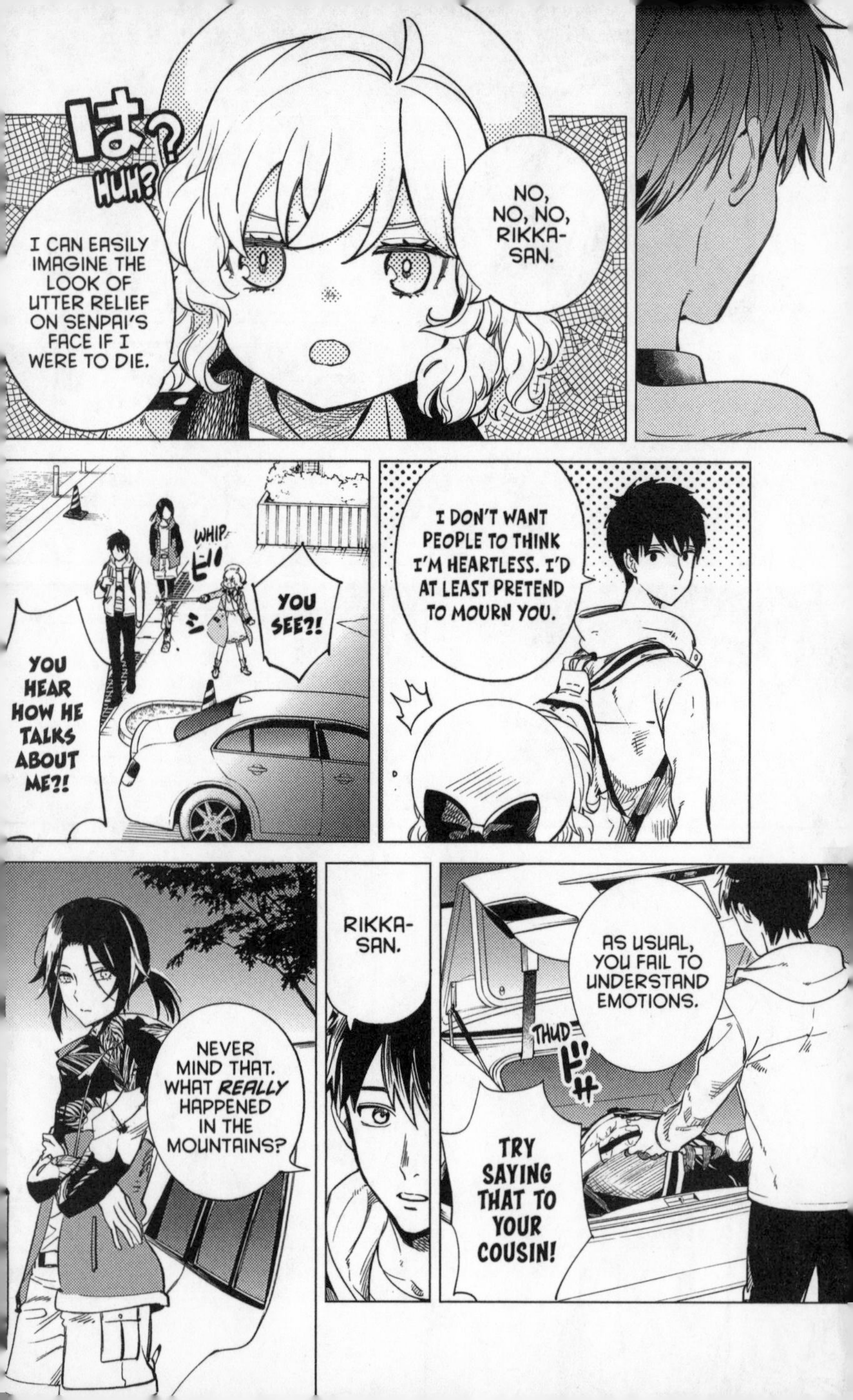
NO, NO, NO, RIKKA-SAN.
は？
HUH?
I CAN EASILY IMAGINE THE LOOK OF UTTER RELIEF ON SENPAI'S FACE IF I WERE TO DIE.
I DON'T WANT PEOPLE TO THINK I'M HEARTLESS. I'D AT LEAST PRETEND TO MOURN YOU.
WHIP
ビッ
YOU SEE?!
シ
YOU HEAR HOW HE TALKS ABOUT ME?!
AS USUAL, YOU FAIL TO UNDERSTAND EMOTIONS.
THUD
ドサ
TRY SAYING THAT TO YOUR COUSIN!
RIKKA-SAN.
NEVER MIND THAT. WHAT *REALLY* HAPPENED IN THE MOUNTAINS?

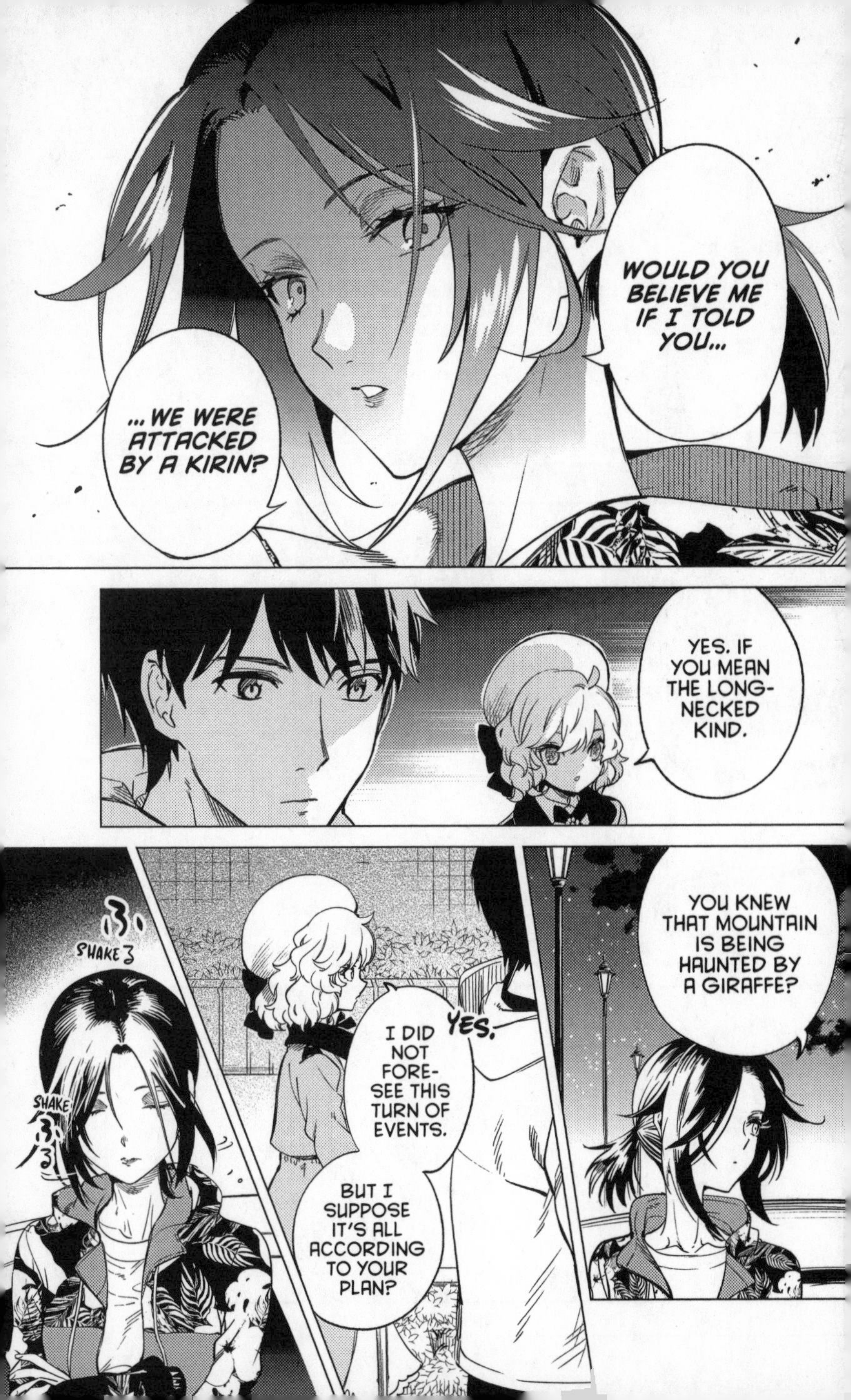
WOULD YOU BELIEVE ME IF I TOLD YOU...
...WE WERE ATTACKED BY A KIRIN?
YES. IF YOU MEAN THE LONG-NECKED KIND.
YOU KNEW THAT MOUNTAIN IS BEING HAUNTED BY A GIRAFFE?
YES.
I DID NOT FORESEE THIS TURN OF EVENTS.
BUT I SUPPOSE IT'S ALL ACCORDING TO YOUR PLAN?
SHAKE
SHAKE

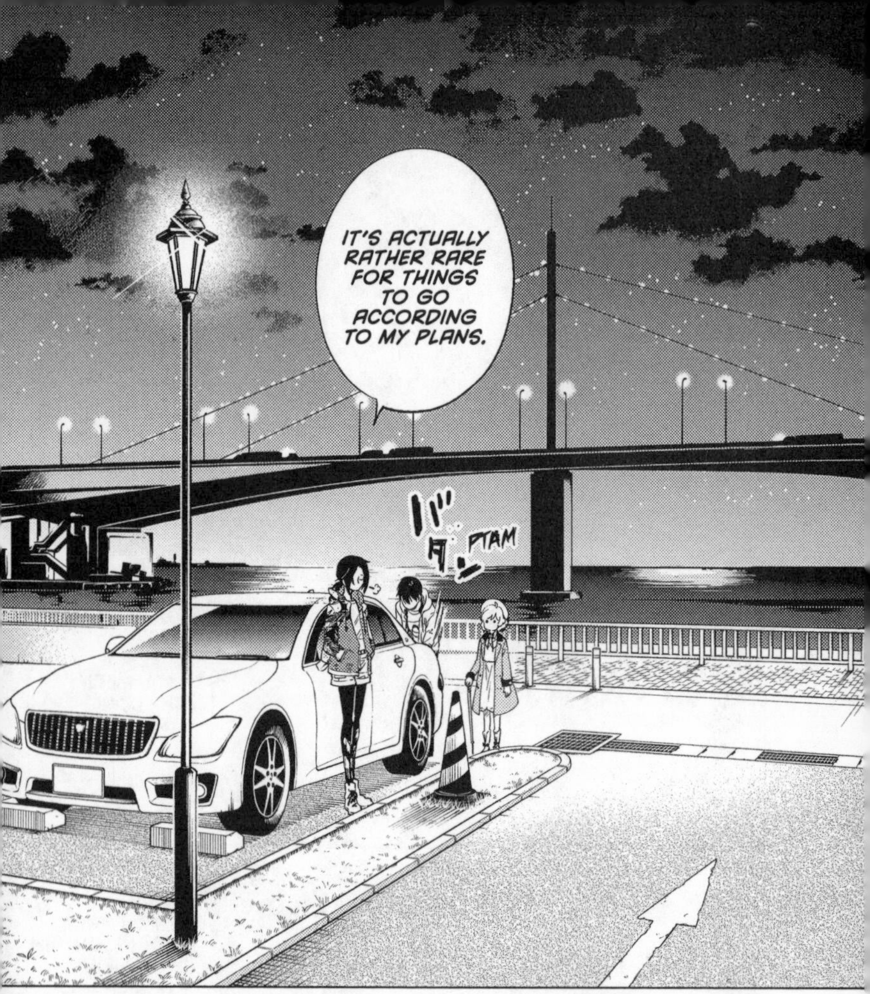
IT'S ACTUALLY RATHER RARE FOR THINGS TO GO ACCORDING TO MY PLANS.
PTAM

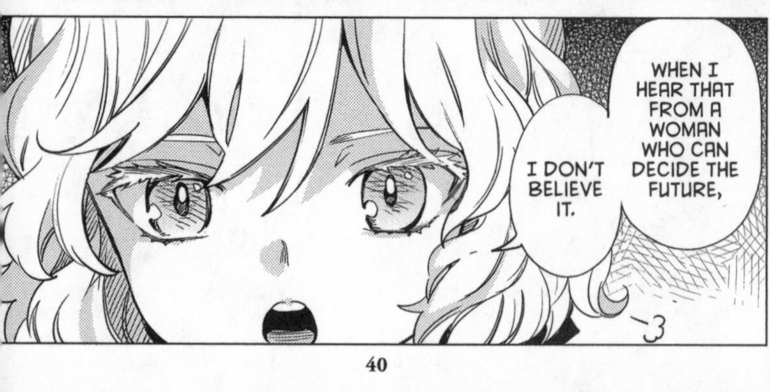
WHEN I HEAR THAT FROM A WOMAN WHO CAN DECIDE THE FUTURE,
I DON'T BELIEVE IT.

IN/SPECTRE

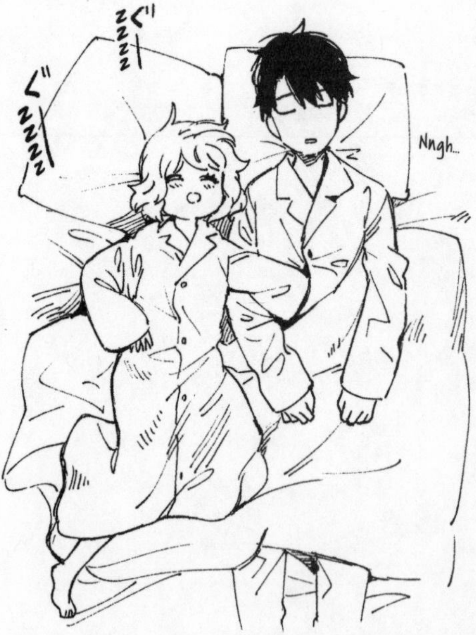
ぐZZZZ
ぐZZZZ
Nngh...

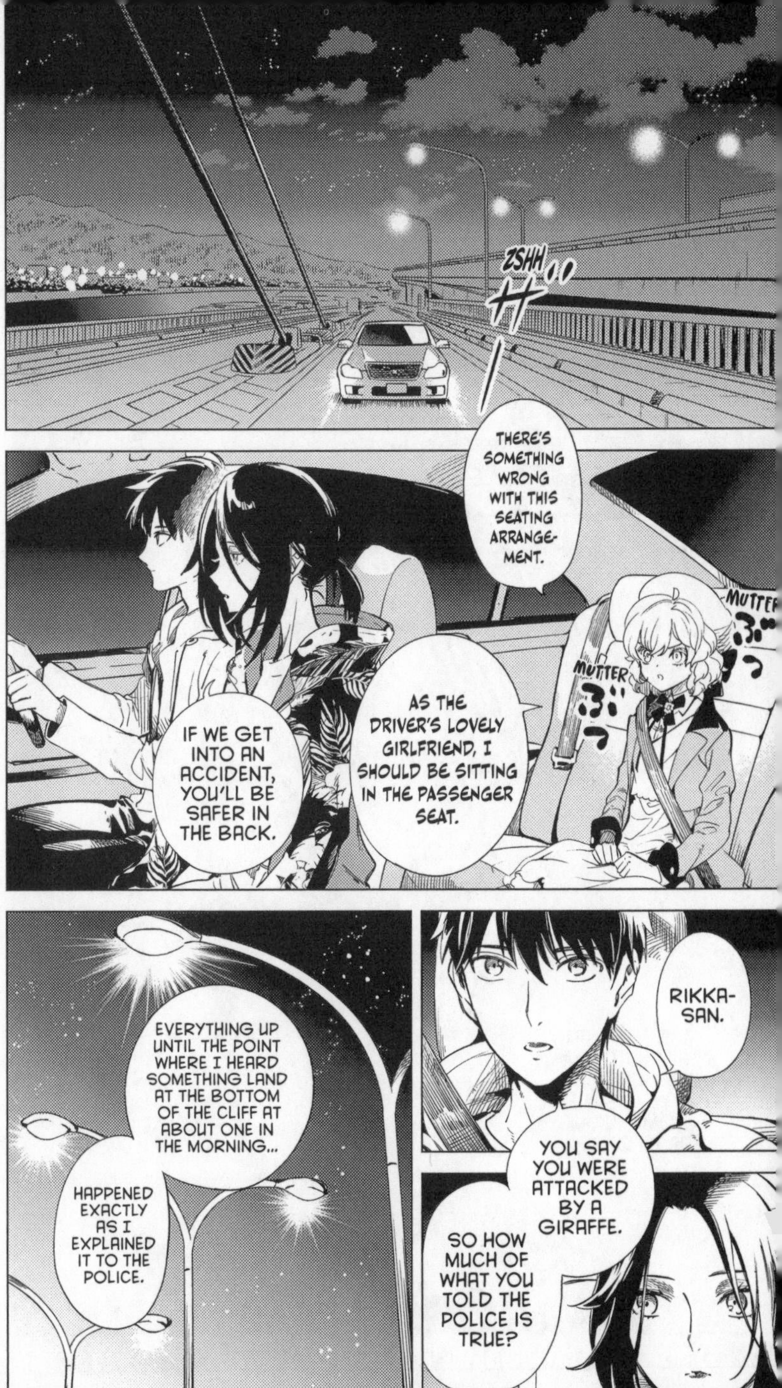
ZSHH
THERE'S SOMETHING WRONG WITH THIS SEATING ARRANGE-MENT.
MUTTER
MUTTER
AS THE DRIVER'S LOVELY GIRLFRIEND, I SHOULD BE SITTING IN THE PASSENGER SEAT.
IF WE GET INTO AN ACCIDENT, YOU'LL BE SAFER IN THE BACK.
RIKKA-SAN.
YOU SAY YOU WERE ATTACKED BY A GIRAFFE.
SO HOW MUCH OF WHAT YOU TOLD THE POLICE IS TRUE?
EVERYTHING UP UNTIL THE POINT WHERE I HEARD SOMETHING LAND AT THE BOTTOM OF THE CLIFF AT ABOUT ONE IN THE MORNING...
HAPPENED EXACTLY AS I EXPLAINED IT TO THE POLICE.

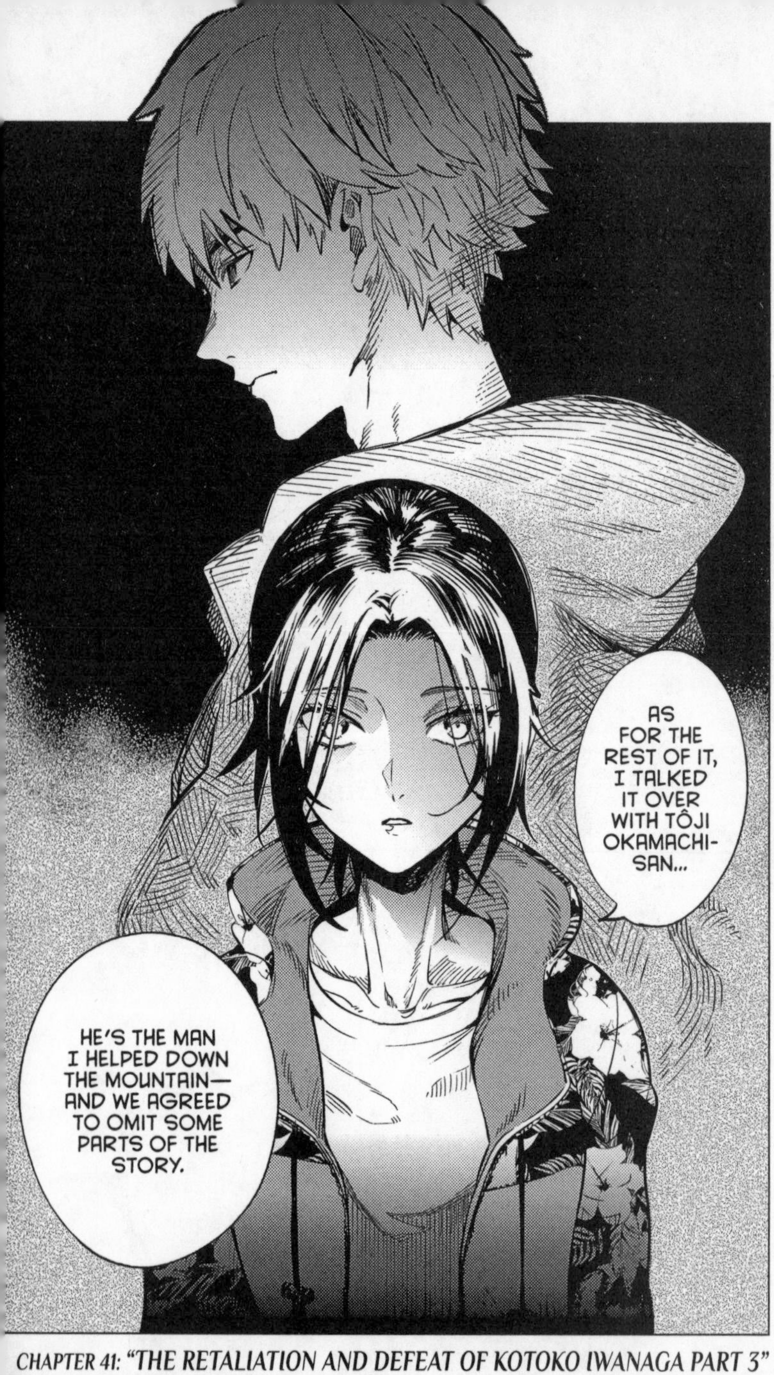
AS FOR THE REST OF IT, I TALKED IT OVER WITH TÔJI OKAMACHI-SAN...
HE'S THE MAN I HELPED DOWN THE MOUNTAIN—AND WE AGREED TO OMIT SOME PARTS OF THE STORY.

CHAPTER 41: "THE RETALIATION AND DEFEAT OF KOTOKO IWANAGA PART 3"

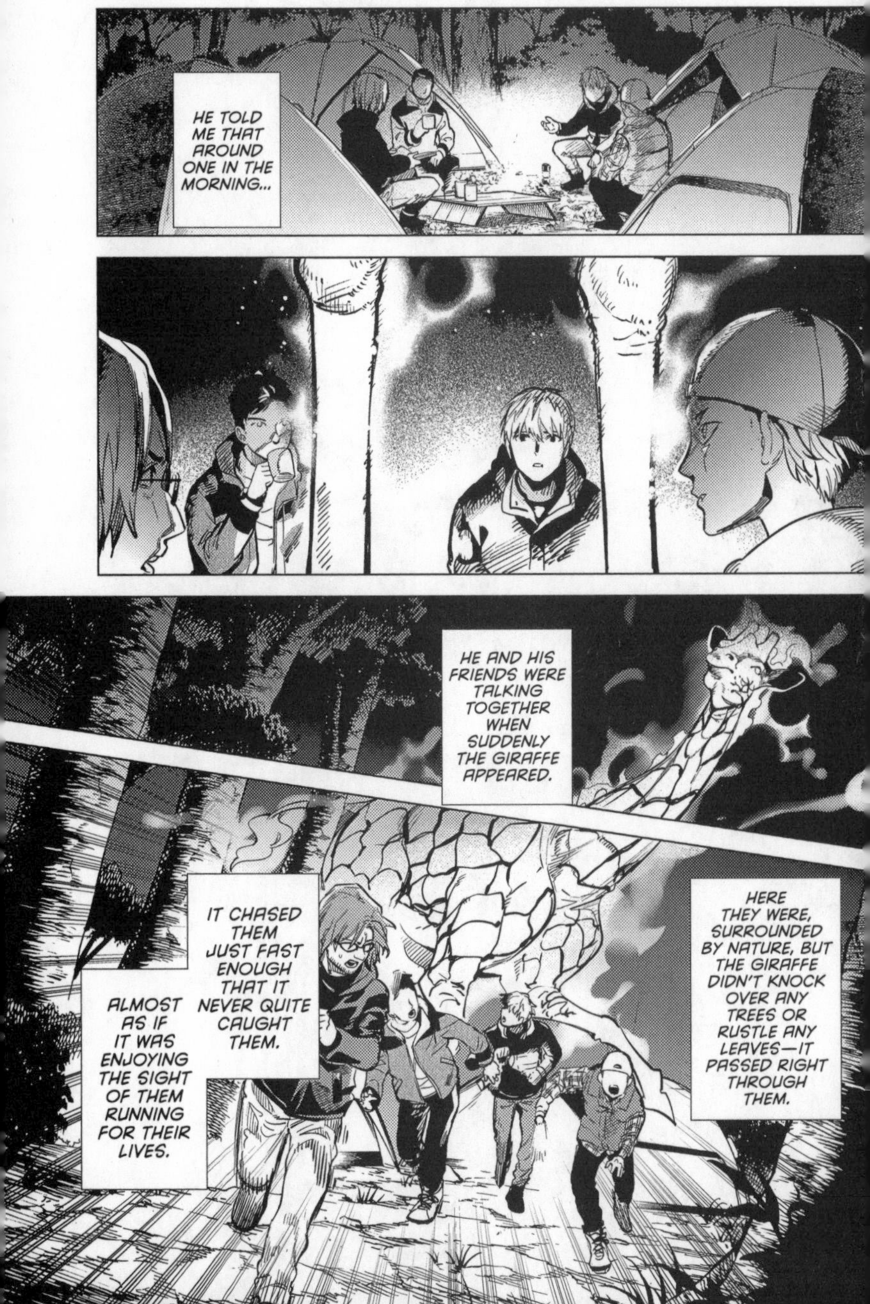
HE TOLD ME THAT AROUND ONE IN THE MORNING...
HE AND HIS FRIENDS WERE TALKING TOGETHER WHEN SUDDENLY THE GIRAFFE APPEARED.
HERE THEY WERE, SURROUNDED BY NATURE, BUT THE GIRAFFE DIDN'T KNOCK OVER ANY TREES OR RUSTLE ANY LEAVES—IT PASSED RIGHT THROUGH THEM.
IT CHASED THEM JUST FAST ENOUGH THAT IT NEVER QUITE CAUGHT THEM.
ALMOST AS IF IT WAS ENJOYING THE SIGHT OF THEM RUNNING FOR THEIR LIVES.

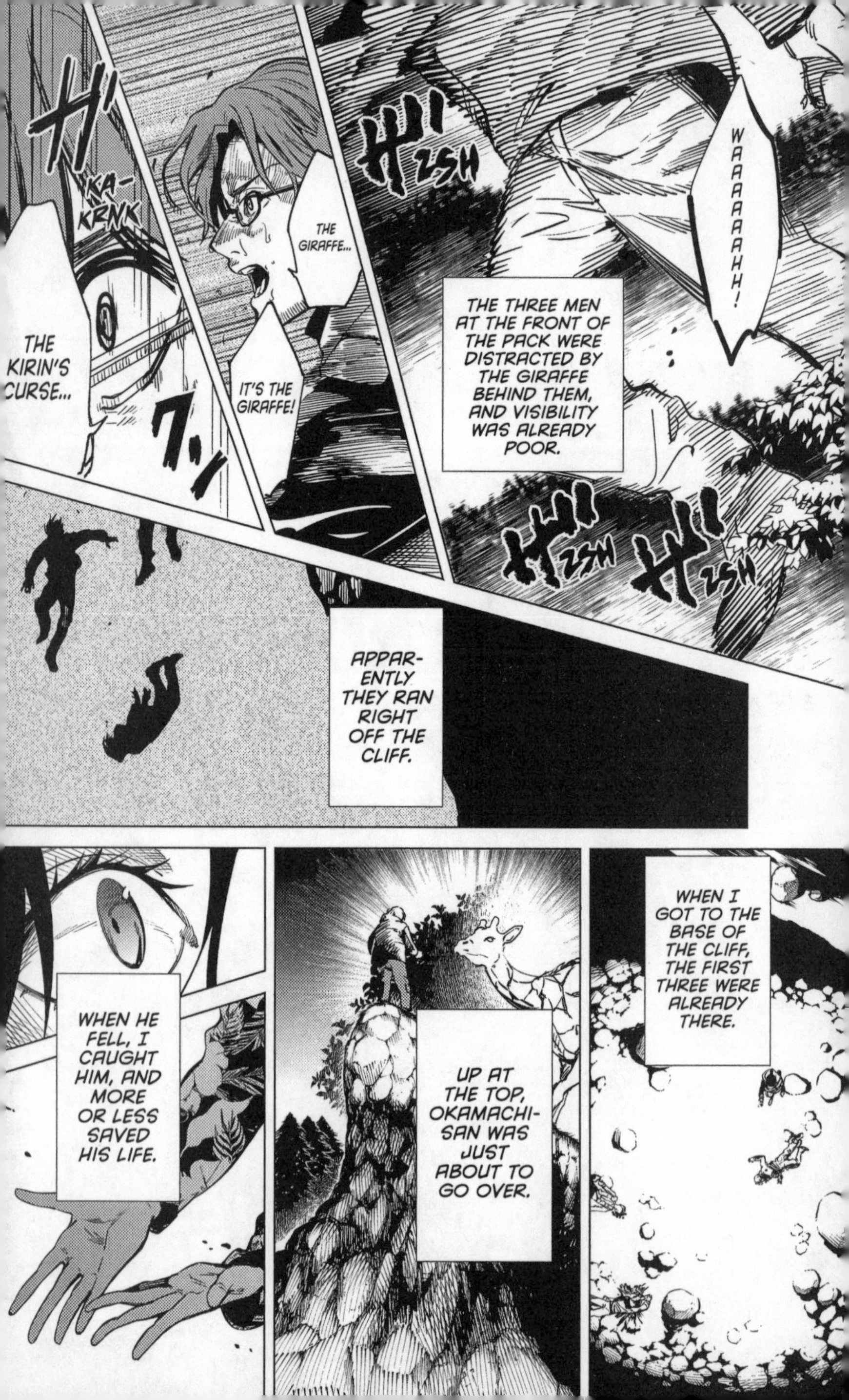
WAAAAAAAHH!
ZSH
THE THREE MEN AT THE FRONT OF THE PACK WERE DISTRACTED BY THE GIRAFFE BEHIND THEM, AND VISIBILITY WAS ALREADY POOR.
ZSH
ZSH
THE GIRAFFE...
IT'S THE GIRAFFE!
KA-KRNK
THE KIRIN'S CURSE...
APPAR-ENTLY THEY RAN RIGHT OFF THE CLIFF.
WHEN I GOT TO THE BASE OF THE CLIFF, THE FIRST THREE WERE ALREADY THERE.
UP AT THE TOP, OKAMACHI-SAN WAS JUST ABOUT TO GO OVER.
WHEN HE FELL, I CAUGHT HIM, AND MORE OR LESS SAVED HIS LIFE.

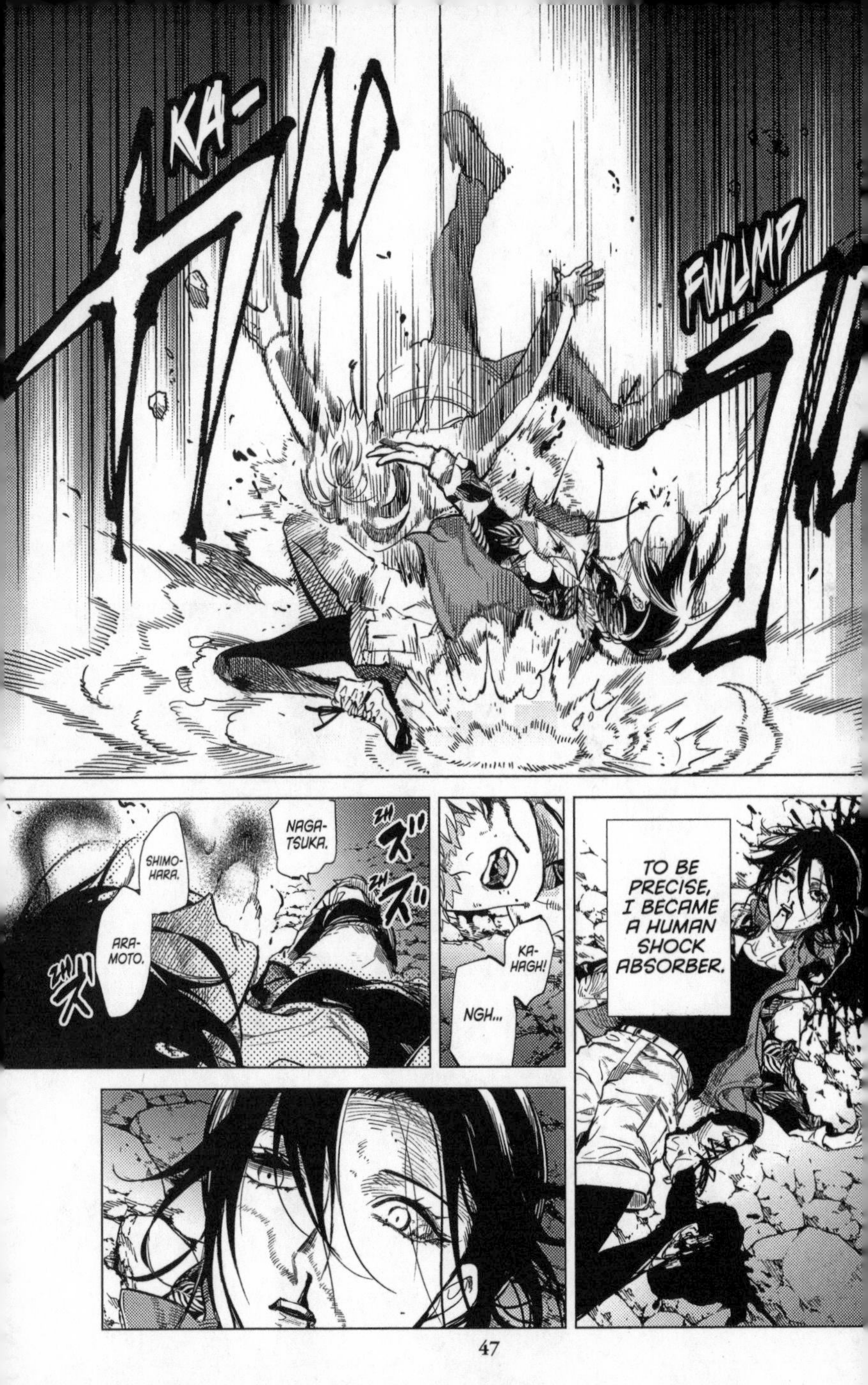
KA-
FWUMP
TO BE PRECISE, I BECAME A HUMAN SHOCK ABSORBER.
KA-HAGH!
NGH...
ZH
ZH
NAGA-TSUKA.
SHIMO-HARA.
ARA-MOTO.
ZH

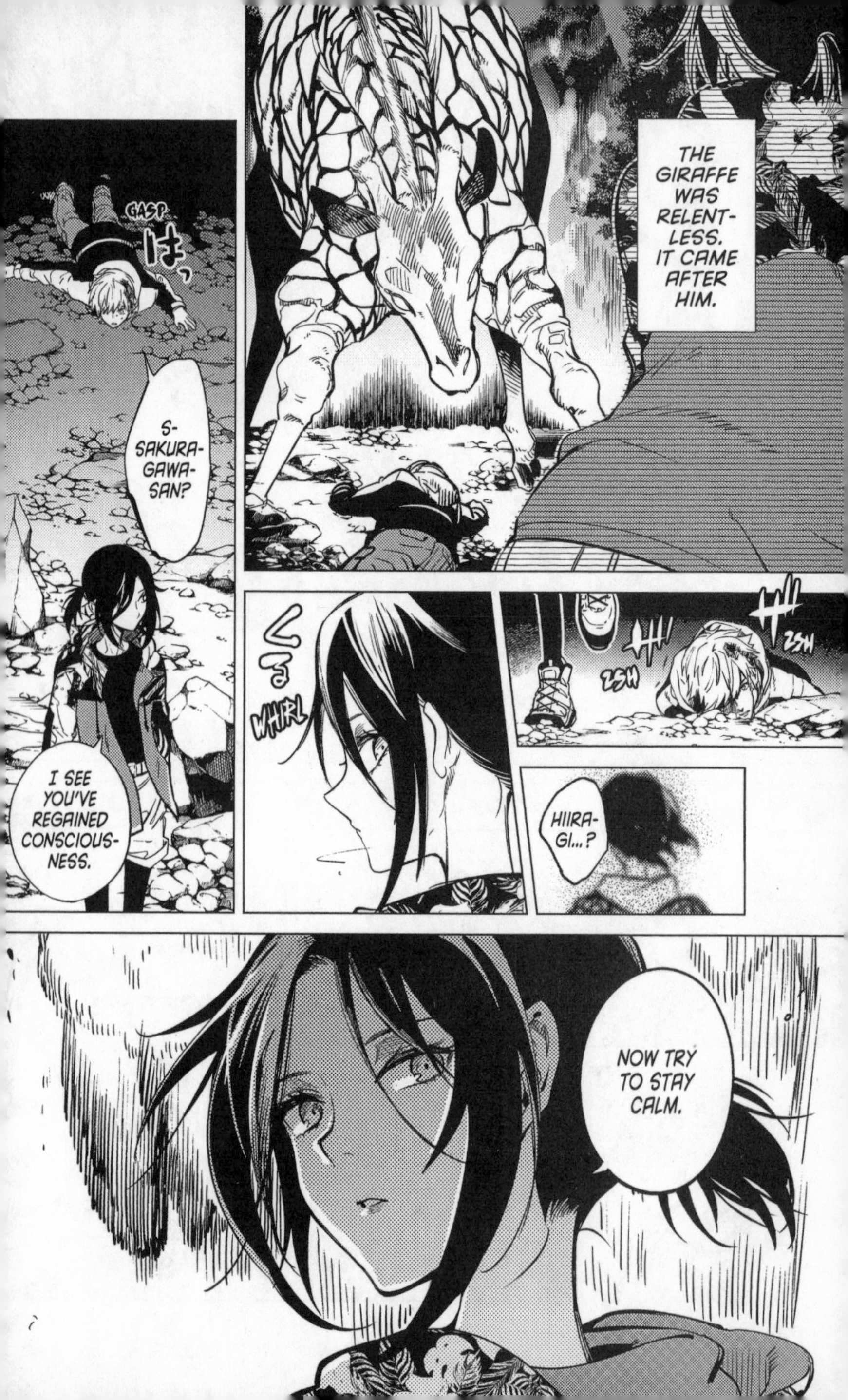
THE GIRAFFE WAS RELENTLESS. IT CAME AFTER HIM.
GASP
は、
S-SAKURAGAWA-SAN?
I SEE YOU'VE REGAINED CONSCIOUSNESS.
ZSH
ZSH
HIIRAGI...?
くる
WHRL
NOW TRY TO STAY CALM.

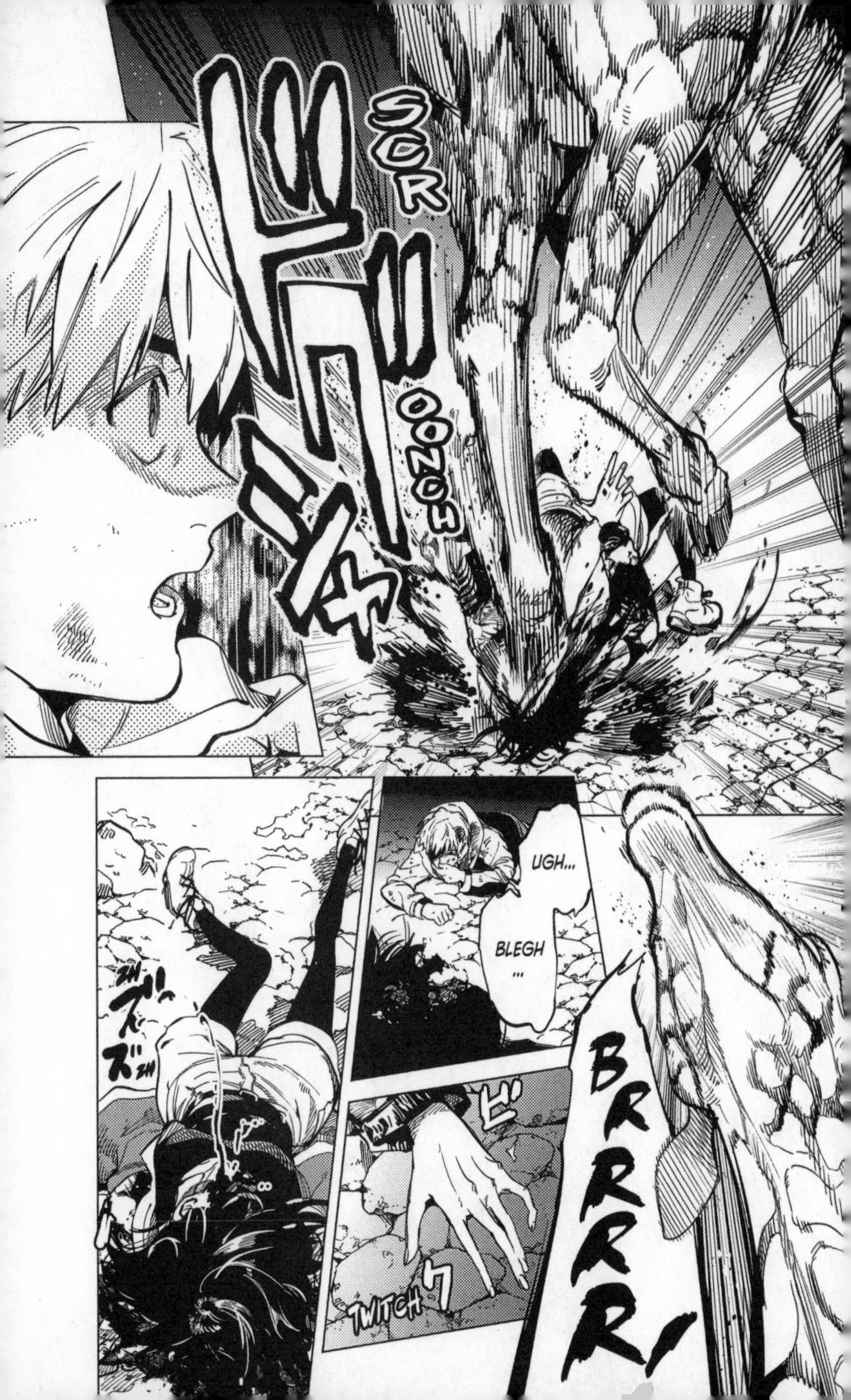
SCROONCH
BRRRR!
UGH...
BLEGH
...
TWITCH
ZH
ZH

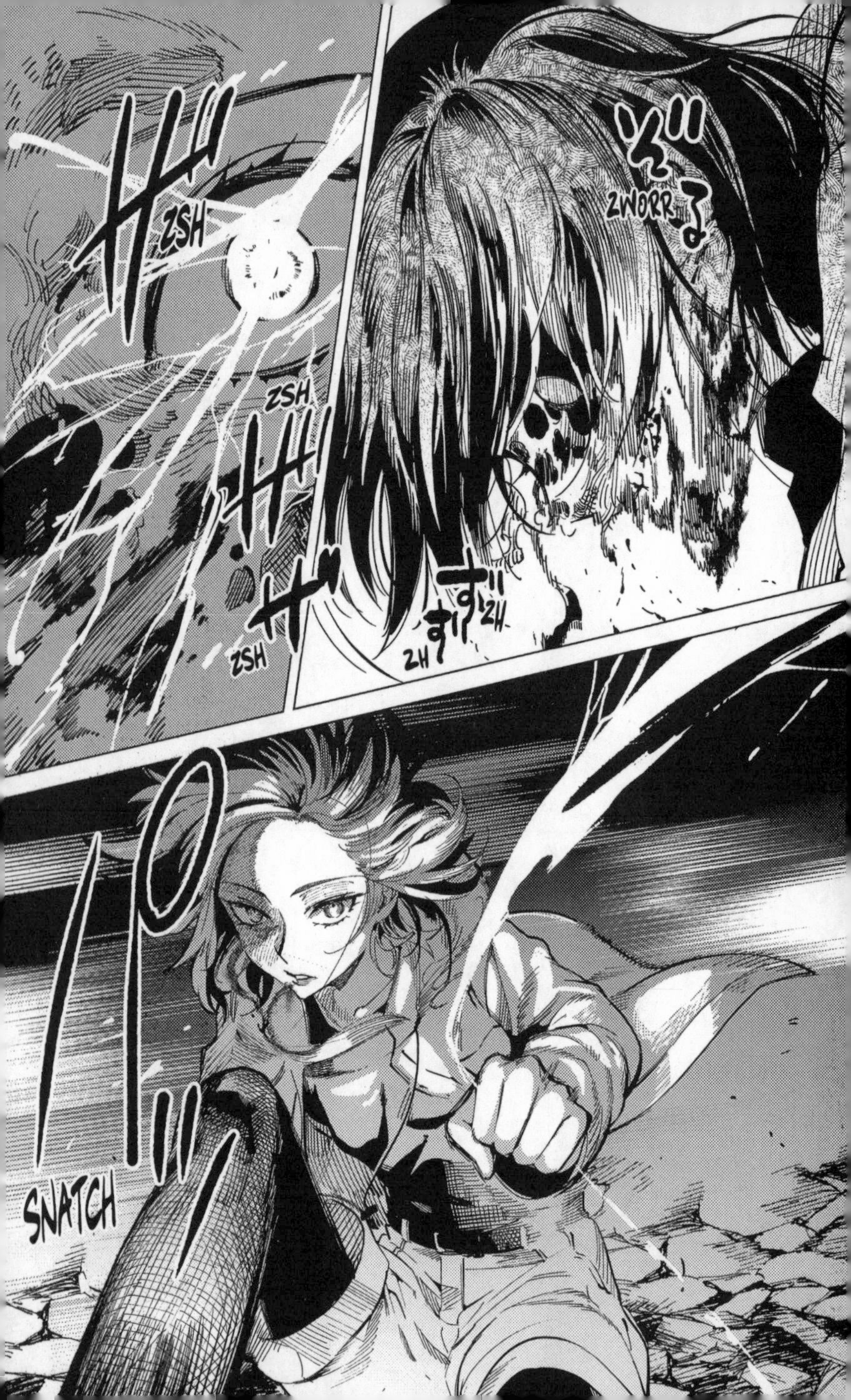
ZWORR
ZH
ZH
ZSH
ZSH
ZSH
SNATCH

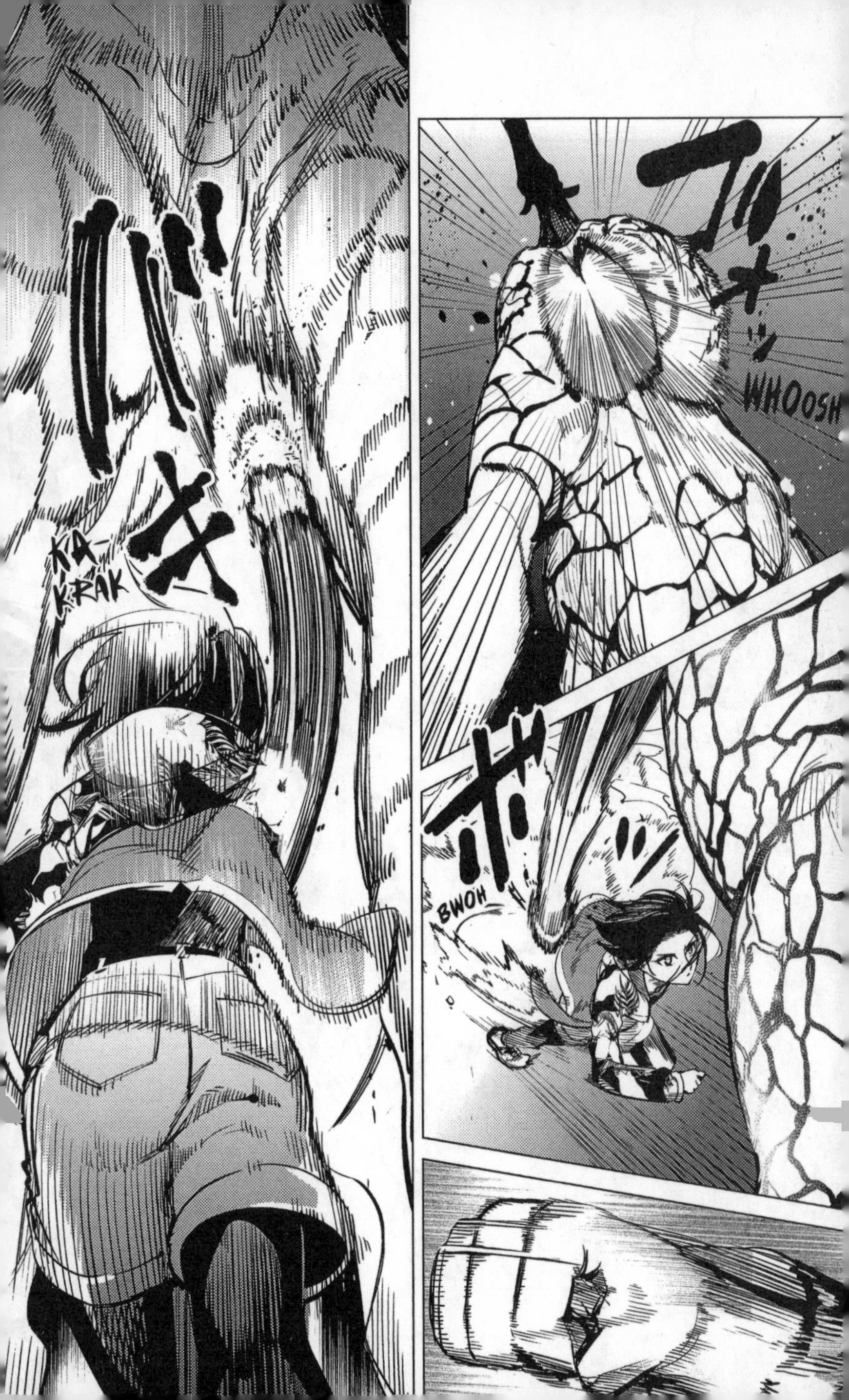
WHOOSH
BWOH
KA-KRAK

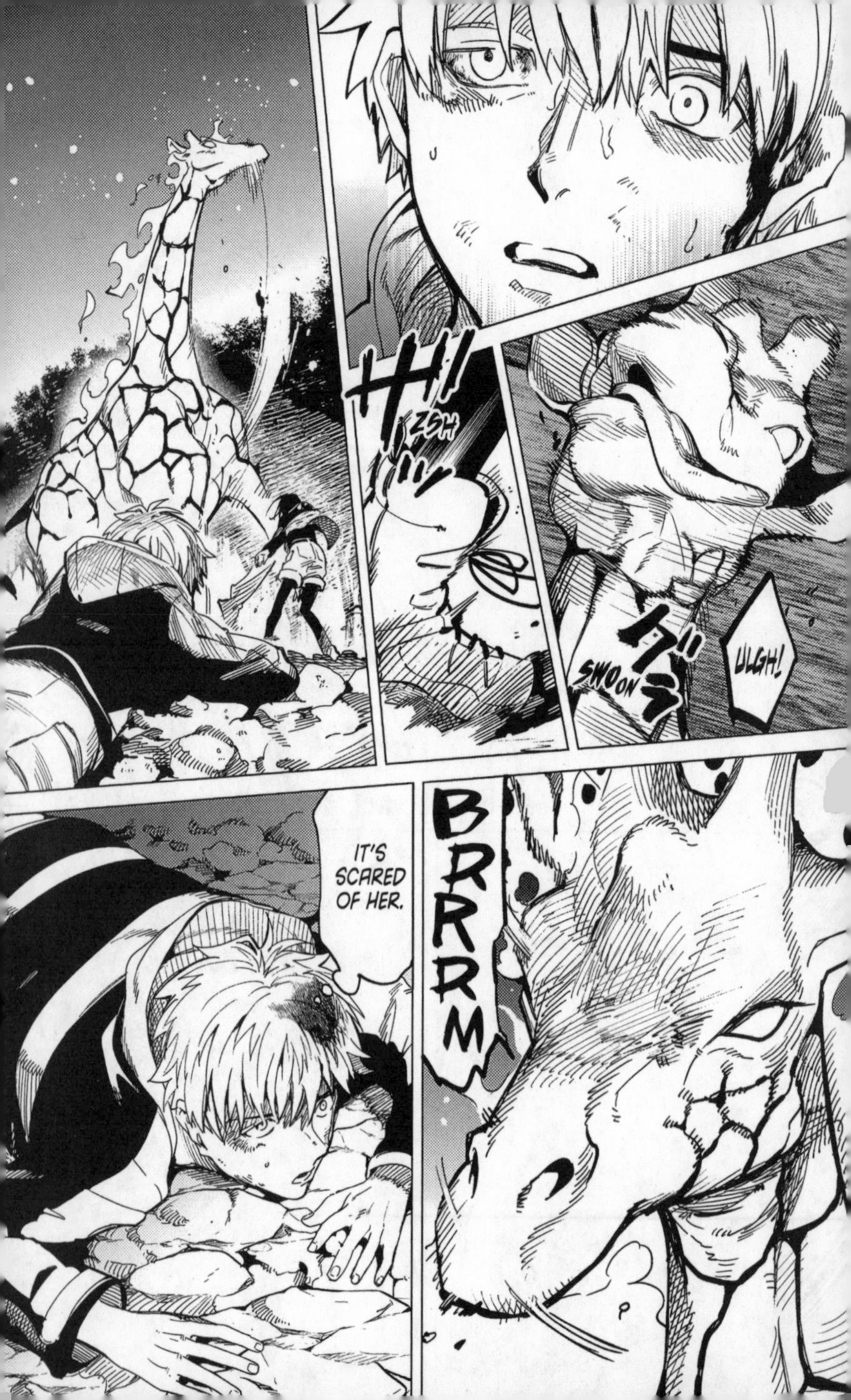
ULGH!
SWOON
HH
ZSH
BRRRM
IT'S SCARED OF HER.

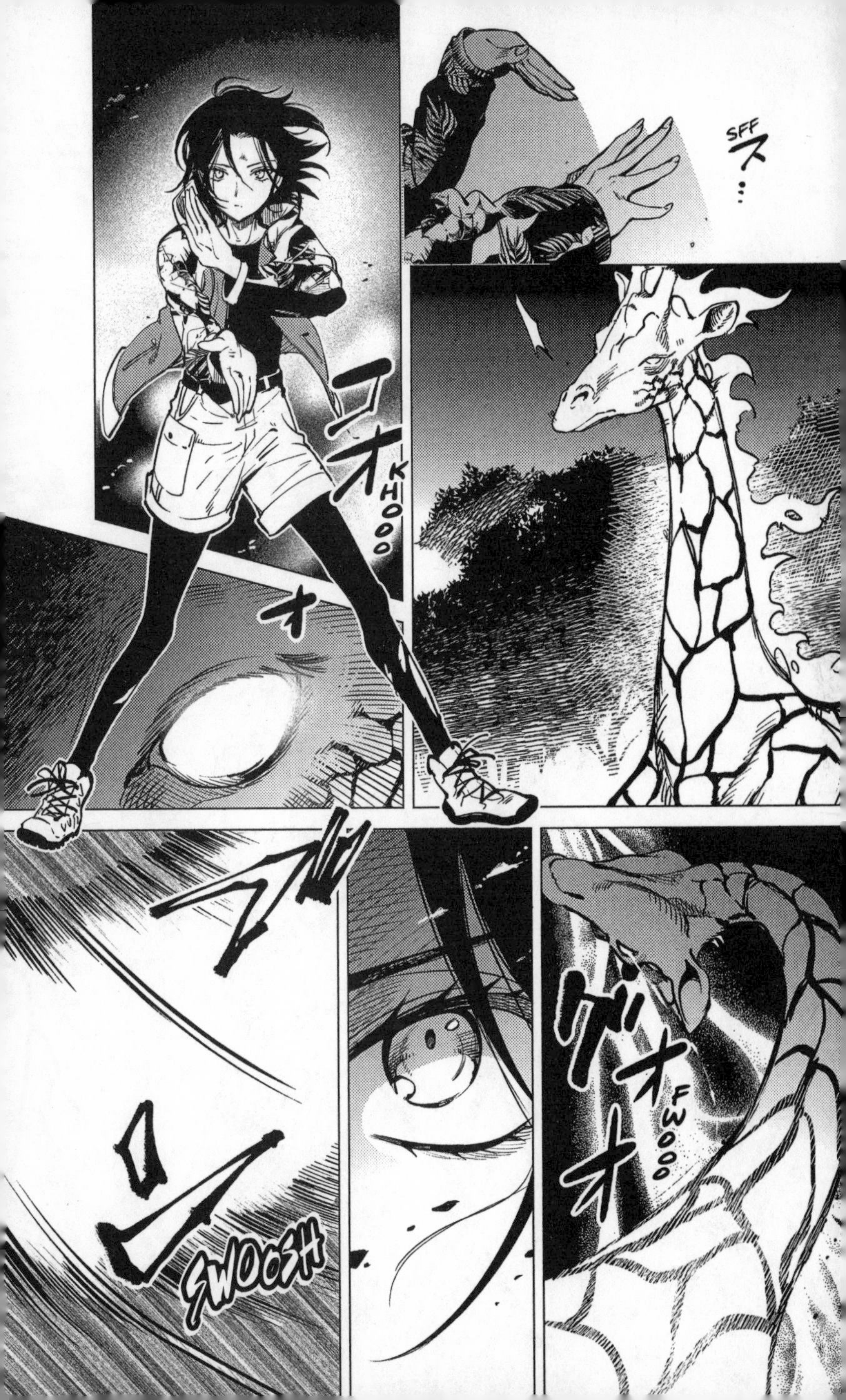

SFF
KHOOOO
FWOOOO
SWOOSH

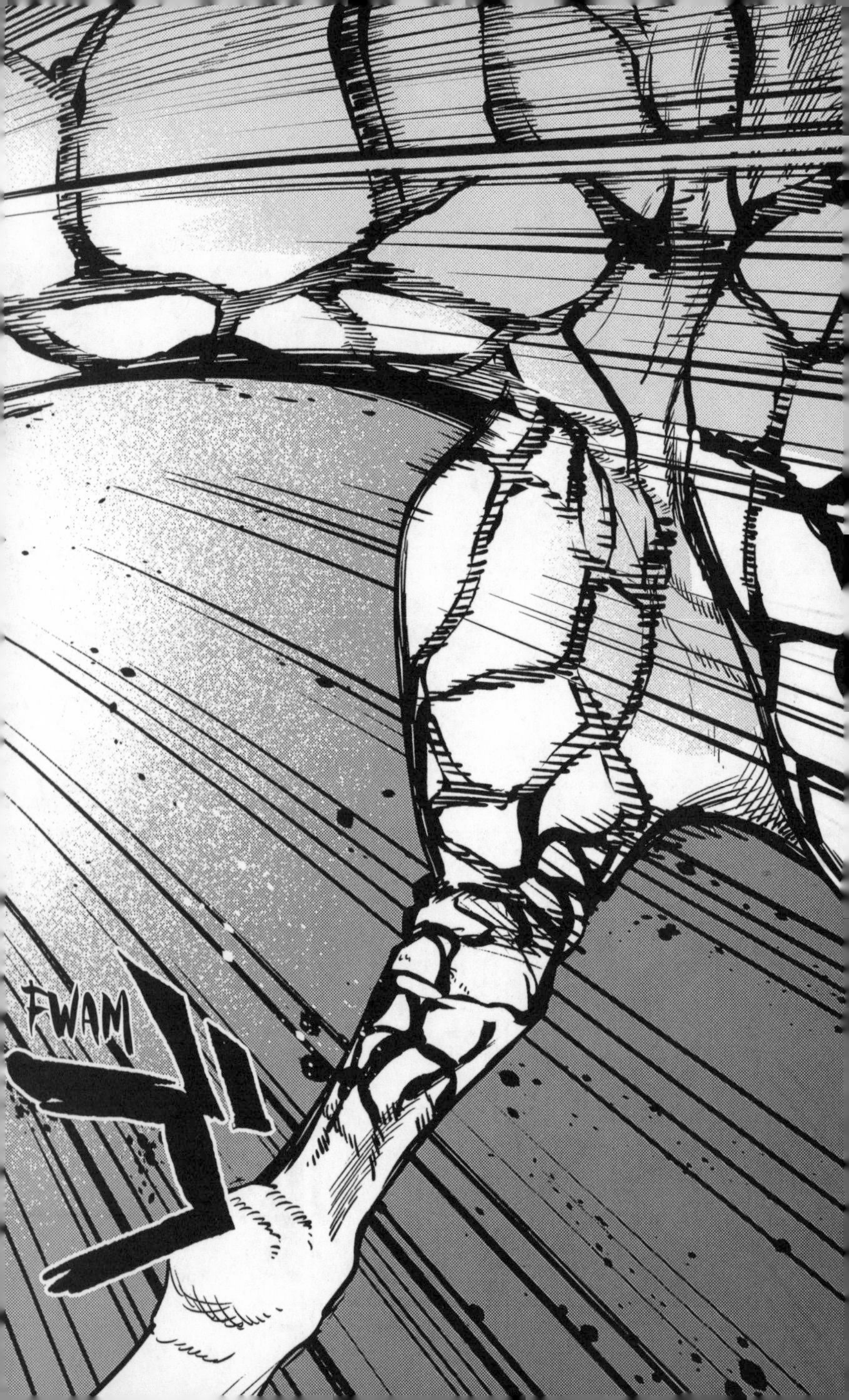
FWAM

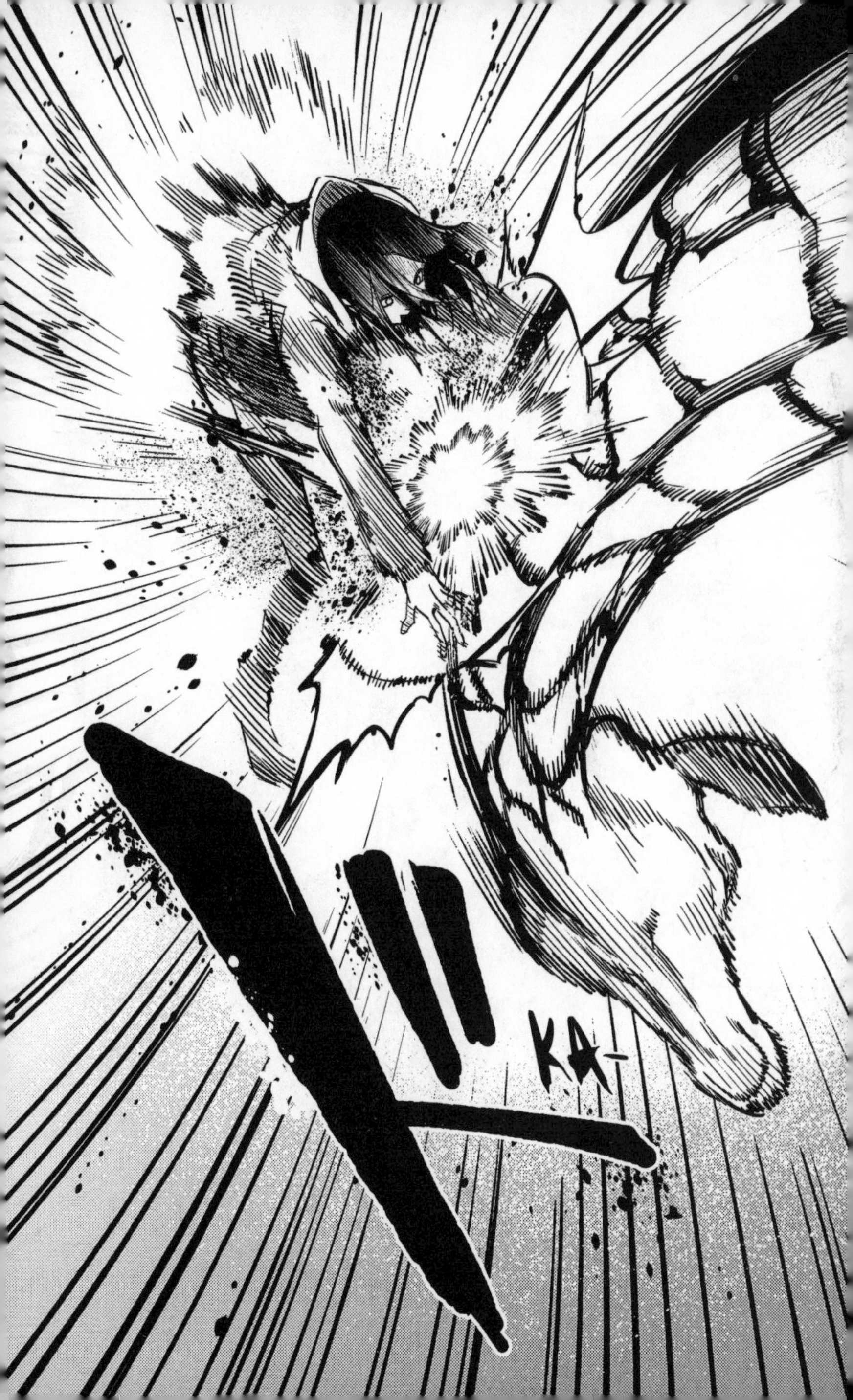
ド
KA-

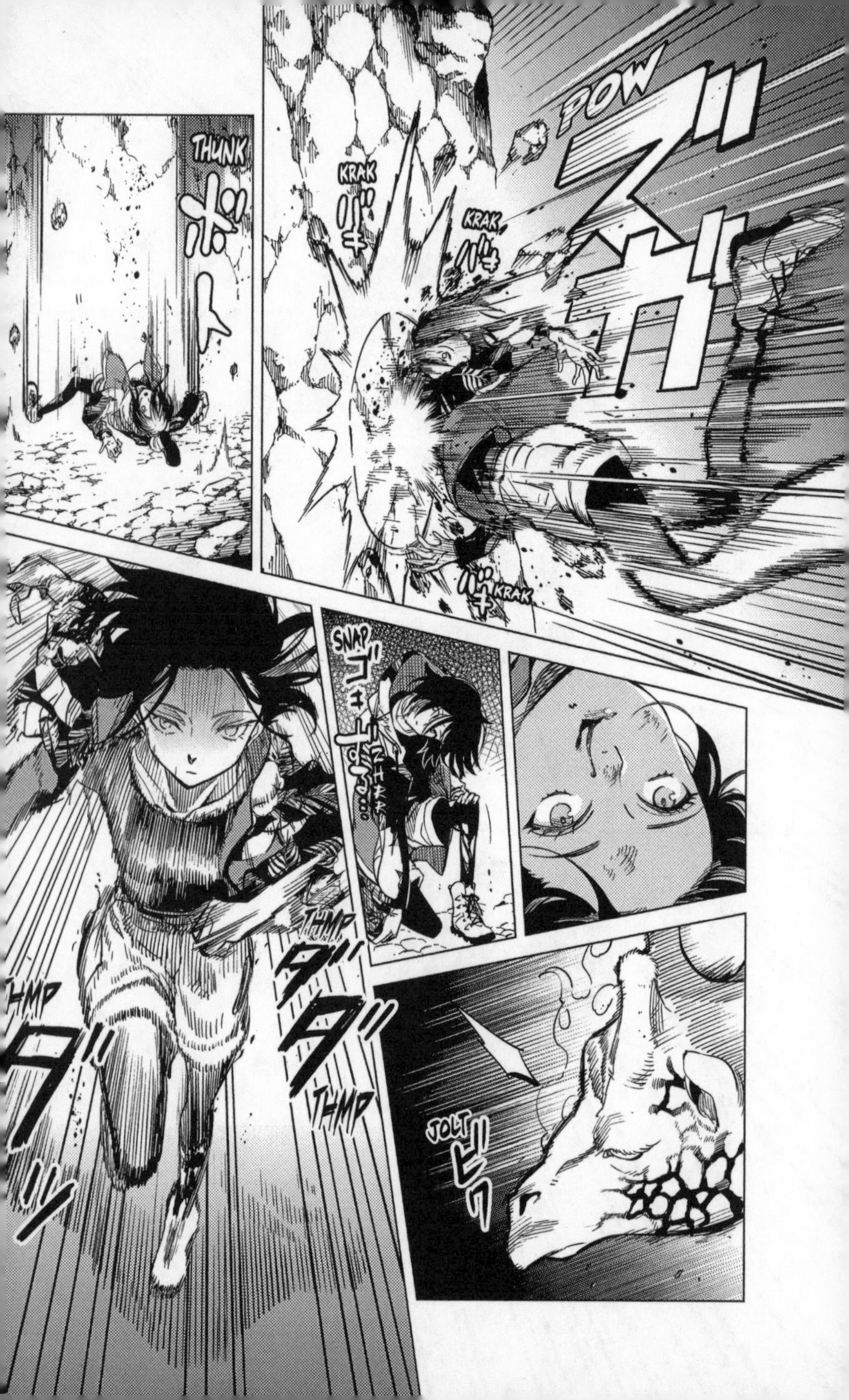

POW
KRAK
KRAK
KRAK
THUNK
SNAP
ZHRR...
THMP
THMP
THMP
JOLT

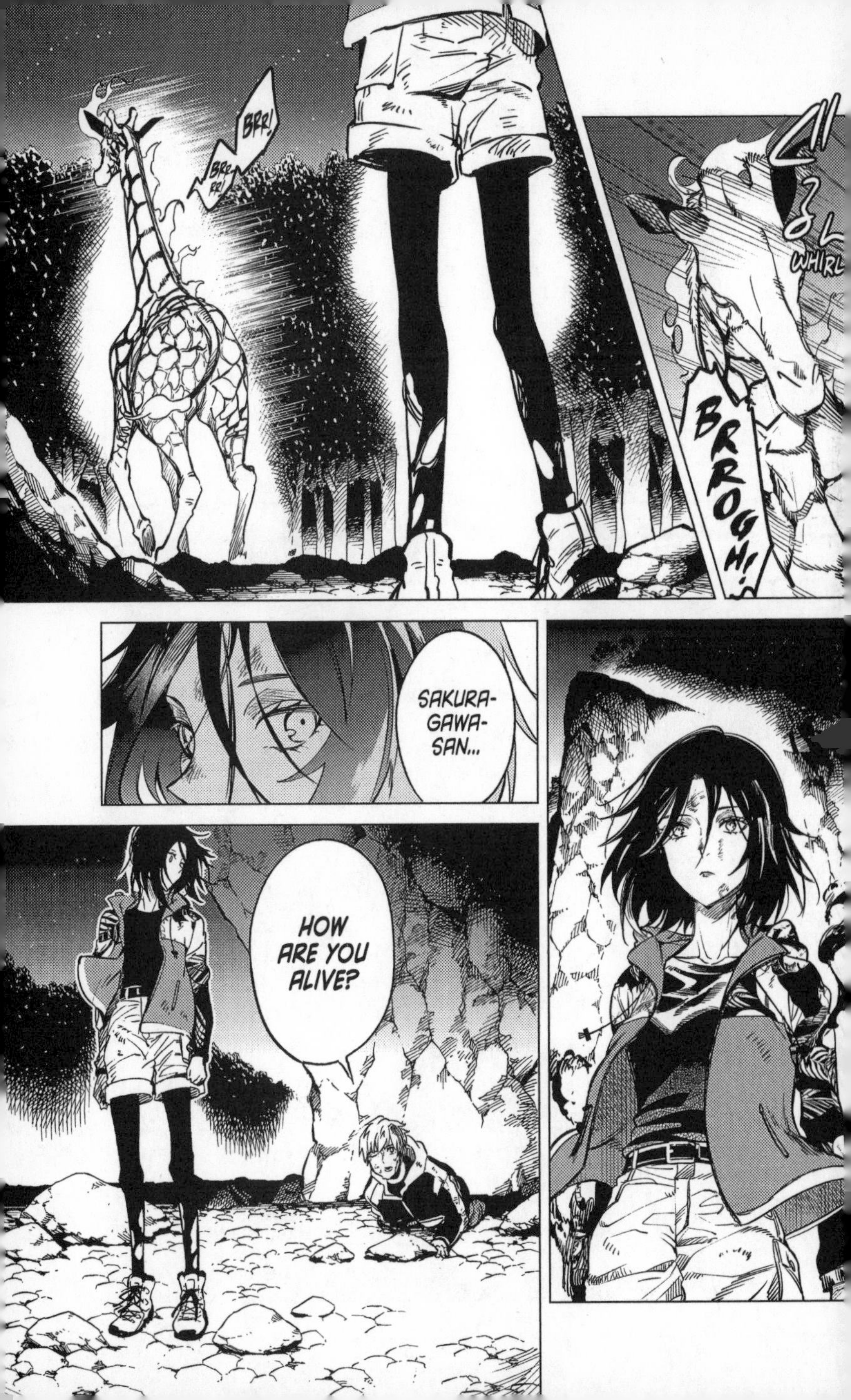
ぐるん
WHIRL
BRROGH!
BRR!
BRR RR!
SAKURA-GAWA-SAN...
HOW ARE YOU ALIVE?

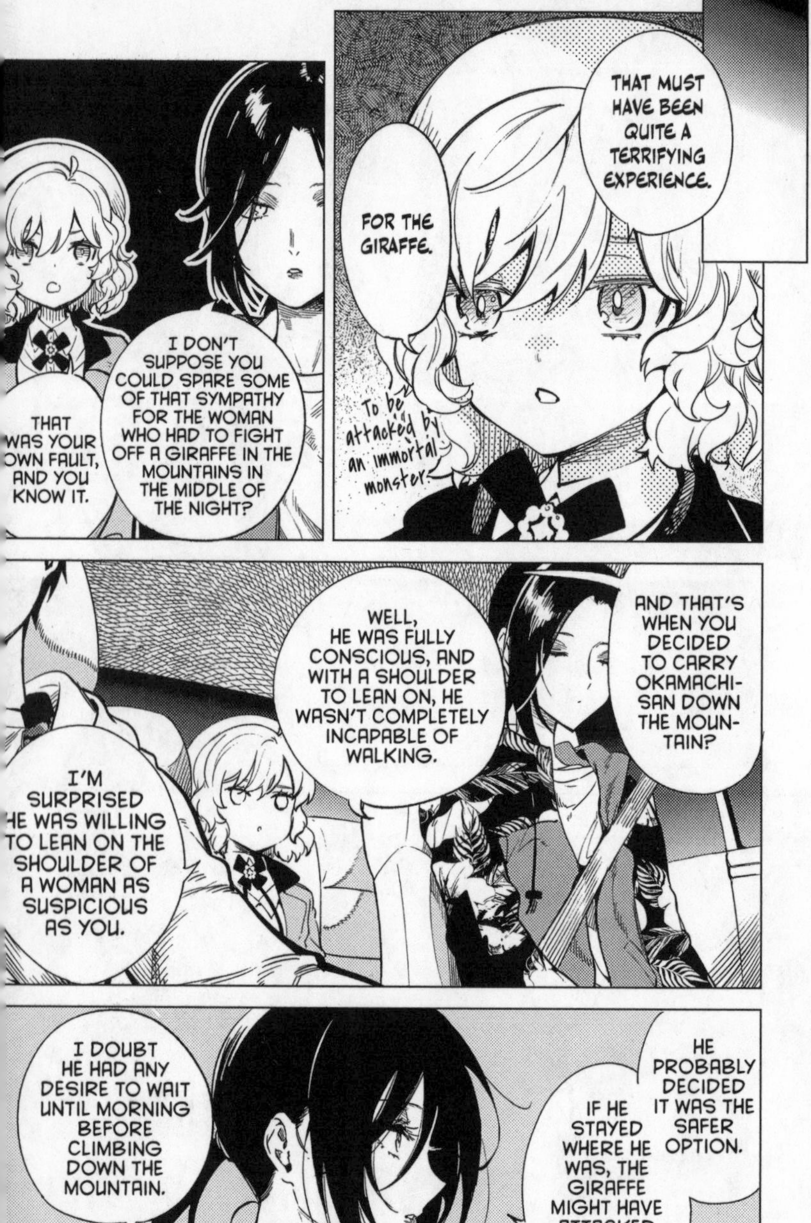
THAT MUST HAVE BEEN QUITE A TERRIFYING EXPERIENCE.
FOR THE GIRAFFE.
To be attacked by an immortal monster.
I DON'T SUPPOSE YOU COULD SPARE SOME OF THAT SYMPATHY FOR THE WOMAN WHO HAD TO FIGHT OFF A GIRAFFE IN THE MOUNTAINS IN THE MIDDLE OF THE NIGHT?
THAT WAS YOUR OWN FAULT, AND YOU KNOW IT.
AND THAT'S WHEN YOU DECIDED TO CARRY OKAMACHI-SAN DOWN THE MOUNTAIN?
WELL, HE WAS FULLY CONSCIOUS, AND WITH A SHOULDER TO LEAN ON, HE WASN'T COMPLETELY INCAPABLE OF WALKING.
I'M SURPRISED HE WAS WILLING TO LEAN ON THE SHOULDER OF A WOMAN AS SUSPICIOUS AS YOU.
HE PROBABLY DECIDED IT WAS THE SAFER OPTION.
IF HE STAYED WHERE HE WAS, THE GIRAFFE MIGHT HAVE ATTACKED AGAIN.
I DOUBT HE HAD ANY DESIRE TO WAIT UNTIL MORNING BEFORE CLIMBING DOWN THE MOUNTAIN.

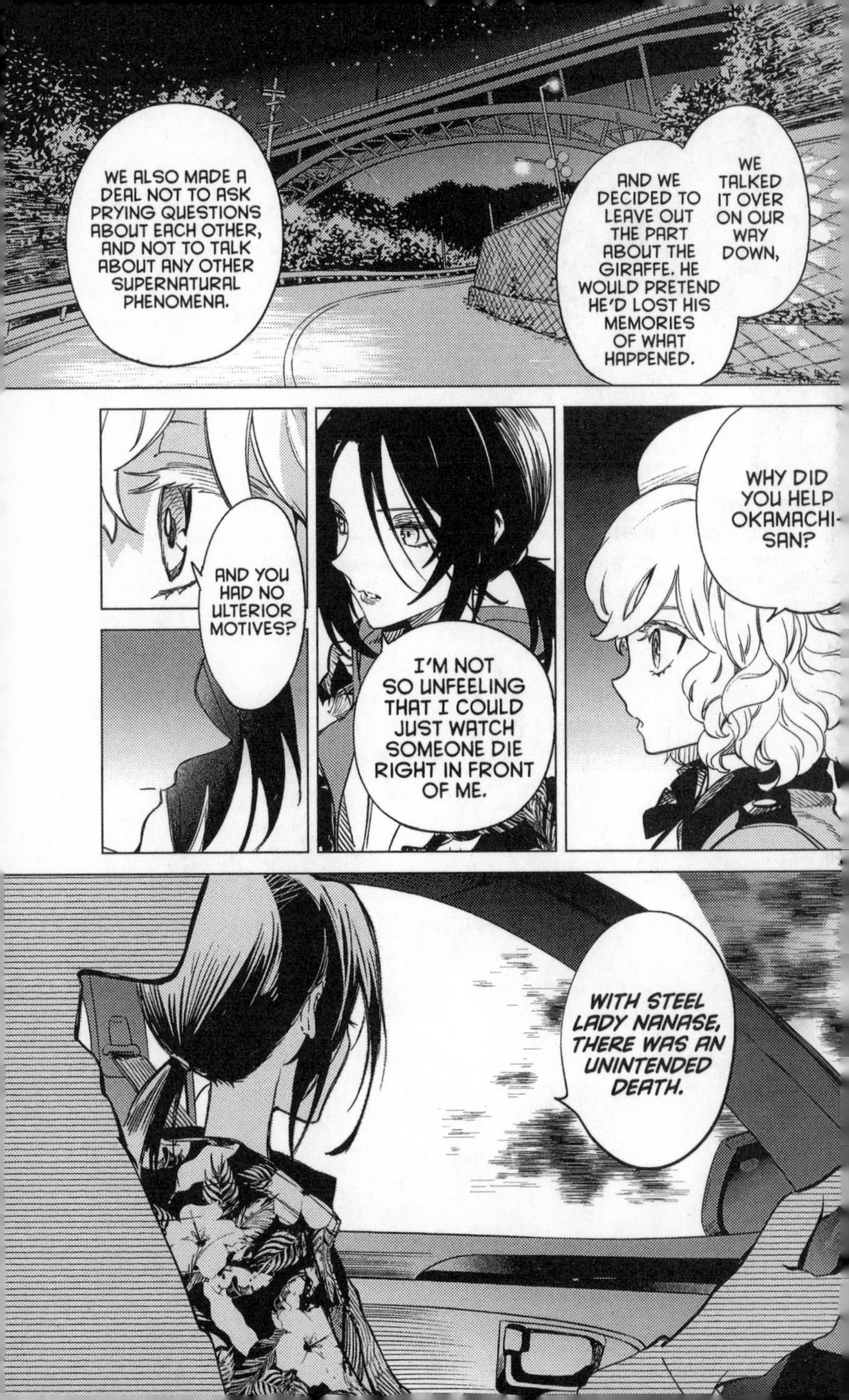
WE TALKED IT OVER ON OUR WAY DOWN,
AND WE DECIDED TO LEAVE OUT THE PART ABOUT THE GIRAFFE. HE WOULD PRETEND HE'D LOST HIS MEMORIES OF WHAT HAPPENED.
WE ALSO MADE A DEAL NOT TO ASK PRYING QUESTIONS ABOUT EACH OTHER, AND NOT TO TALK ABOUT ANY OTHER SUPERNATURAL PHENOMENA.
WHY DID YOU HELP OKAMACHI-SAN?
I'M NOT SO UNFEELING THAT I COULD JUST WATCH SOMEONE DIE RIGHT IN FRONT OF ME.
AND YOU HAD NO ULTERIOR MOTIVES?
*WITH STEEL LADY NANASE, THERE WAS AN UNINTENDED DEATH.*

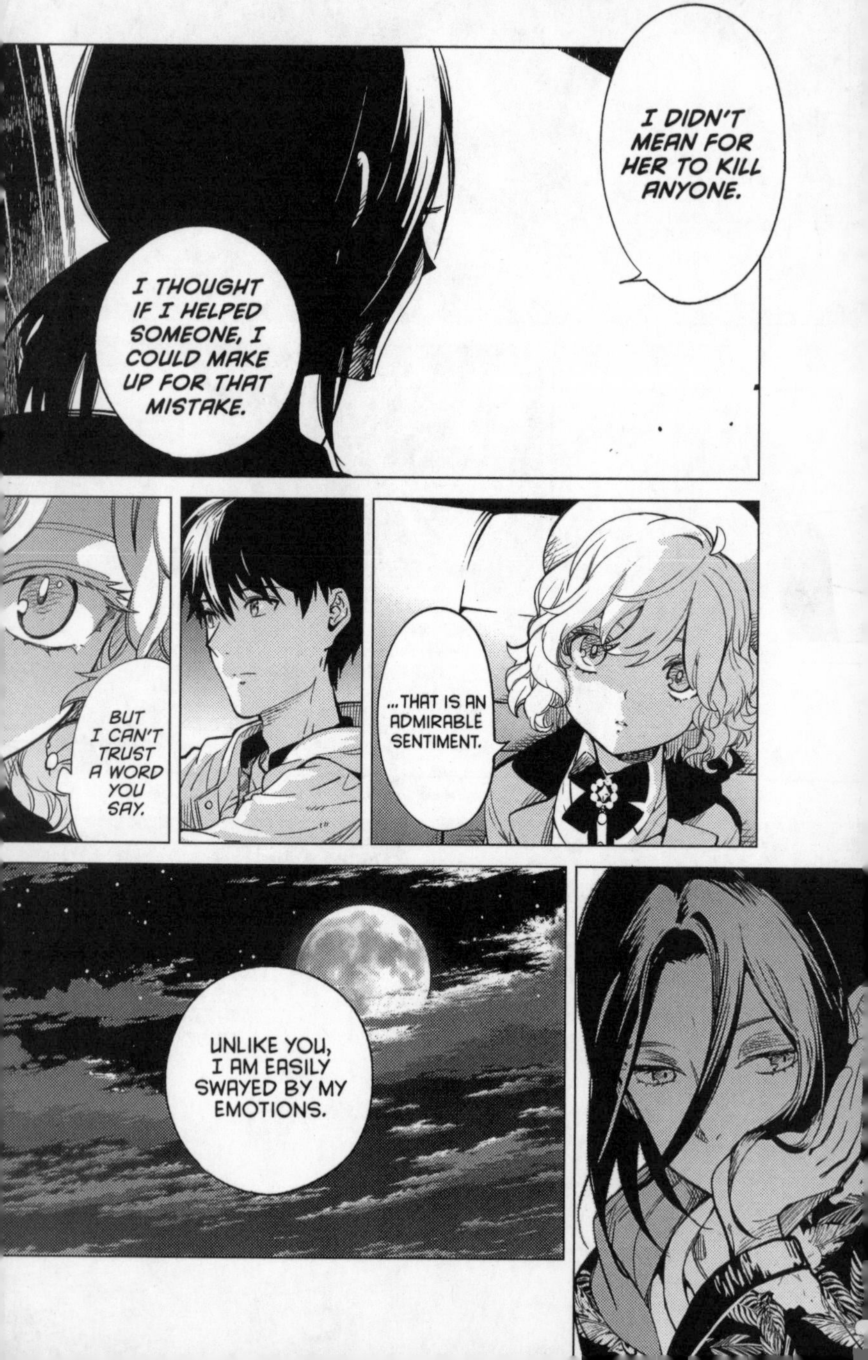
I DIDN'T MEAN FOR HER TO KILL ANYONE.
I THOUGHT IF I HELPED SOMEONE, I COULD MAKE UP FOR THAT MISTAKE.
...THAT IS AN ADMIRABLE SENTIMENT.
BUT I CAN'T TRUST A WORD YOU SAY.
UNLIKE YOU, I AM EASILY SWAYED BY MY EMOTIONS.

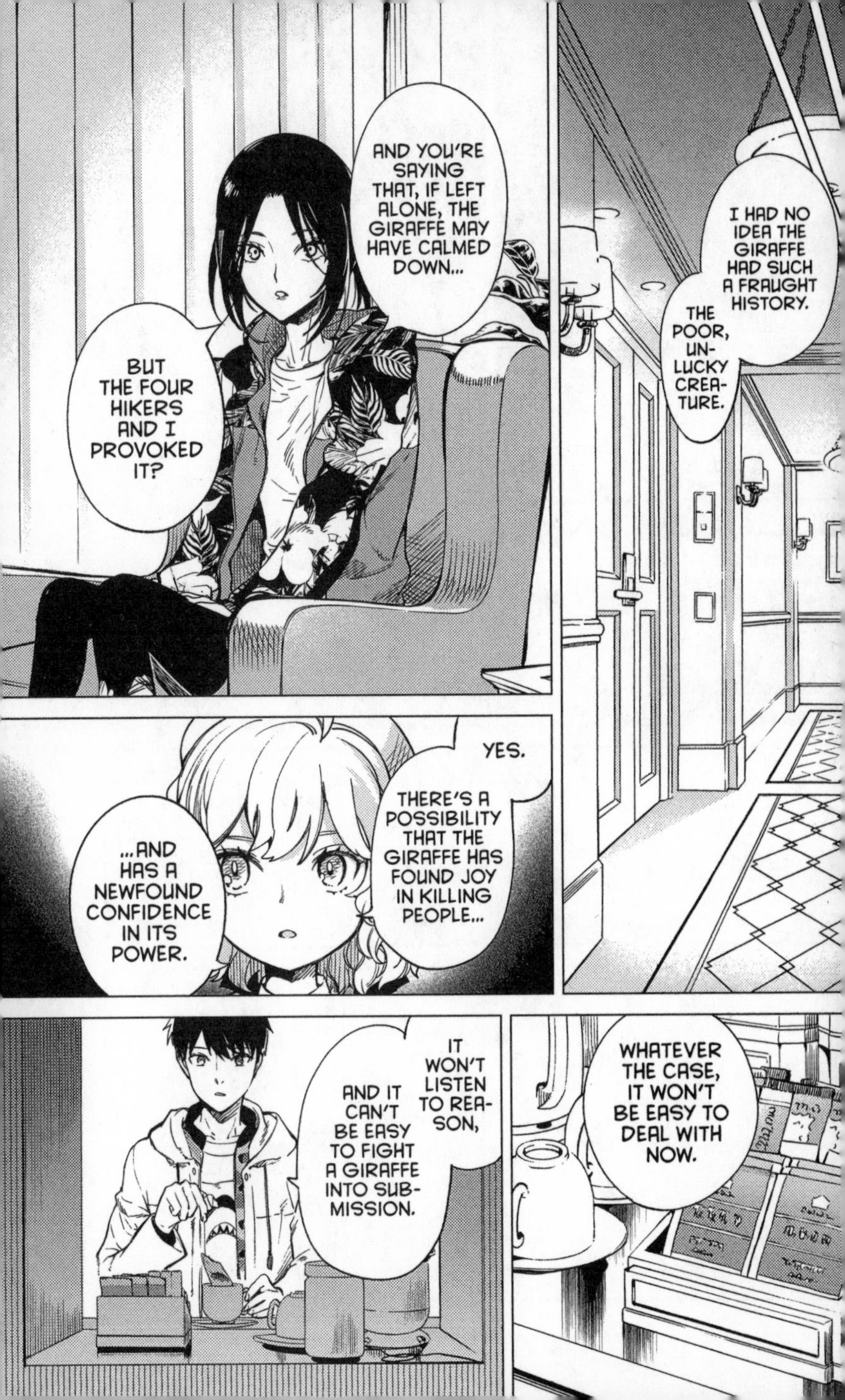
I HAD NO IDEA THE GIRAFFE HAD SUCH A FRAUGHT HISTORY.
THE POOR, UNLUCKY CREATURE.
AND YOU'RE SAYING THAT, IF LEFT ALONE, THE GIRAFFE MAY HAVE CALMED DOWN...
BUT THE FOUR HIKERS AND I PROVOKED IT?
YES.
THERE'S A POSSIBILITY THAT THE GIRAFFE HAS FOUND JOY IN KILLING PEOPLE...
...AND HAS A NEWFOUND CONFIDENCE IN ITS POWER.
WHATEVER THE CASE, IT WON'T BE EASY TO DEAL WITH NOW.
IT WON'T LISTEN TO REASON,
AND IT CAN'T BE EASY TO FIGHT A GIRAFFE INTO SUBMISSION.

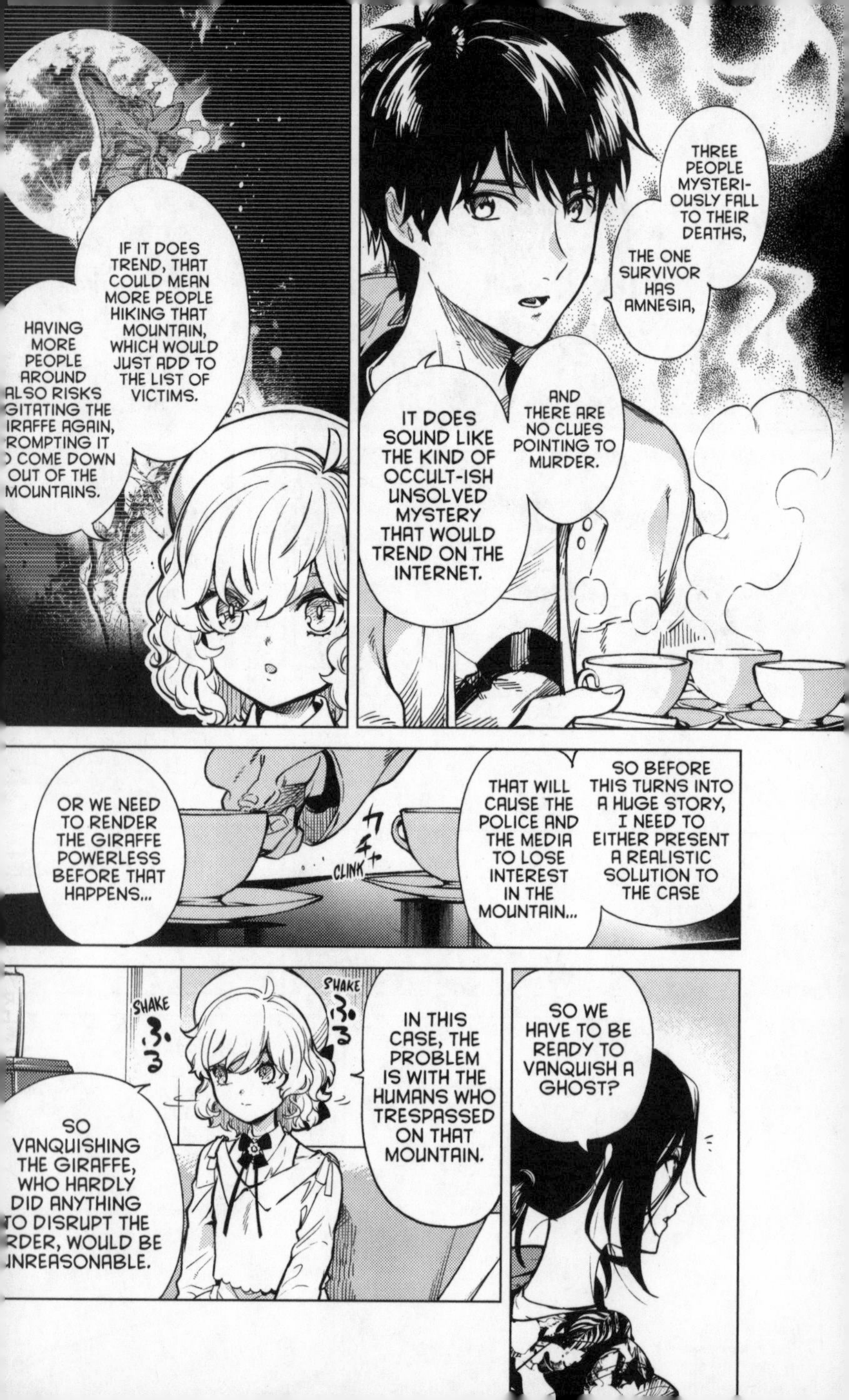
THREE PEOPLE MYSTERIOUSLY FALL TO THEIR DEATHS,
THE ONE SURVIVOR HAS AMNESIA,
AND THERE ARE NO CLUES POINTING TO MURDER.
IT DOES SOUND LIKE THE KIND OF OCCULT-ISH UNSOLVED MYSTERY THAT WOULD TREND ON THE INTERNET.
IF IT DOES TREND, THAT COULD MEAN MORE PEOPLE HIKING THAT MOUNTAIN, WHICH WOULD JUST ADD TO THE LIST OF VICTIMS.
HAVING MORE PEOPLE AROUND ALSO RISKS GITATING THE IRAFFE AGAIN, ROMPTING IT O COME DOWN OUT OF THE MOUNTAINS.
SO BEFORE THIS TURNS INTO A HUGE STORY, I NEED TO EITHER PRESENT A REALISTIC SOLUTION TO THE CASE
THAT WILL CAUSE THE POLICE AND THE MEDIA TO LOSE INTEREST IN THE MOUNTAIN...
CLINK
OR WE NEED TO RENDER THE GIRAFFE POWERLESS BEFORE THAT HAPPENS...
SO WE HAVE TO BE READY TO VANQUISH A GHOST?
SHAKE
SHAKE
IN THIS CASE, THE PROBLEM IS WITH THE HUMANS WHO TRESPASSED ON THAT MOUNTAIN.
SO VANQUISHING THE GIRAFFE, WHO HARDLY DID ANYTHING TO DISRUPT THE RDER, WOULD BE NREASONABLE.

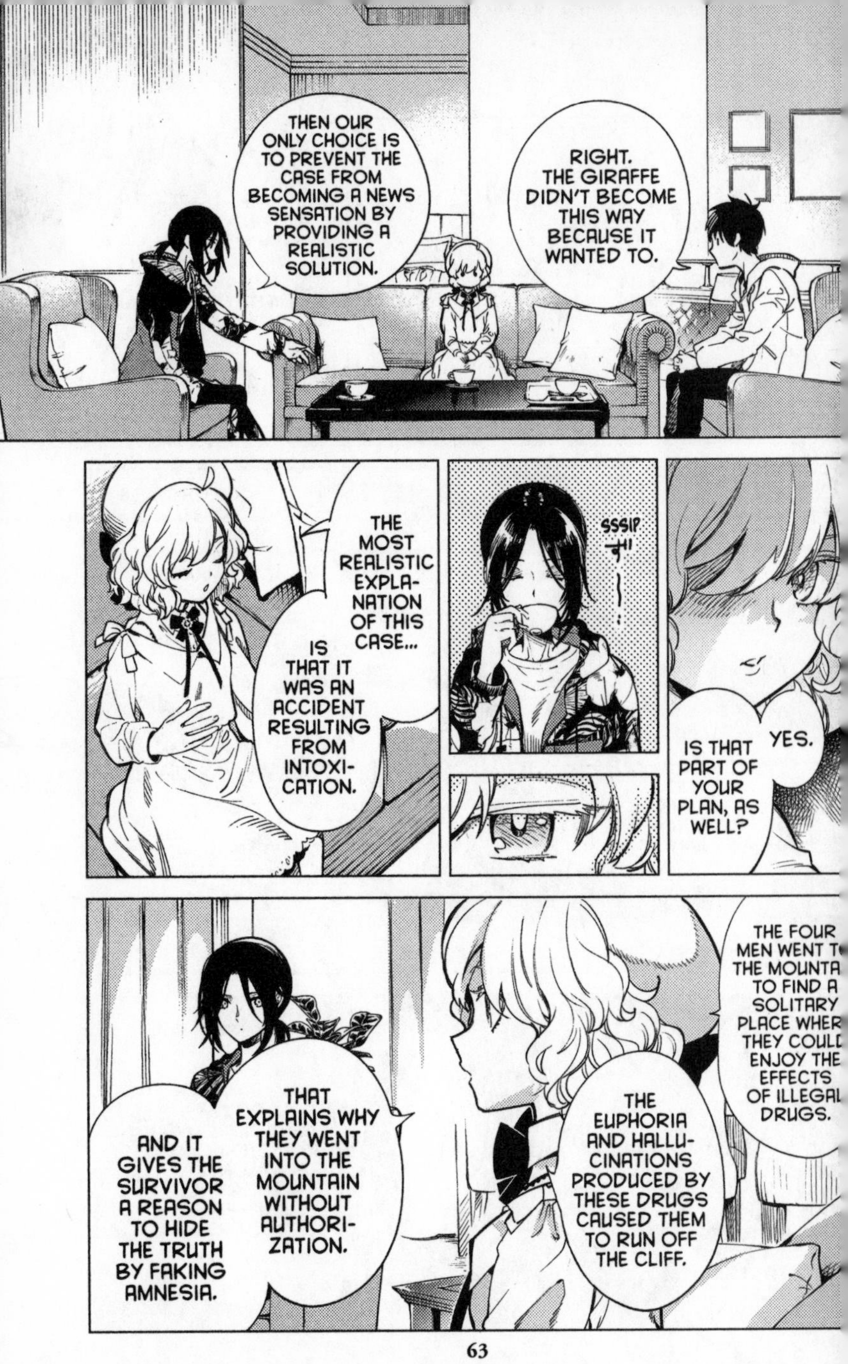
RIGHT. THE GIRAFFE DIDN'T BECOME THIS WAY BECAUSE IT WANTED TO.
THEN OUR ONLY CHOICE IS TO PREVENT THE CASE FROM BECOMING A NEWS SENSATION BY PROVIDING A REALISTIC SOLUTION.
YES.
IS THAT PART OF YOUR PLAN, AS WELL?
SSSIP
THE MOST REALISTIC EXPLA-NATION OF THIS CASE...
IS THAT IT WAS AN ACCIDENT RESULTING FROM INTOXI-CATION.
THE FOUR MEN WENT T THE MOUNTA TO FIND A SOLITARY PLACE WHER THEY COUL ENJOY THE EFFECTS OF ILLEGAL DRUGS.
THE EUPHORIA AND HALLU-CINATIONS PRODUCED BY THESE DRUGS CAUSED THEM TO RUN OFF THE CLIFF.
THAT EXPLAINS WHY THEY WENT INTO THE MOUNTAIN WITHOUT AUTHORI-ZATION.
AND IT GIVES THE SURVIVOR A REASON TO HIDE THE TRUTH BY FAKING AMNESIA.

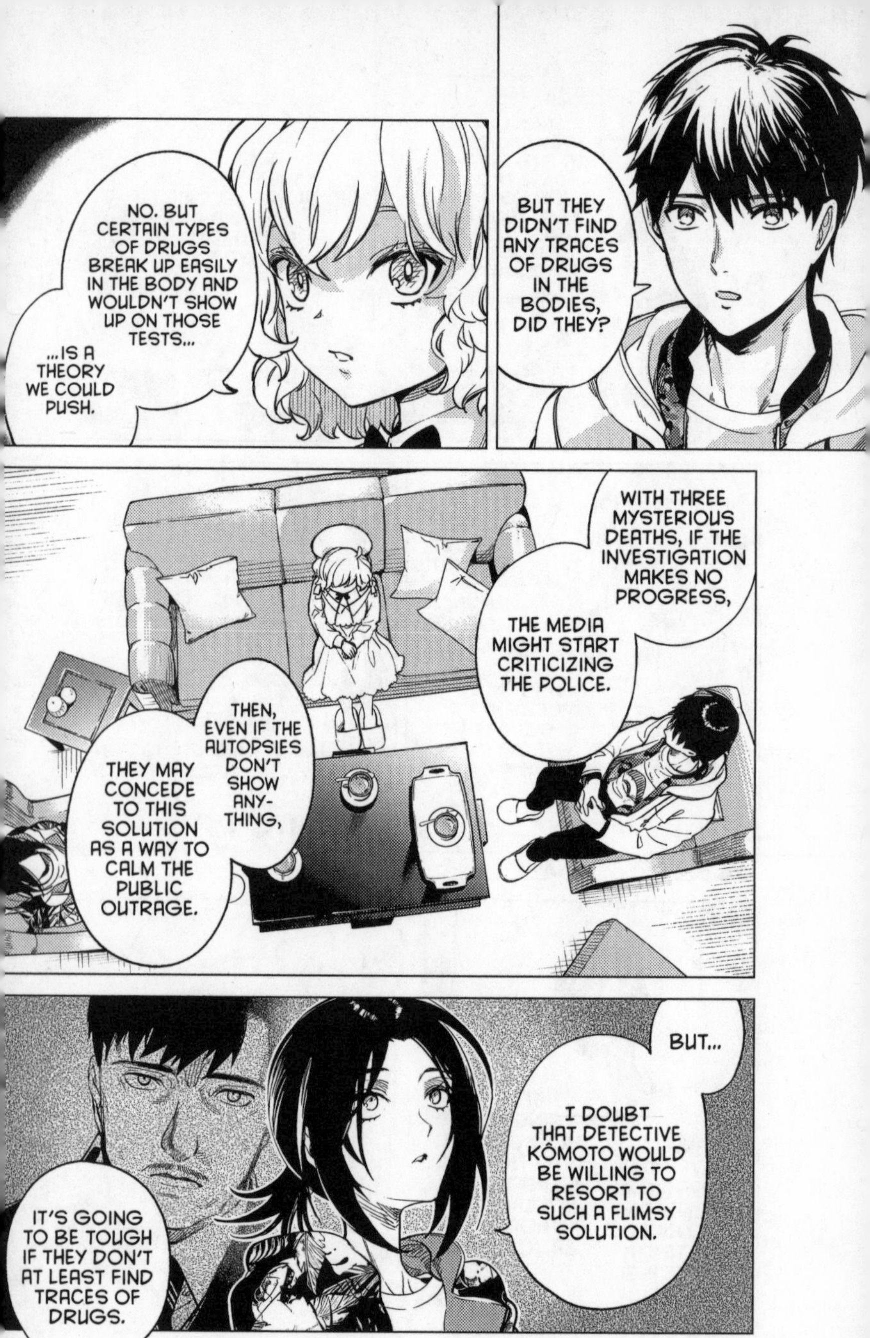
BUT THEY DIDN'T FIND ANY TRACES OF DRUGS IN THE BODIES, DID THEY?
NO. BUT CERTAIN TYPES OF DRUGS BREAK UP EASILY IN THE BODY AND WOULDN'T SHOW UP ON THOSE TESTS...
...IS A THEORY WE COULD PUSH.
WITH THREE MYSTERIOUS DEATHS, IF THE INVESTIGATION MAKES NO PROGRESS,
THE MEDIA MIGHT START CRITICIZING THE POLICE.
THEN, EVEN IF THE AUTOPSIES DON'T SHOW ANY-THING,
THEY MAY CONCEDE TO THIS SOLUTION AS A WAY TO CALM THE PUBLIC OUTRAGE.
BUT...
I DOUBT THAT DETECTIVE KÔMOTO WOULD BE WILLING TO RESORT TO SUCH A FLIMSY SOLUTION.
IT'S GOING TO BE TOUGH IF THEY DON'T AT LEAST FIND TRACES OF DRUGS.

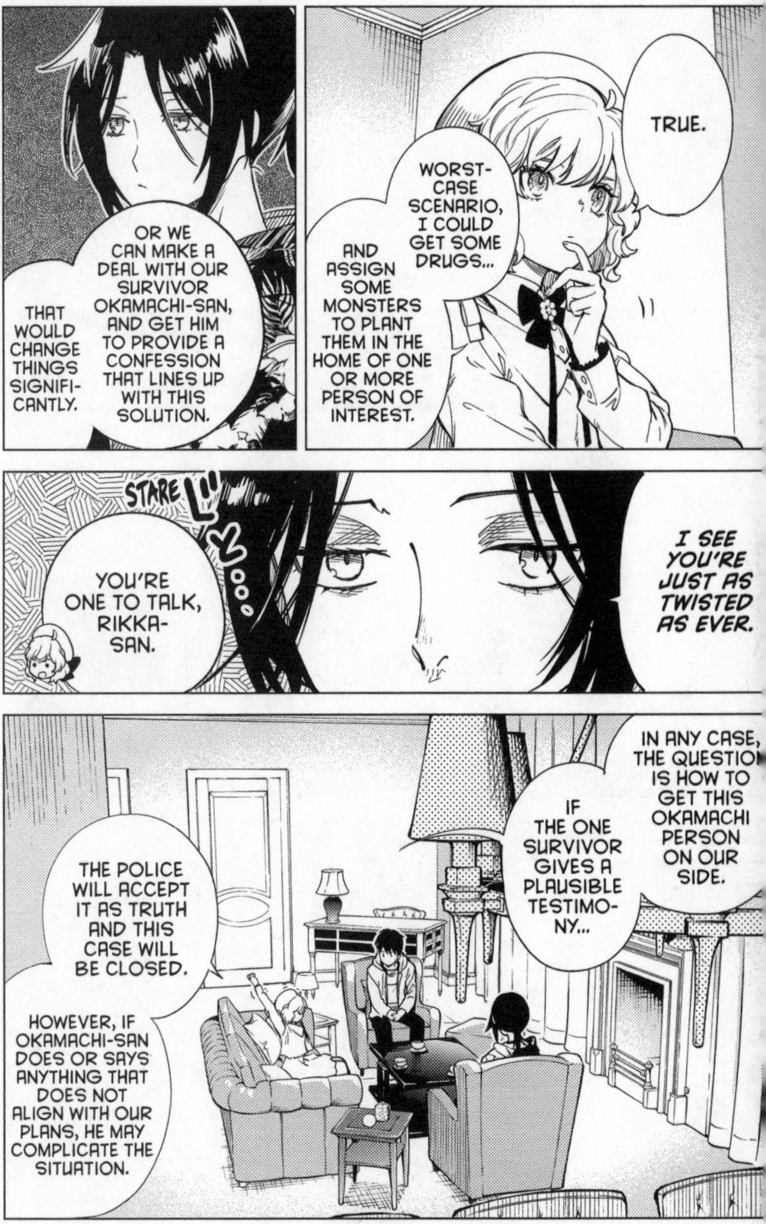

TRUE.
WORST-CASE SCENARIO, I COULD GET SOME DRUGS...
AND ASSIGN SOME MONSTERS TO PLANT THEM IN THE HOME OF ONE OR MORE PERSON OF INTEREST.
OR WE CAN MAKE A DEAL WITH OUR SURVIVOR OKAMACHI-SAN, AND GET HIM TO PROVIDE A CONFESSION THAT LINES UP WITH THIS SOLUTION.
THAT WOULD CHANGE THINGS SIGNIFI-CANTLY.
I SEE YOU'RE JUST AS TWISTED AS EVER.
STARE
YOU'RE ONE TO TALK, RIKKA-SAN.
IN ANY CASE, THE QUESTIO IS HOW TO GET THIS OKAMACHI PERSON ON OUR SIDE.
IF THE ONE SURVIVOR GIVES A PLAUSIBLE TESTIMO-NY...
THE POLICE WILL ACCEPT IT AS TRUTH AND THIS CASE WILL BE CLOSED.
HOWEVER, IF OKAMACHI-SAN DOES OR SAYS ANYTHING THAT DOES NOT ALIGN WITH OUR PLANS, HE MAY COMPLICATE THE SITUATION.

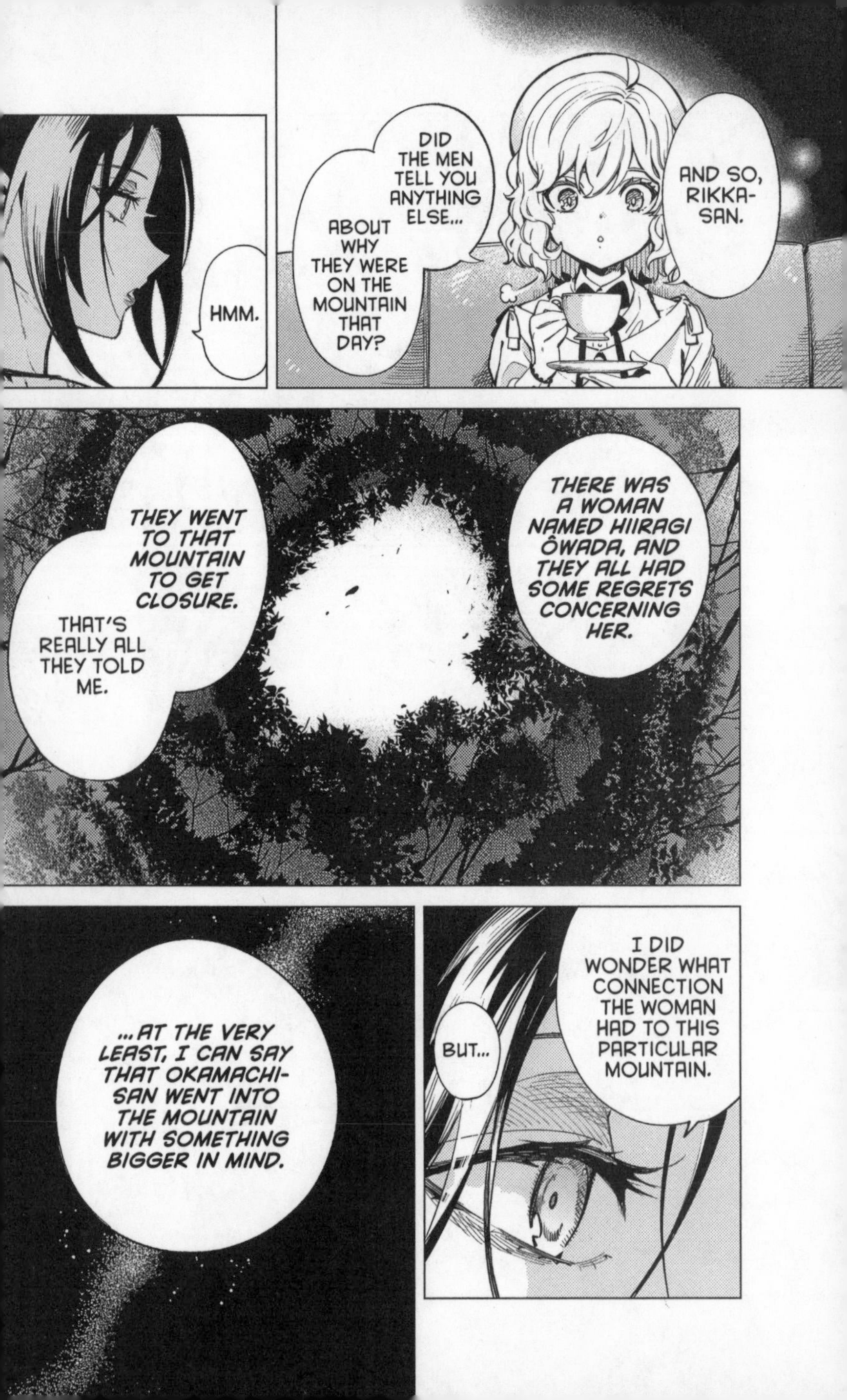
AND SO, RIKKA-SAN.
DID THE MEN TELL YOU ANYTHING ELSE...
ABOUT WHY THEY WERE ON THE MOUNTAIN THAT DAY?
HMM.
THERE WAS A WOMAN NAMED HIIRAGI ÔWADA, AND THEY ALL HAD SOME REGRETS CONCERNING HER.
THEY WENT TO THAT MOUNTAIN TO GET CLOSURE.
THAT'S REALLY ALL THEY TOLD ME.
I DID WONDER WHAT CONNECTION THE WOMAN HAD TO THIS PARTICULAR MOUNTAIN.
BUT...
...AT THE VERY LEAST, I CAN SAY THAT OKAMACHI-SAN WENT INTO THE MOUNTAIN WITH SOMETHING BIGGER IN MIND.

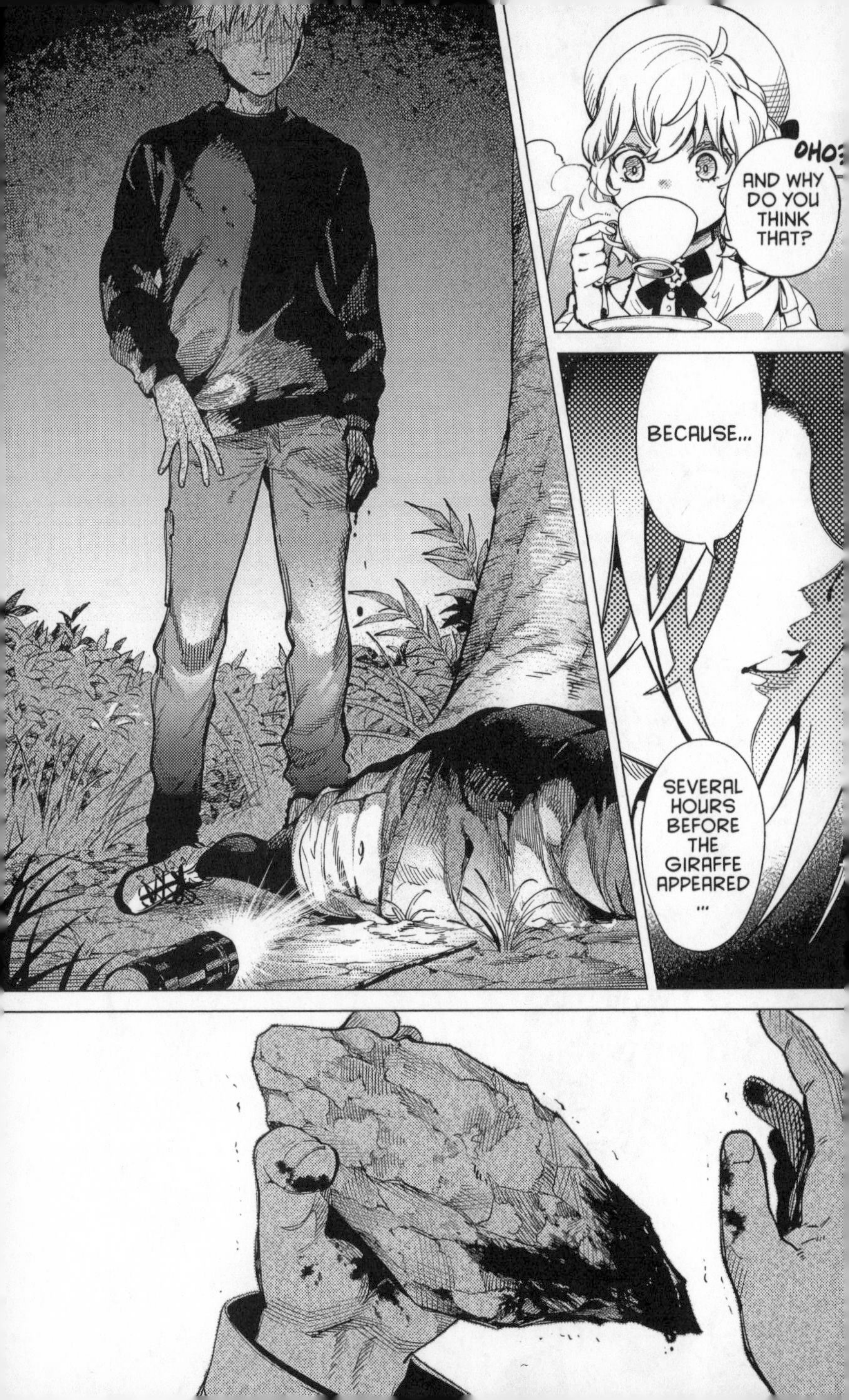
OHO?
AND WHY DO YOU THINK THAT?
BECAUSE...
SEVERAL HOURS BEFORE THE GIRAFFE APPEARED ...

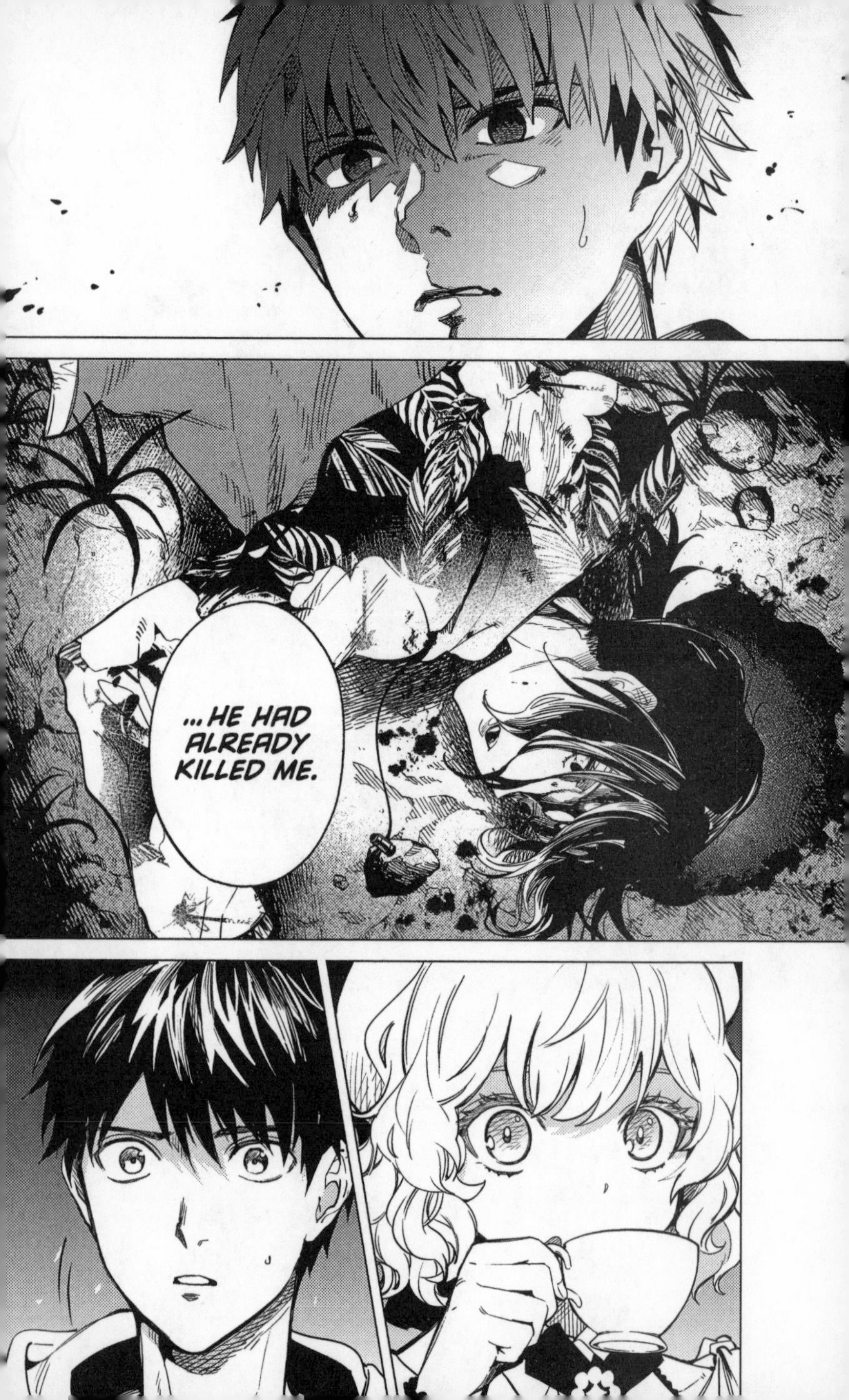
...HE HAD ALREADY KILLED ME.

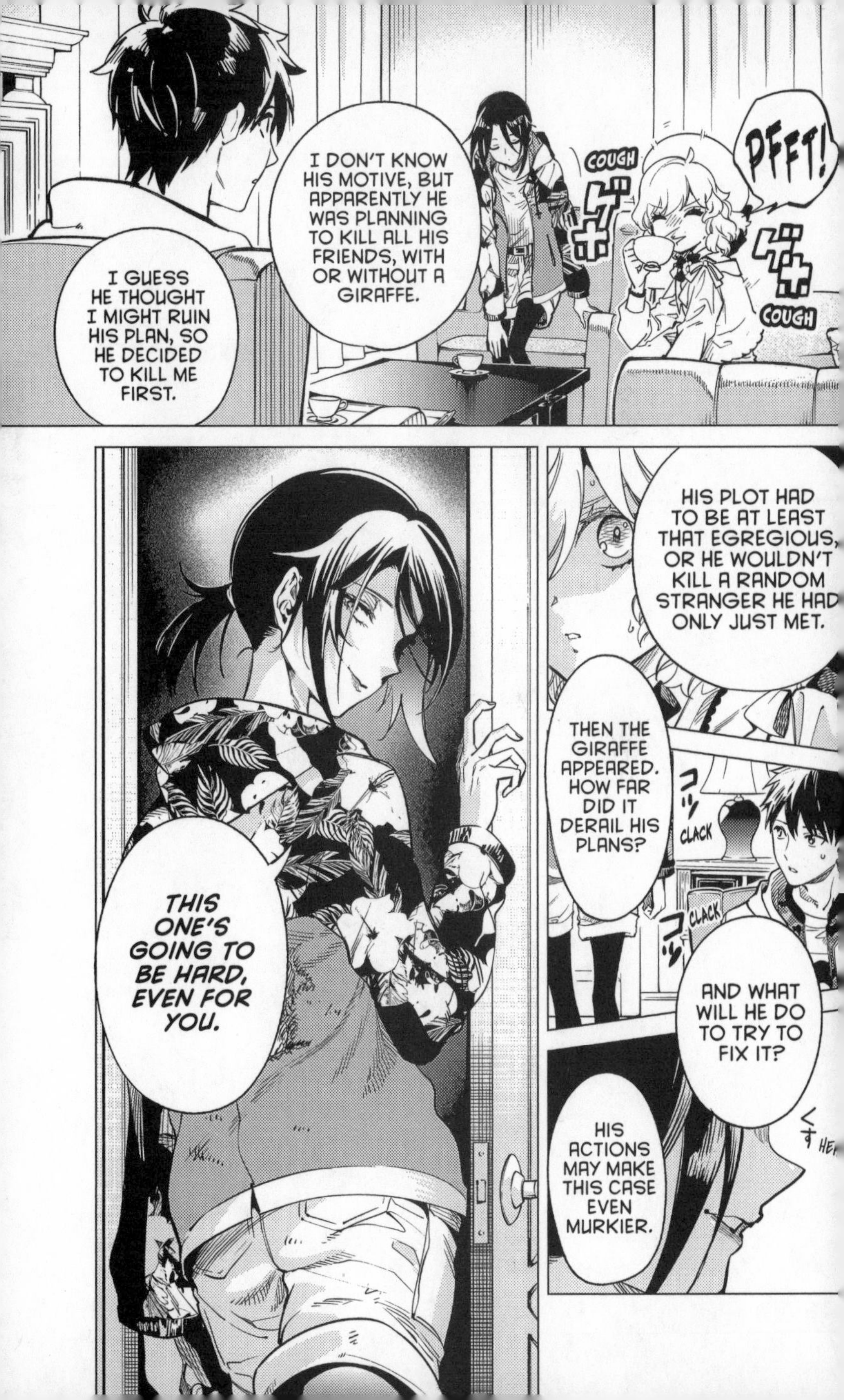
PFFT!
ゲホ
COUGH
COUGH
ゲホ
I DON'T KNOW HIS MOTIVE, BUT APPARENTLY HE WAS PLANNING TO KILL ALL HIS FRIENDS, WITH OR WITHOUT A GIRAFFE.
I GUESS HE THOUGHT I MIGHT RUIN HIS PLAN, SO HE DECIDED TO KILL ME FIRST.
HIS PLOT HAD TO BE AT LEAST THAT EGREGIOUS, OR HE WOULDN'T KILL A RANDOM STRANGER HE HAD ONLY JUST MET.
THEN THE GIRAFFE APPEARED. HOW FAR DID IT DERAIL HIS PLANS?
コツ
CLACK
CLACK
コツ
AND WHAT WILL HE DO TO TRY TO FIX IT?
HIS ACTIONS MAY MAKE THIS CASE EVEN MURKIER.
くす
THIS ONE'S GOING TO BE HARD, EVEN FOR YOU.

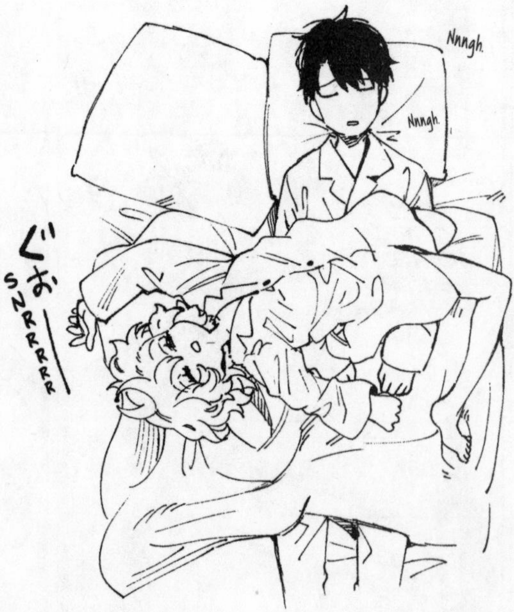
Nnngh.
Nnngh.
ぐお
SNRRRRRR

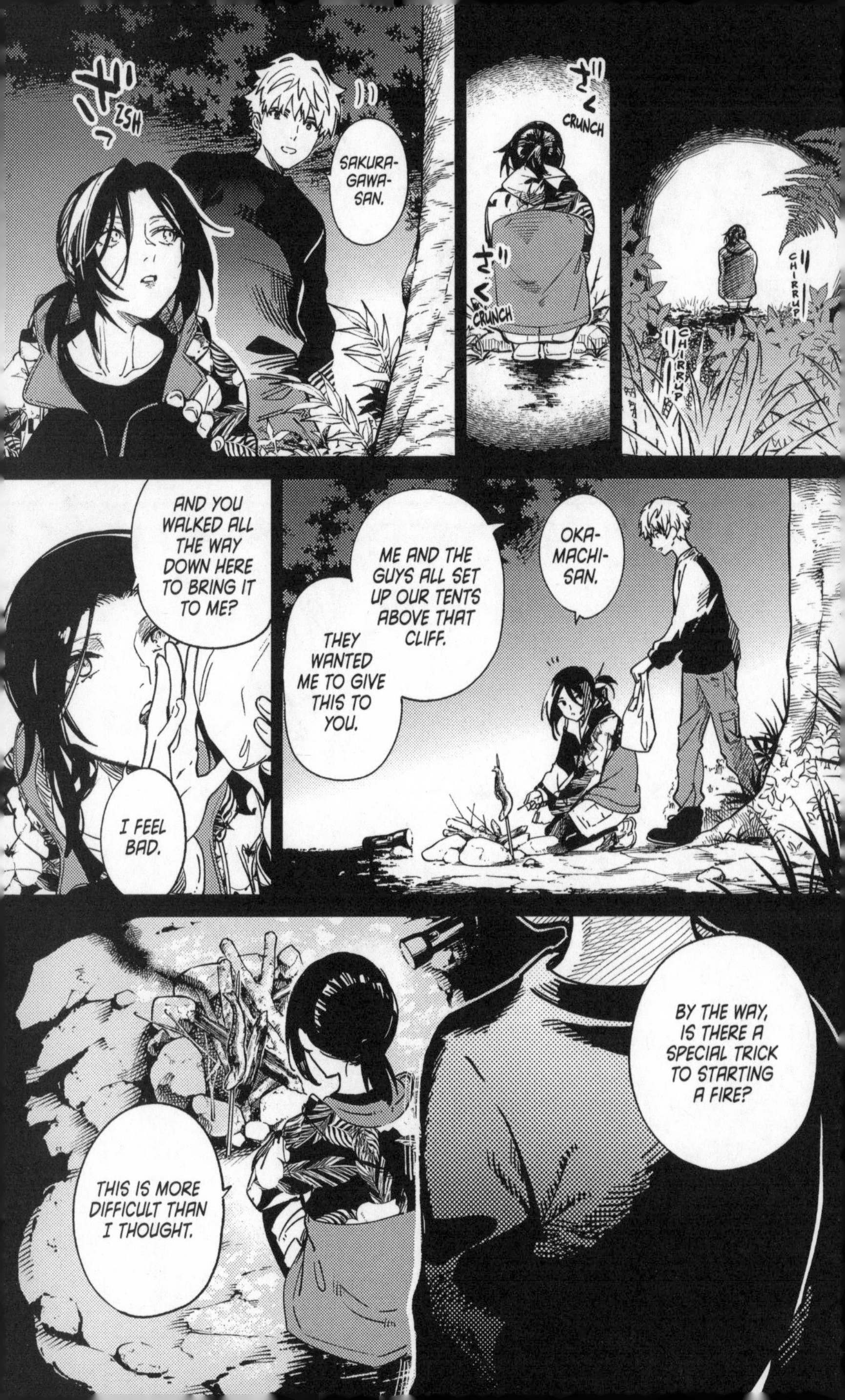

CHIRRUP
CHIRRUP
CRUNCH
CRUNCH
ZSH
SAKURA-GAWA-SAN.
OKA-MACHI-SAN.
ME AND THE GUYS ALL SET UP OUR TENTS ABOVE THAT CLIFF.
THEY WANTED ME TO GIVE THIS TO YOU.
AND YOU WALKED ALL THE WAY DOWN HERE TO BRING IT TO ME?
I FEEL BAD.
BY THE WAY, IS THERE A SPECIAL TRICK TO STARTING A FIRE?
THIS IS MORE DIFFICULT THAN I THOUGHT.

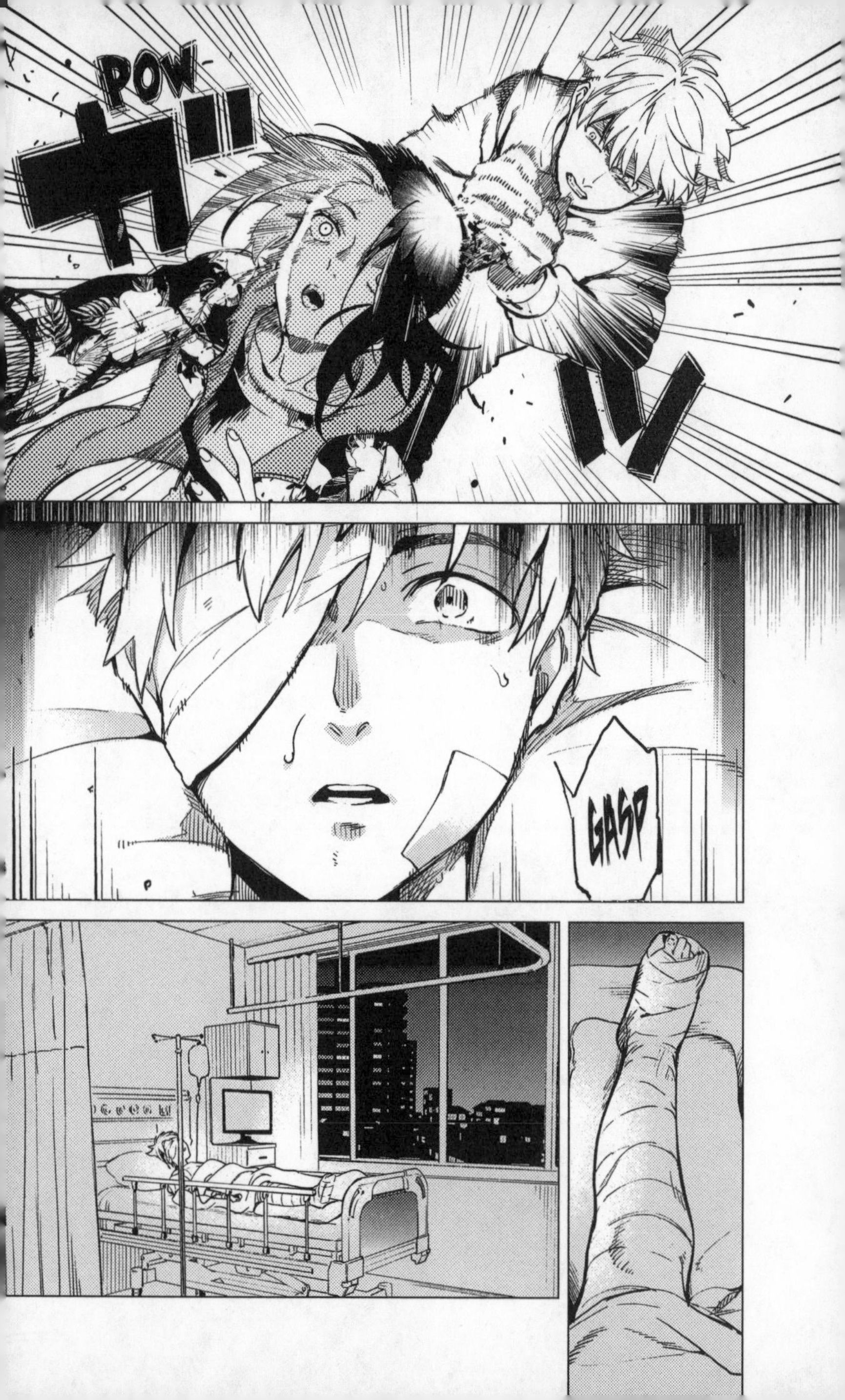
POW
GASP

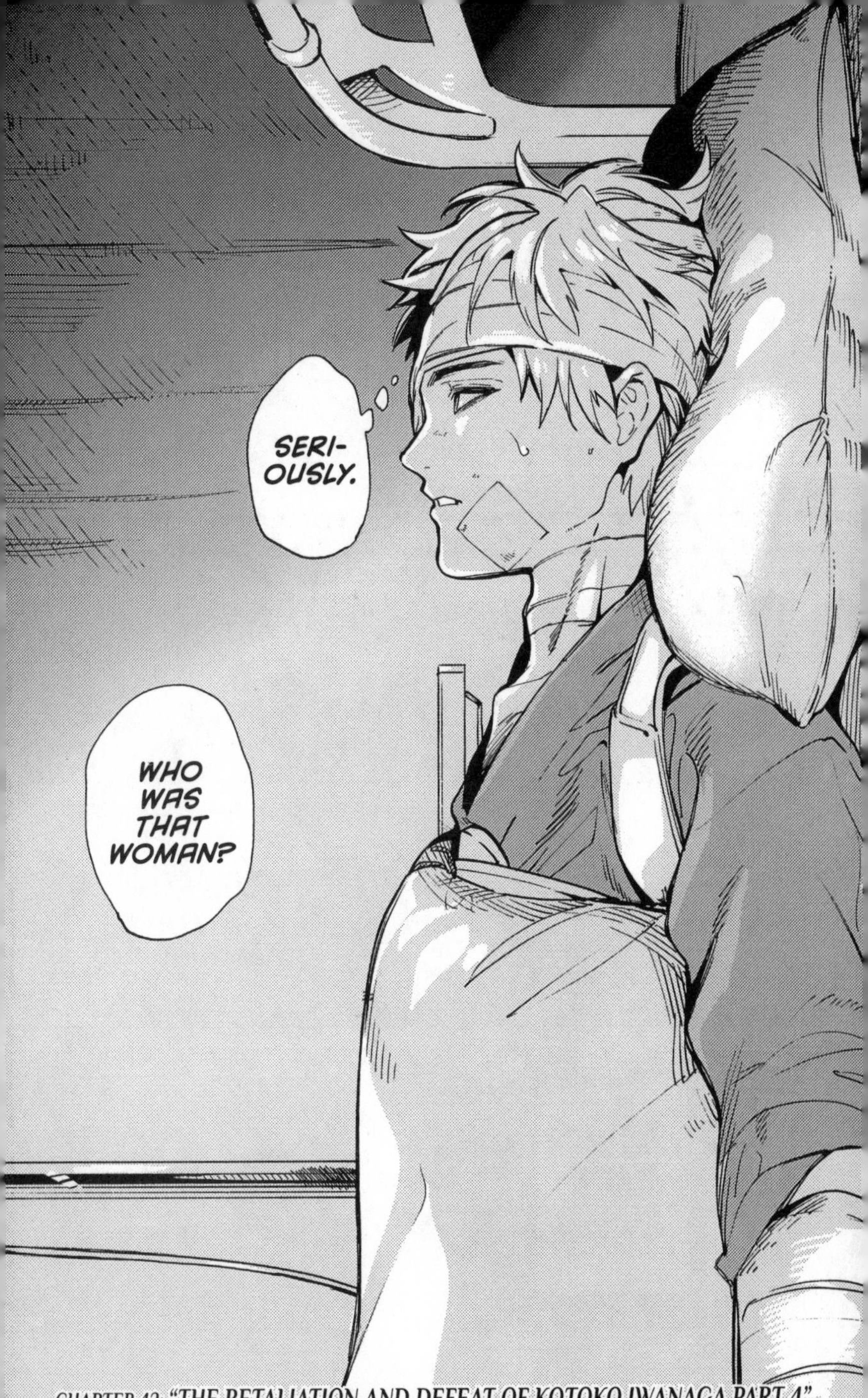
SERI-
OUSLY.
WHO WAS THAT WOMAN?

CHAPTER 42: "THE RETALIATION AND DEFEAT OF KOTOKO IWANAGA PART 4"

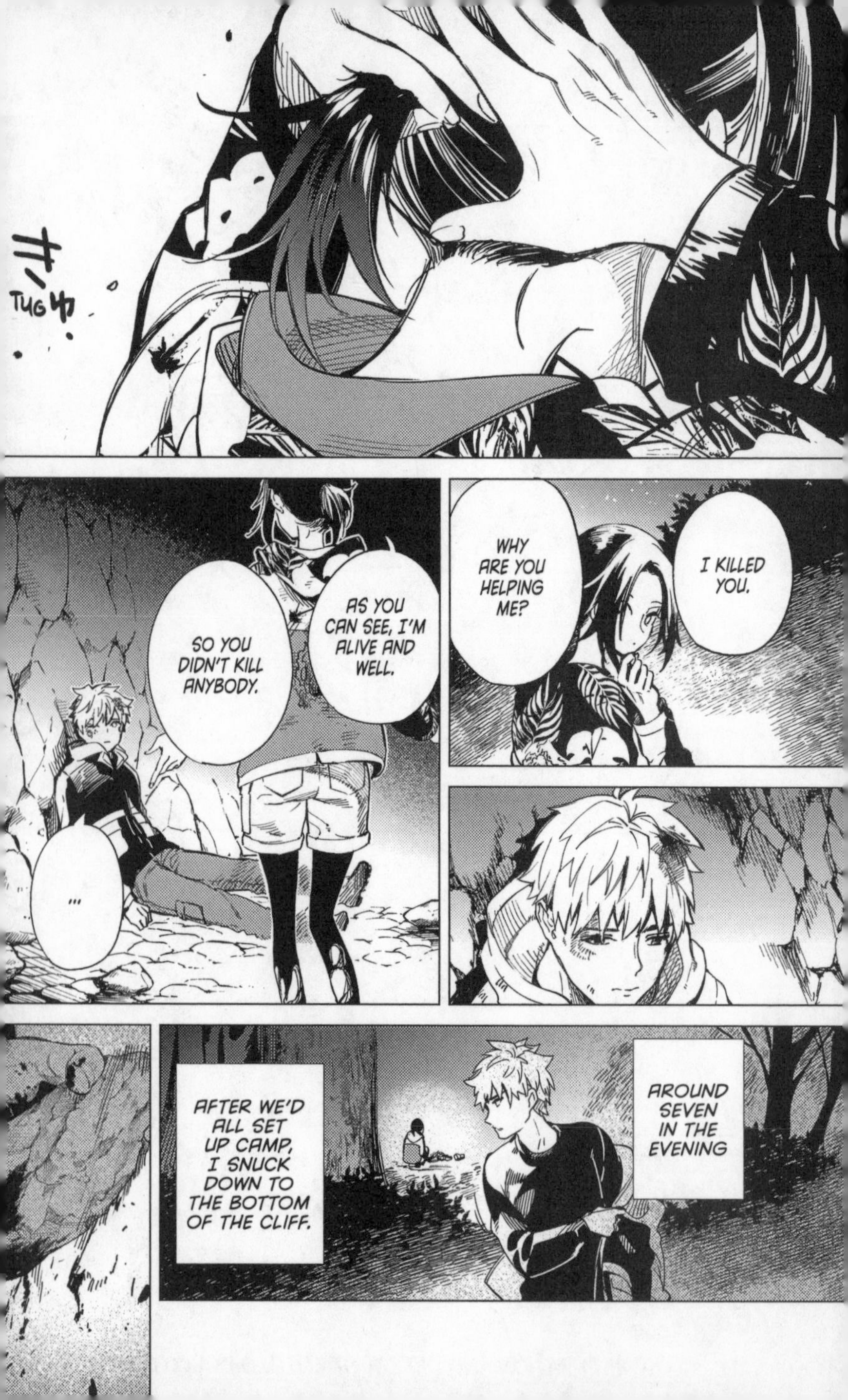
ぎゅ
TUG
I KILLED YOU.
WHY ARE YOU HELPING ME?
AS YOU CAN SEE, I'M ALIVE AND WELL.
SO YOU DIDN'T KILL ANYBODY.
...
AROUND SEVEN IN THE EVENING
AFTER WE'D ALL SET UP CAMP, I SNUCK DOWN TO THE BOTTOM OF THE CLIFF.

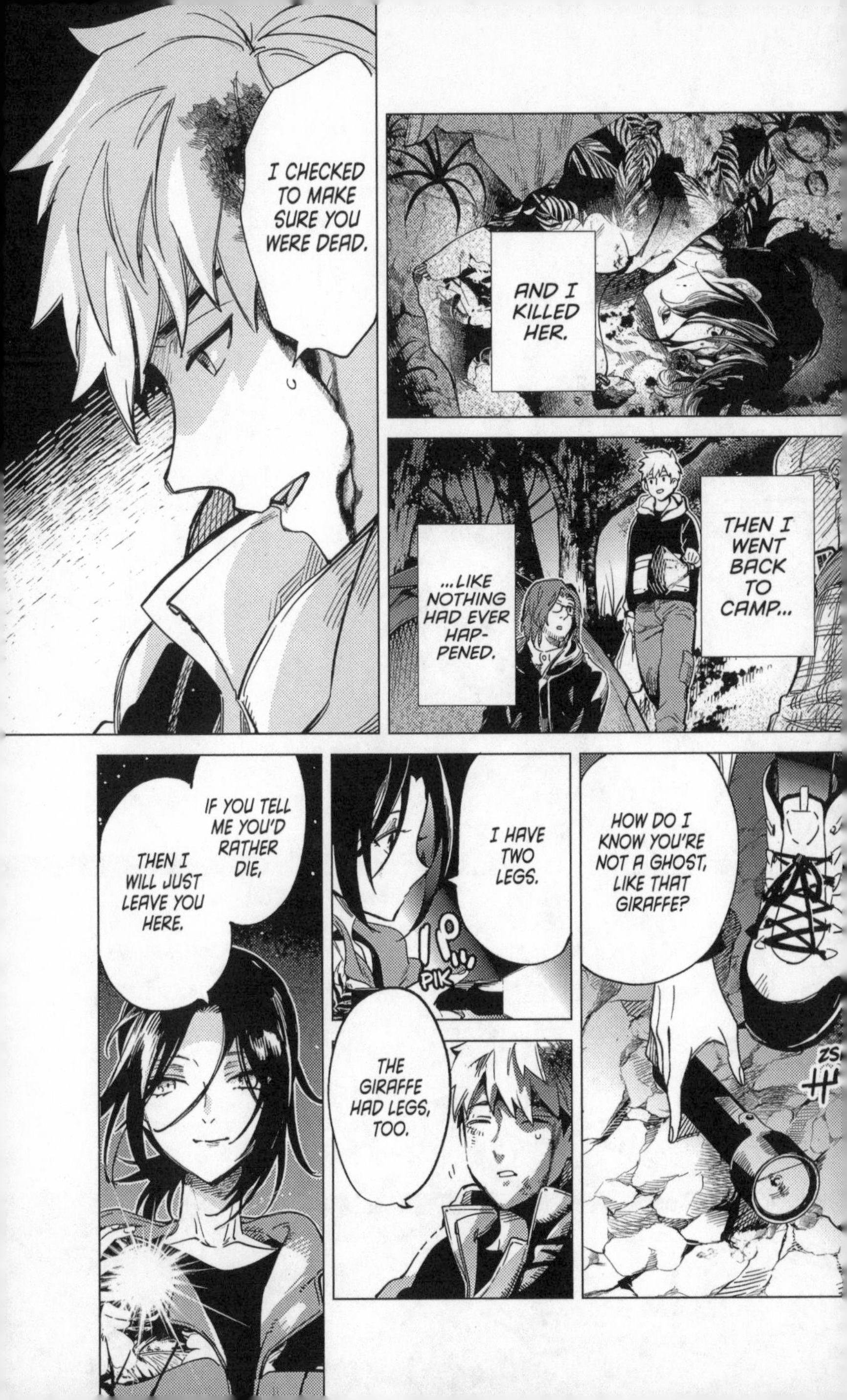
AND I KILLED HER.
THEN I WENT BACK TO CAMP...
...LIKE NOTHING HAD EVER HAP-PENED.
I CHECKED TO MAKE SURE YOU WERE DEAD.
ZSH
HOW DO I KNOW YOU'RE NOT A GHOST, LIKE THAT GIRAFFE?
I HAVE TWO LEGS.
PIK
THE GIRAFFE HAD LEGS, TOO.
IF YOU TELL ME YOU'D RATHER DIE,
THEN I WILL JUST LEAVE YOU HERE.

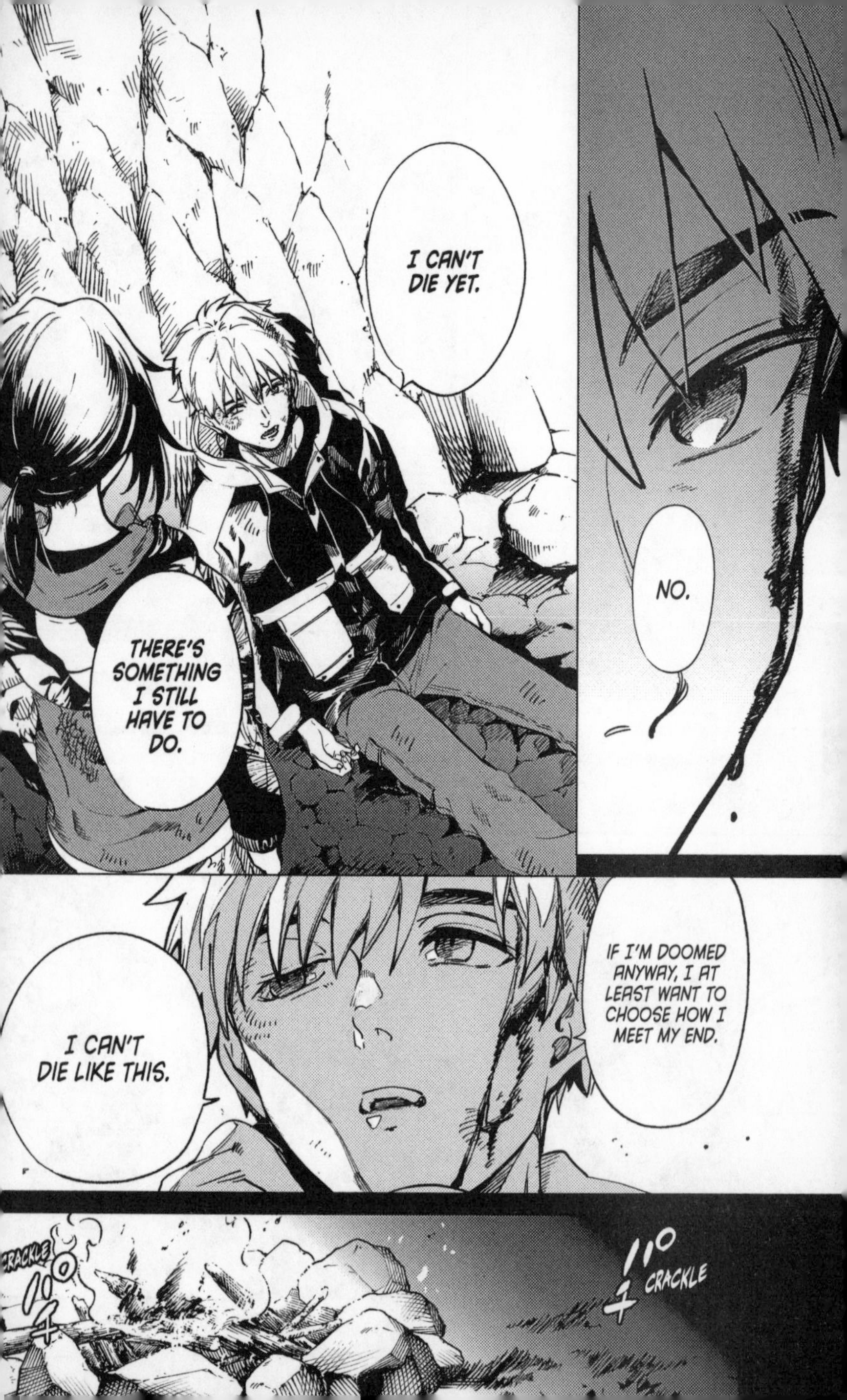
NO.
I CAN'T DIE YET.
THERE'S SOMETHING I STILL HAVE TO DO.
IF I'M DOOMED ANYWAY, I AT LEAST WANT TO CHOOSE HOW I MEET MY END.
I CAN'T DIE LIKE THIS.
CRACKLE
CRACKLE

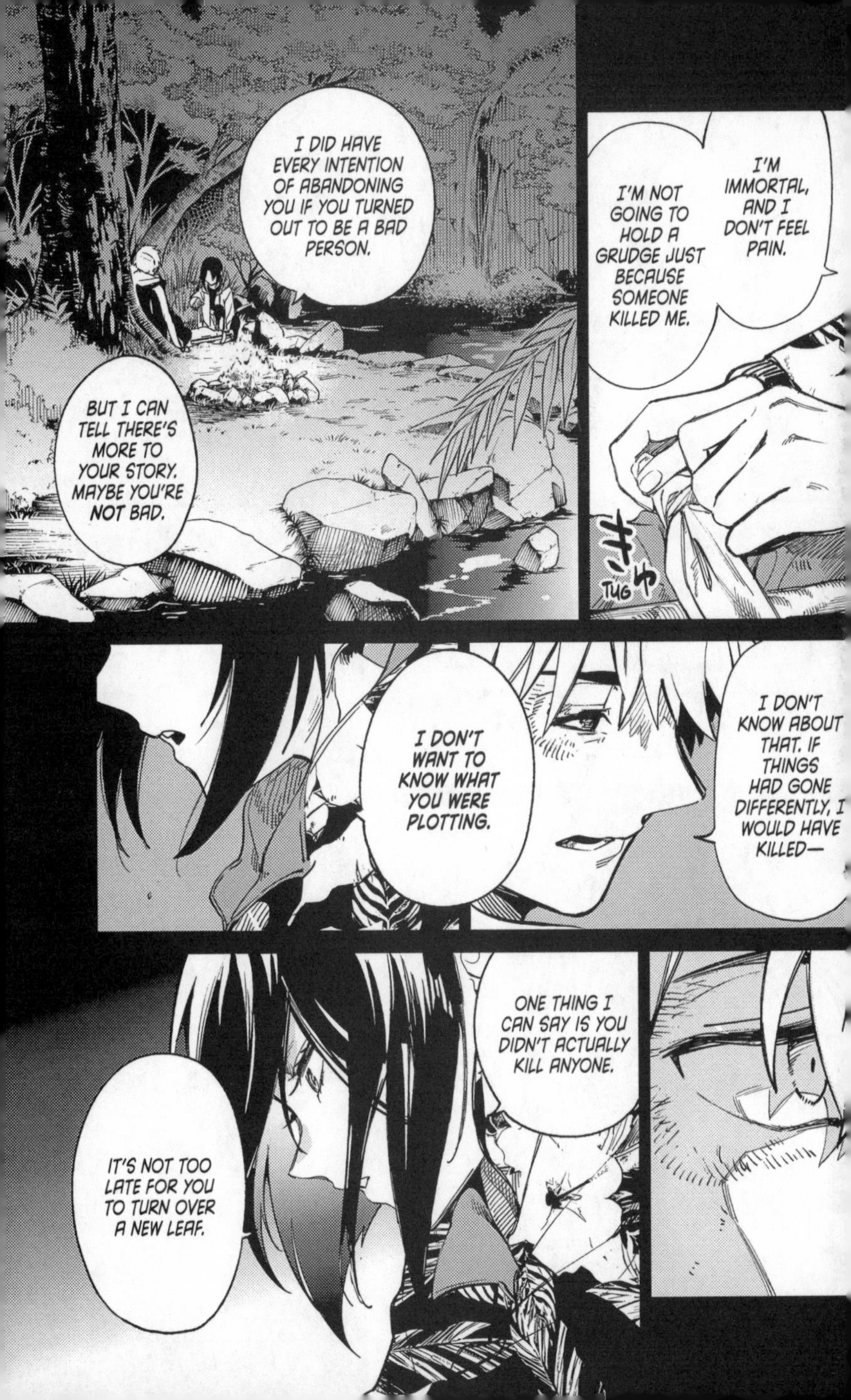
I'M IMMORTAL, AND I DON'T FEEL PAIN.
I'M NOT GOING TO HOLD A GRUDGE JUST BECAUSE SOMEONE KILLED ME.
きゅ TUG
I DID HAVE EVERY INTENTION OF ABANDONING YOU IF YOU TURNED OUT TO BE A BAD PERSON.
BUT I CAN TELL THERE'S MORE TO YOUR STORY. MAYBE YOU'RE NOT BAD.
I DON'T KNOW ABOUT THAT. IF THINGS HAD GONE DIFFERENTLY, I WOULD HAVE KILLED—
I DON'T WANT TO KNOW WHAT YOU WERE PLOTTING.
ONE THING I CAN SAY IS YOU DIDN'T ACTUALLY KILL ANYONE.
IT'S NOT TOO LATE FOR YOU TO TURN OVER A NEW LEAF.

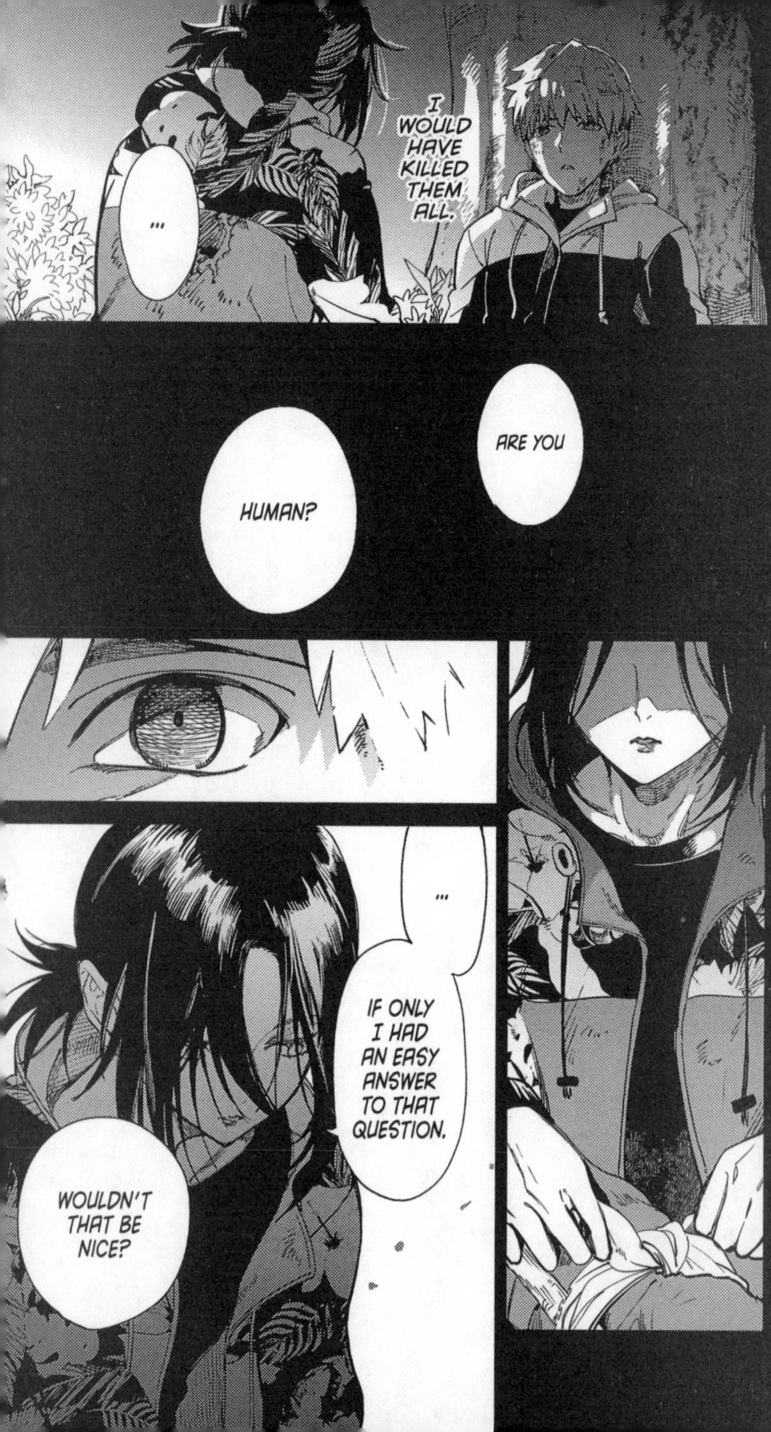
I WOULD HAVE KILLED THEM ALL.
...
ARE YOU
HUMAN?
...
IF ONLY I HAD AN EASY ANSWER TO THAT QUESTION.
WOULDN'T THAT BE NICE?

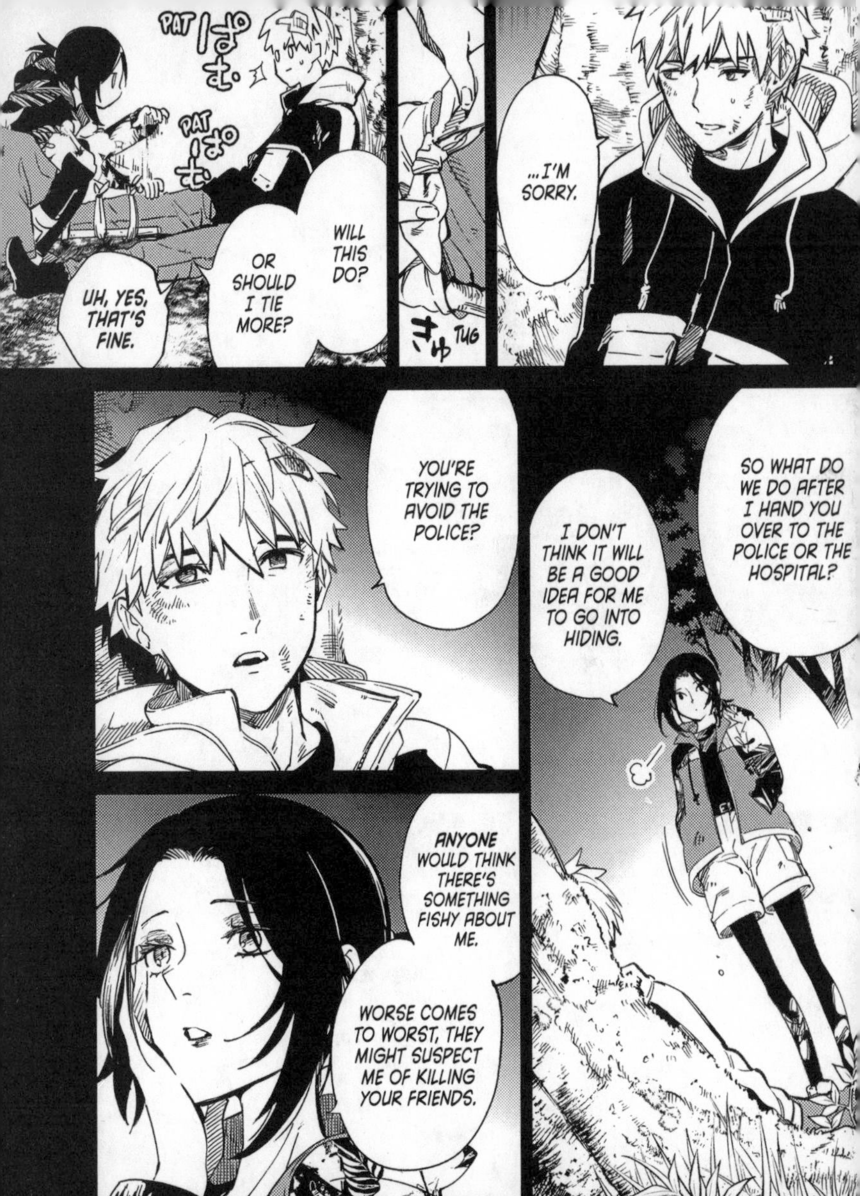
...I'M SORRY.
きゅ TUG
PAT ぽむ
PAT ぽむ
WILL THIS DO?
OR SHOULD I TIE MORE?
UH, YES, THAT'S FINE.
SO WHAT DO WE DO AFTER I HAND YOU OVER TO THE POLICE OR THE HOSPITAL?
I DON'T THINK IT WILL BE A GOOD IDEA FOR ME TO GO INTO HIDING.
YOU'RE TRYING TO AVOID THE POLICE?
ANYONE WOULD THINK THERE'S SOMETHING FISHY ABOUT ME.
WORSE COMES TO WORST, THEY MIGHT SUSPECT ME OF KILLING YOUR FRIENDS.

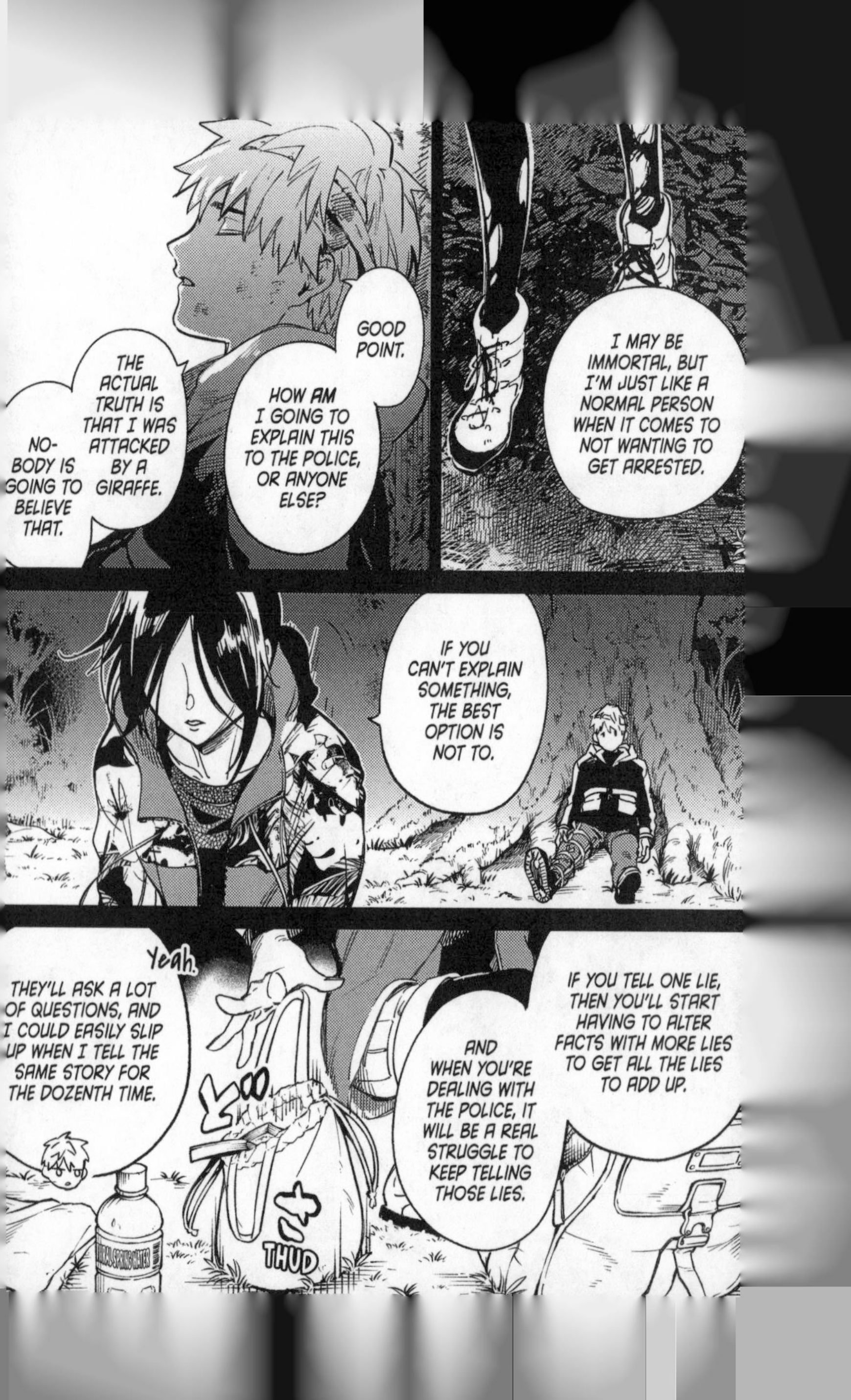
I MAY BE IMMORTAL, BUT I'M JUST LIKE A NORMAL PERSON WHEN IT COMES TO NOT WANTING TO GET ARRESTED.
GOOD POINT.
HOW AM I GOING TO EXPLAIN THIS TO THE POLICE, OR ANYONE ELSE?
THE ACTUAL TRUTH IS THAT I WAS ATTACKED BY A GIRAFFE.
NO-BODY IS GOING TO BELIEVE THAT.
IF YOU CAN'T EXPLAIN SOMETHING, THE BEST OPTION IS NOT TO.
IF YOU TELL ONE LIE, THEN YOU'LL START HAVING TO ALTER FACTS WITH MORE LIES TO GET ALL THE LIES TO ADD UP.
AND WHEN YOU'RE DEALING WITH THE POLICE, IT WILL BE A REAL STRUGGLE TO KEEP TELLING THOSE LIES.
Yeah.
THEY'LL ASK A LOT OF QUESTIONS, AND I COULD EASILY SLIP UP WHEN I TELL THE SAME STORY FOR THE DOZENTH TIME.
THUD

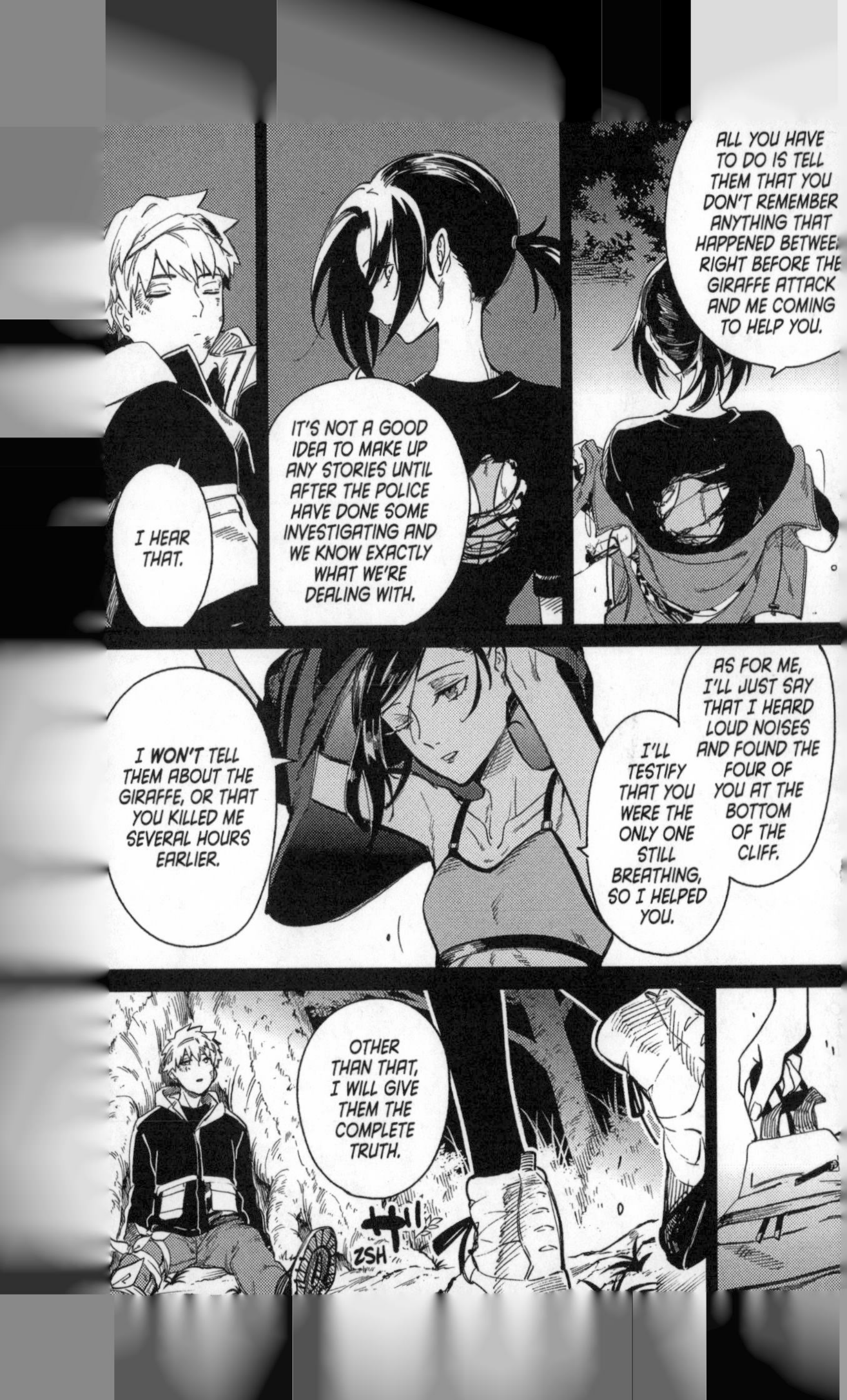
ALL YOU HAVE TO DO IS TELL THEM THAT YOU DON'T REMEMBER ANYTHING THAT HAPPENED BETWEE RIGHT BEFORE THE GIRAFFE ATTACK AND ME COMING TO HELP YOU.
IT'S NOT A GOOD IDEA TO MAKE UP ANY STORIES UNTIL AFTER THE POLICE HAVE DONE SOME INVESTIGATING AND WE KNOW EXACTLY WHAT WE'RE DEALING WITH.
I HEAR THAT.
AS FOR ME, I'LL JUST SAY THAT I HEARD LOUD NOISES AND FOUND THE FOUR OF YOU AT THE BOTTOM OF THE CLIFF.
I'LL TESTIFY THAT YOU WERE THE ONLY ONE STILL BREATHING, SO I HELPED YOU.
I WON'T TELL THEM ABOUT THE GIRAFFE, OR THAT YOU KILLED ME SEVERAL HOURS EARLIER.
OTHER THAN THAT, I WILL GIVE THEM THE COMPLETE TRUTH.
ZSH

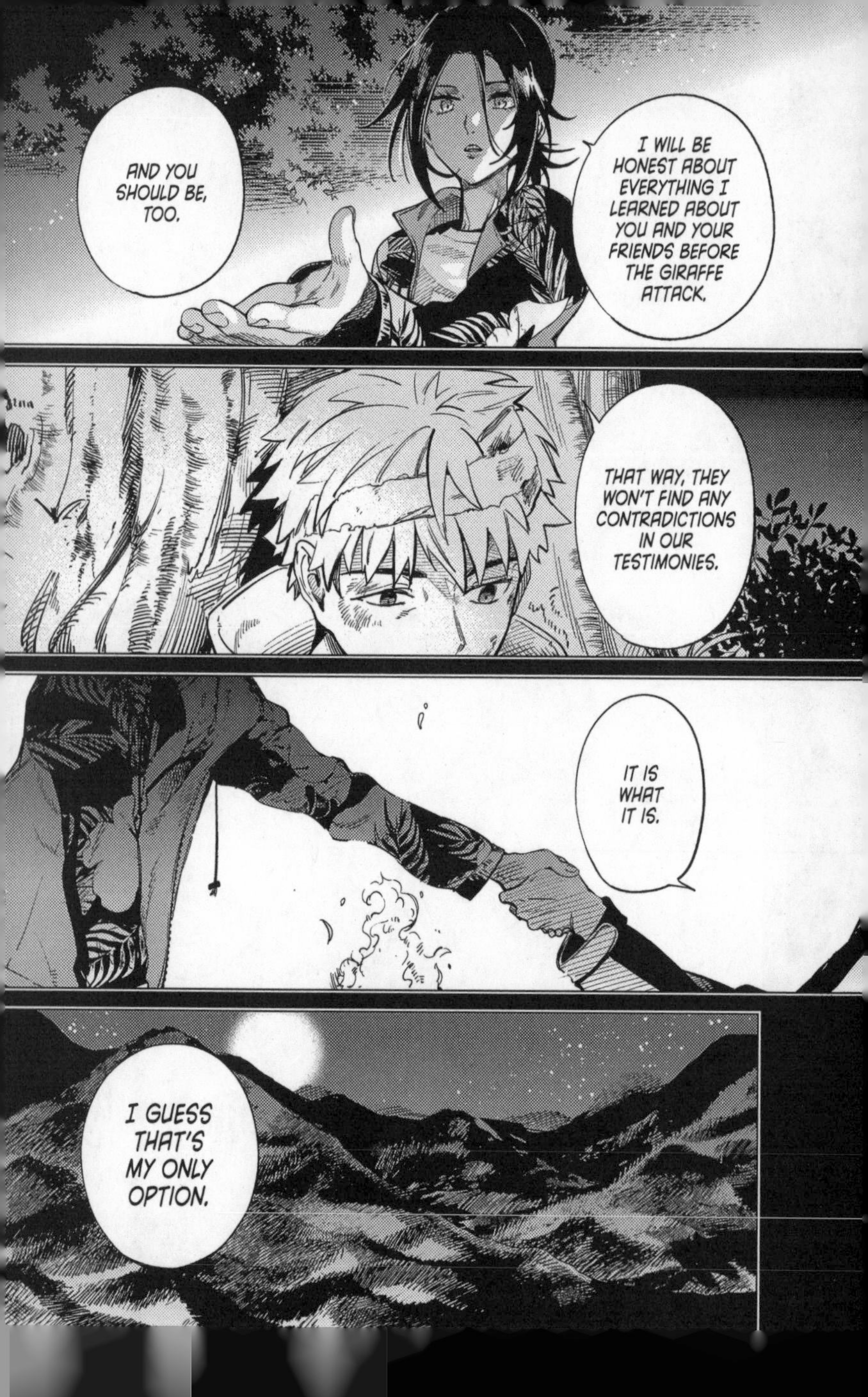
I WILL BE HONEST ABOUT EVERYTHING I LEARNED ABOUT YOU AND YOUR FRIENDS BEFORE THE GIRAFFE ATTACK.
AND YOU SHOULD BE, TOO.
THAT WAY, THEY WON'T FIND ANY CONTRADICTIONS IN OUR TESTIMONIES.
IT IS WHAT IT IS.
I GUESS THAT'S MY ONLY OPTION.

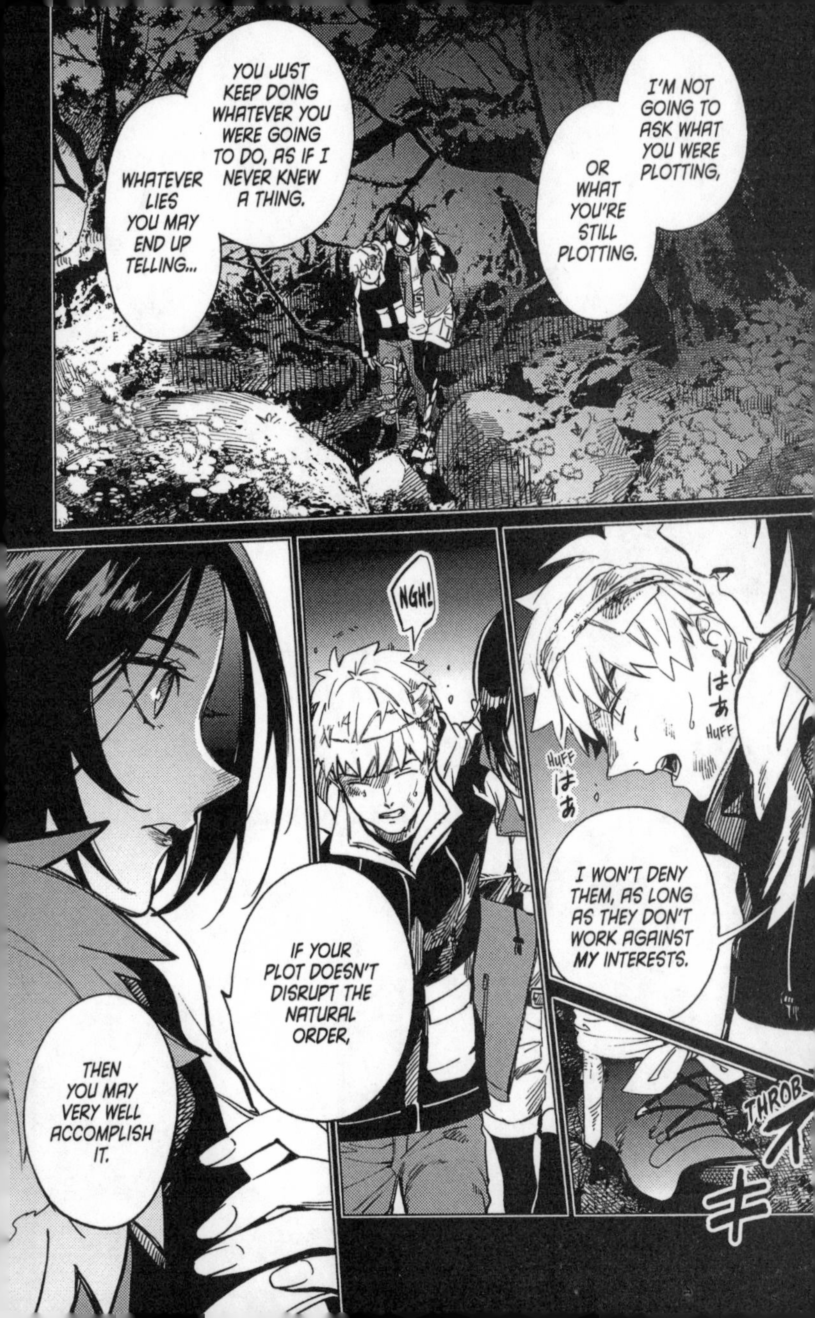
I'M NOT GOING TO ASK WHAT YOU WERE PLOTTING,
OR WHAT YOU'RE STILL PLOTTING.
YOU JUST KEEP DOING WHATEVER YOU WERE GOING TO DO, AS IF I NEVER KNEW A THING.
WHATEVER LIES YOU MAY END UP TELLING...
はあ HUFF
HUFF はあ
I WON'T DENY THEM, AS LONG AS THEY DON'T WORK AGAINST MY INTERESTS.
THROB
キ
NGH!
IF YOUR PLOT DOESN'T DISRUPT THE NATURAL ORDER,
THEN YOU MAY VERY WELL ACCOMPLISH IT.

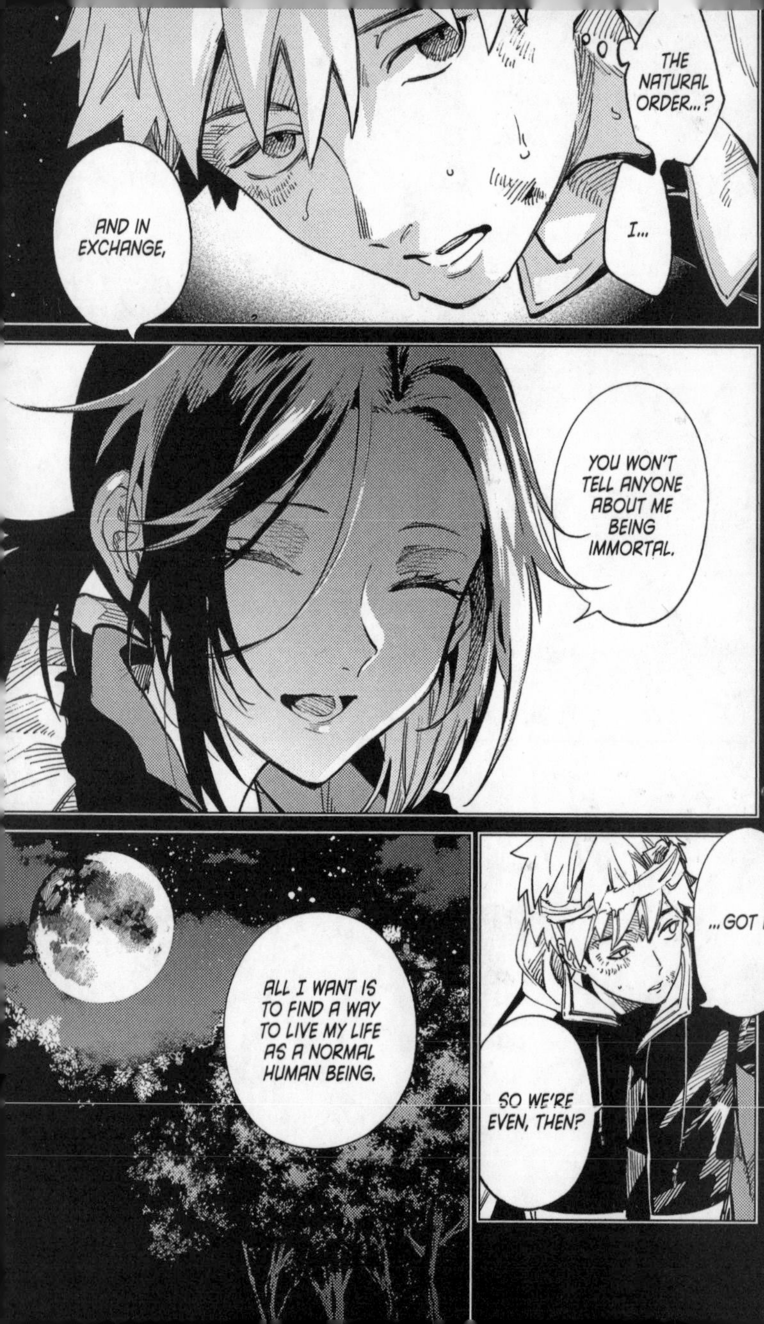
THE NATURAL ORDER...?
I...
AND IN EXCHANGE,
YOU WON'T TELL ANYONE ABOUT ME BEING IMMORTAL.
...GOT IT.
SO WE'RE EVEN, THEN?
ALL I WANT IS TO FIND A WAY TO LIVE MY LIFE AS A NORMAL HUMAN BEING.

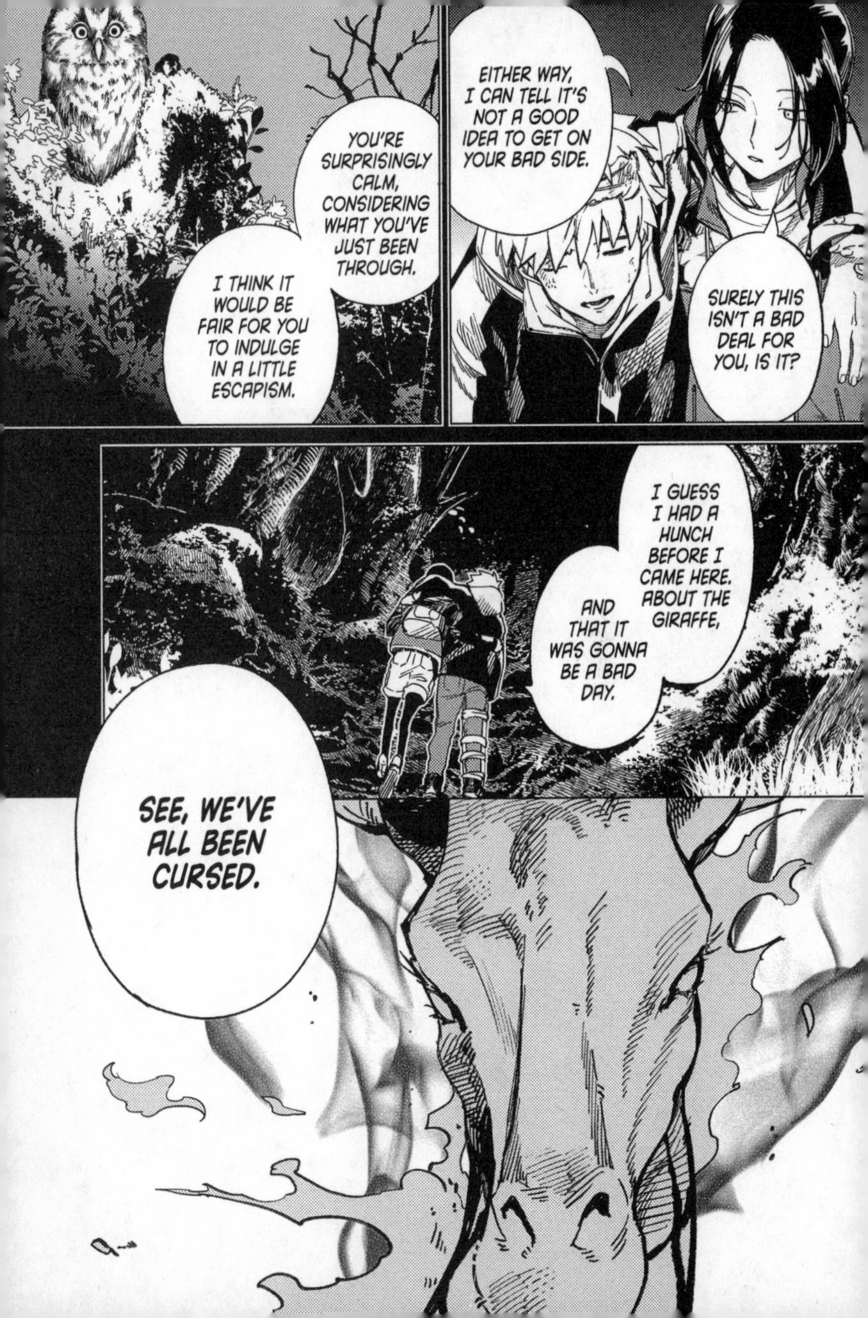
EITHER WAY, I CAN TELL IT'S NOT A GOOD IDEA TO GET ON YOUR BAD SIDE.
SURELY THIS ISN'T A BAD DEAL FOR YOU, IS IT?
YOU'RE SURPRISINGLY CALM, CONSIDERING WHAT YOU'VE JUST BEEN THROUGH.
I THINK IT WOULD BE FAIR FOR YOU TO INDULGE IN A LITTLE ESCAPISM.
I GUESS I HAD A HUNCH BEFORE I CAME HERE. ABOUT THE GIRAFFE,
AND THAT IT WAS GONNA BE A BAD DAY.
SEE, WE'VE ALL BEEN CURSED.

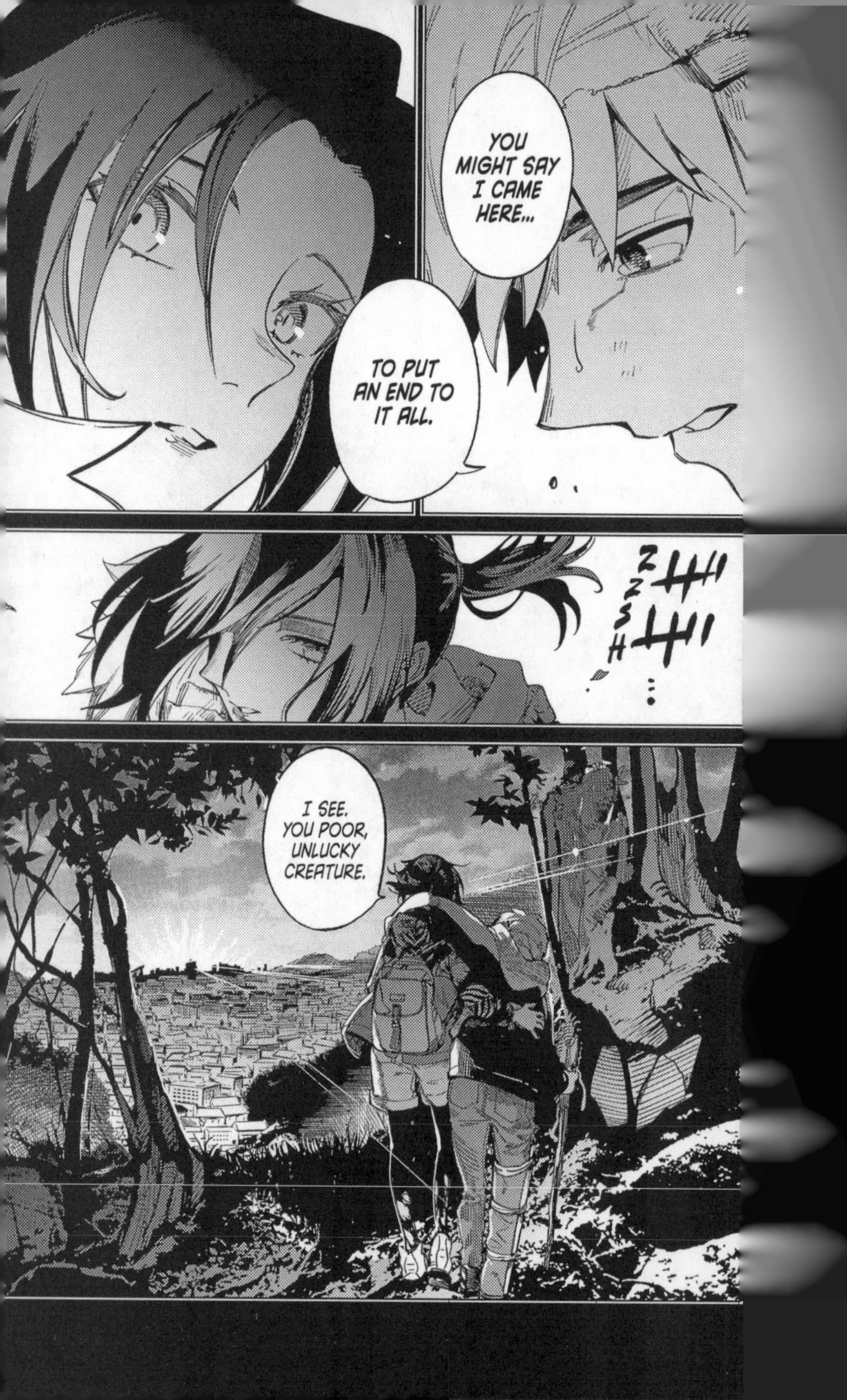
YOU MIGHT SAY I CAME HERE...
TO PUT AN END TO IT ALL.
ZZSH
I SEE. YOU POOR, UNLUCKY CREATURE.

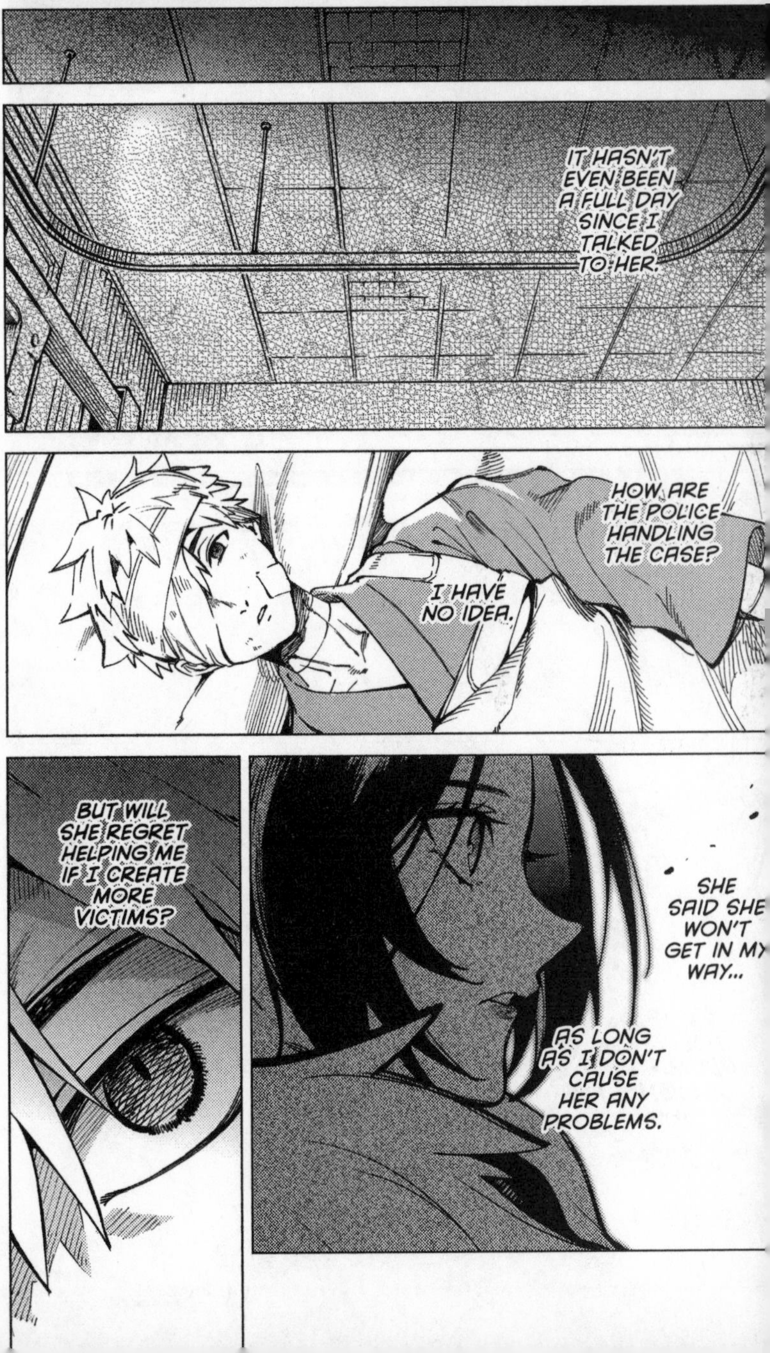
IT HASN'T EVEN BEEN A FULL DAY SINCE I TALKED TO HER.
HOW ARE THE POLICE HANDLING THE CASE?
I HAVE NO IDEA.
SHE SAID SHE WON'T GET IN MY WAY...
AS LONG AS I DON'T CAUSE HER ANY PROBLEMS.
BUT WILL SHE REGRET HELPING ME IF I CREATE MORE VICTIMS?

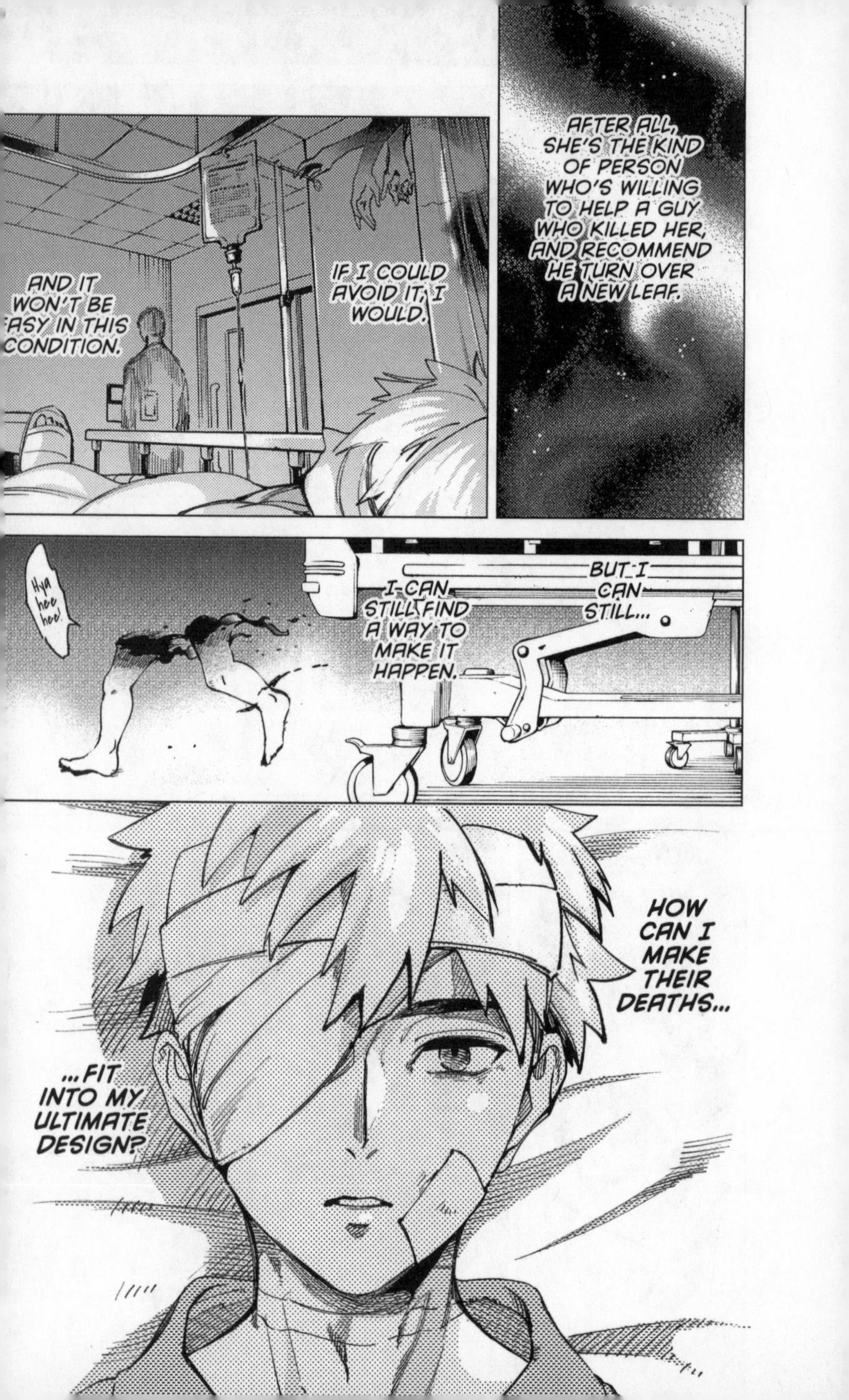
AFTER ALL, SHE'S THE KIND OF PERSON WHO'S WILLING TO HELP A GUY WHO KILLED HER, AND RECOMMEND HE TURN OVER A NEW LEAF.
IF I COULD AVOID IT, I WOULD.
AND IT WON'T BE EASY IN THIS CONDITION.
BUT I CAN STILL...
I CAN STILL FIND A WAY TO MAKE IT HAPPEN.
Hya hee hee!
HOW CAN I MAKE THEIR DEATHS...
...FIT INTO MY ULTIMATE DESIGN?

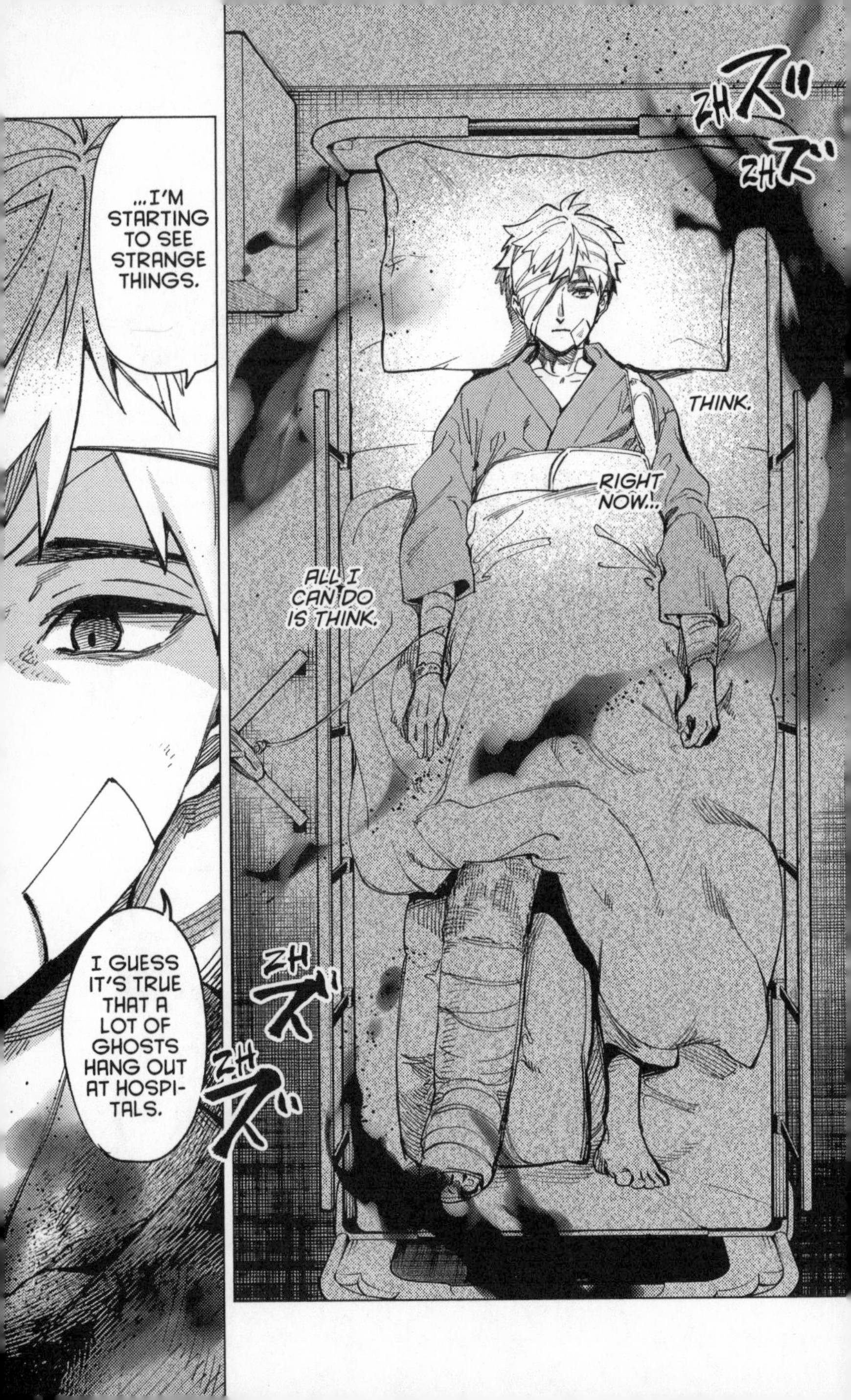
ZH ズ
ZH ズ
THINK.
RIGHT NOW...
ALL I CAN DO IS THINK.
ZH ズ
ZH ズ
...I'M STARTING TO SEE STRANGE THINGS.
I GUESS IT'S TRUE THAT A LOT OF GHOSTS HANG OUT AT HOSPI-TALS.

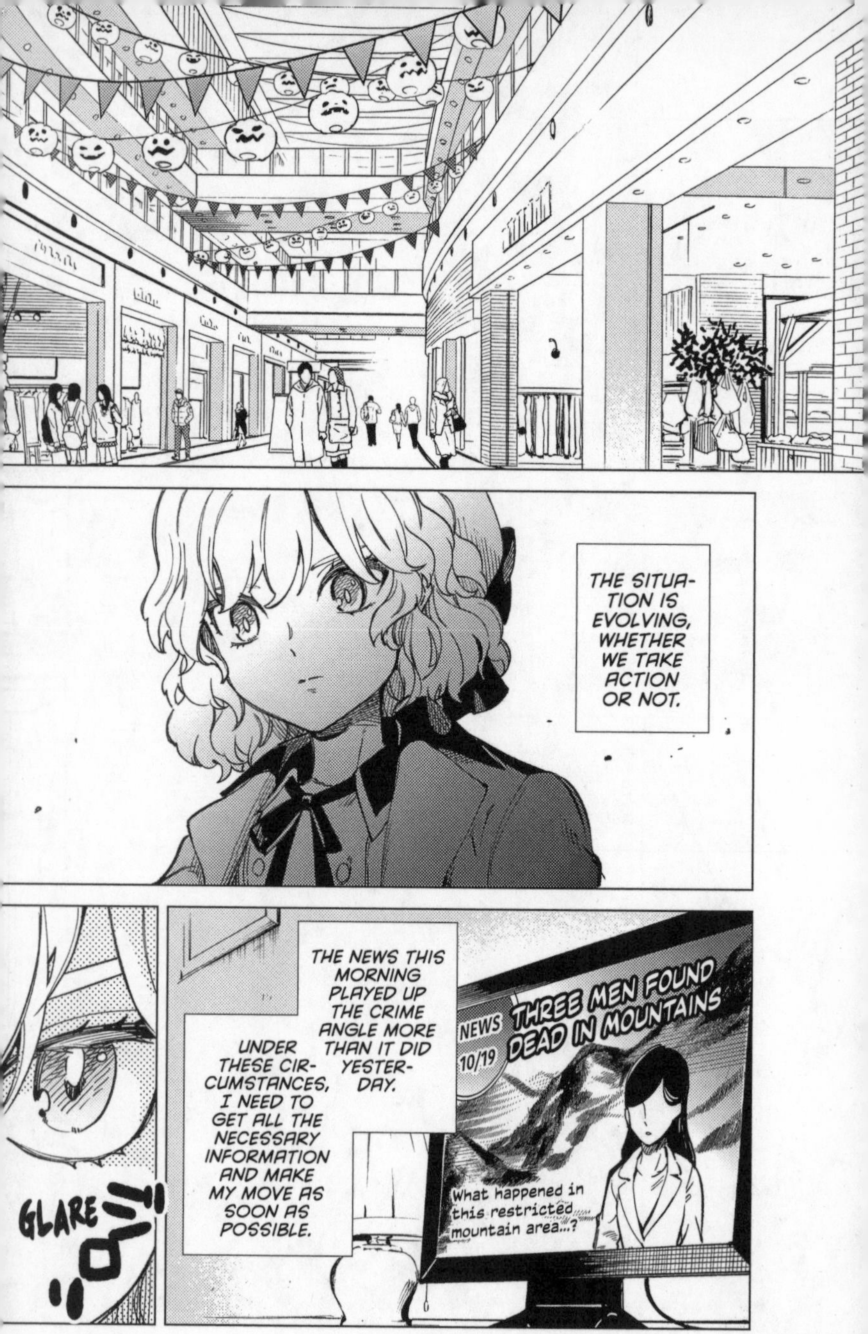
THE SITUATION IS EVOLVING, WHETHER WE TAKE ACTION OR NOT.
NEWS 10/19
THREE MEN FOUND DEAD IN MOUNTAINS
THE NEWS THIS MORNING PLAYED UP THE CRIME ANGLE MORE THAN IT DID YESTERDAY.
UNDER THESE CIRCUMSTANCES, I NEED TO GET ALL THE NECESSARY INFORMATION AND MAKE MY MOVE AS SOON AS POSSIBLE.
What happened in this restricted mountain area...?
GLARE

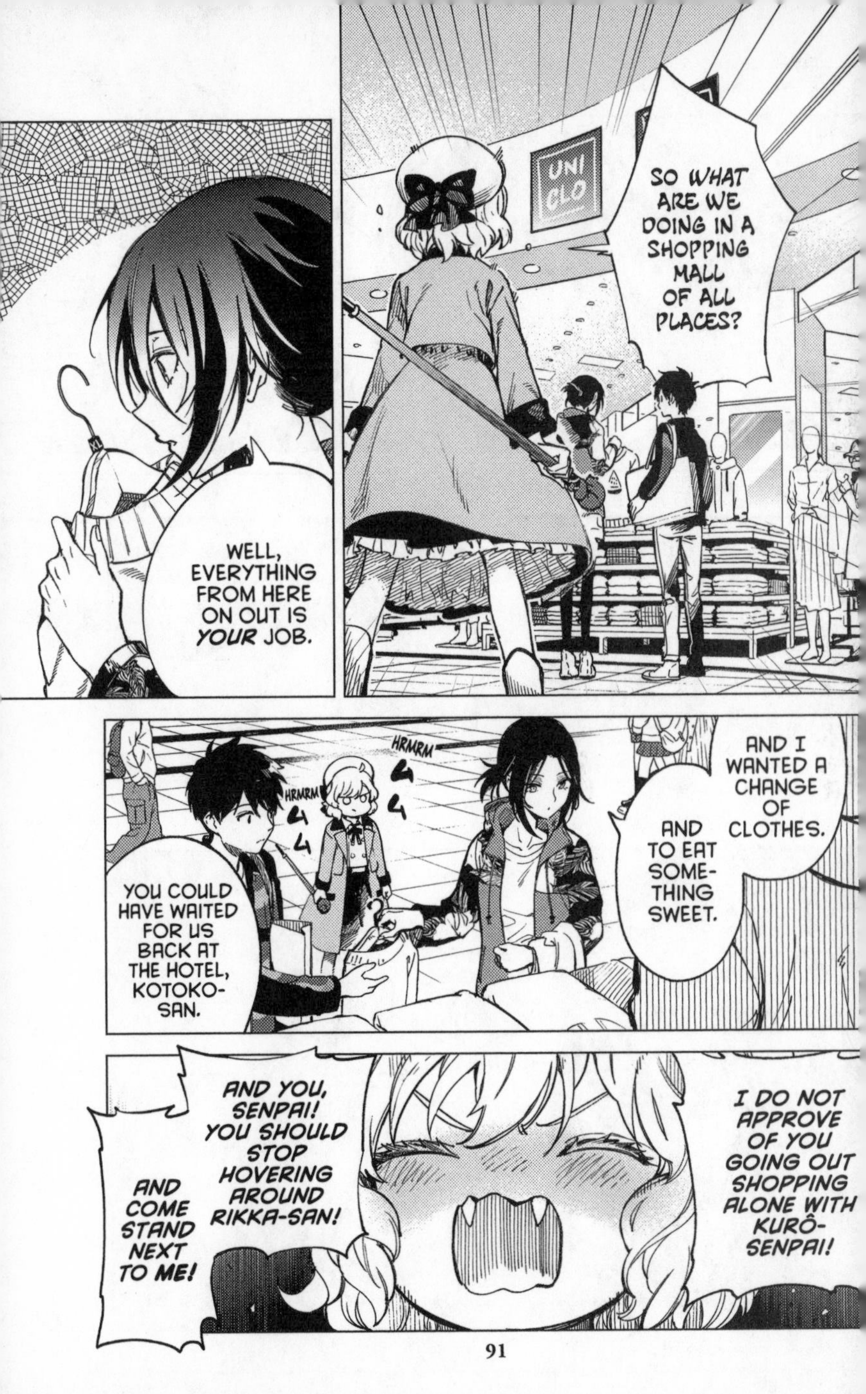

SO WHAT ARE WE DOING IN A SHOPPING MALL OF ALL PLACES?
UNI CLO
WELL, EVERYTHING FROM HERE ON OUT IS *YOUR* JOB.
AND I WANTED A CHANGE OF CLOTHES.
AND TO EAT SOMETHING SWEET.
HRMRM
HRMRM
YOU COULD HAVE WAITED FOR US BACK AT THE HOTEL, KOTOKO-SAN.
I DO NOT APPROVE OF YOU GOING OUT SHOPPING ALONE WITH KURÔ-SENPAI!
AND YOU, SENPAI! YOU SHOULD STOP HOVERING AROUND RIKKA-SAN!
AND COME STAND NEXT TO ME!

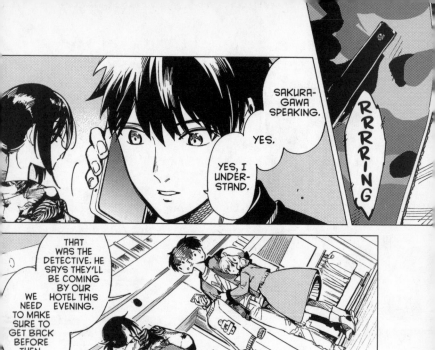

SAKURA-GAWA SPEAKING.

YES.

YES, I UNDER-STAND.

RRRRING

THAT WAS THE DETECTIVE. HE SAYS THEY'LL BE COMING BY OUR HOTEL THIS EVENING. WE NEED TO MAKE SURE TO GET BACK BEFORE THEN.

PLOP

SORRY FOR TAKING SO MUCH OF YOUR TIME, SAKURA-GAWA-SAN.

A suite...

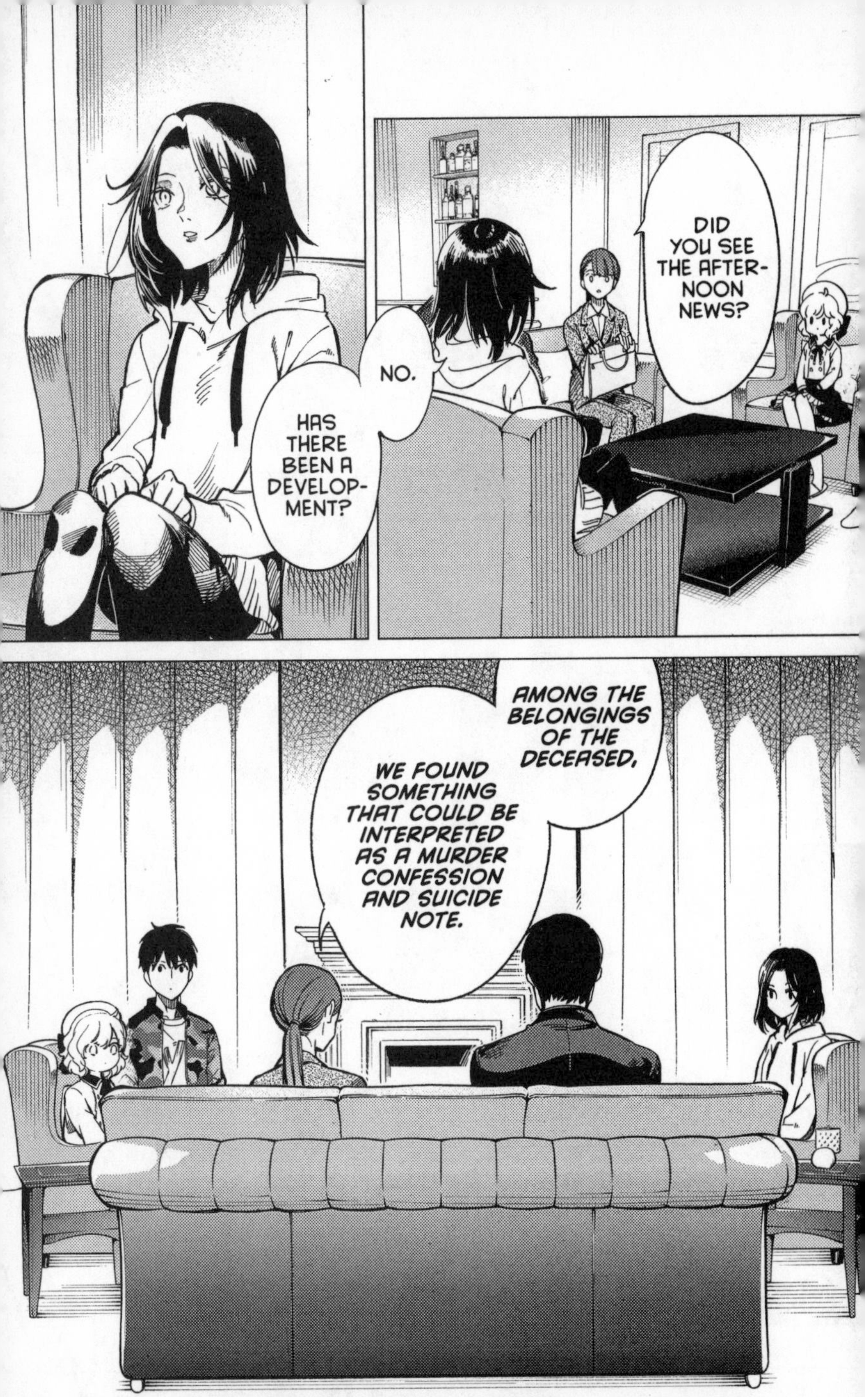
DID YOU SEE THE AFTER-NOON NEWS?
NO.
HAS THERE BEEN A DEVELOP-MENT?
AMONG THE BELONGINGS OF THE DECEASED,
WE FOUND SOMETHING THAT COULD BE INTERPRETED AS A MURDER CONFESSION AND SUICIDE NOTE.

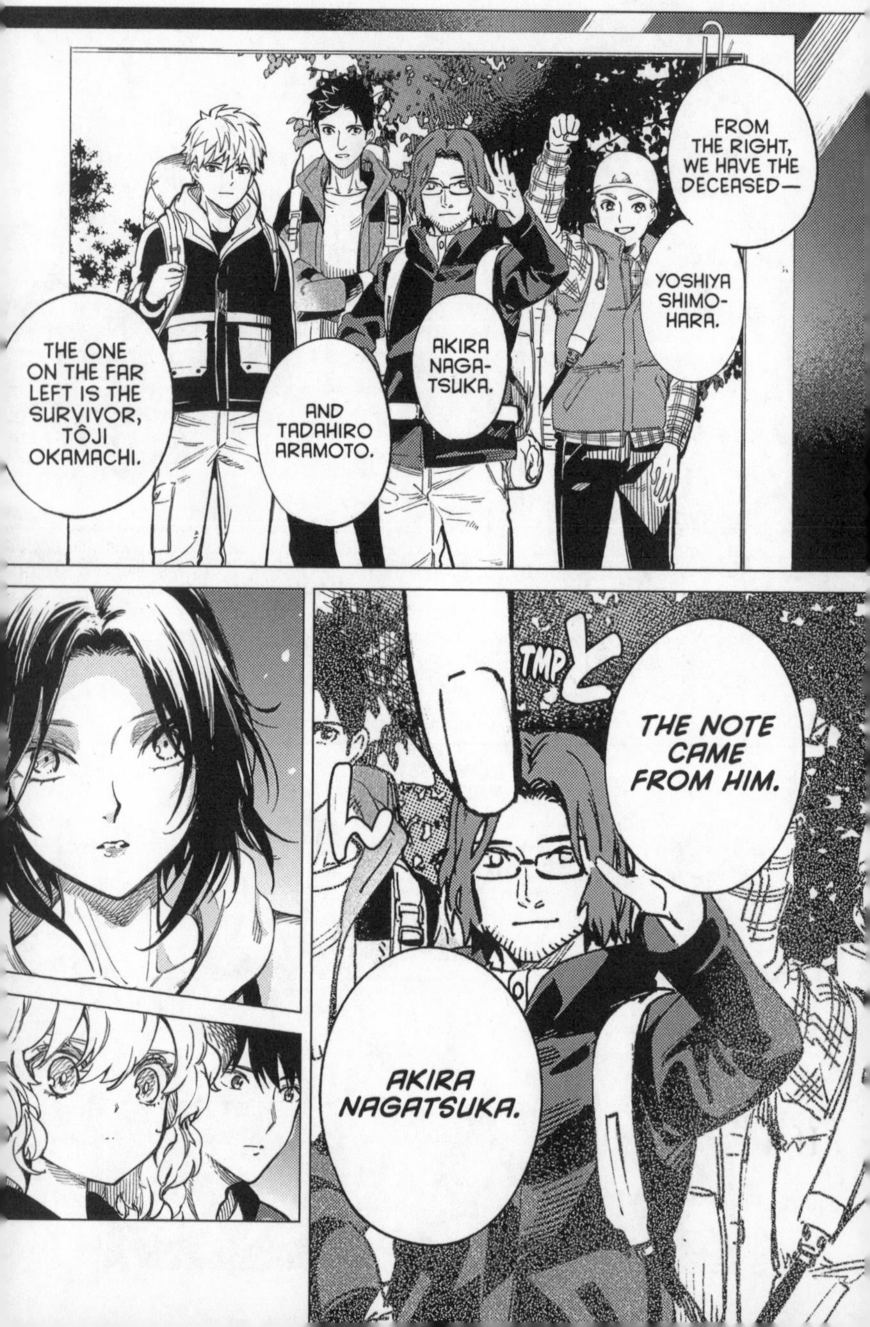
FROM THE RIGHT, WE HAVE THE DECEASED—
YOSHIYA SHIMOHARA.
AKIRA NAGATSUKA.
AND TADAHIRO ARAMOTO.
THE ONE ON THE FAR LEFT IS THE SURVIVOR, TÔJI OKAMACHI.
TMP
THE NOTE CAME FROM HIM.
AKIRA NAGATSUKA.

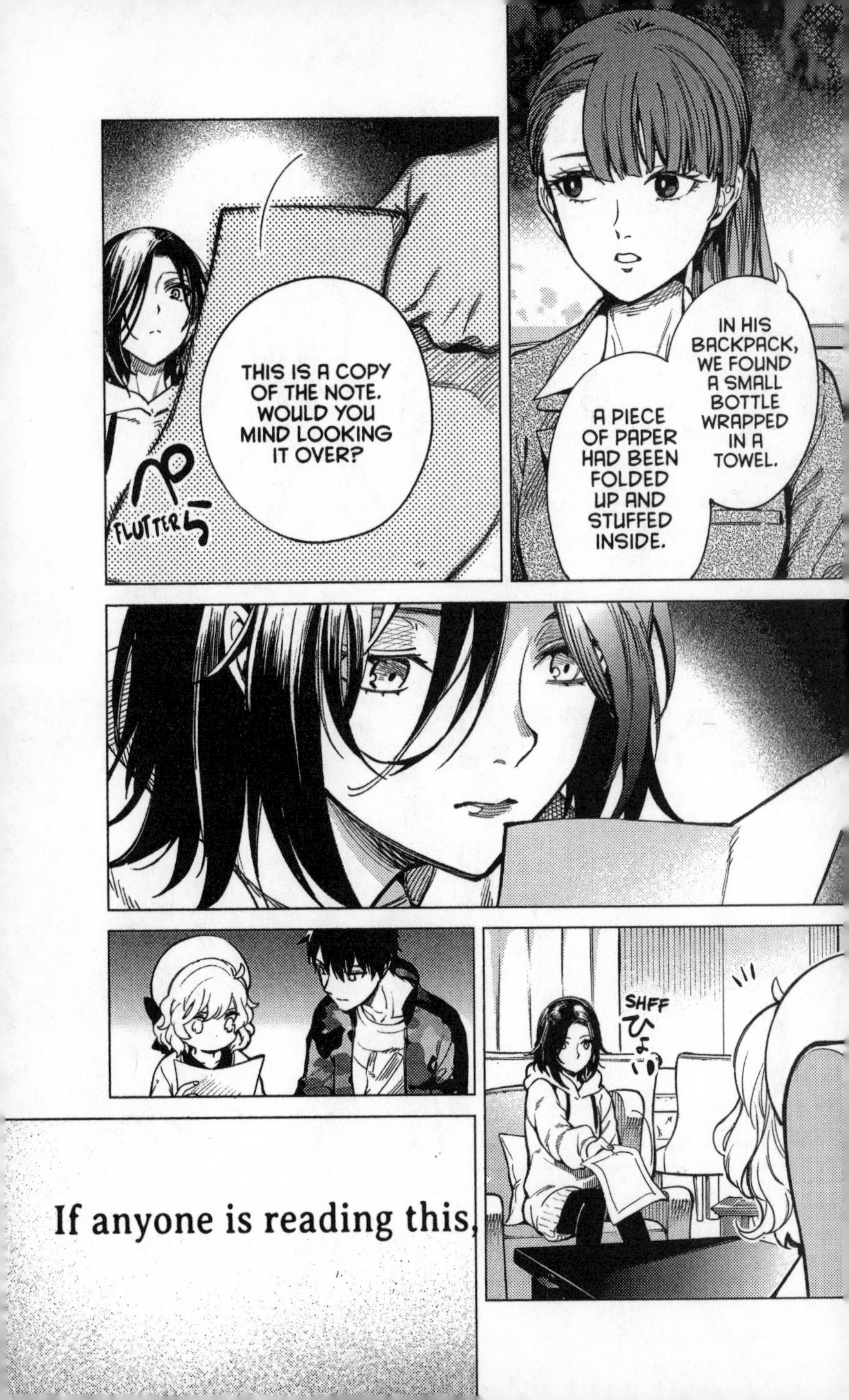
IN HIS BACKPACK, WE FOUND A SMALL BOTTLE WRAPPED IN A TOWEL.
A PIECE OF PAPER HAD BEEN FOLDED UP AND STUFFED INSIDE.
THIS IS A COPY OF THE NOTE. WOULD YOU MIND LOOKING IT OVER?
FLUTTER
SHFF
If anyone is reading this,

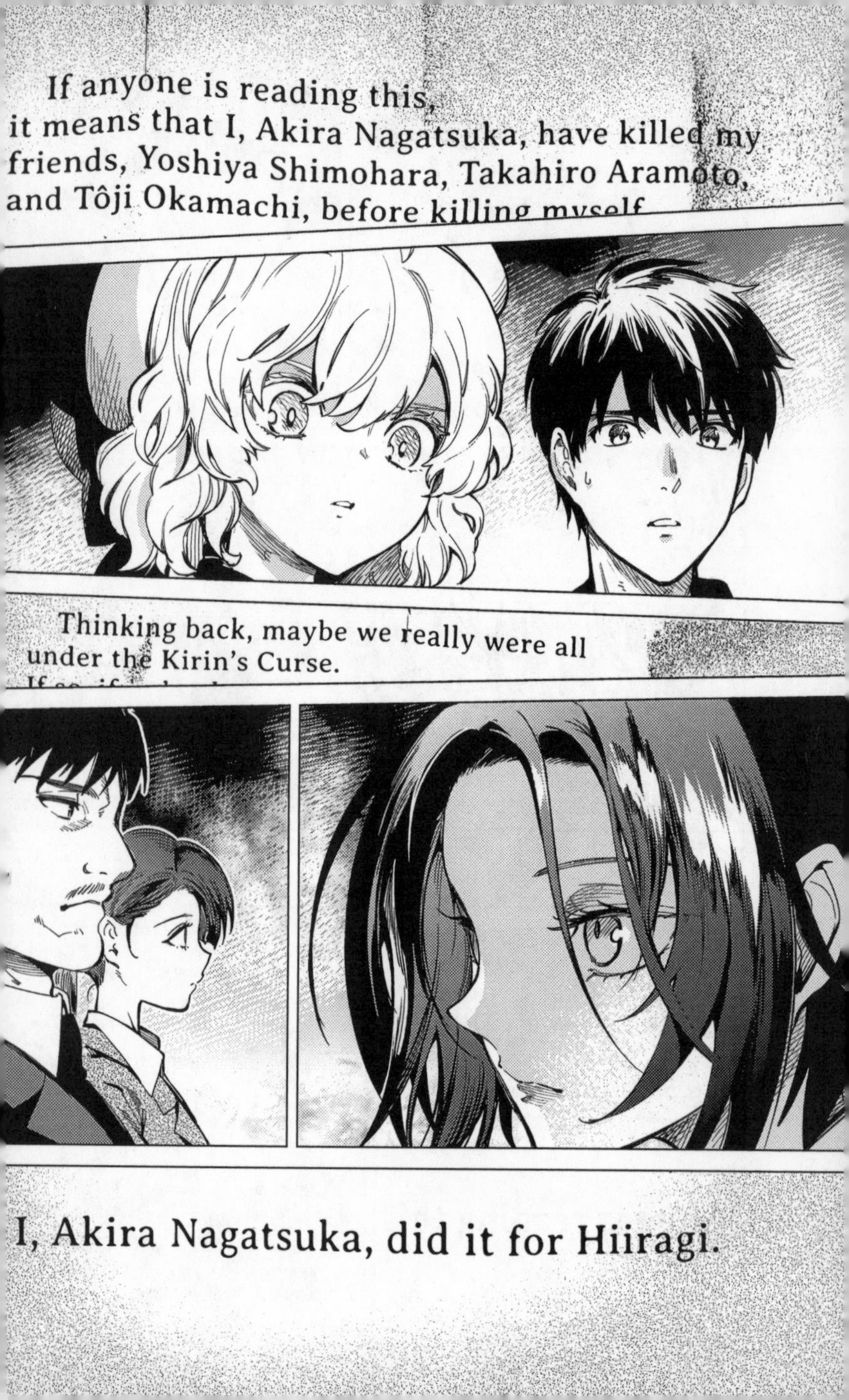
If anyone is reading this,
it means that I, Akira Nagatsuka, have killed my friends, Yoshiya Shimohara, Takahiro Aramoto, and Tôji Okamachi, before killing myself
Thinking back, maybe we really were all under the Kirin's Curse.
I, Akira Nagatsuka, did it for Hiiragi.

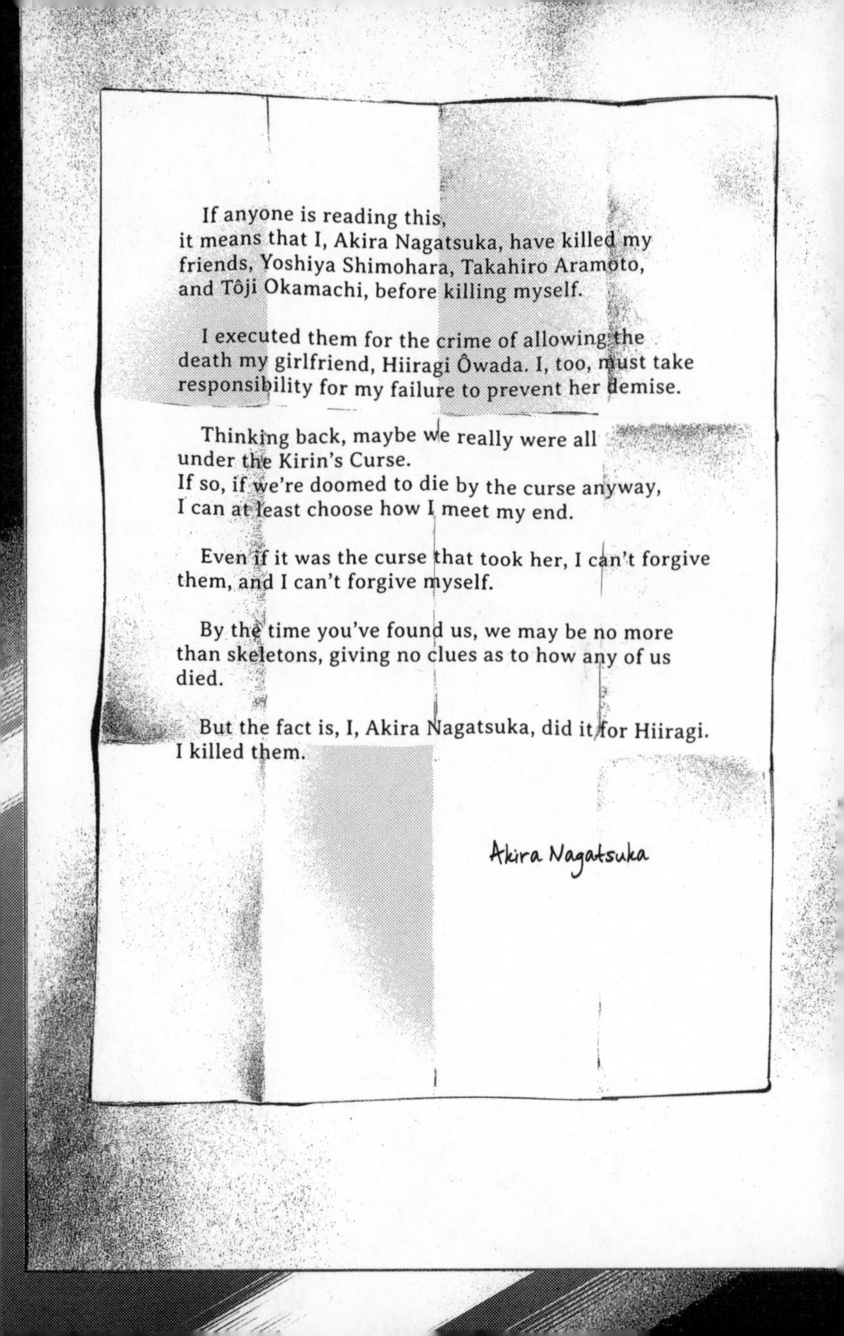

If anyone is reading this,
it means that I, Akira Nagatsuka, have killed my friends, Yoshiya Shimohara, Takahiro Aramoto, and Tôji Okamachi, before killing myself.

I executed them for the crime of allowing the death my girlfriend, Hiiragi Ôwada. I, too, must take responsibility for my failure to prevent her demise.

Thinking back, maybe we really were all under the Kirin's Curse.
If so, if we're doomed to die by the curse anyway, I can at least choose how I meet my end.

Even if it was the curse that took her, I can't forgive them, and I can't forgive myself.

By the time you've found us, we may be no more than skeletons, giving no clues as to how any of us died.

But the fact is, I, Akira Nagatsuka, did it for Hiiragi. I killed them.

Akira Nagatsuka

IN/SPECTRE

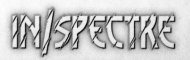

If anyone is reading this,
it means that I, Akira Nagatsuka, have killed my friends, Yoshiya Shimohara, Takahiro Aramoto, and Tôji Okamachi, before killing myself.

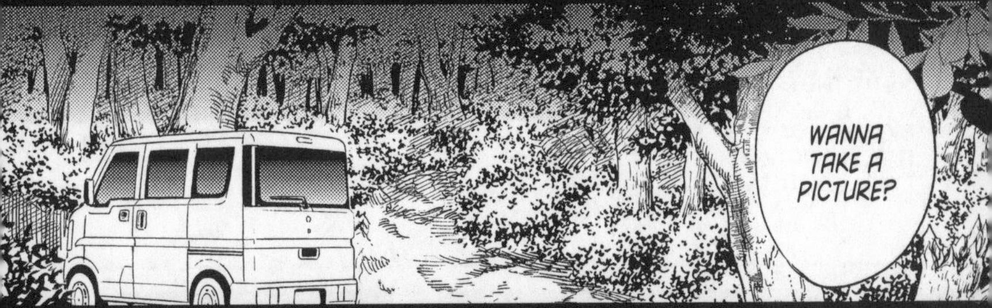
WANNA TAKE A PICTURE?

I executed them for the crime of allowing the death my girlfriend, Hiiragi Ôwada. I, too, must take responsibility for my failure to prevent her demise.

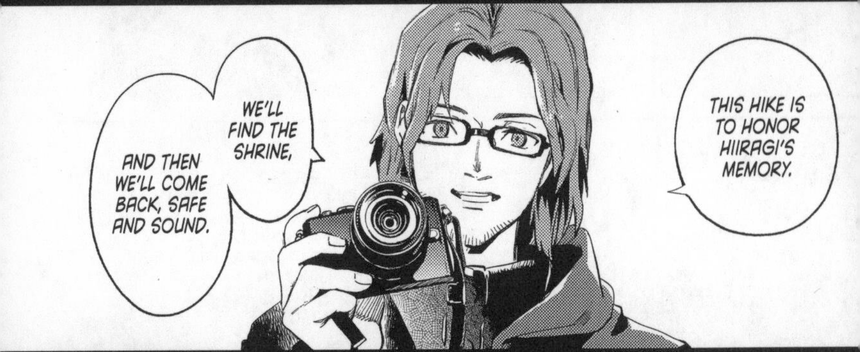
THIS HIKE IS TO HONOR HIIRAGI'S MEMORY.
WE'LL FIND THE SHRINE,
AND THEN WE'LL COME BACK, SAFE AND SOUND.

Thinking back, maybe we really were all under the Kirin's Curse.
If so, if we're doomed to die by the curse anyway,
I can at least choose how I meet my end.

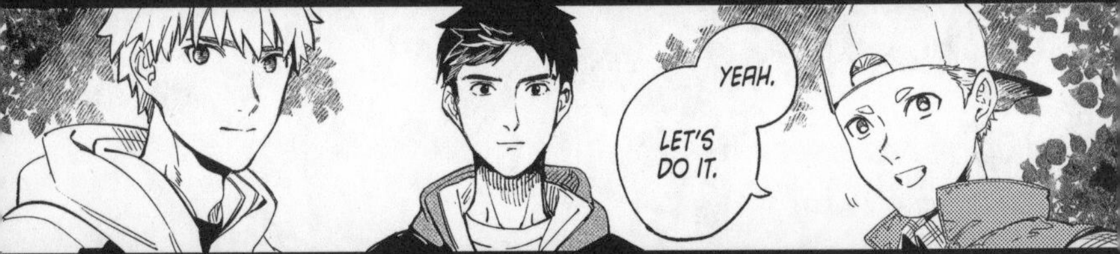
YEAH.
LET'S DO IT.

Even if it was the curse that took her, I can't forgive them, and I can't forgive myself.

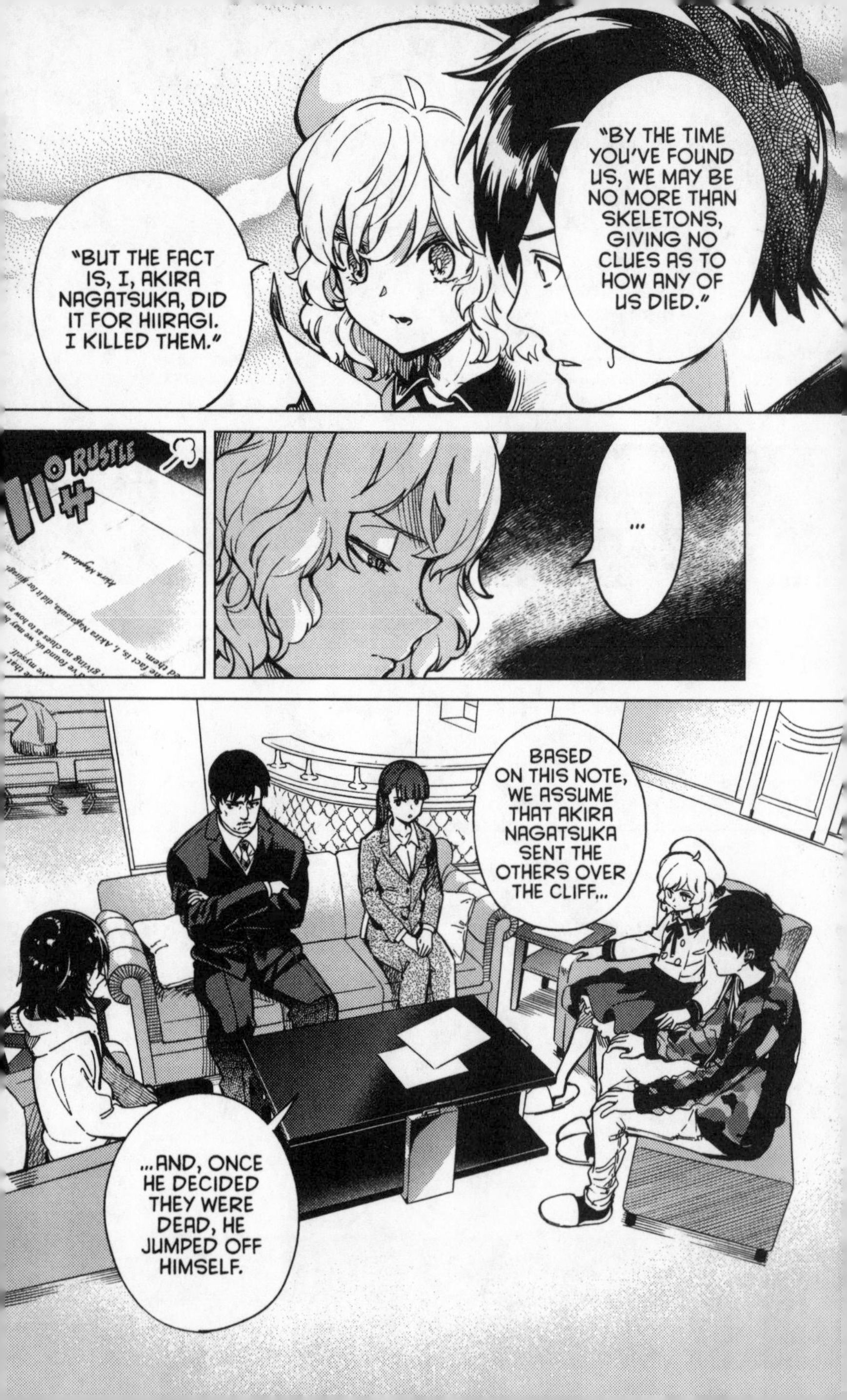
"BY THE TIME YOU'VE FOUND US, WE MAY BE NO MORE THAN SKELETONS, GIVING NO CLUES AS TO HOW ANY OF US DIED."
"BUT THE FACT IS, I, AKIRA NAGATSUKA, DID IT FOR HIIRAGI. I KILLED THEM."
...
RUSTLE
BASED ON THIS NOTE, WE ASSUME THAT AKIRA NAGATSUKA SENT THE OTHERS OVER THE CLIFF...
...AND, ONCE HE DECIDED THEY WERE DEAD, HE JUMPED OFF HIMSELF.

# CHAPTER 43: "THE RETALIATION AND DEFEAT OF KOTOKO IWANAGA PART 5"

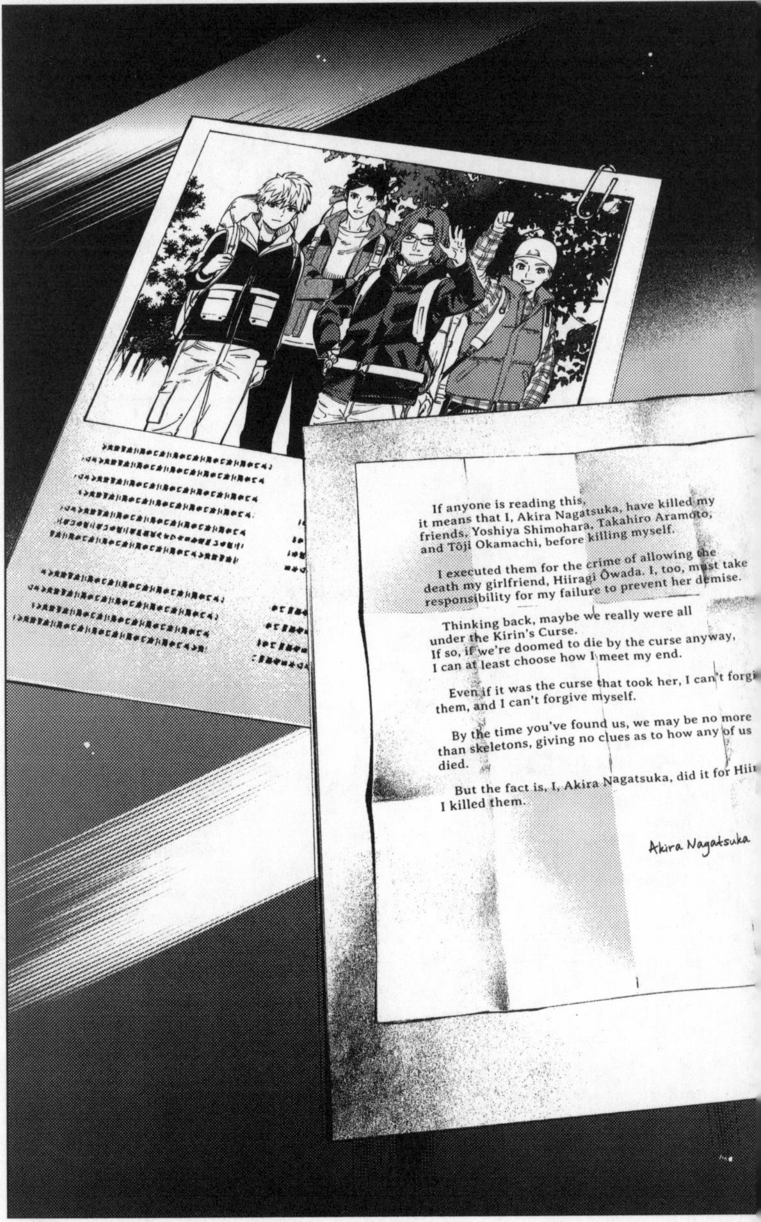
If anyone is reading this,
it means that I, Akira Nagatsuka, have killed my
friends, Yoshiya Shimohara, Takahiro Aramoto,
and Tōji Okamachi, before killing myself.
I executed them for the crime of allowing the
death my girlfriend, Hiiragi Ōwada. I, too, must take
responsibility for my failure to prevent her demise.
Thinking back, maybe we really were all
under the Kirin's Curse.
If so, if we're doomed to die by the curse anyway,
I can at least choose how I meet my end.
Even if it was the curse that took her, I can't forgi
them, and I can't forgive myself.
By the time you've found us, we may be no more
than skeletons, giving no clues as to how any of us
died.
But the fact is, I, Akira Nagatsuka, did it for Hii
I killed them.
Akira Nagatsuka

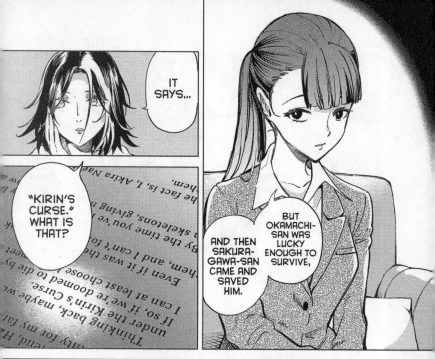

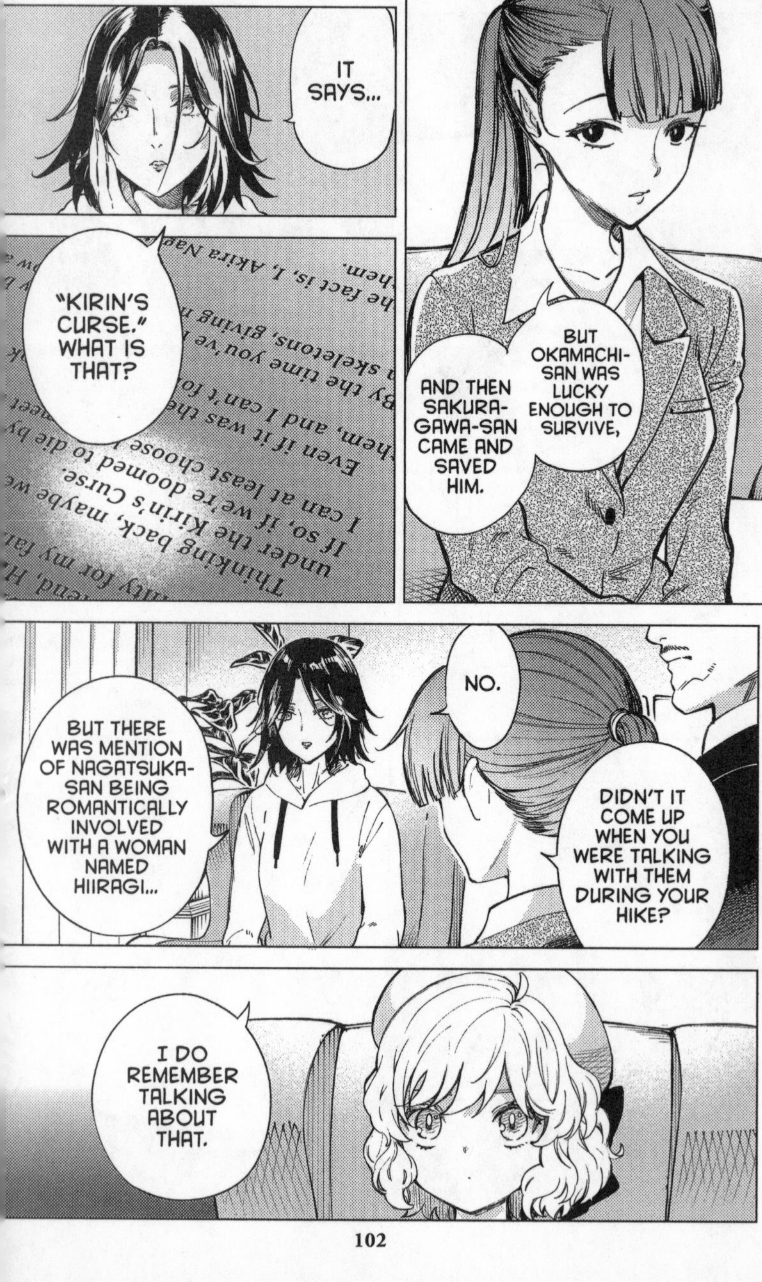
BUT OKAMACHI-SAN WAS LUCKY ENOUGH TO SURVIVE,
AND THEN SAKURA-GAWA-SAN CAME AND SAVED HIM.
IT SAYS...
"KIRIN'S CURSE." WHAT IS THAT?
NO.
DIDN'T IT COME UP WHEN YOU WERE TALKING WITH THEM DURING YOUR HIKE?
BUT THERE WAS MENTION OF NAGATSUKA-SAN BEING ROMANTICALLY INVOLVED WITH A WOMAN NAMED HIIRAGI...
I DO REMEMBER TALKING ABOUT THAT.

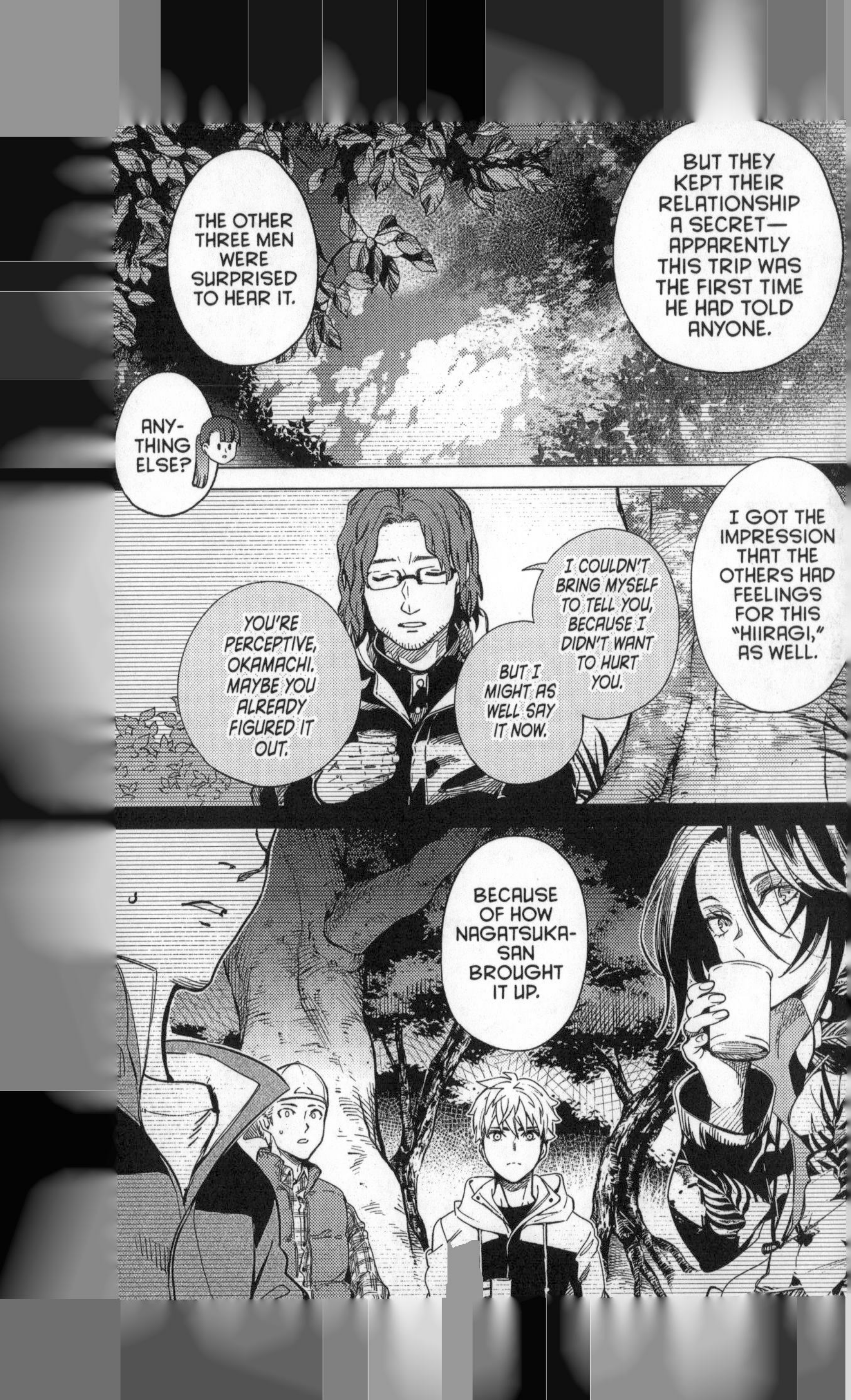
BUT THEY KEPT THEIR RELATIONSHIP A SECRET—APPARENTLY THIS TRIP WAS THE FIRST TIME HE HAD TOLD ANYONE.
THE OTHER THREE MEN WERE SURPRISED TO HEAR IT.
ANY-THING ELSE?
I GOT THE IMPRESSION THAT THE OTHERS HAD FEELINGS FOR THIS "HIIRAGI," AS WELL.
I COULDN'T BRING MYSELF TO TELL YOU, BECAUSE I DIDN'T WANT TO HURT YOU.
BUT I MIGHT AS WELL SAY IT NOW.
YOU'RE PERCEPTIVE, OKAMACHI. MAYBE YOU ALREADY FIGURED IT OUT.
BECAUSE OF HOW NAGATSUKA-SAN BROUGHT IT UP.

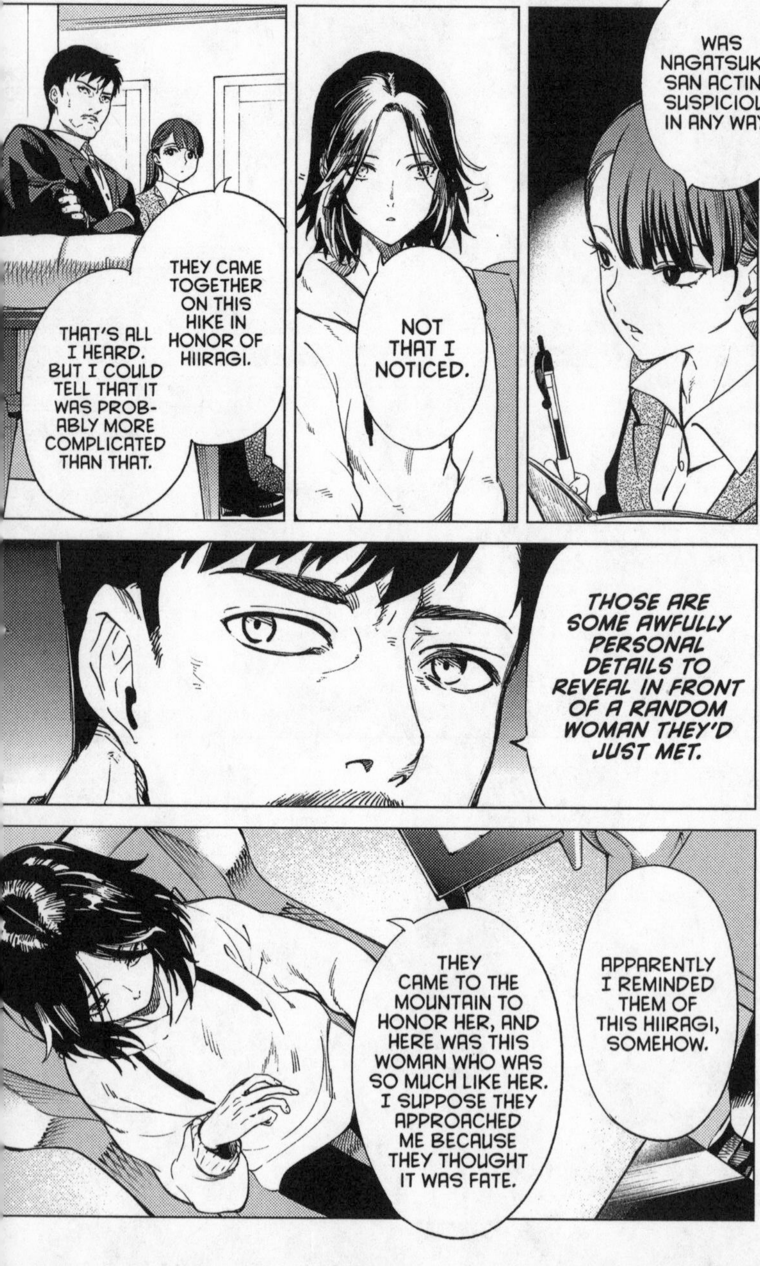
WAS NAGATSUKA-SAN ACTING SUSPICIOUS IN ANY WAY?
NOT THAT I NOTICED.
THEY CAME TOGETHER ON THIS HIKE IN HONOR OF HIIRAGI.
THAT'S ALL I HEARD. BUT I COULD TELL THAT IT WAS PROB-ABLY MORE COMPLICATED THAN THAT.
THOSE ARE SOME AWFULLY PERSONAL DETAILS TO REVEAL IN FRONT OF A RANDOM WOMAN THEY'D JUST MET.
APPARENTLY I REMINDED THEM OF THIS HIIRAGI, SOMEHOW.
THEY CAME TO THE MOUNTAIN TO HONOR HER, AND HERE WAS THIS WOMAN WHO WAS SO MUCH LIKE HER. I SUPPOSE THEY APPROACHED ME BECAUSE THEY THOUGHT IT WAS FATE.

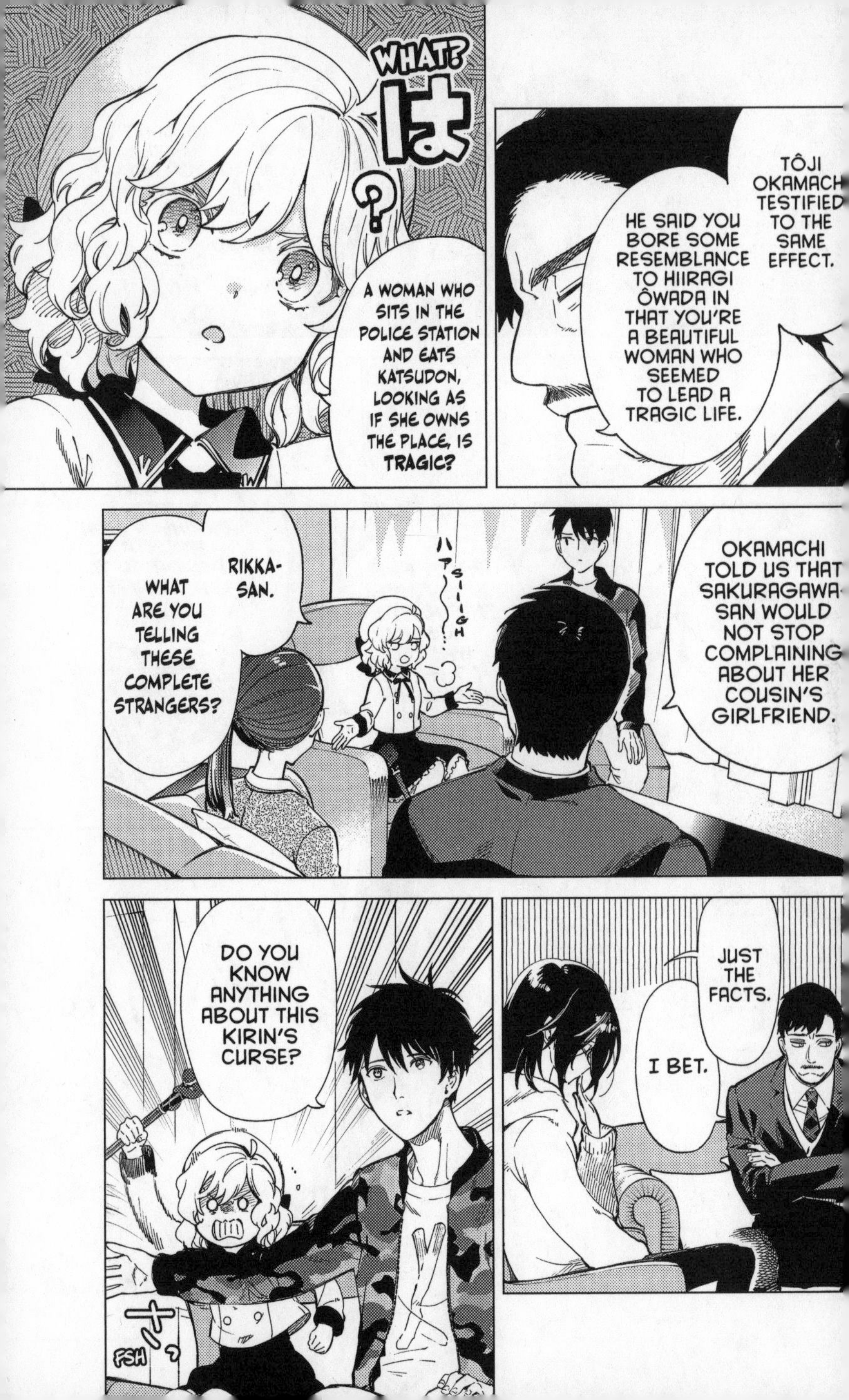
TÔJI OKAMACHI TESTIFIED TO THE SAME EFFECT.
HE SAID YOU BORE SOME RESEMBLANCE TO HIIRAGI ÔWADA IN THAT YOU'RE A BEAUTIFUL WOMAN WHO SEEMED TO LEAD A TRAGIC LIFE.
WHAT?
は？
A WOMAN WHO SITS IN THE POLICE STATION AND EATS KATSUDON, LOOKING AS IF SHE OWNS THE PLACE, IS TRAGIC?
OKAMACHI TOLD US THAT SAKURAGAWA-SAN WOULD NOT STOP COMPLAINING ABOUT HER COUSIN'S GIRLFRIEND.
ハア～～…
SIIIGH
RIKKA-SAN.
WHAT ARE YOU TELLING THESE COMPLETE STRANGERS?
JUST THE FACTS.
I BET.
DO YOU KNOW ANYTHING ABOUT THIS KIRIN'S CURSE?
FSH

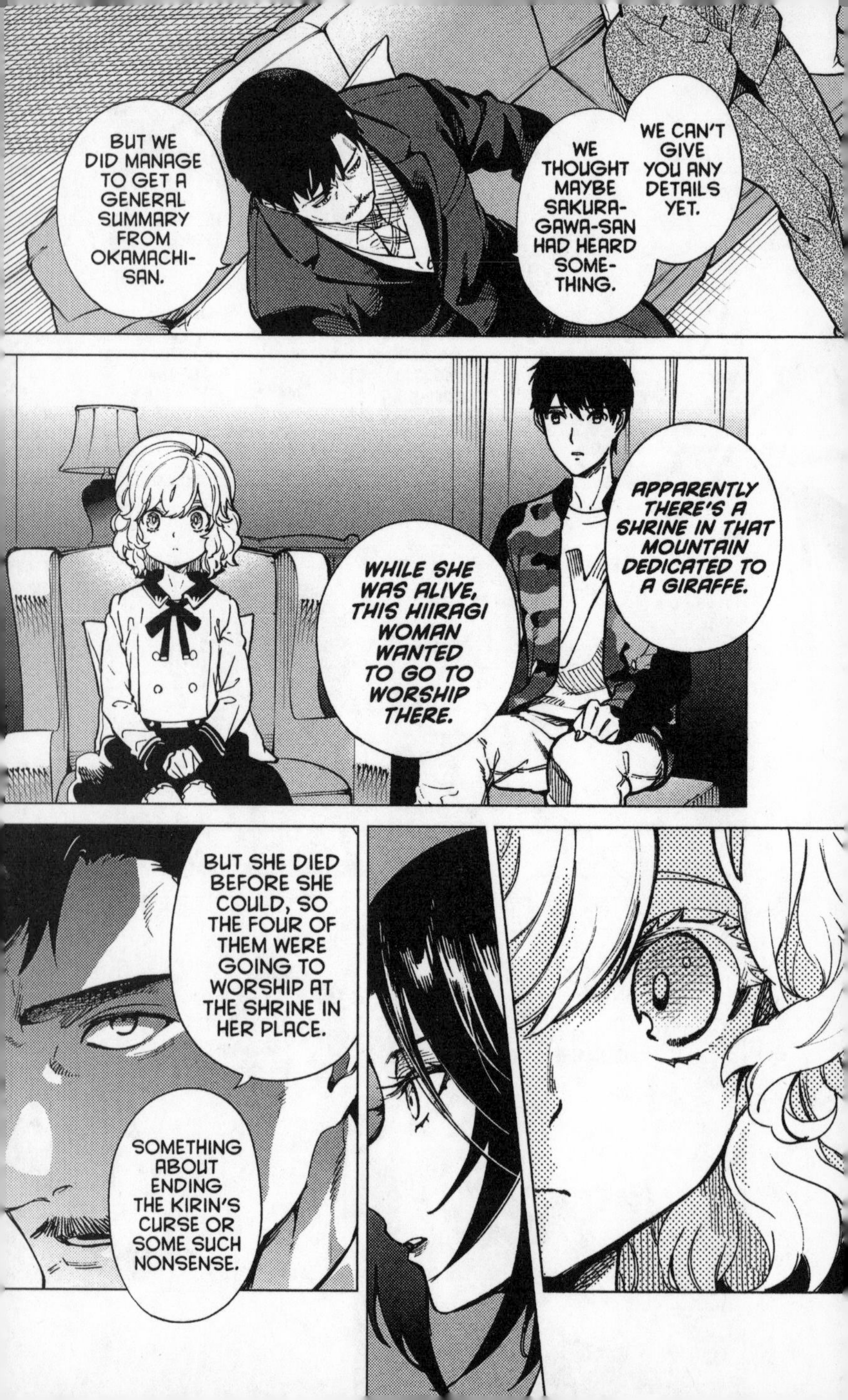
WE CAN'T GIVE YOU ANY DETAILS YET.
WE THOUGHT MAYBE SAKURA-GAWA-SAN HAD HEARD SOME-THING.
BUT WE DID MANAGE TO GET A GENERAL SUMMARY FROM OKAMACHI-SAN.
APPARENTLY THERE'S A SHRINE IN THAT MOUNTAIN DEDICATED TO A GIRAFFE.
WHILE SHE WAS ALIVE, THIS HIIRAGI WOMAN WANTED TO GO TO WORSHIP THERE.
BUT SHE DIED BEFORE SHE COULD, SO THE FOUR OF THEM WERE GOING TO WORSHIP AT THE SHRINE IN HER PLACE.
SOMETHING ABOUT ENDING THE KIRIN'S CURSE OR SOME SUCH NONSENSE.

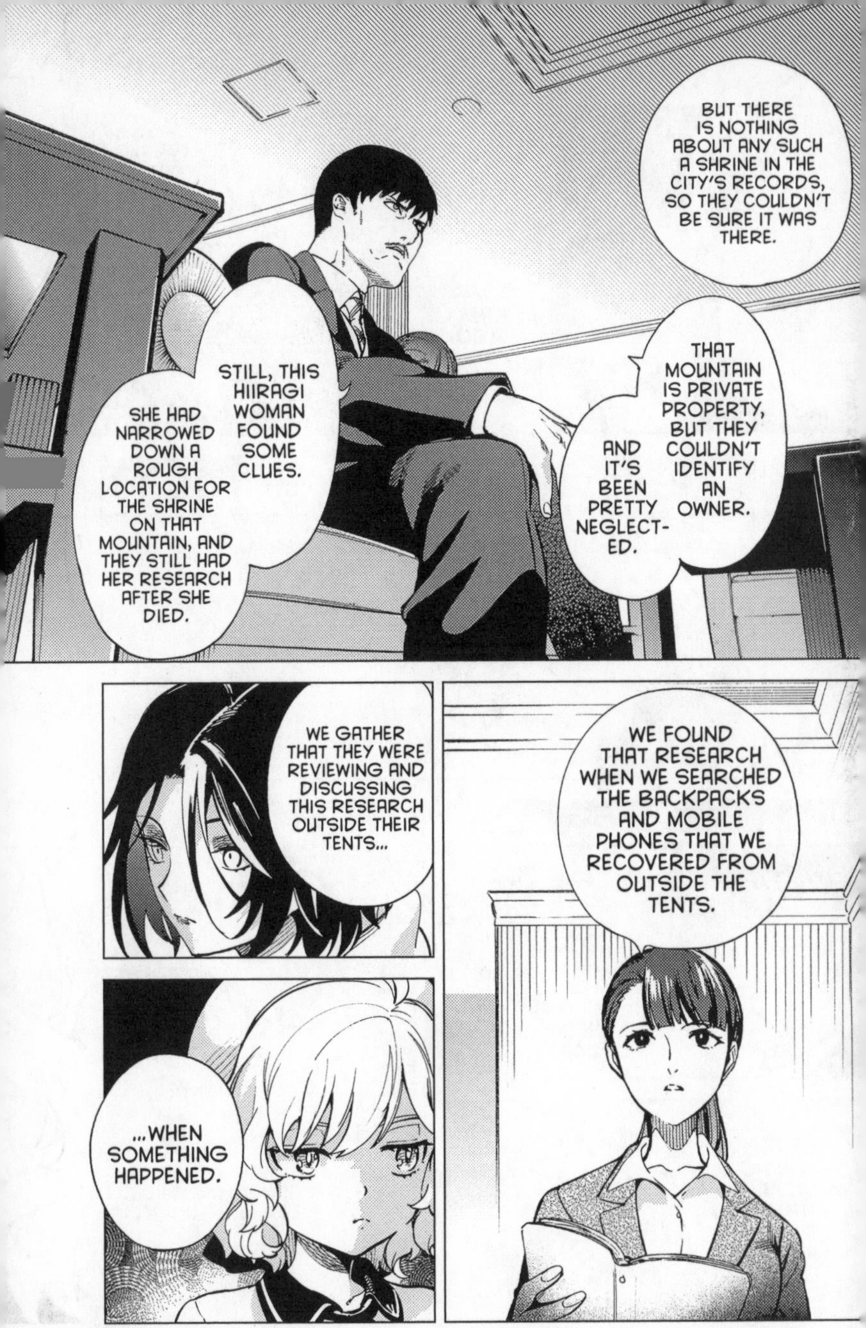
BUT THERE IS NOTHING ABOUT ANY SUCH A SHRINE IN THE CITY'S RECORDS, SO THEY COULDN'T BE SURE IT WAS THERE.
THAT MOUNTAIN IS PRIVATE PROPERTY, BUT THEY COULDN'T IDENTIFY AN OWNER.
AND IT'S BEEN PRETTY NEGLECT-ED.
STILL, THIS HIIRAGI WOMAN FOUND SOME CLUES.
SHE HAD NARROWED DOWN A ROUGH LOCATION FOR THE SHRINE ON THAT MOUNTAIN, AND THEY STILL HAD HER RESEARCH AFTER SHE DIED.
WE FOUND THAT RESEARCH WHEN WE SEARCHED THE BACKPACKS AND MOBILE PHONES THAT WE RECOVERED FROM OUTSIDE THE TENTS.
WE GATHER THAT THEY WERE REVIEWING AND DISCUSSING THIS RESEARCH OUTSIDE THEIR TENTS...
...WHEN SOMETHING HAPPENED.

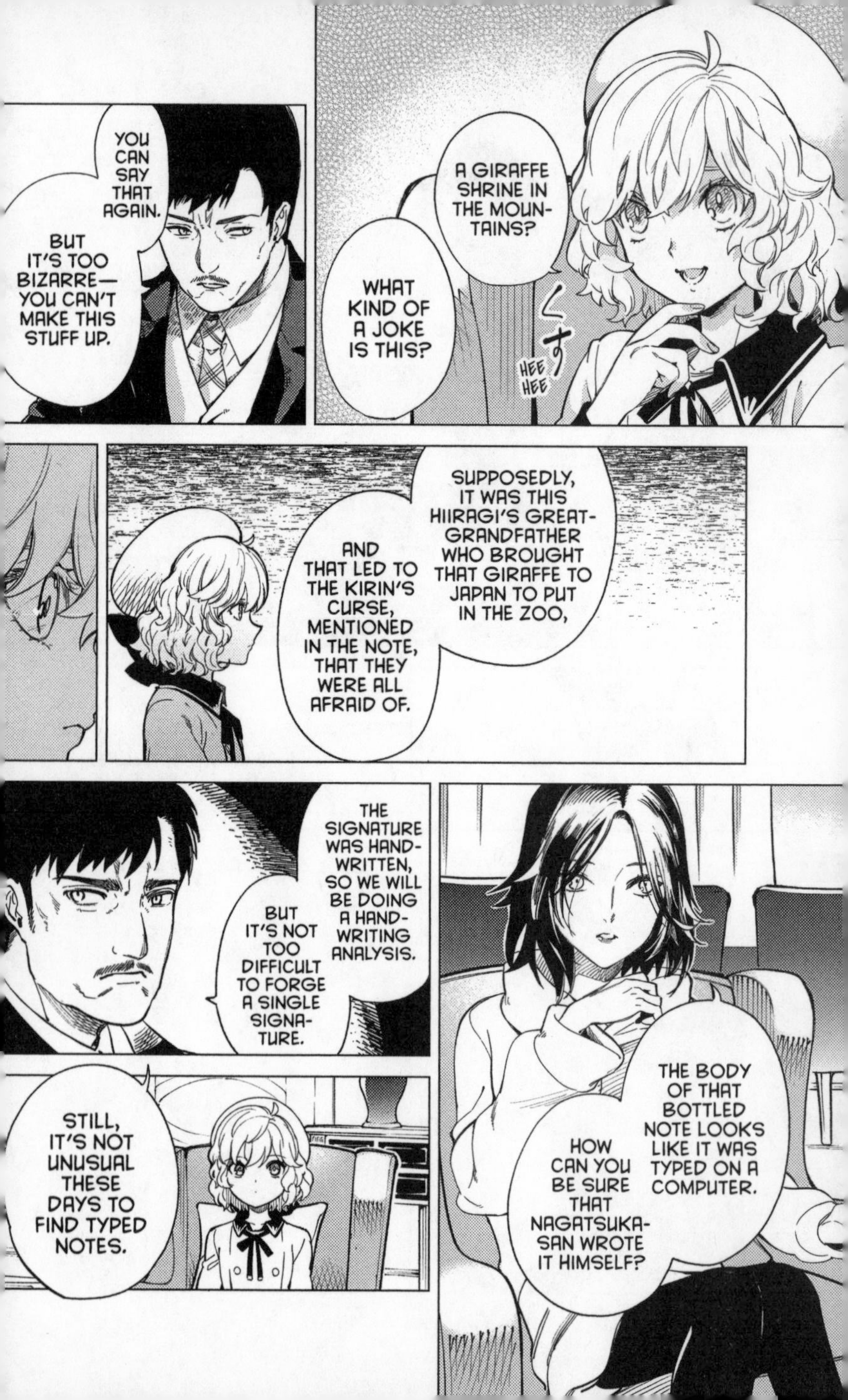
A GIRAFFE SHRINE IN THE MOUN-TAINS?
WHAT KIND OF A JOKE IS THIS?
くす
HEE HEE
YOU CAN SAY THAT AGAIN.
BUT IT'S TOO BIZARRE—YOU CAN'T MAKE THIS STUFF UP.
SUPPOSEDLY, IT WAS THIS HIIRAGI'S GREAT-GRANDFATHER WHO BROUGHT THAT GIRAFFE TO JAPAN TO PUT IN THE ZOO,
AND THAT LED TO THE KIRIN'S CURSE, MENTIONED IN THE NOTE, THAT THEY WERE ALL AFRAID OF.
THE BODY OF THAT BOTTLED NOTE LOOKS LIKE IT WAS TYPED ON A COMPUTER.
HOW CAN YOU BE SURE THAT NAGATSUKA-SAN WROTE IT HIMSELF?
THE SIGNATURE WAS HAND-WRITTEN, SO WE WILL BE DOING A HAND-WRITING ANALYSIS.
BUT IT'S NOT TOO DIFFICULT TO FORGE A SINGLE SIGNA-TURE.
STILL, IT'S NOT UNUSUAL THESE DAYS TO FIND TYPED NOTES.

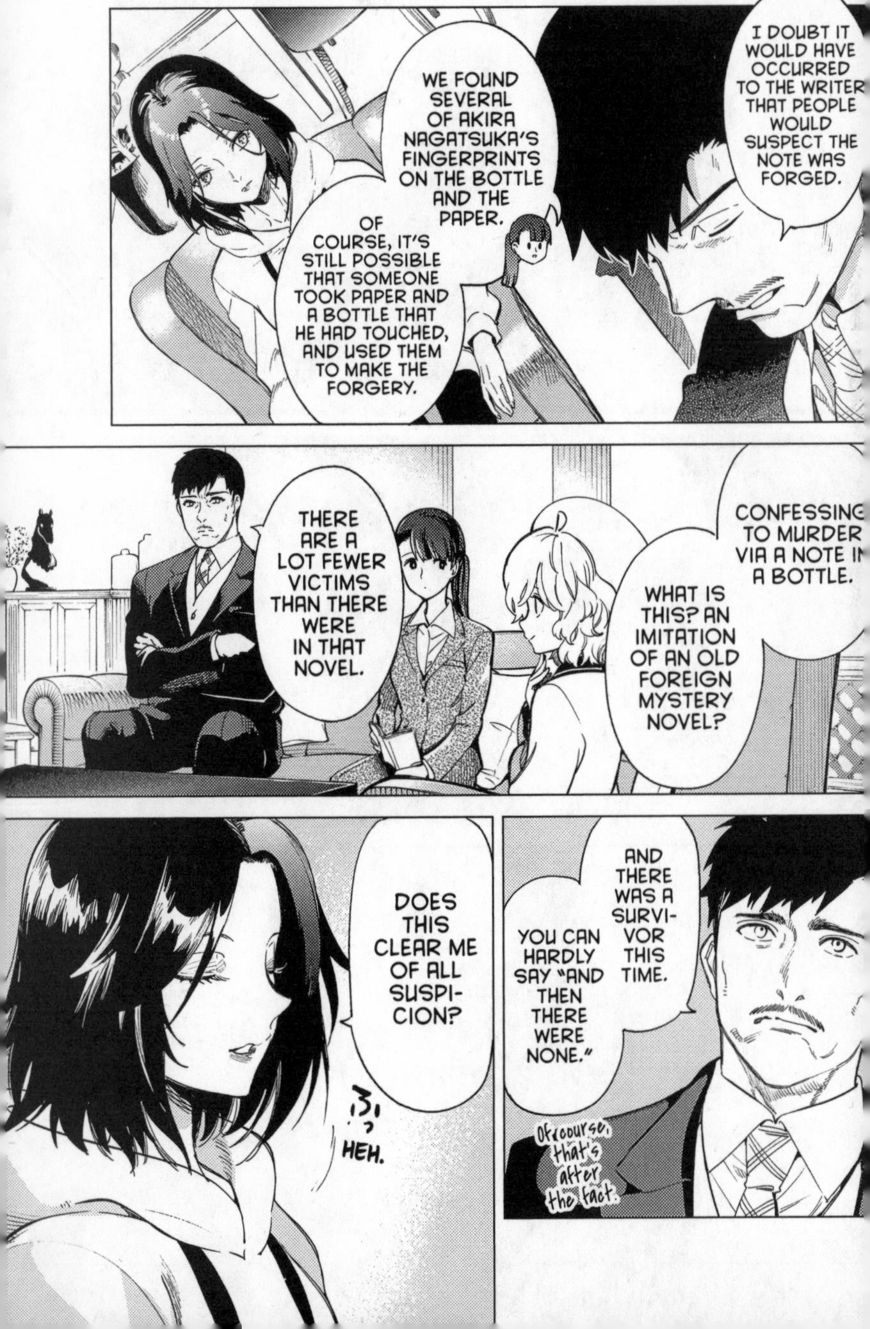
I DOUBT IT WOULD HAVE OCCURRED TO THE WRITER THAT PEOPLE WOULD SUSPECT THE NOTE WAS FORGED.
WE FOUND SEVERAL OF AKIRA NAGATSUKA'S FINGERPRINTS ON THE BOTTLE AND THE PAPER.
OF COURSE, IT'S STILL POSSIBLE THAT SOMEONE TOOK PAPER AND A BOTTLE THAT HE HAD TOUCHED, AND USED THEM TO MAKE THE FORGERY.
CONFESSING TO MURDER VIA A NOTE IN A BOTTLE.
WHAT IS THIS? AN IMITATION OF AN OLD FOREIGN MYSTERY NOVEL?
THERE ARE A LOT FEWER VICTIMS THAN THERE WERE IN THAT NOVEL.
AND THERE WAS A SURVIVOR THIS TIME.
YOU CAN HARDLY SAY "AND THEN THERE WERE NONE."
Of course, that's after the fact.
DOES THIS CLEAR ME OF ALL SUSPICION?
HEH.

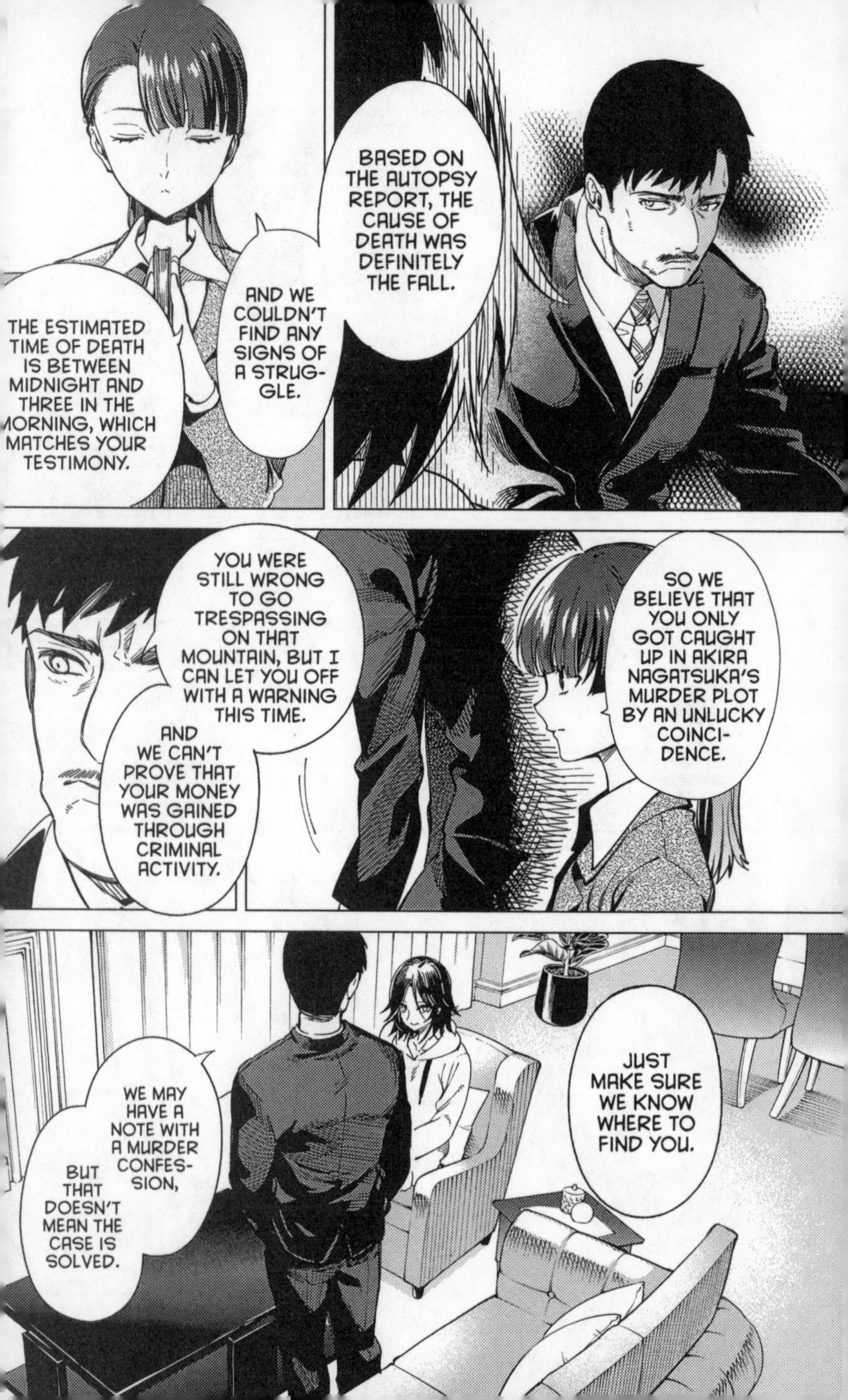
BASED ON THE AUTOPSY REPORT, THE CAUSE OF DEATH WAS DEFINITELY THE FALL.
AND WE COULDN'T FIND ANY SIGNS OF A STRUG-GLE.
THE ESTIMATED TIME OF DEATH IS BETWEEN MIDNIGHT AND THREE IN THE ORNING, WHICH MATCHES YOUR TESTIMONY.
SO WE BELIEVE THAT YOU ONLY GOT CAUGHT UP IN AKIRA NAGATSUKA'S MURDER PLOT BY AN UNLUCKY COINCI-DENCE.
YOU WERE STILL WRONG TO GO TRESPASSING ON THAT MOUNTAIN, BUT I CAN LET YOU OFF WITH A WARNING THIS TIME.
AND WE CAN'T PROVE THAT YOUR MONEY WAS GAINED THROUGH CRIMINAL ACTIVITY.
WE MAY HAVE A NOTE WITH A MURDER CONFES-SION,
BUT THAT DOESN'T MEAN THE CASE IS SOLVED.
JUST MAKE SURE WE KNOW WHERE TO FIND YOU.

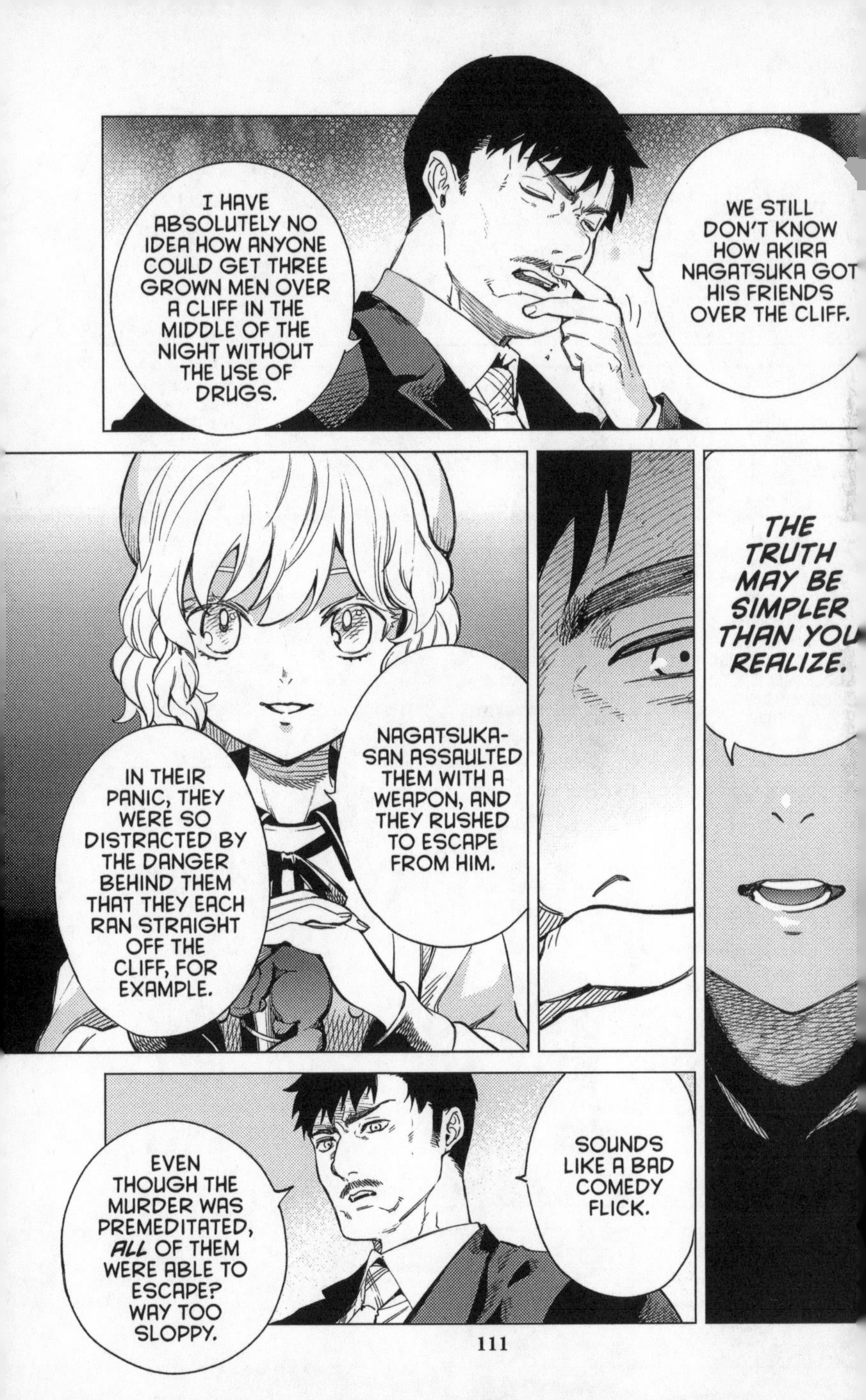
WE STILL DON'T KNOW HOW AKIRA NAGATSUKA GOT HIS FRIENDS OVER THE CLIFF.
I HAVE ABSOLUTELY NO IDEA HOW ANYONE COULD GET THREE GROWN MEN OVER A CLIFF IN THE MIDDLE OF THE NIGHT WITHOUT THE USE OF DRUGS.
THE TRUTH MAY BE SIMPLER THAN YOU REALIZE.
NAGATSUKA-SAN ASSAULTED THEM WITH A WEAPON, AND THEY RUSHED TO ESCAPE FROM HIM.
IN THEIR PANIC, THEY WERE SO DISTRACTED BY THE DANGER BEHIND THEM THAT THEY EACH RAN STRAIGHT OFF THE CLIFF, FOR EXAMPLE.
SOUNDS LIKE A BAD COMEDY FLICK.
EVEN THOUGH THE MURDER WAS PREMEDITATED, ALL OF THEM WERE ABLE TO ESCAPE? WAY TOO SLOPPY.

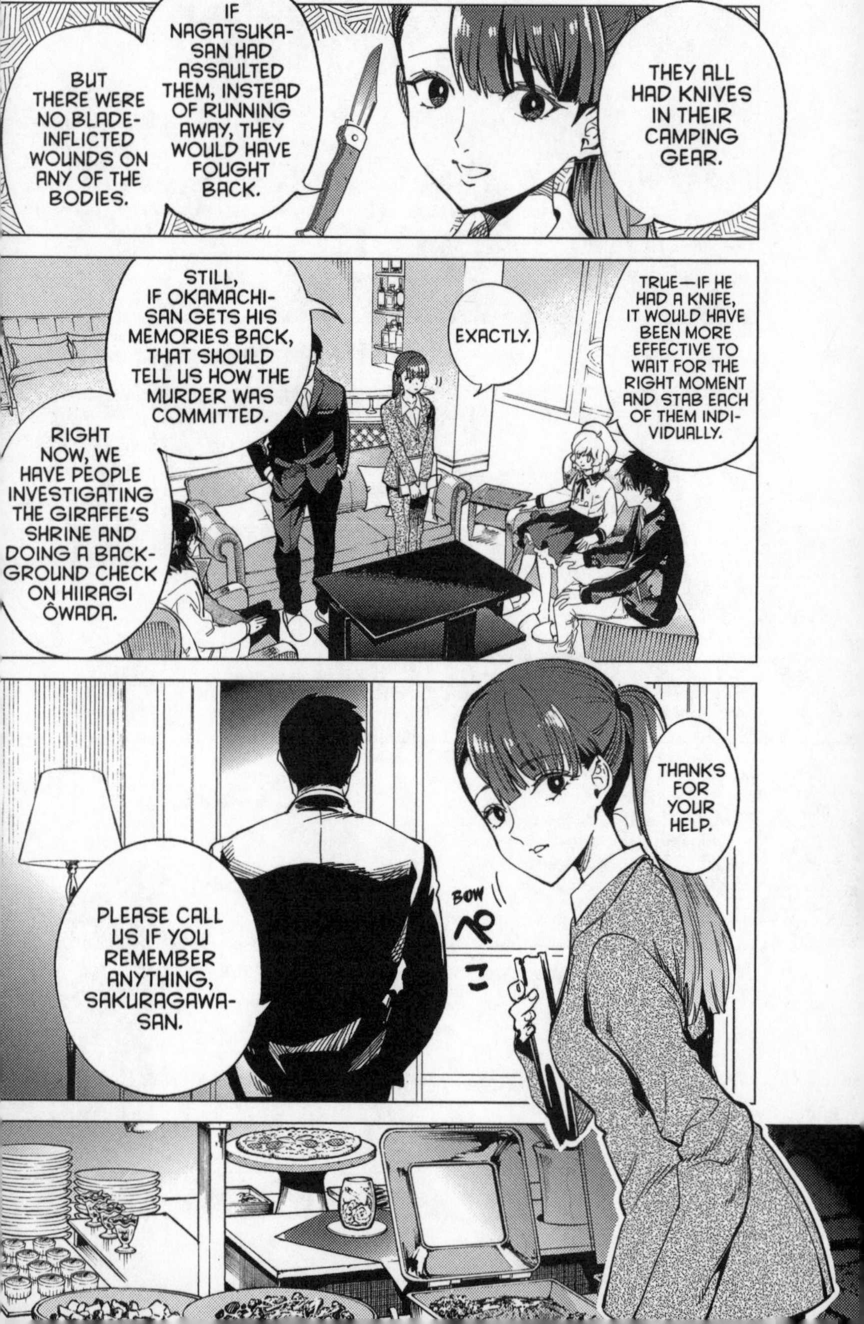
THEY ALL HAD KNIVES IN THEIR CAMPING GEAR.
IF NAGATSUKA-SAN HAD ASSAULTED THEM, INSTEAD OF RUNNING AWAY, THEY WOULD HAVE FOUGHT BACK.
BUT THERE WERE NO BLADE-INFLICTED WOUNDS ON ANY OF THE BODIES.
TRUE—IF HE HAD A KNIFE, IT WOULD HAVE BEEN MORE EFFECTIVE TO WAIT FOR THE RIGHT MOMENT AND STAB EACH OF THEM INDIVIDUALLY.
EXACTLY.
STILL, IF OKAMACHI-SAN GETS HIS MEMORIES BACK, THAT SHOULD TELL US HOW THE MURDER WAS COMMITTED.
RIGHT NOW, WE HAVE PEOPLE INVESTIGATING THE GIRAFFE'S SHRINE AND DOING A BACKGROUND CHECK ON HIIRAGI ÔWADA.
THANKS FOR YOUR HELP.
BOW
ぺこ
PLEASE CALL US IF YOU REMEMBER ANYTHING, SAKURAGAWA-SAN.

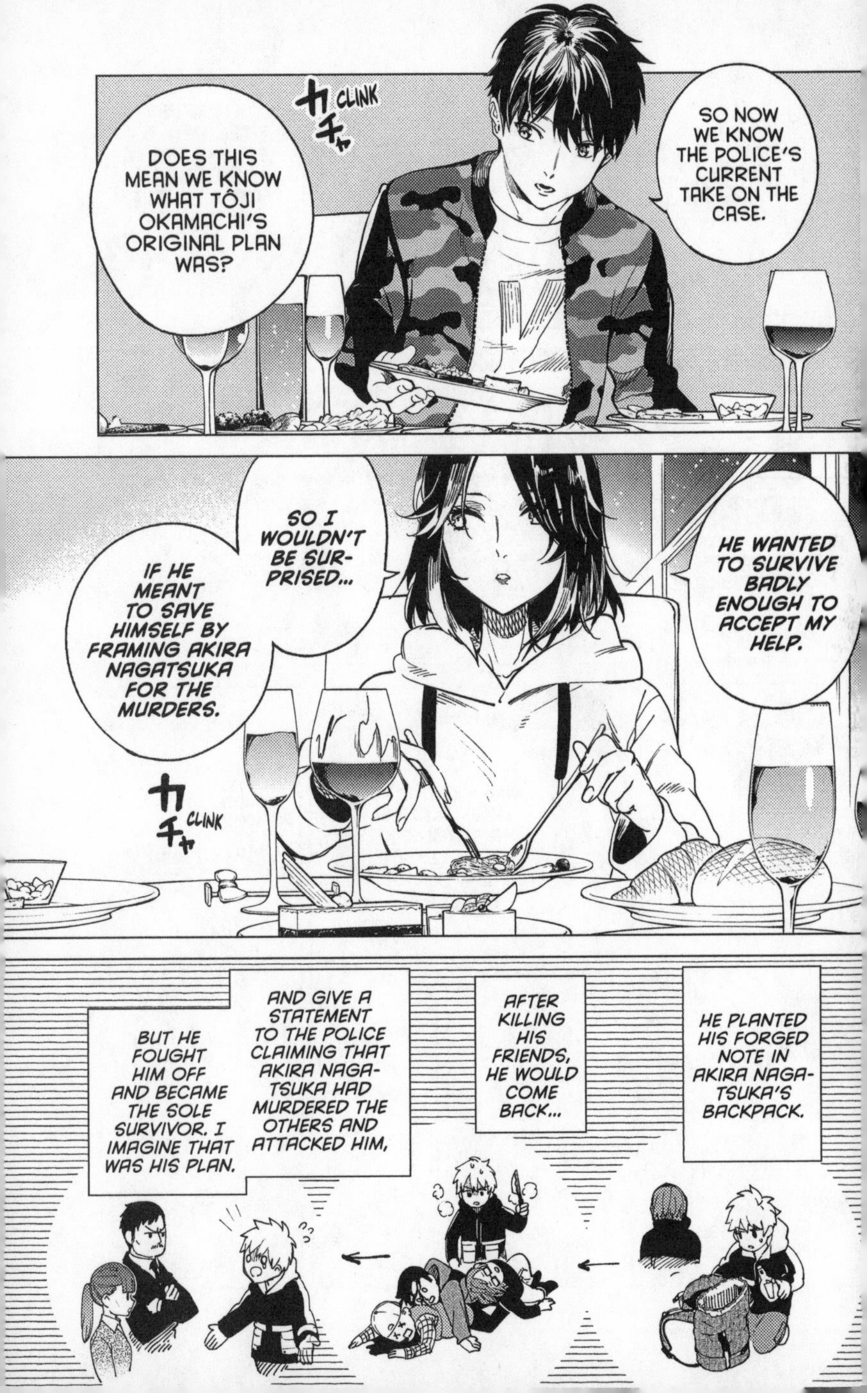
CLINK
SO NOW WE KNOW THE POLICE'S CURRENT TAKE ON THE CASE.
DOES THIS MEAN WE KNOW WHAT TÔJI OKAMACHI'S ORIGINAL PLAN WAS?
HE WANTED TO SURVIVE BADLY ENOUGH TO ACCEPT MY HELP.
SO I WOULDN'T BE SUR-PRISED...
IF HE MEANT TO SAVE HIMSELF BY FRAMING AKIRA NAGATSUKA FOR THE MURDERS.
CLINK
HE PLANTED HIS FORGED NOTE IN AKIRA NAGA-TSUKA'S BACKPACK.
AFTER KILLING HIS FRIENDS, HE WOULD COME BACK...
AND GIVE A STATEMENT TO THE POLICE CLAIMING THAT AKIRA NAGA-TSUKA HAD MURDERED THE OTHERS AND ATTACKED HIM,
BUT HE FOUGHT HIM OFF AND BECAME THE SOLE SURVIVOR. I IMAGINE THAT WAS HIS PLAN.

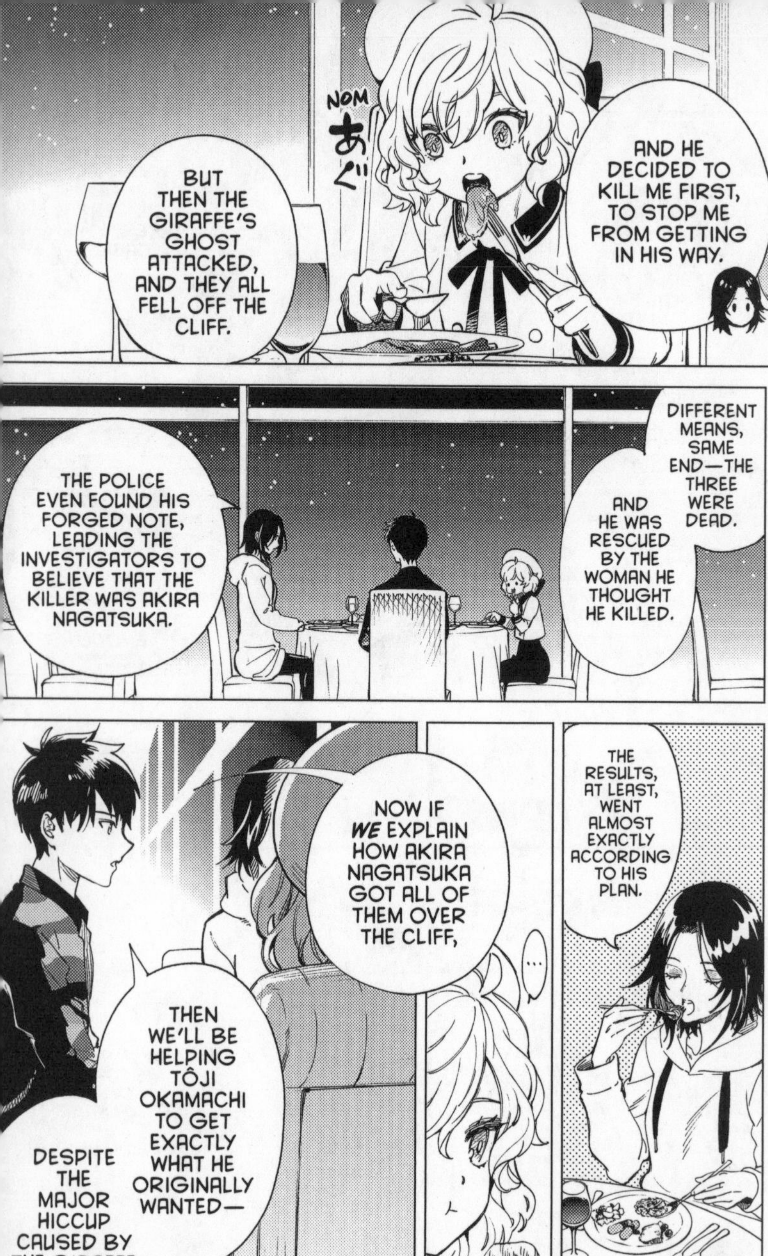

AND HE DECIDED TO KILL ME FIRST, TO STOP ME FROM GETTING IN HIS WAY.
NOM
あぐ
BUT THEN THE GIRAFFE'S GHOST ATTACKED, AND THEY ALL FELL OFF THE CLIFF.
DIFFERENT MEANS, SAME END—THE THREE WERE DEAD.
AND HE WAS RESCUED BY THE WOMAN HE THOUGHT HE KILLED.
THE POLICE EVEN FOUND HIS FORGED NOTE, LEADING THE INVESTIGATORS TO BELIEVE THAT THE KILLER WAS AKIRA NAGATSUKA.
THE RESULTS, AT LEAST, WENT ALMOST EXACTLY ACCORDING TO HIS PLAN.
...
NOW IF *WE* EXPLAIN HOW AKIRA NAGATSUKA GOT ALL OF THEM OVER THE CLIFF,
THEN WE'LL BE HELPING TÔJI OKAMACHI TO GET EXACTLY WHAT HE ORIGINALLY WANTED—
DESPITE THE MAJOR HICCUP CAUSED BY THE GIRAFFE GHOST...

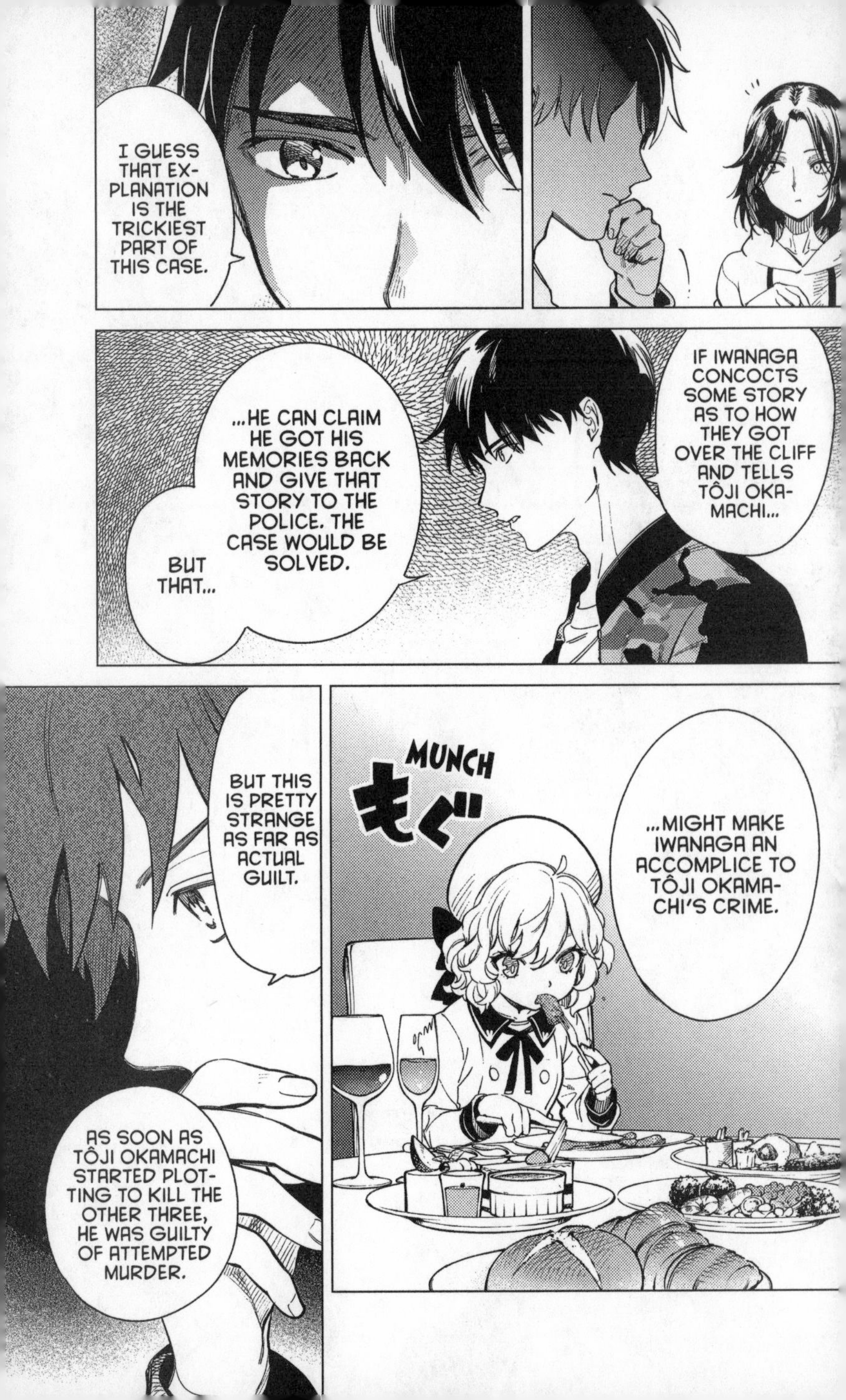
I GUESS THAT EX-PLANATION IS THE TRICKIEST PART OF THIS CASE.
IF IWANAGA CONCOCTS SOME STORY AS TO HOW THEY GOT OVER THE CLIFF AND TELLS TÔJI OKA-MACHI...
...HE CAN CLAIM HE GOT HIS MEMORIES BACK AND GIVE THAT STORY TO THE POLICE. THE CASE WOULD BE SOLVED.
BUT THAT...
...MIGHT MAKE IWANAGA AN ACCOMPLICE TO TÔJI OKAMA-CHI'S CRIME.
MUNCH
もぐ
BUT THIS IS PRETTY STRANGE AS FAR AS ACTUAL GUILT.
AS SOON AS TÔJI OKAMACHI STARTED PLOT-TING TO KILL THE OTHER THREE, HE WAS GUILTY OF ATTEMPTED MURDER.

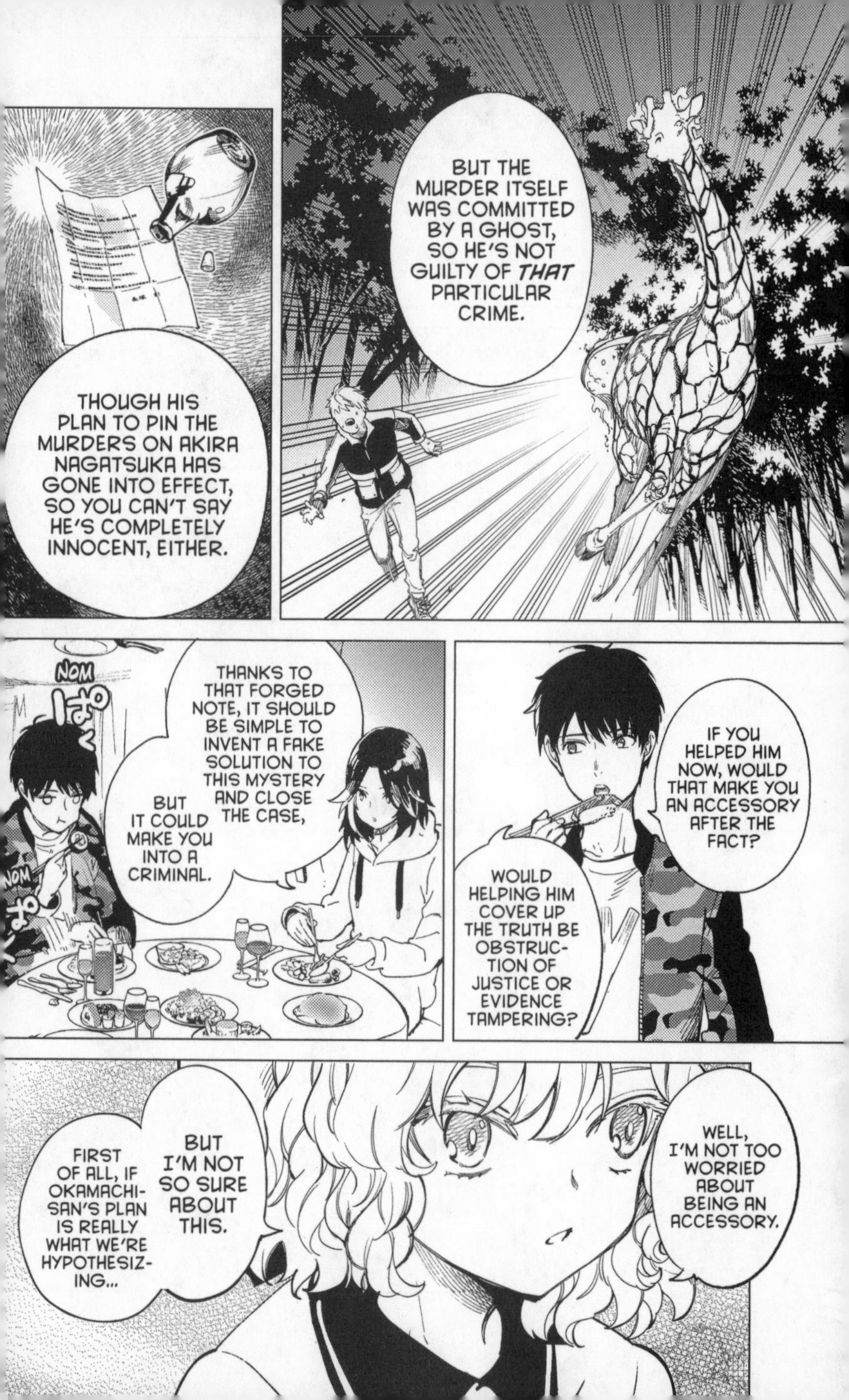
BUT THE MURDER ITSELF WAS COMMITTED BY A GHOST, SO HE'S NOT GUILTY OF *THAT* PARTICULAR CRIME.
THOUGH HIS PLAN TO PIN THE MURDERS ON AKIRA NAGATSUKA HAS GONE INTO EFFECT, SO YOU CAN'T SAY HE'S COMPLETELY INNOCENT, EITHER.
IF YOU HELPED HIM NOW, WOULD THAT MAKE YOU AN ACCESSORY AFTER THE FACT?
WOULD HELPING HIM COVER UP THE TRUTH BE OBSTRUCTION OF JUSTICE OR EVIDENCE TAMPERING?
THANKS TO THAT FORGED NOTE, IT SHOULD BE SIMPLE TO INVENT A FAKE SOLUTION TO THIS MYSTERY AND CLOSE THE CASE,
BUT IT COULD MAKE YOU INTO A CRIMINAL.
NOM ぱく
NOM ぱく
WELL, I'M NOT TOO WORRIED ABOUT BEING AN ACCESSORY.
BUT I'M NOT SO SURE ABOUT THIS.
FIRST OF ALL, IF OKAMACHI-SAN'S PLAN IS REALLY WHAT WE'RE HYPOTHESIZ-ING...

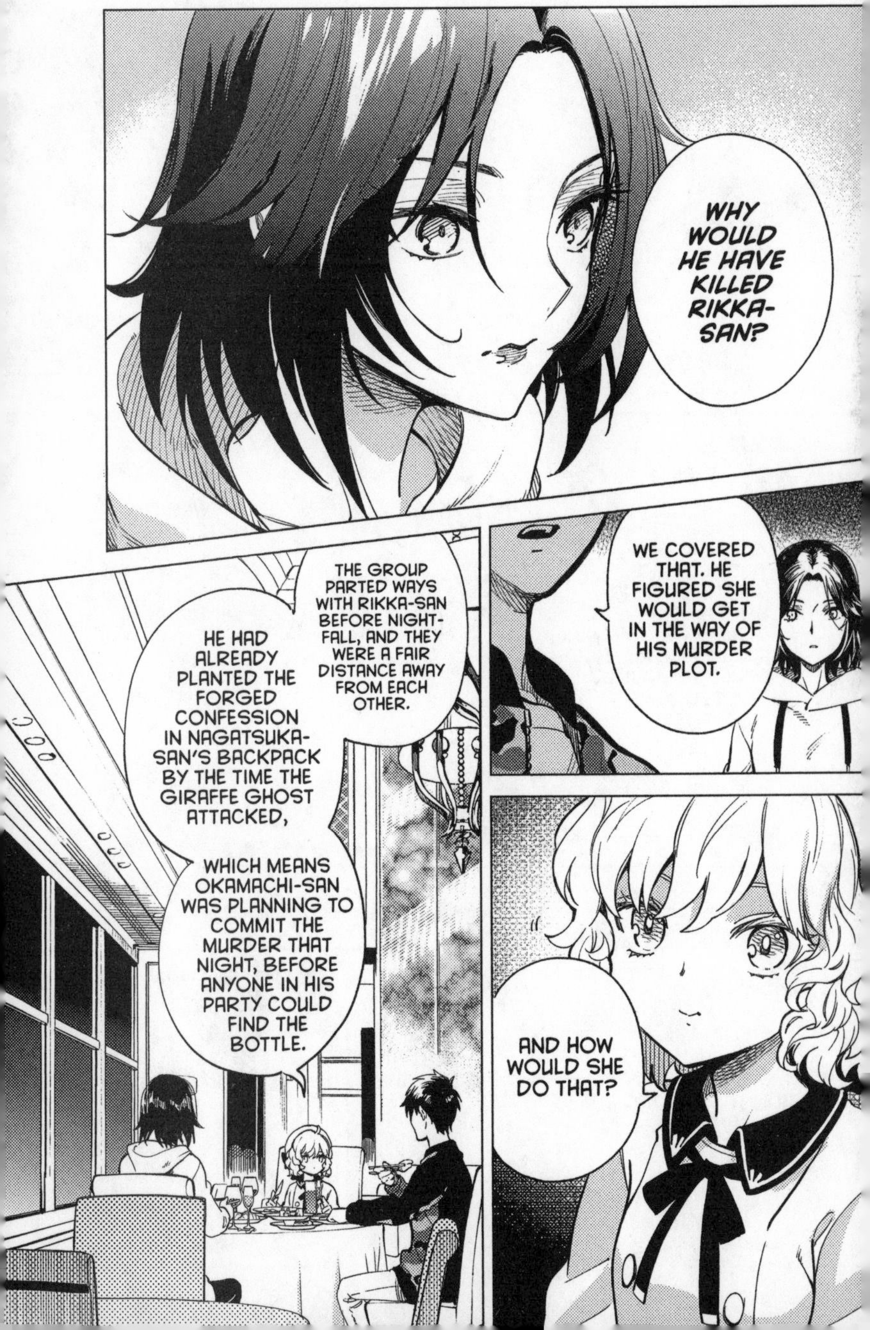
WHY WOULD HE HAVE KILLED RIKKA-SAN?
WE COVERED THAT. HE FIGURED SHE WOULD GET IN THE WAY OF HIS MURDER PLOT.
AND HOW WOULD SHE DO THAT?
THE GROUP PARTED WAYS WITH RIKKA-SAN BEFORE NIGHT-FALL, AND THEY WERE A FAIR DISTANCE AWAY FROM EACH OTHER.
HE HAD ALREADY PLANTED THE FORGED CONFESSION IN NAGATSUKA-SAN'S BACKPACK BY THE TIME THE GIRAFFE GHOST ATTACKED,
WHICH MEANS OKAMACHI-SAN WAS PLANNING TO COMMIT THE MURDER THAT NIGHT, BEFORE ANYONE IN HIS PARTY COULD FIND THE BOTTLE.

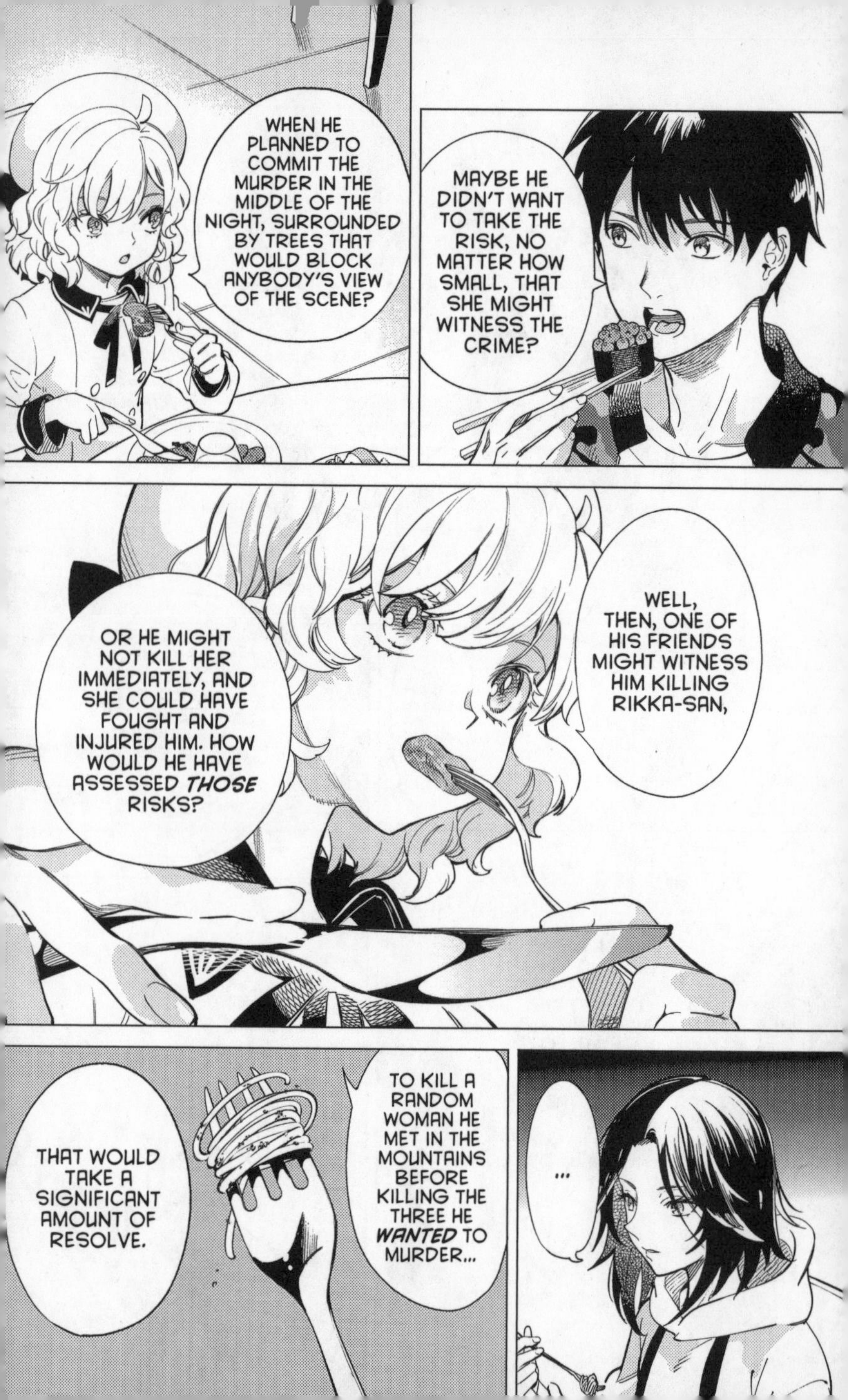
MAYBE HE DIDN'T WANT TO TAKE THE RISK, NO MATTER HOW SMALL, THAT SHE MIGHT WITNESS THE CRIME?
WHEN HE PLANNED TO COMMIT THE MURDER IN THE MIDDLE OF THE NIGHT, SURROUNDED BY TREES THAT WOULD BLOCK ANYBODY'S VIEW OF THE SCENE?
WELL, THEN, ONE OF HIS FRIENDS MIGHT WITNESS HIM KILLING RIKKA-SAN,
OR HE MIGHT NOT KILL HER IMMEDIATELY, AND SHE COULD HAVE FOUGHT AND INJURED HIM. HOW WOULD HE HAVE ASSESSED *THOSE* RISKS?
...
TO KILL A RANDOM WOMAN HE MET IN THE MOUNTAINS BEFORE KILLING THE THREE HE *WANTED* TO MURDER...
THAT WOULD TAKE A SIGNIFICANT AMOUNT OF RESOLVE.

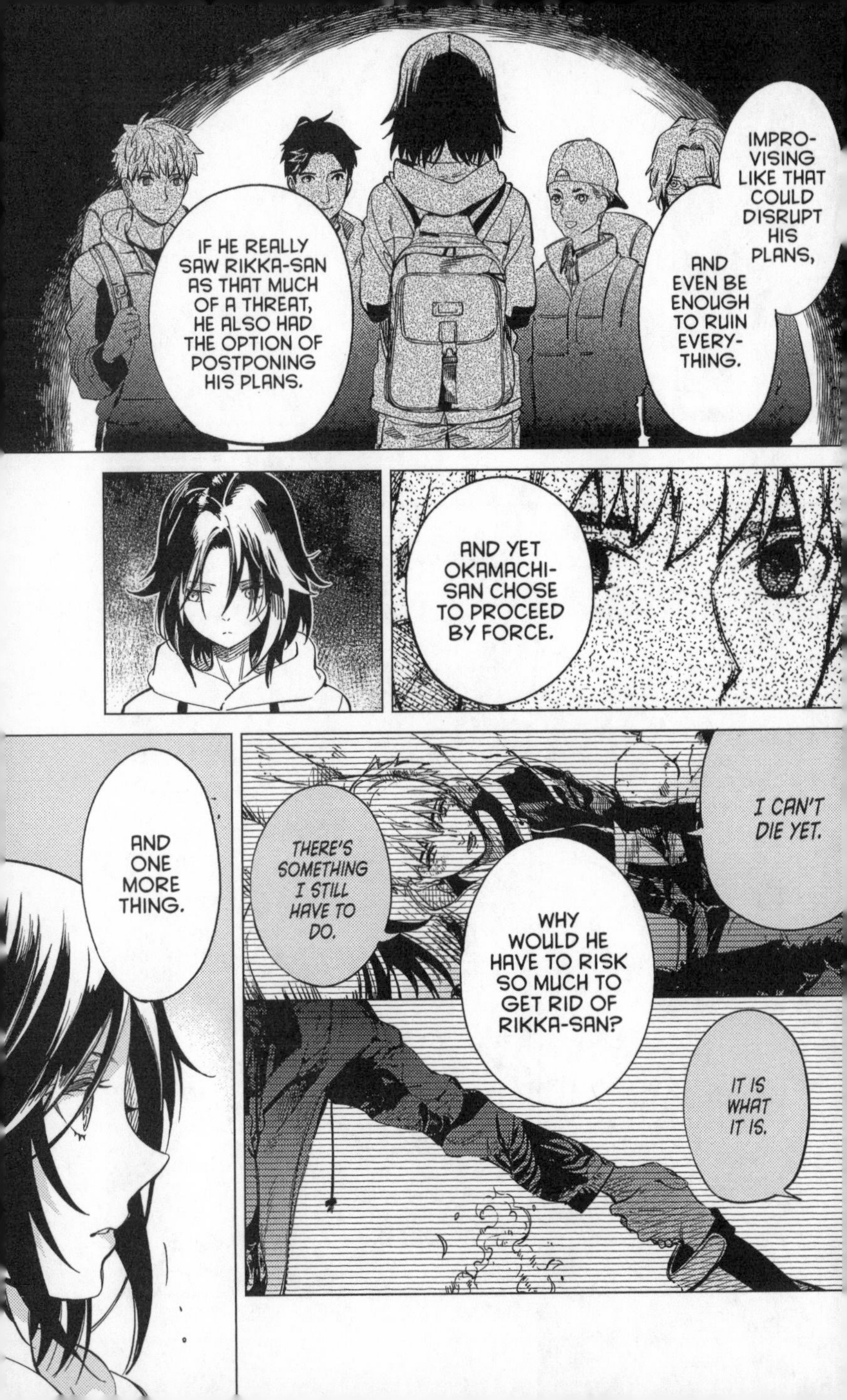
IMPRO-VISING LIKE THAT COULD DISRUPT HIS PLANS,
AND EVEN BE ENOUGH TO RUIN EVERY-THING.
IF HE REALLY SAW RIKKA-SAN AS THAT MUCH OF A THREAT, HE ALSO HAD THE OPTION OF POSTPONING HIS PLANS.
AND YET OKAMACHI-SAN CHOSE TO PROCEED BY FORCE.
I CAN'T DIE YET.
THERE'S SOMETHING I STILL HAVE TO DO.
WHY WOULD HE HAVE TO RISK SO MUCH TO GET RID OF RIKKA-SAN?
IT IS WHAT IT IS.
AND ONE MORE THING.

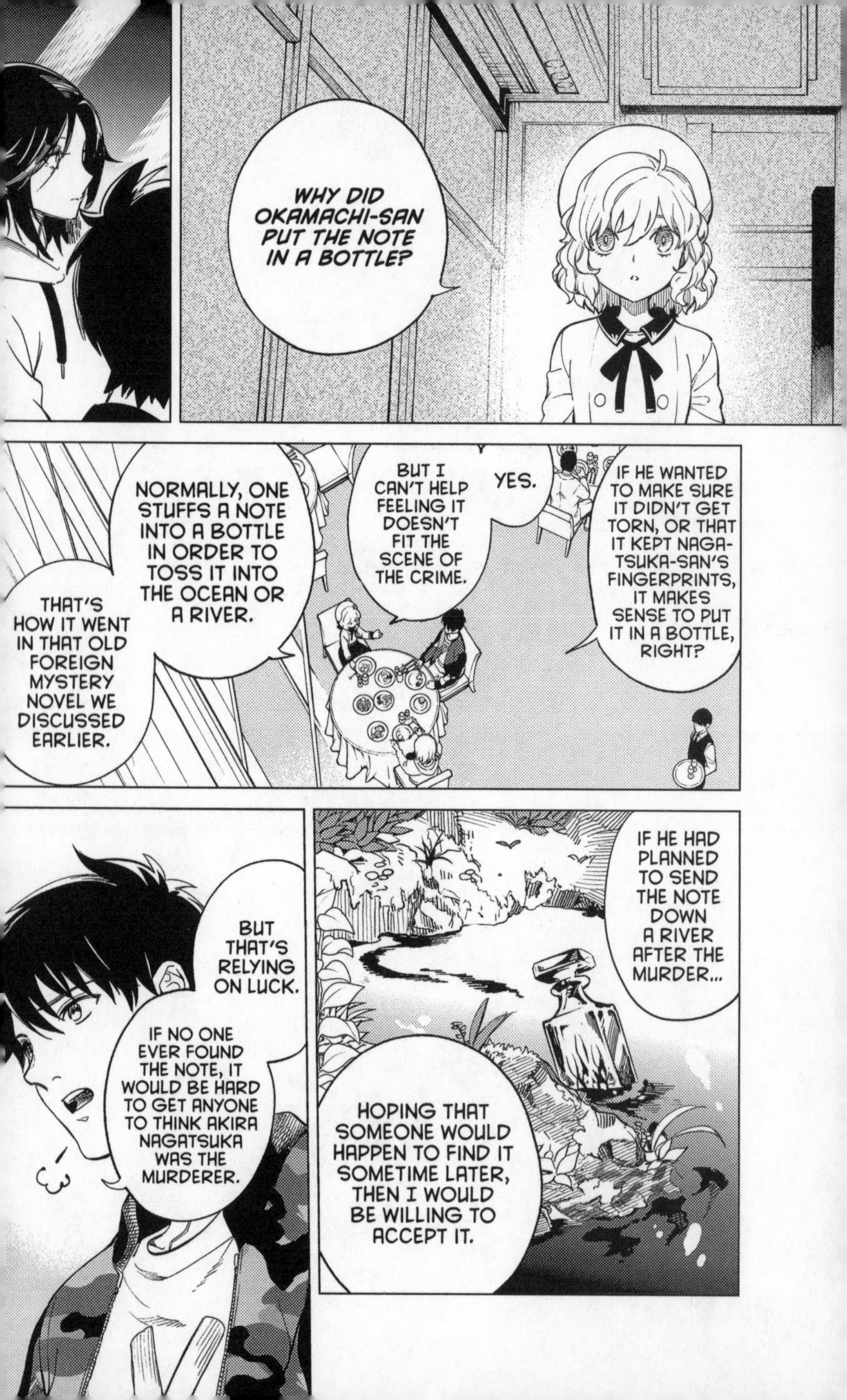
WHY DID OKAMACHI-SAN PUT THE NOTE IN A BOTTLE?
IF HE WANTED TO MAKE SURE IT DIDN'T GET TORN, OR THAT IT KEPT NAGA-TSUKA-SAN'S FINGERPRINTS, IT MAKES SENSE TO PUT IT IN A BOTTLE, RIGHT?
YES.
BUT I CAN'T HELP FEELING IT DOESN'T FIT THE SCENE OF THE CRIME.
NORMALLY, ONE STUFFS A NOTE INTO A BOTTLE IN ORDER TO TOSS IT INTO THE OCEAN OR A RIVER.
THAT'S HOW IT WENT IN THAT OLD FOREIGN MYSTERY NOVEL WE DISCUSSED EARLIER.
IF HE HAD PLANNED TO SEND THE NOTE DOWN A RIVER AFTER THE MURDER...
HOPING THAT SOMEONE WOULD HAPPEN TO FIND IT SOMETIME LATER, THEN I WOULD BE WILLING TO ACCEPT IT.
BUT THAT'S RELYING ON LUCK.
IF NO ONE EVER FOUND THE NOTE, IT WOULD BE HARD TO GET ANYONE TO THINK AKIRA NAGATSUKA WAS THE MURDERER.

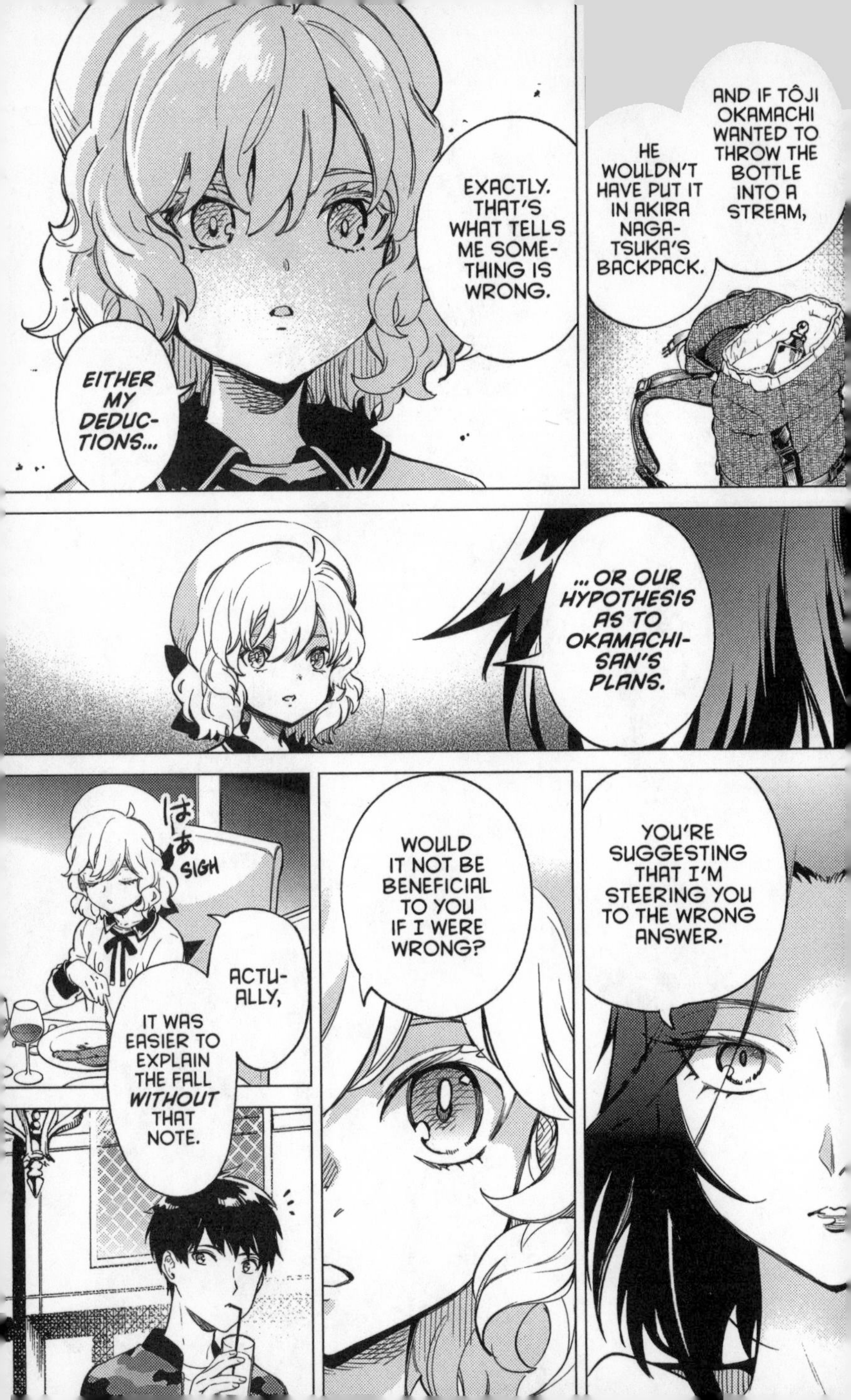
AND IF TÔJI OKAMACHI WANTED TO THROW THE BOTTLE INTO A STREAM,
HE WOULDN'T HAVE PUT IT IN AKIRA NAGA-TSUKA'S BACKPACK.
EXACTLY. THAT'S WHAT TELLS ME SOME-THING IS WRONG.
*EITHER MY DEDUC-TIONS...*
*...OR OUR HYPOTHESIS AS TO OKAMACHI-SAN'S PLANS.*
YOU'RE SUGGESTING THAT I'M STEERING YOU TO THE WRONG ANSWER.
WOULD IT NOT BE BENEFICIAL TO YOU IF I WERE WRONG?
はあ SIGH
ACTU-ALLY,
IT WAS EASIER TO EXPLAIN THE FALL *WITHOUT* THAT NOTE.

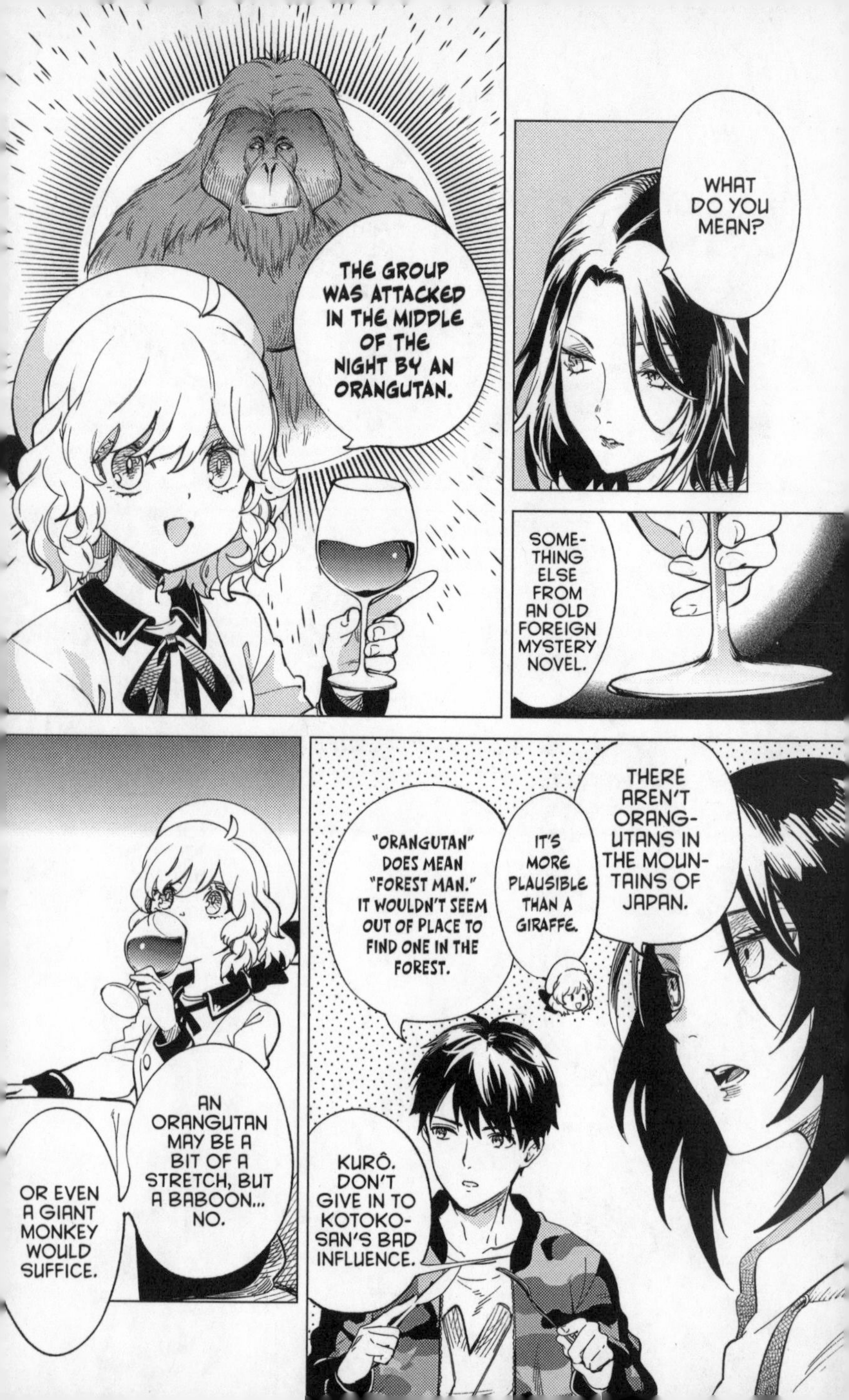
WHAT DO YOU MEAN?
SOME-THING ELSE FROM AN OLD FOREIGN MYSTERY NOVEL.
THE GROUP WAS ATTACKED IN THE MIDDLE OF THE NIGHT BY AN ORANGUTAN.
THERE AREN'T ORANG-UTANS IN THE MOUN-TAINS OF JAPAN.
IT'S MORE PLAUSIBLE THAN A GIRAFFE.
"ORANGUTAN" DOES MEAN "FOREST MAN." IT WOULDN'T SEEM OUT OF PLACE TO FIND ONE IN THE FOREST.
KURÔ. DON'T GIVE IN TO KOTOKO-SAN'S BAD INFLUENCE.
AN ORANGUTAN MAY BE A BIT OF A STRETCH, BUT A BABOON... NO.
OR EVEN A GIANT MONKEY WOULD SUFFICE.

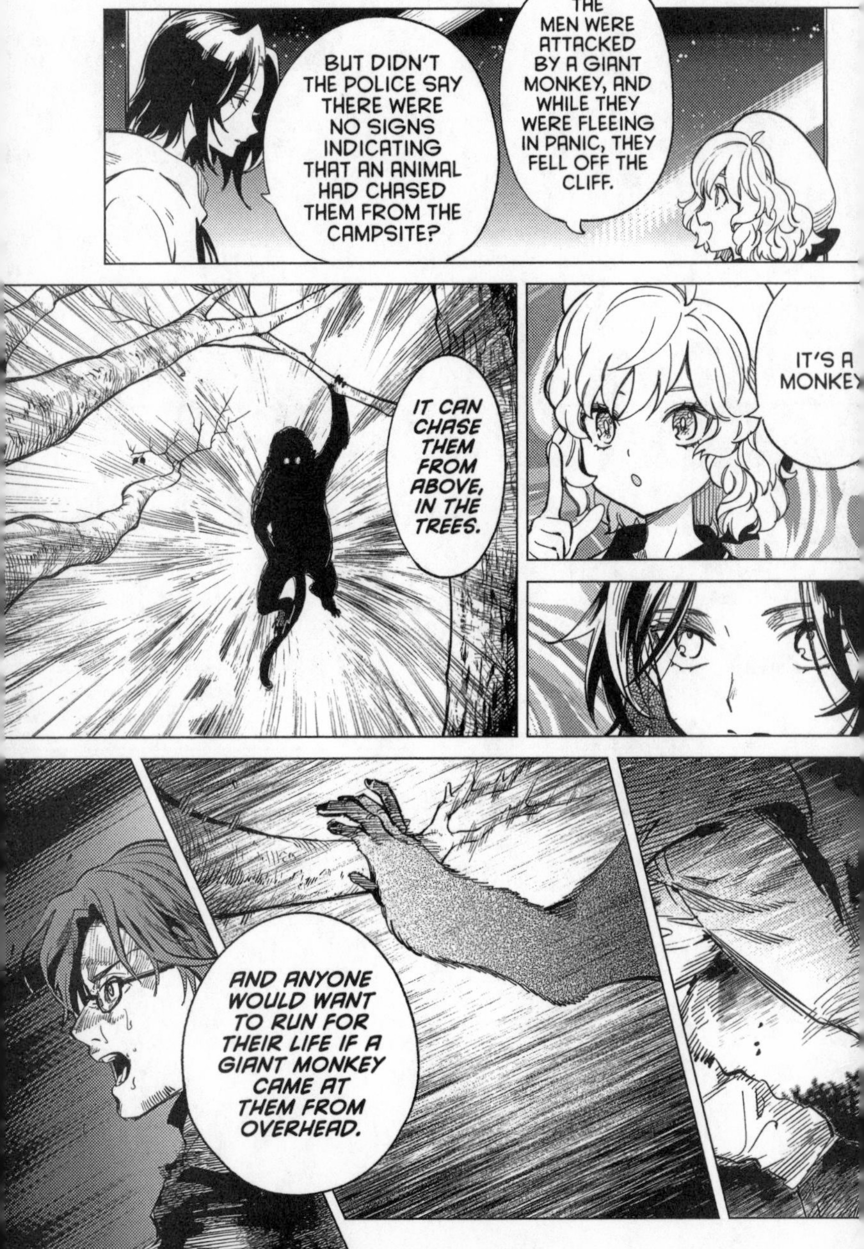
THE MEN WERE ATTACKED BY A GIANT MONKEY, AND WHILE THEY WERE FLEEING IN PANIC, THEY FELL OFF THE CLIFF.
BUT DIDN'T THE POLICE SAY THERE WERE NO SIGNS INDICATING THAT AN ANIMAL HAD CHASED THEM FROM THE CAMPSITE?
IT'S A MONKEY
IT CAN CHASE THEM FROM ABOVE, IN THE TREES.
AND ANYONE WOULD WANT TO RUN FOR THEIR LIFE IF A GIANT MONKEY CAME AT THEM FROM OVERHEAD.

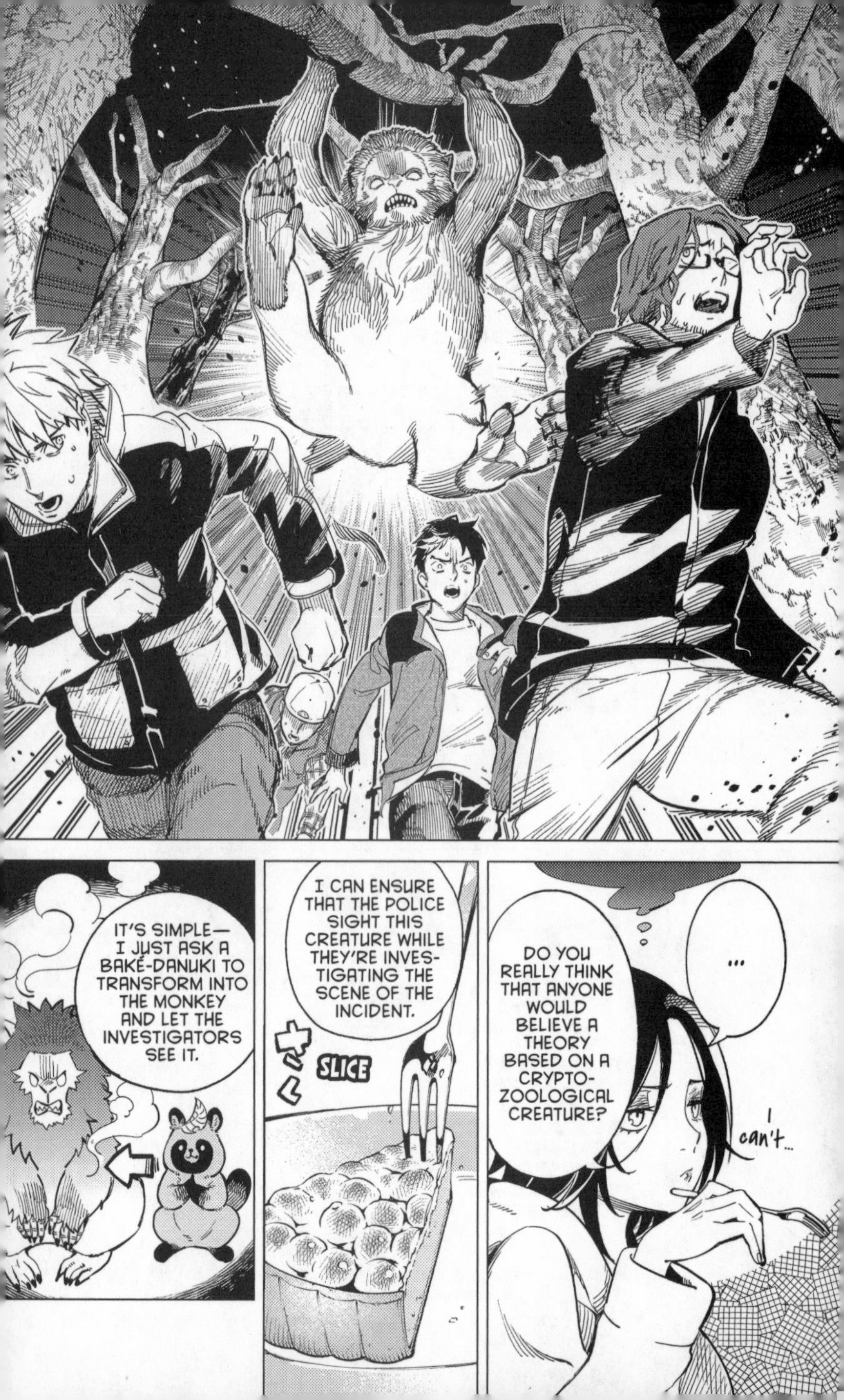
...
DO YOU REALLY THINK THAT ANYONE WOULD BELIEVE A THEORY BASED ON A CRYPTO-ZOOLOGICAL CREATURE?
I can't...
I CAN ENSURE THAT THE POLICE SIGHT THIS CREATURE WHILE THEY'RE INVES-TIGATING THE SCENE OF THE INCIDENT.
SLICE
IT'S SIMPLE— I JUST ASK A BAKÉ-DANUKI TO TRANSFORM INTO THE MONKEY AND LET THE INVESTIGATORS SEE IT.

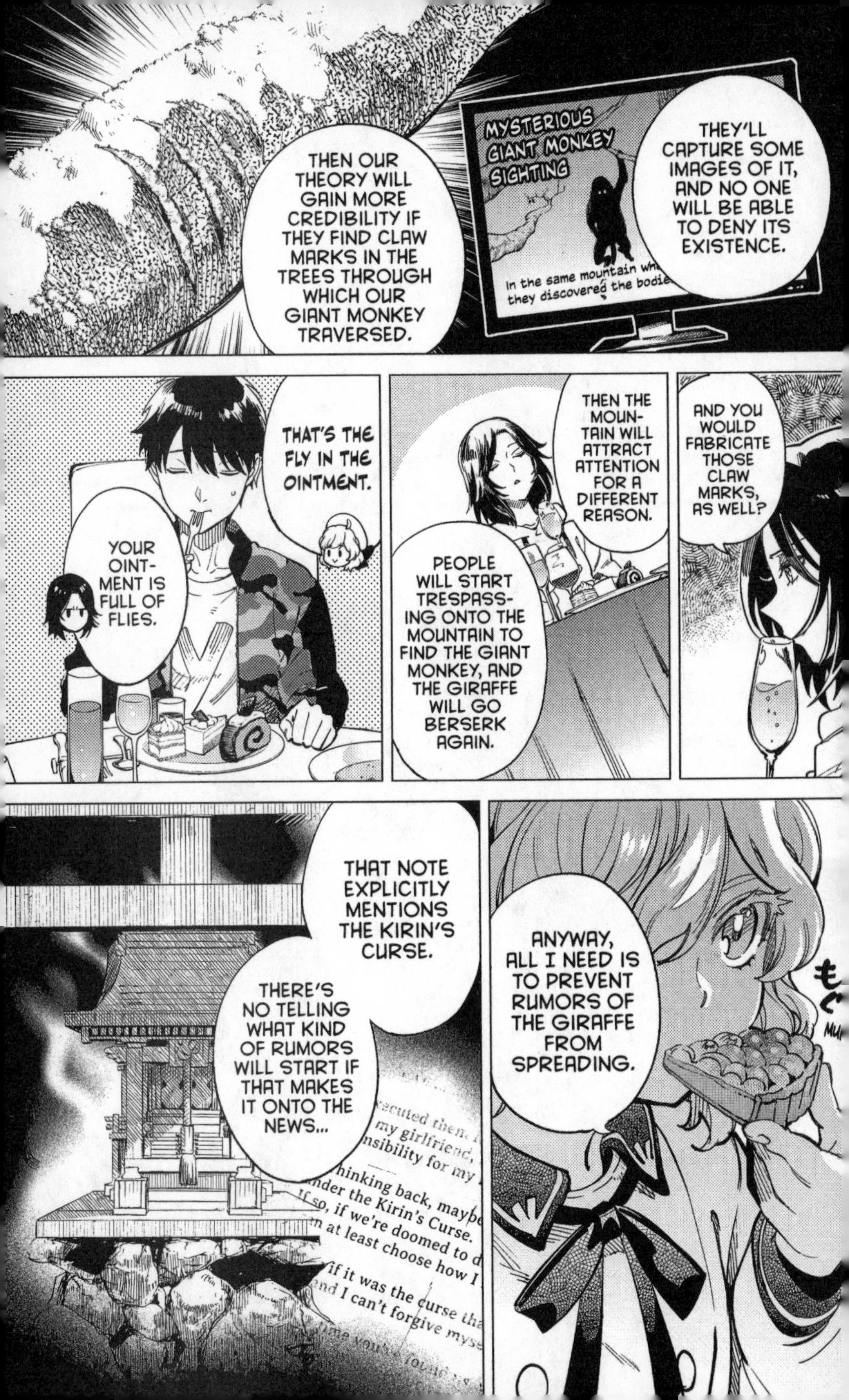
THEY'LL CAPTURE SOME IMAGES OF IT, AND NO ONE WILL BE ABLE TO DENY ITS EXISTENCE.
MYSTERIOUS GIANT MONKEY SIGHTING
In the same mountain wh
they discovered the bodie
THEN OUR THEORY WILL GAIN MORE CREDIBILITY IF THEY FIND CLAW MARKS IN THE TREES THROUGH WHICH OUR GIANT MONKEY TRAVERSED.
AND YOU WOULD FABRICATE THOSE CLAW MARKS, AS WELL?
THEN THE MOUNTAIN WILL ATTRACT ATTENTION FOR A DIFFERENT REASON.
PEOPLE WILL START TRESPASSING ONTO THE MOUNTAIN TO FIND THE GIANT MONKEY, AND THE GIRAFFE WILL GO BERSERK AGAIN.
THAT'S THE FLY IN THE OINTMENT.
YOUR OINTMENT IS FULL OF FLIES.
ANYWAY, ALL I NEED IS TO PREVENT RUMORS OF THE GIRAFFE FROM SPREADING.
もぐ
THAT NOTE EXPLICITLY MENTIONS THE KIRIN'S CURSE.
THERE'S NO TELLING WHAT KIND OF RUMORS WILL START IF THAT MAKES IT ONTO THE NEWS...
my girlfriend,
nder the Kirin's Curse.
If so, if we're doomed to
n at least choose how I
if it was the curse th
and I can't forgive myse

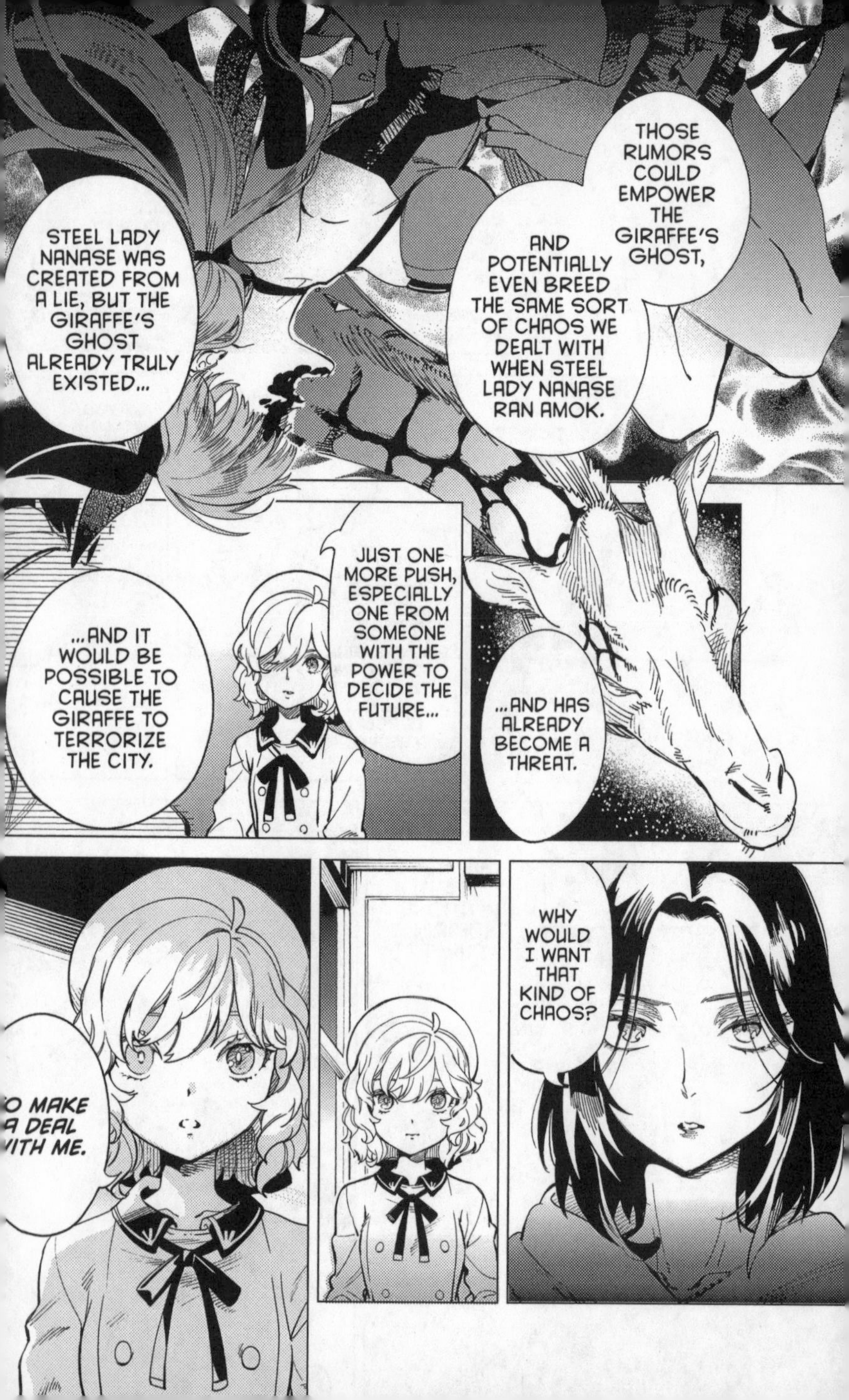
THOSE RUMORS COULD EMPOWER THE GIRAFFE'S GHOST,
AND POTENTIALLY EVEN BREED THE SAME SORT OF CHAOS WE DEALT WITH WHEN STEEL LADY NANASE RAN AMOK.
STEEL LADY NANASE WAS CREATED FROM A LIE, BUT THE GIRAFFE'S GHOST ALREADY TRULY EXISTED...
...AND HAS ALREADY BECOME A THREAT.
JUST ONE MORE PUSH, ESPECIALLY ONE FROM SOMEONE WITH THE POWER TO DECIDE THE FUTURE...
...AND IT WOULD BE POSSIBLE TO CAUSE THE GIRAFFE TO TERRORIZE THE CITY.
WHY WOULD I WANT THAT KIND OF CHAOS?
O MAKE A DEAL WITH ME.

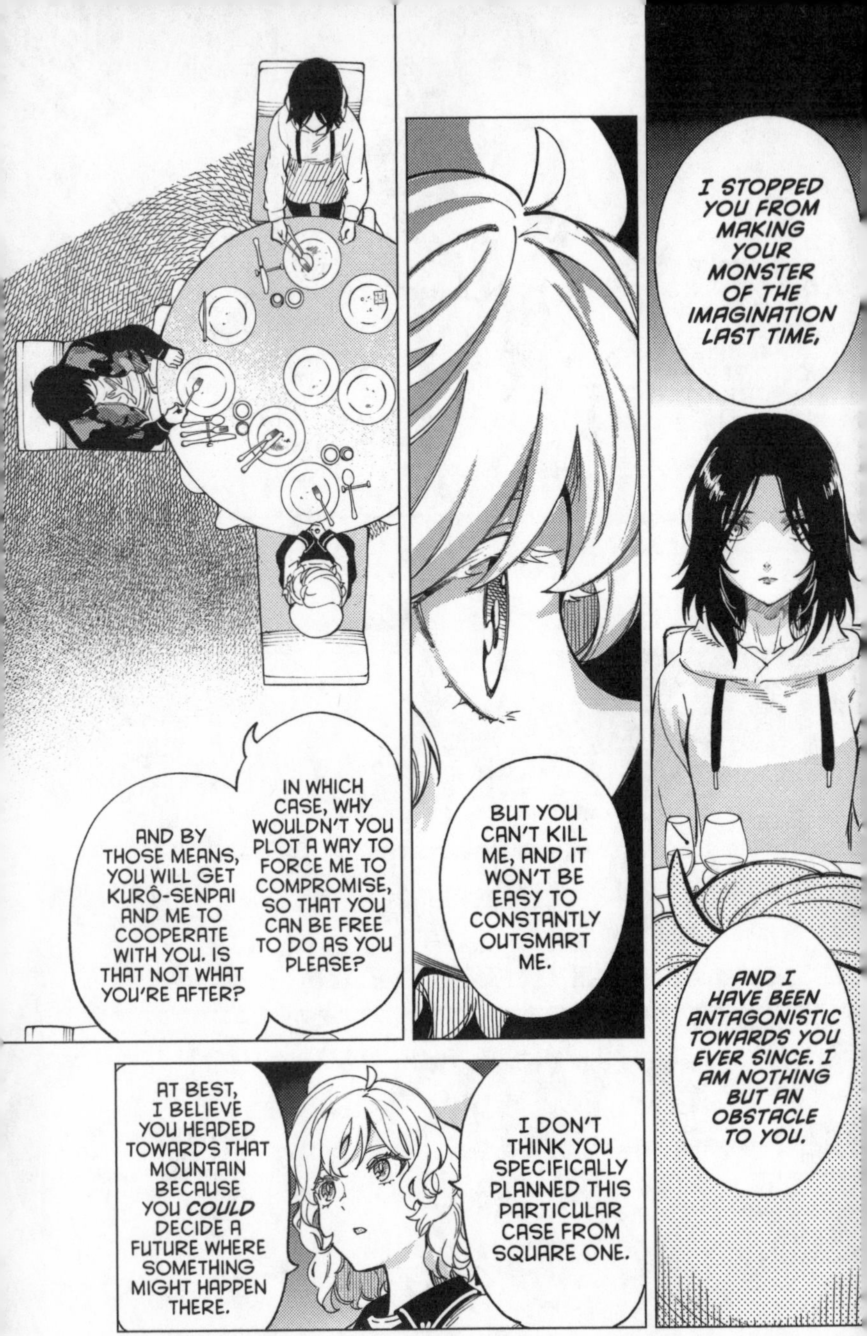
I STOPPED YOU FROM MAKING YOUR MONSTER OF THE IMAGINATION LAST TIME,
AND I HAVE BEEN ANTAGONISTIC TOWARDS YOU EVER SINCE. I AM NOTHING BUT AN OBSTACLE TO YOU.
BUT YOU CAN'T KILL ME, AND IT WON'T BE EASY TO CONSTANTLY OUTSMART ME.
IN WHICH CASE, WHY WOULDN'T YOU PLOT A WAY TO FORCE ME TO COMPROMISE, SO THAT YOU CAN BE FREE TO DO AS YOU PLEASE?
AND BY THOSE MEANS, YOU WILL GET KURÔ-SENPAI AND ME TO COOPERATE WITH YOU. IS THAT NOT WHAT YOU'RE AFTER?
I DON'T THINK YOU SPECIFICALLY PLANNED THIS PARTICULAR CASE FROM SQUARE ONE.
AT BEST, I BELIEVE YOU HEADED TOWARDS THAT MOUNTAIN BECAUSE YOU *COULD* DECIDE A FUTURE WHERE SOMETHING MIGHT HAPPEN THERE.

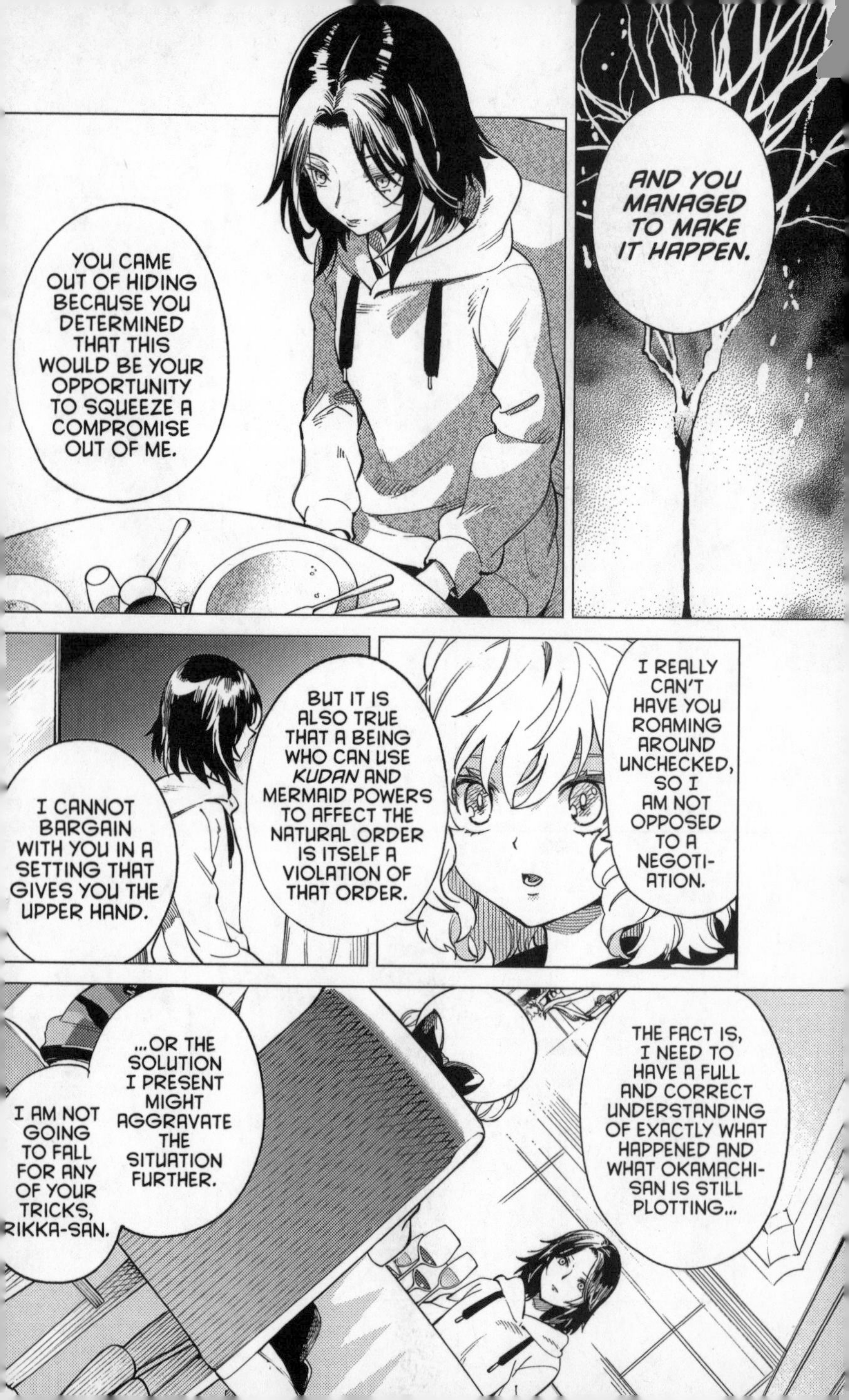
AND YOU MANAGED TO MAKE IT HAPPEN.
YOU CAME OUT OF HIDING BECAUSE YOU DETERMINED THAT THIS WOULD BE YOUR OPPORTUNITY TO SQUEEZE A COMPROMISE OUT OF ME.
I REALLY CAN'T HAVE YOU ROAMING AROUND UNCHECKED, SO I AM NOT OPPOSED TO A NEGOTI-ATION.
BUT IT IS ALSO TRUE THAT A BEING WHO CAN USE *KUDAN* AND MERMAID POWERS TO AFFECT THE NATURAL ORDER IS ITSELF A VIOLATION OF THAT ORDER.
I CANNOT BARGAIN WITH YOU IN A SETTING THAT GIVES YOU THE UPPER HAND.
THE FACT IS, I NEED TO HAVE A FULL AND CORRECT UNDERSTANDING OF EXACTLY WHAT HAPPENED AND WHAT OKAMACHI-SAN IS STILL PLOTTING...
...OR THE SOLUTION I PRESENT MIGHT AGGRAVATE THE SITUATION FURTHER.
I AM NOT GOING TO FALL FOR ANY OF YOUR TRICKS, RIKKA-SAN.

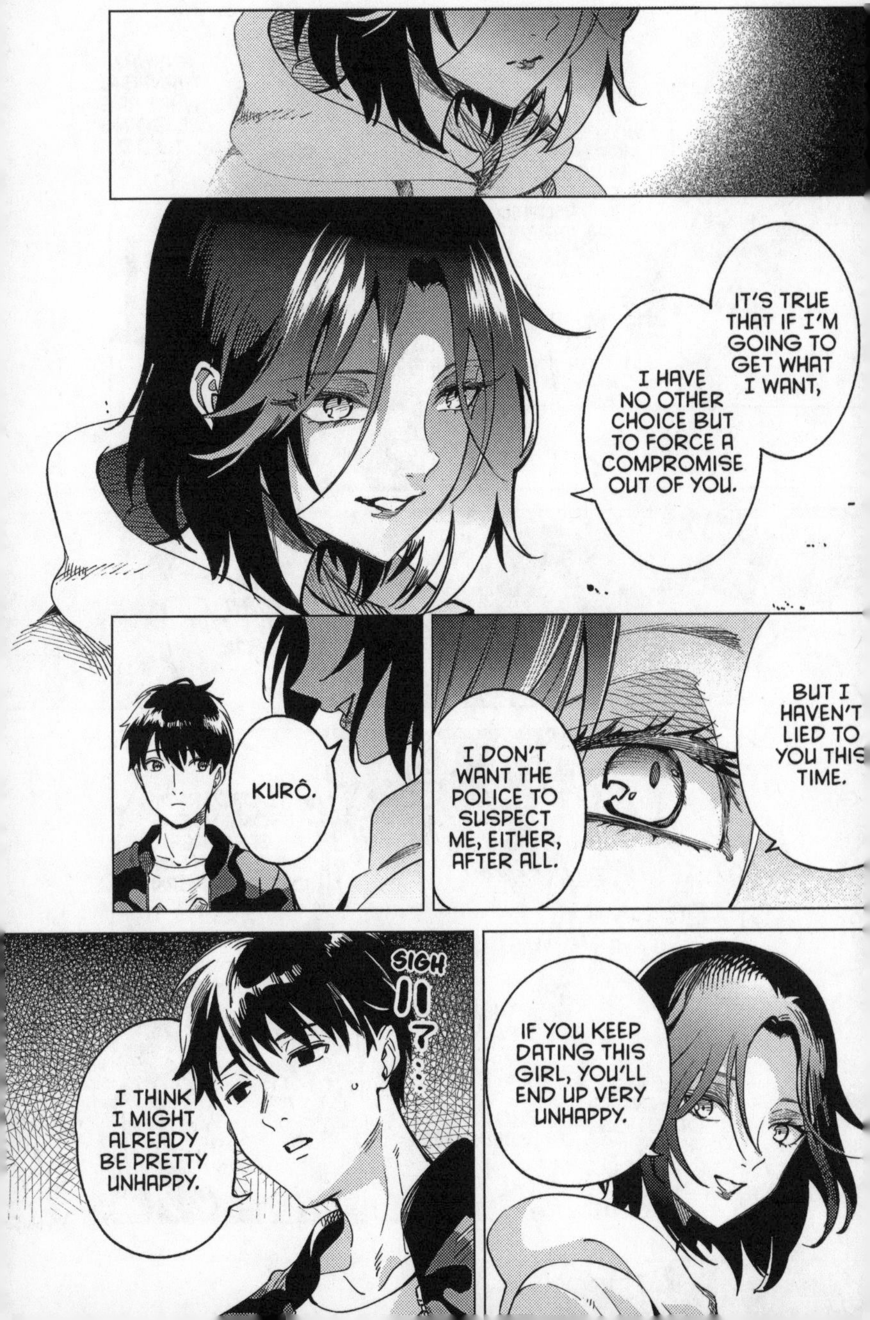
IT'S TRUE THAT IF I'M GOING TO GET WHAT I WANT,
I HAVE NO OTHER CHOICE BUT TO FORCE A COMPROMISE OUT OF YOU.
BUT I HAVEN'T LIED TO YOU THIS TIME.
I DON'T WANT THE POLICE TO SUSPECT ME, EITHER, AFTER ALL.
KURÔ.
IF YOU KEEP DATING THIS GIRL, YOU'LL END UP VERY UNHAPPY.
SIGH
I THINK I MIGHT ALREADY BE PRETTY UNHAPPY.

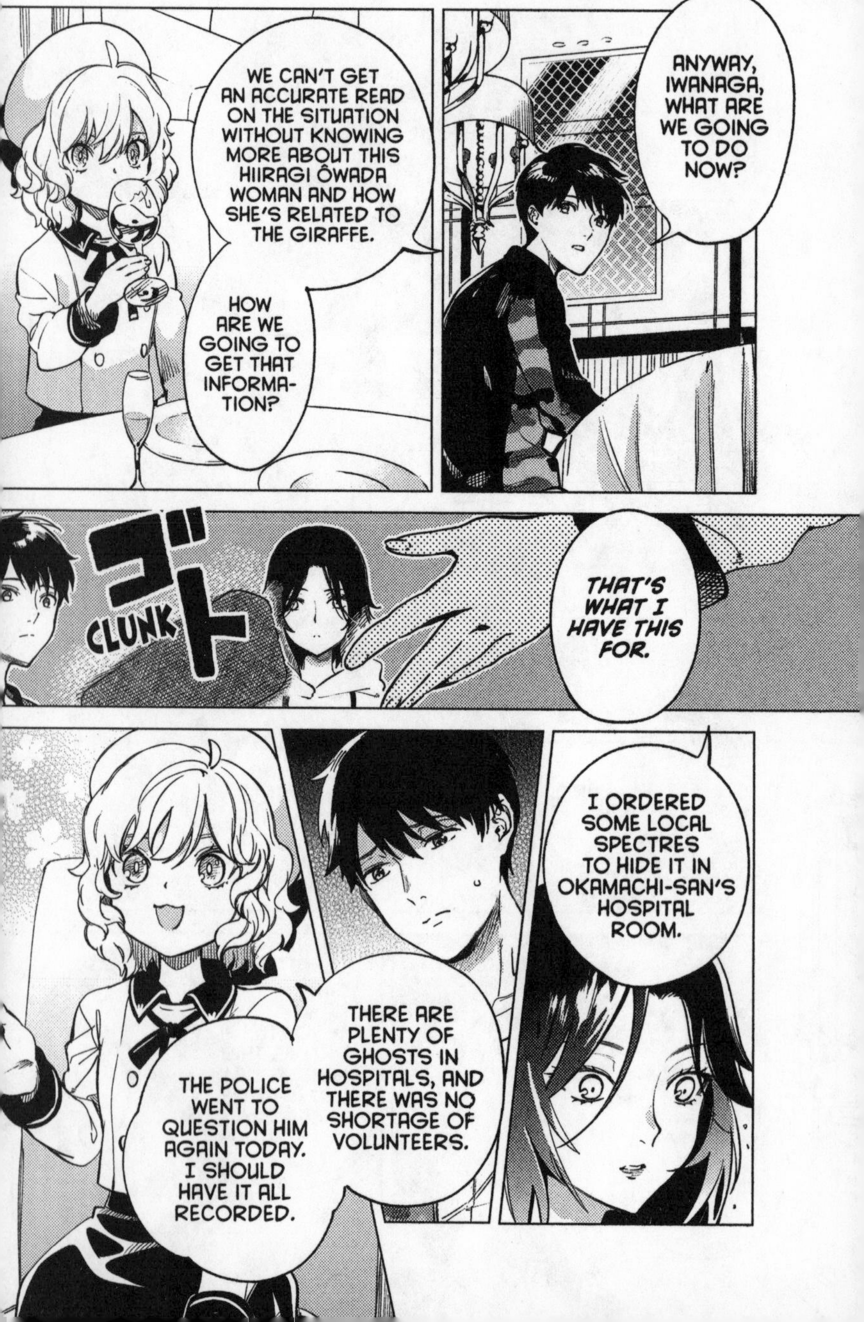
ANYWAY, IWANAGA, WHAT ARE WE GOING TO DO NOW?
WE CAN'T GET AN ACCURATE READ ON THE SITUATION WITHOUT KNOWING MORE ABOUT THIS HIIRAGI ÔWADA WOMAN AND HOW SHE'S RELATED TO THE GIRAFFE.
HOW ARE WE GOING TO GET THAT INFORMATION?
THAT'S WHAT I HAVE THIS FOR.
ゴト
CLUNK
I ORDERED SOME LOCAL SPECTRES TO HIDE IT IN OKAMACHI-SAN'S HOSPITAL ROOM.
THERE ARE PLENTY OF GHOSTS IN HOSPITALS, AND THERE WAS NO SHORTAGE OF VOLUNTEERS.
THE POLICE WENT TO QUESTION HIM AGAIN TODAY. I SHOULD HAVE IT ALL RECORDED.

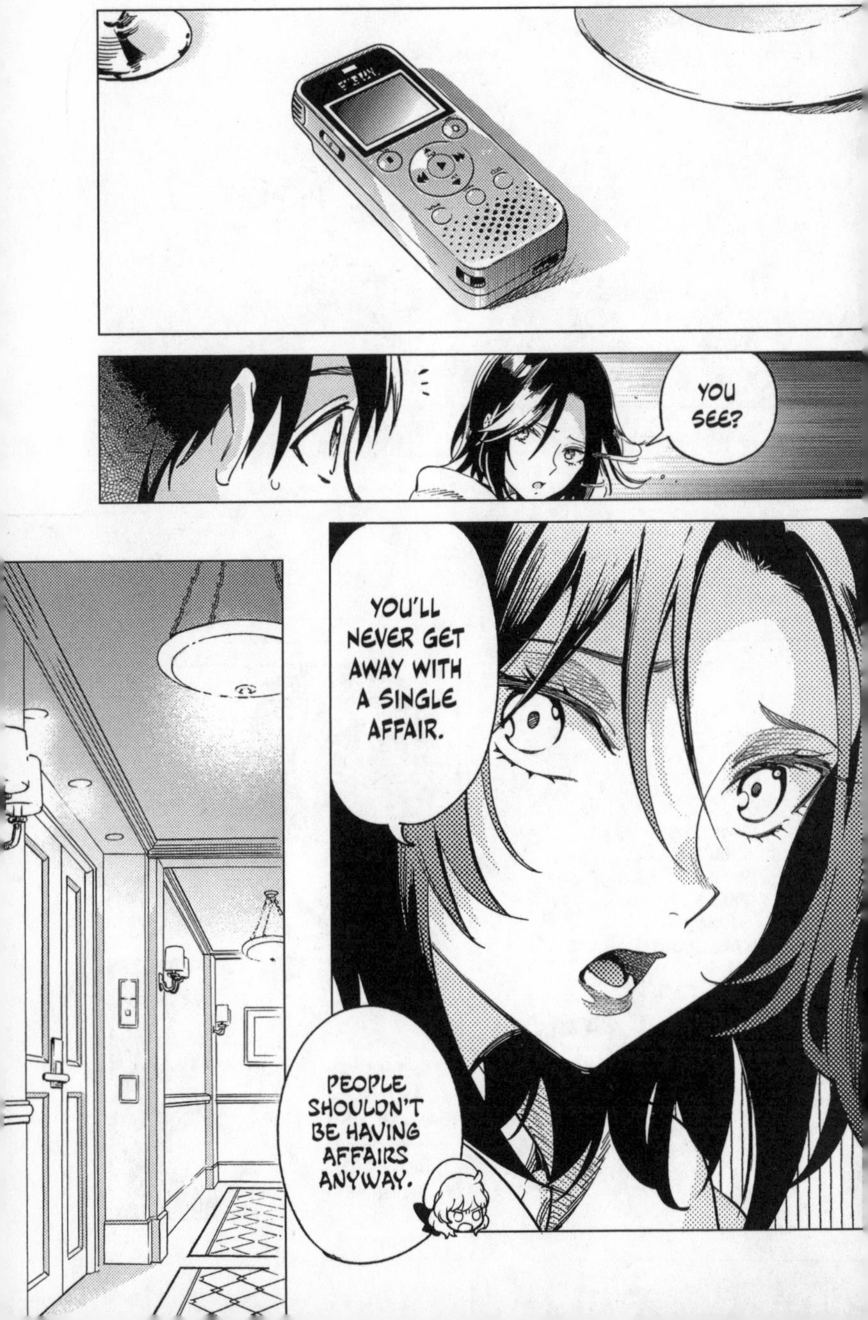
YOU SEE?
YOU'LL NEVER GET AWAY WITH A SINGLE AFFAIR.
PEOPLE SHOULDN'T BE HAVING AFFAIRS ANYWAY.

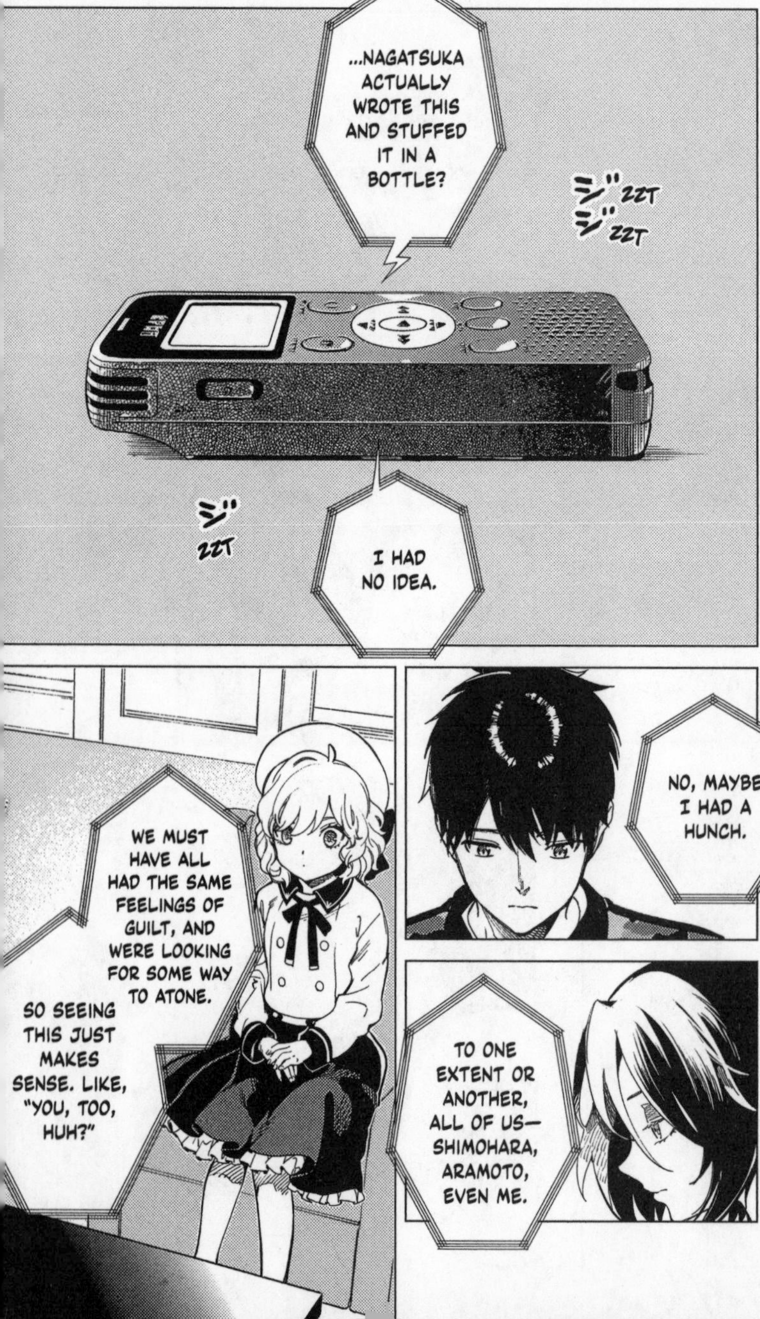
...NAGATSUKA ACTUALLY WROTE THIS AND STUFFED IT IN A BOTTLE?
ジ ZZT
ジ ZZT
I HAD NO IDEA.
ジ ZZT
NO, MAYBE I HAD A HUNCH.
TO ONE EXTENT OR ANOTHER, ALL OF US— SHIMOHARA, ARAMOTO, EVEN ME.
WE MUST HAVE ALL HAD THE SAME FEELINGS OF GUILT, AND WERE LOOKING FOR SOME WAY TO ATONE.
SO SEEING THIS JUST MAKES SENSE. LIKE, "YOU, TOO, HUH?"

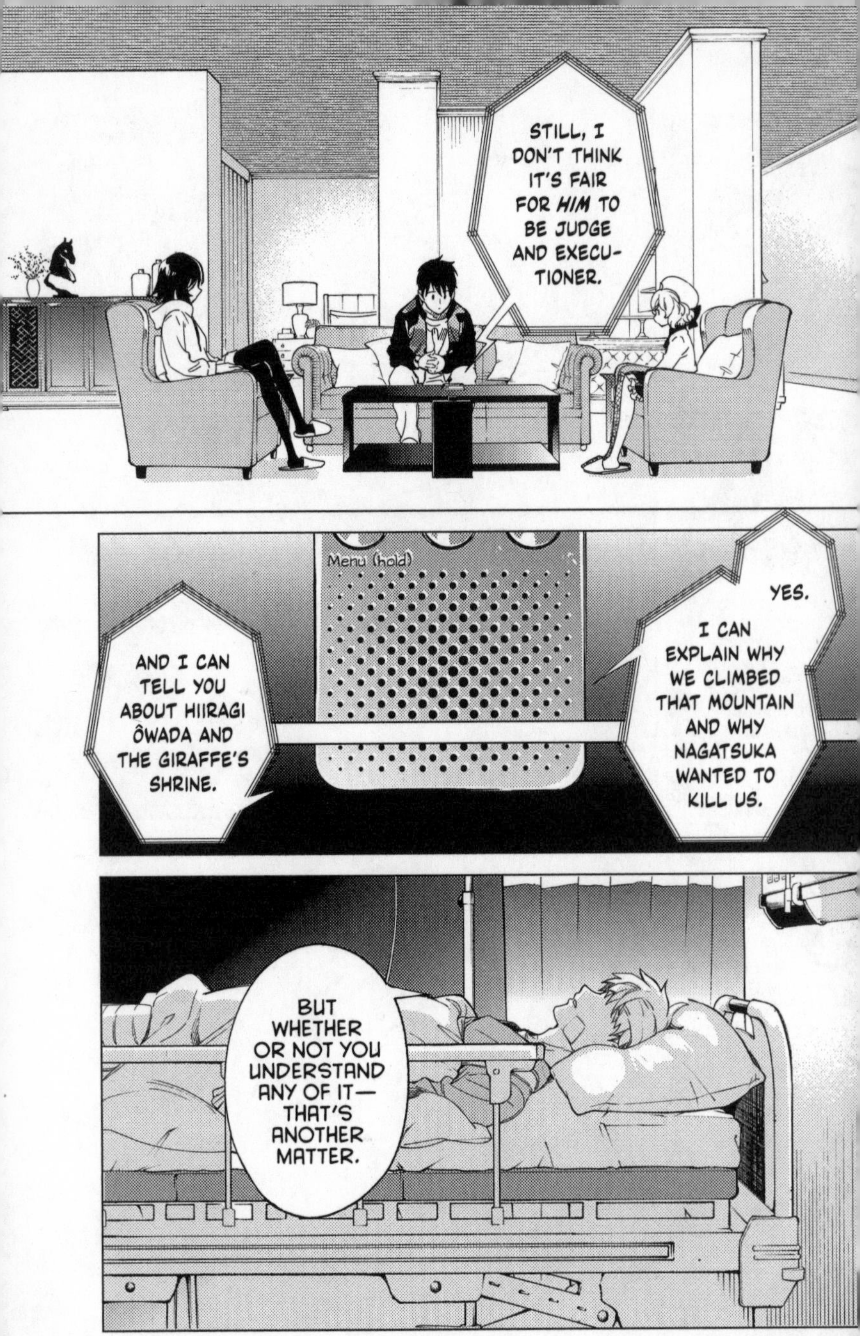
STILL, I DON'T THINK IT'S FAIR FOR *HIM* TO BE JUDGE AND EXECU-TIONER.
YES. I CAN EXPLAIN WHY WE CLIMBED THAT MOUNTAIN AND WHY NAGATSUKA WANTED TO KILL US.
Menu (hold)
AND I CAN TELL YOU ABOUT HIIRAGI ÔWADA AND THE GIRAFFE'S SHRINE.
BUT WHETHER OR NOT YOU UNDERSTAND ANY OF IT—THAT'S ANOTHER MATTER.

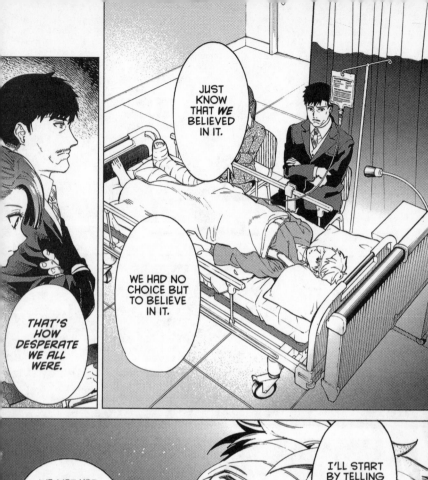

JUST KNOW THAT *WE* BELIEVED IN IT.

WE HAD NO CHOICE BUT TO BELIEVE IN IT.

*THAT'S HOW DESPERATE WE ALL WERE.*

I'LL START BY TELLING YOU ABOUT HIIRAGI.

WE MET HER IN COLLEGE. SHE WAS A YEAR YOUNGER THAN US, AND SHE JOINED OUR OUTDOOR RECREATION CLUB AS A FIRST-YEAR.

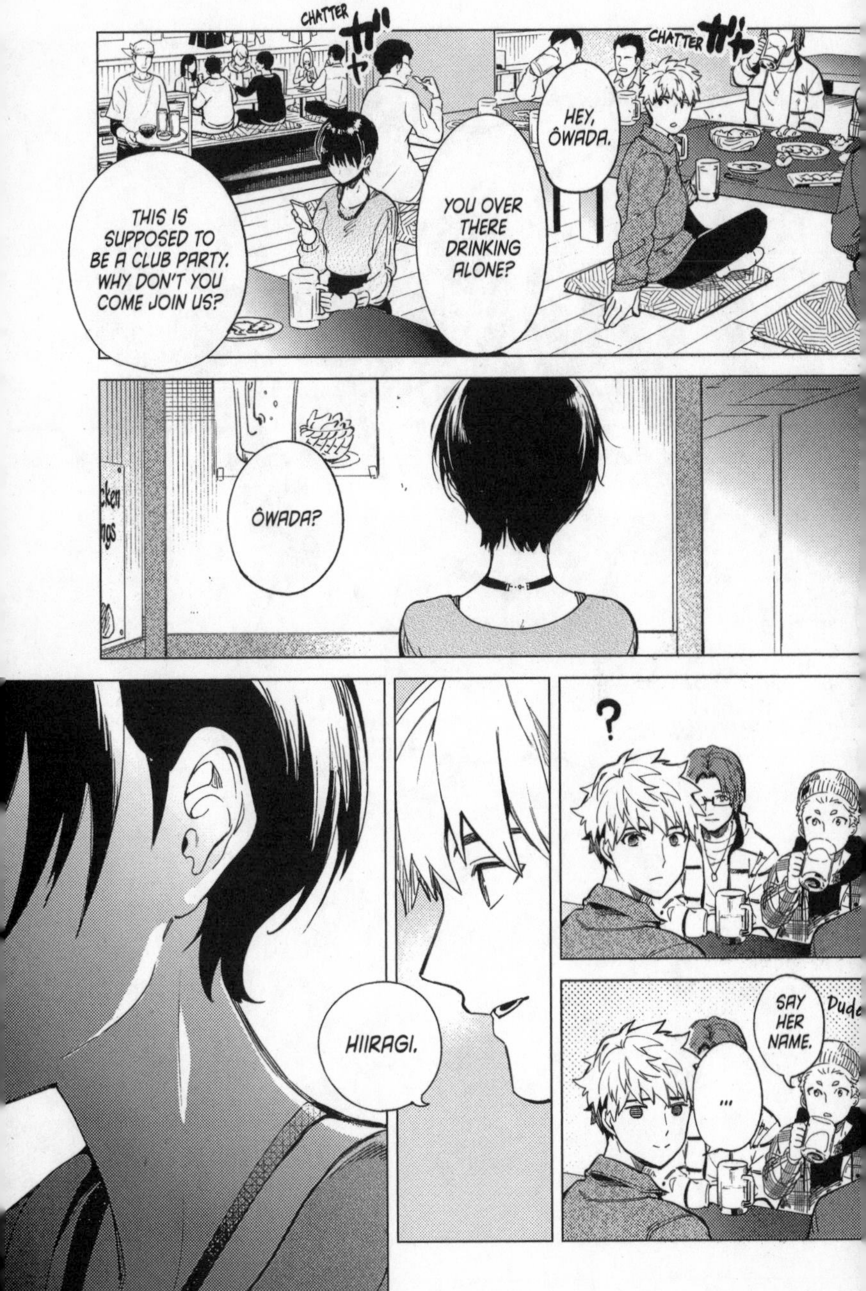
CHATTER
CHATTER
HEY, ÔWADA.
YOU OVER THERE DRINKING ALONE?
THIS IS SUPPOSED TO BE A CLUB PARTY. WHY DON'T YOU COME JOIN US?
ÔWADA?
?
Dude
SAY HER NAME.
...
HIIRAGI.

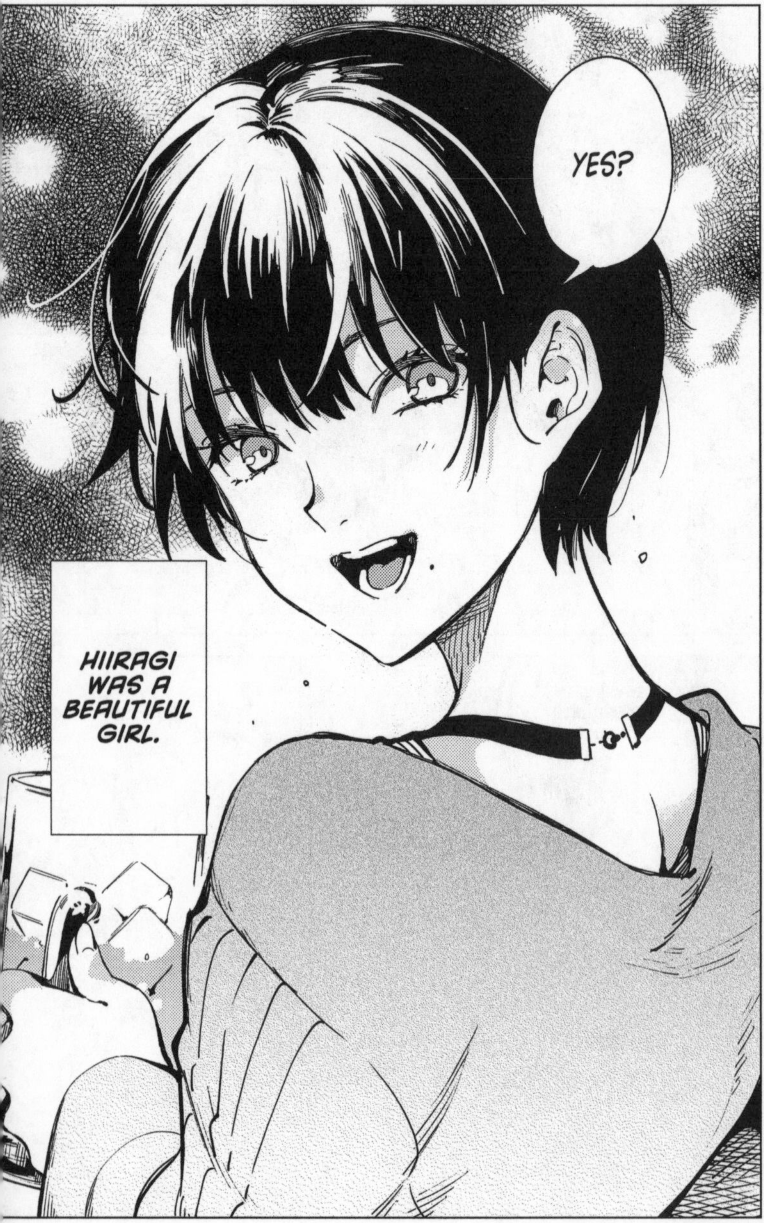
YES?
HIIRAGI WAS A BEAUTIFUL GIRL.

IN/SPECTRE

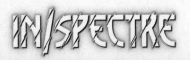

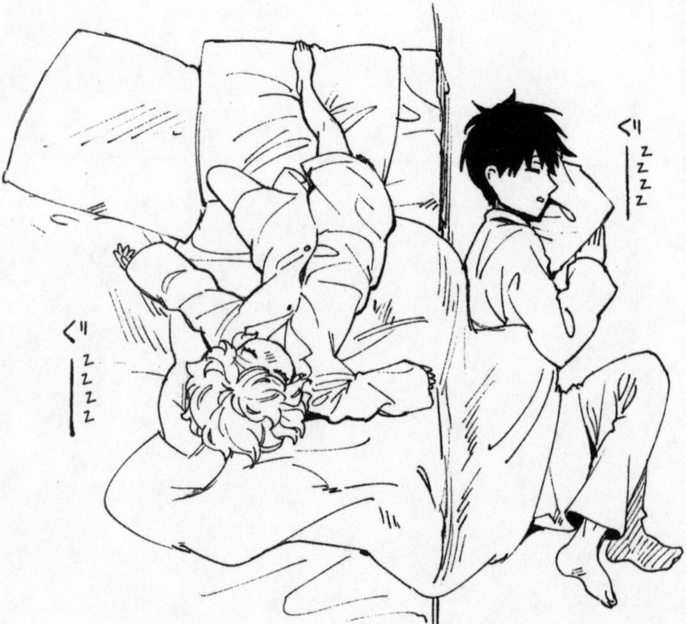
ぐー
zzzz
ぐー
zzzz

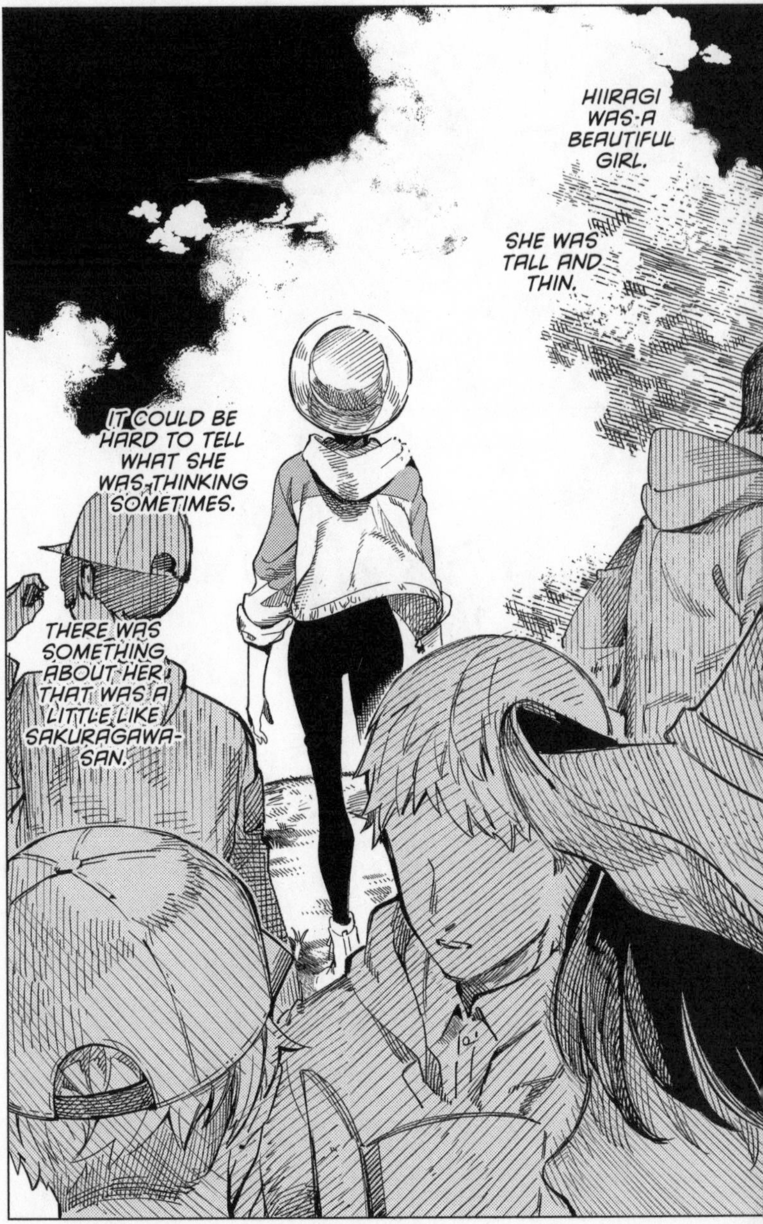
HIIRAGI WAS A BEAUTIFUL GIRL.
SHE WAS TALL AND THIN.
IT COULD BE HARD TO TELL WHAT SHE WAS THINKING SOMETIMES.
THERE WAS SOMETHING ABOUT HER THAT WAS A LITTLE LIKE SAKURAGAWA-SAN.

CHAPTER 44: "THE RETALIATION AND DEFEAT OF KOTOKO IWANAGA PART 6"

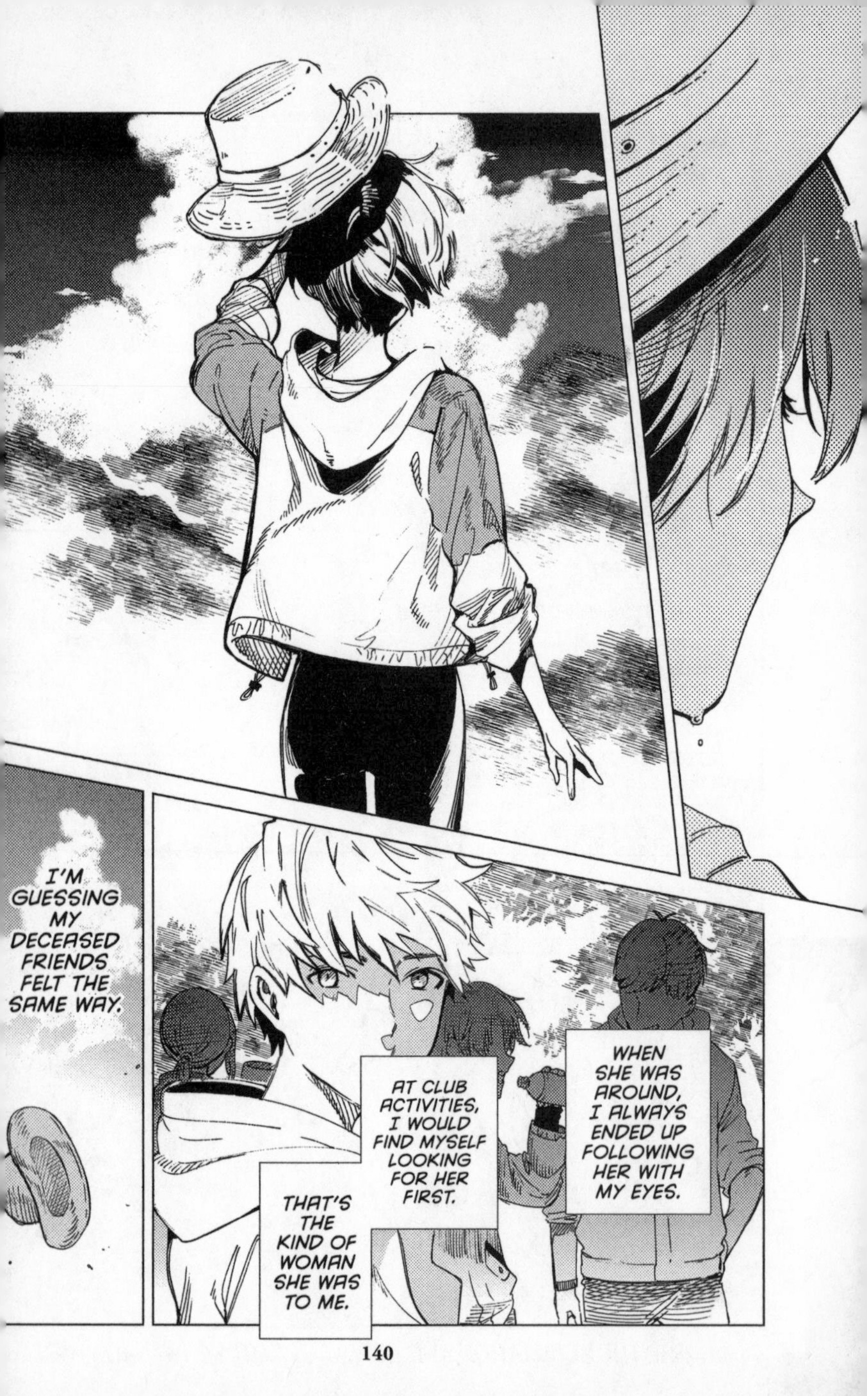
WHEN SHE WAS AROUND, I ALWAYS ENDED UP FOLLOWING HER WITH MY EYES.
AT CLUB ACTIVITIES, I WOULD FIND MYSELF LOOKING FOR HER FIRST.
THAT'S THE KIND OF WOMAN SHE WAS TO ME.
I'M GUESSING MY DECEASED FRIENDS FELT THE SAME WAY.

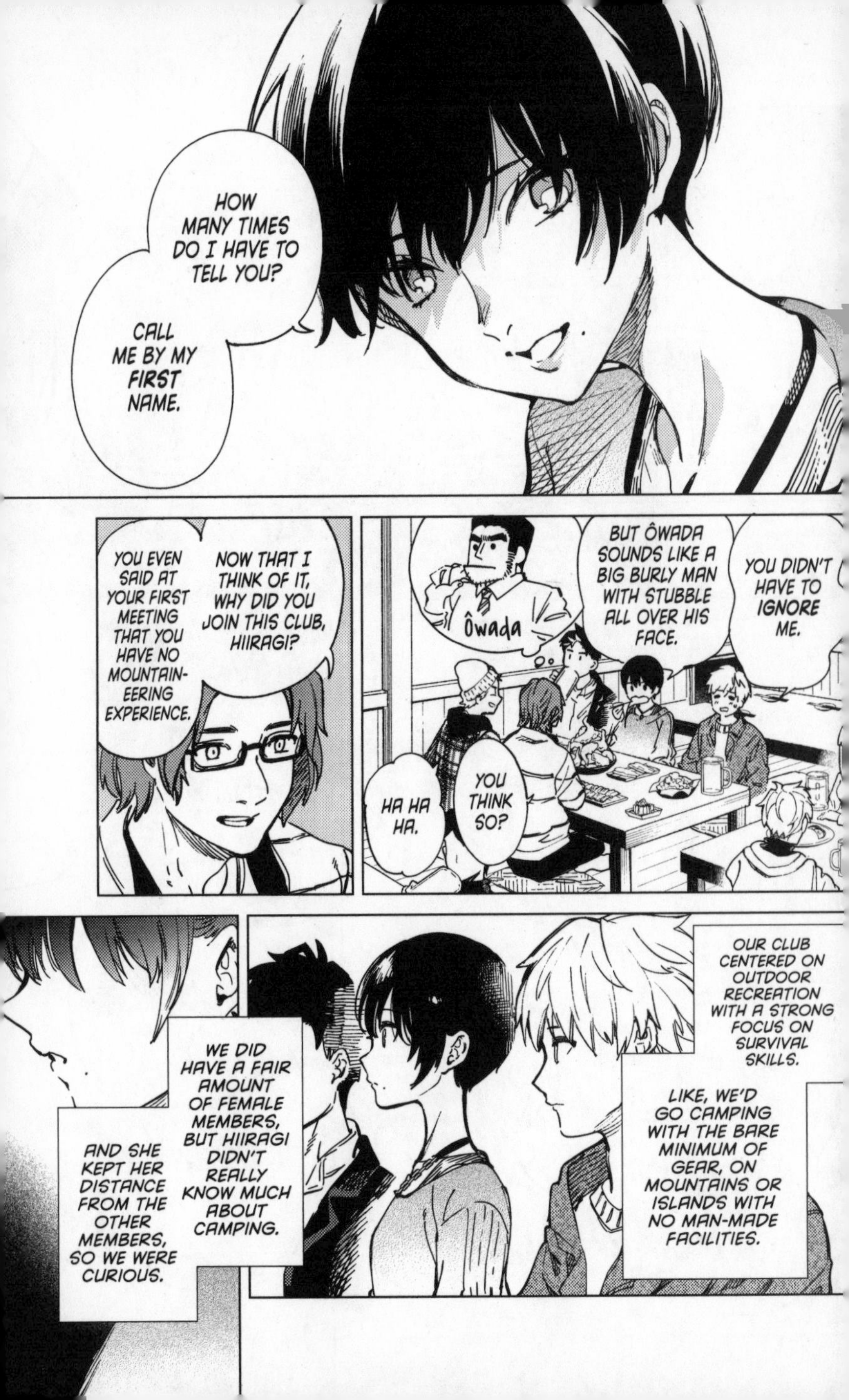
HOW MANY TIMES DO I HAVE TO TELL YOU?
CALL ME BY MY FIRST NAME.
YOU DIDN'T HAVE TO IGNORE ME.
BUT ÔWADA SOUNDS LIKE A BIG BURLY MAN WITH STUBBLE ALL OVER HIS FACE.
Ôwada
YOU THINK SO?
HA HA HA.
NOW THAT I THINK OF IT, WHY DID YOU JOIN THIS CLUB, HIIRAGI?
YOU EVEN SAID AT YOUR FIRST MEETING THAT YOU HAVE NO MOUNTAIN-EERING EXPERIENCE.
OUR CLUB CENTERED ON OUTDOOR RECREATION WITH A STRONG FOCUS ON SURVIVAL SKILLS.
LIKE, WE'D GO CAMPING WITH THE BARE MINIMUM OF GEAR, ON MOUNTAINS OR ISLANDS WITH NO MAN-MADE FACILITIES.
WE DID HAVE A FAIR AMOUNT OF FEMALE MEMBERS, BUT HIIRAGI DIDN'T REALLY KNOW MUCH ABOUT CAMPING.
AND SHE KEPT HER DISTANCE FROM THE OTHER MEMBERS, SO WE WERE CURIOUS.

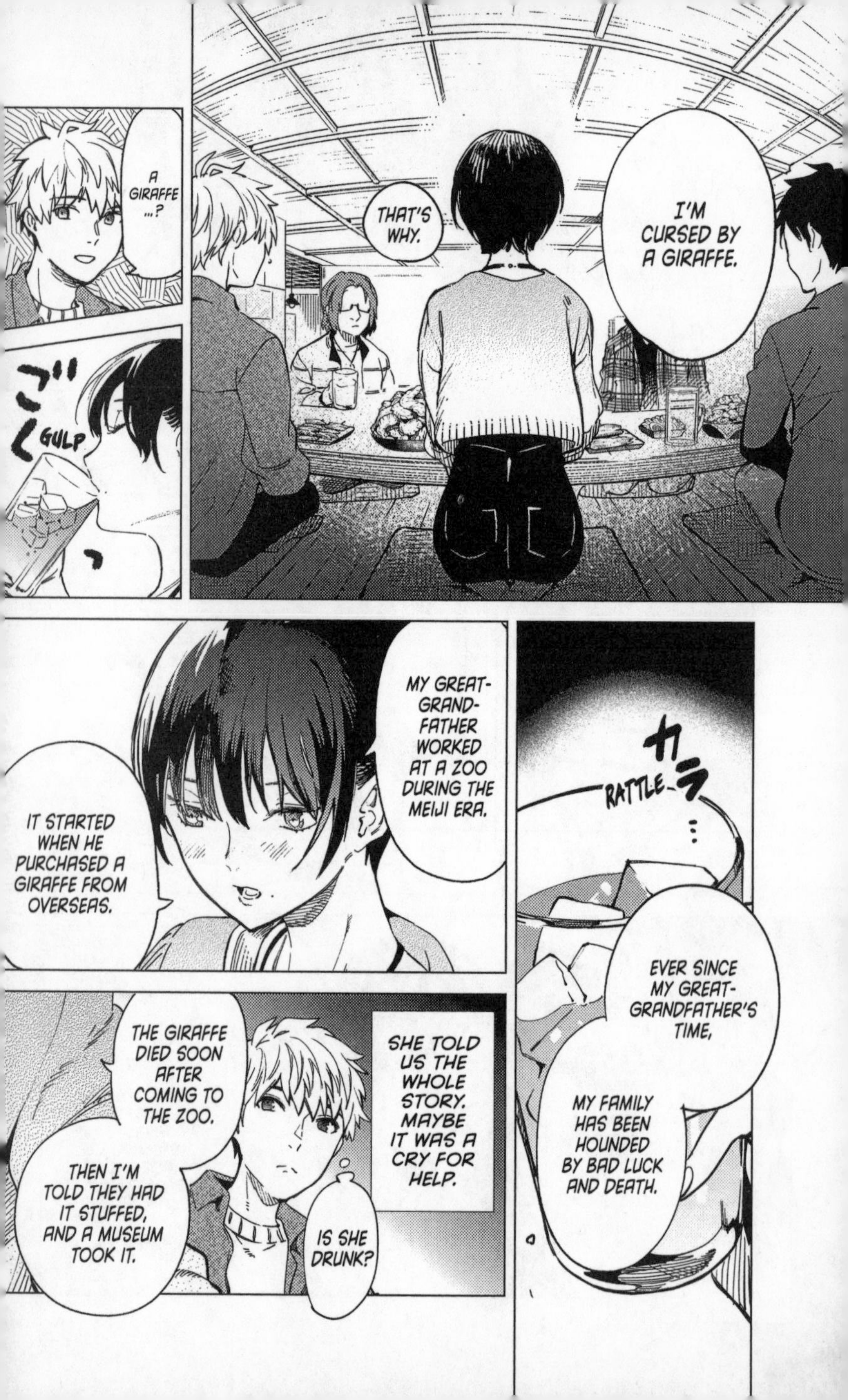
I'M CURSED BY A GIRAFFE.
THAT'S WHY.
A GIRAFFE ...?
ごく
GULP
カラ
RATTLE
...
EVER SINCE MY GREAT-GRANDFATHER'S TIME,
MY FAMILY HAS BEEN HOUNDED BY BAD LUCK AND DEATH.
MY GREAT-GRAND-FATHER WORKED AT A ZOO DURING THE MEIJI ERA.
IT STARTED WHEN HE PURCHASED A GIRAFFE FROM OVERSEAS.
THE GIRAFFE DIED SOON AFTER COMING TO THE ZOO.
THEN I'M TOLD THEY HAD IT STUFFED, AND A MUSEUM TOOK IT.
SHE TOLD US THE WHOLE STORY. MAYBE IT WAS A CRY FOR HELP.
IS SHE DRUNK?

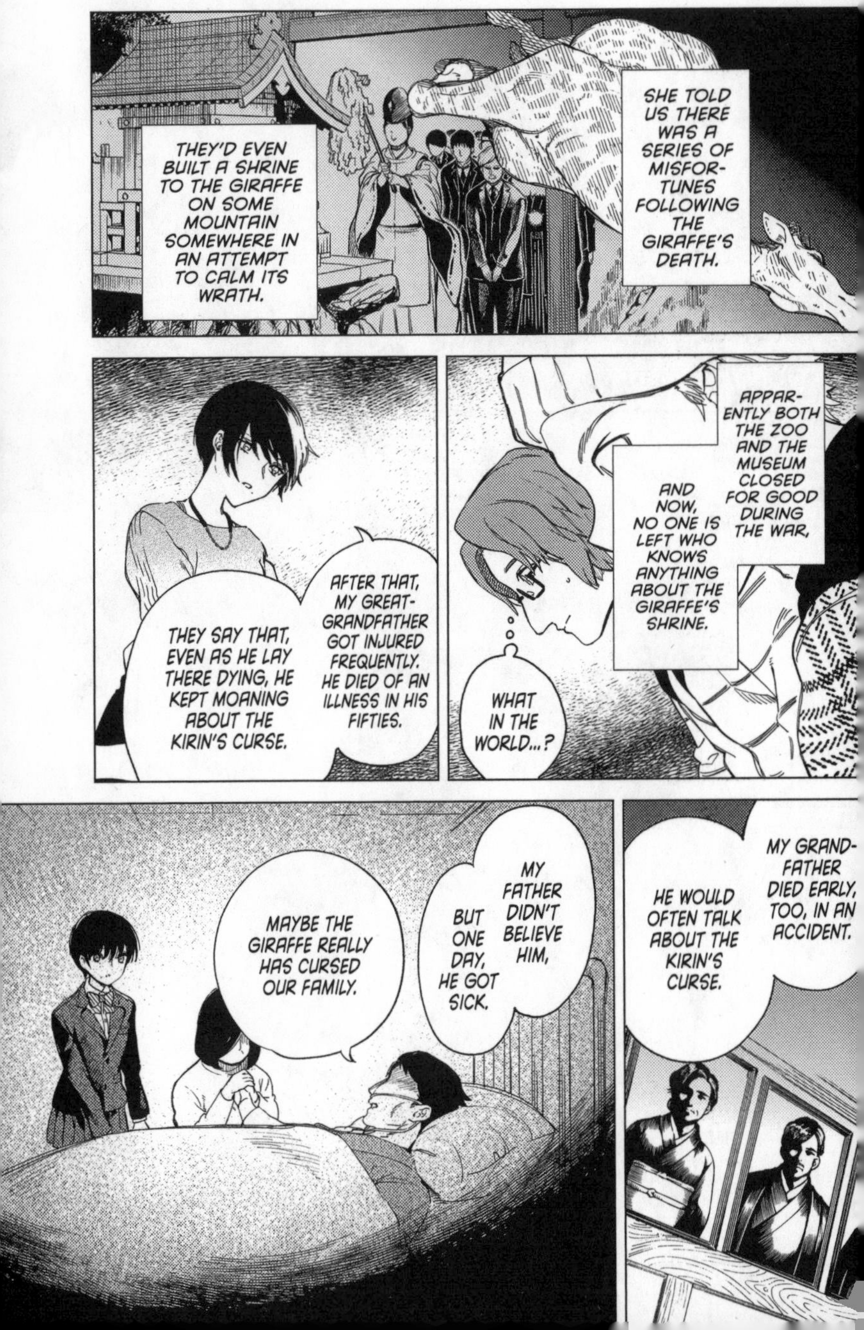
SHE TOLD US THERE WAS A SERIES OF MISFORTUNES FOLLOWING THE GIRAFFE'S DEATH.
THEY'D EVEN BUILT A SHRINE TO THE GIRAFFE ON SOME MOUNTAIN SOMEWHERE IN AN ATTEMPT TO CALM ITS WRATH.
APPARENTLY BOTH THE ZOO AND THE MUSEUM CLOSED FOR GOOD DURING THE WAR,
AND NOW, NO ONE IS LEFT WHO KNOWS ANYTHING ABOUT THE GIRAFFE'S SHRINE.
WHAT IN THE WORLD...?
AFTER THAT, MY GREAT-GRANDFATHER GOT INJURED FREQUENTLY. HE DIED OF AN ILLNESS IN HIS FIFTIES.
THEY SAY THAT, EVEN AS HE LAY THERE DYING, HE KEPT MOANING ABOUT THE KIRIN'S CURSE.
MY GRANDFATHER DIED EARLY, TOO, IN AN ACCIDENT.
HE WOULD OFTEN TALK ABOUT THE KIRIN'S CURSE.
MY FATHER DIDN'T BELIEVE HIM,
BUT ONE DAY, HE GOT SICK.
MAYBE THE GIRAFFE REALLY HAS CURSED OUR FAMILY.

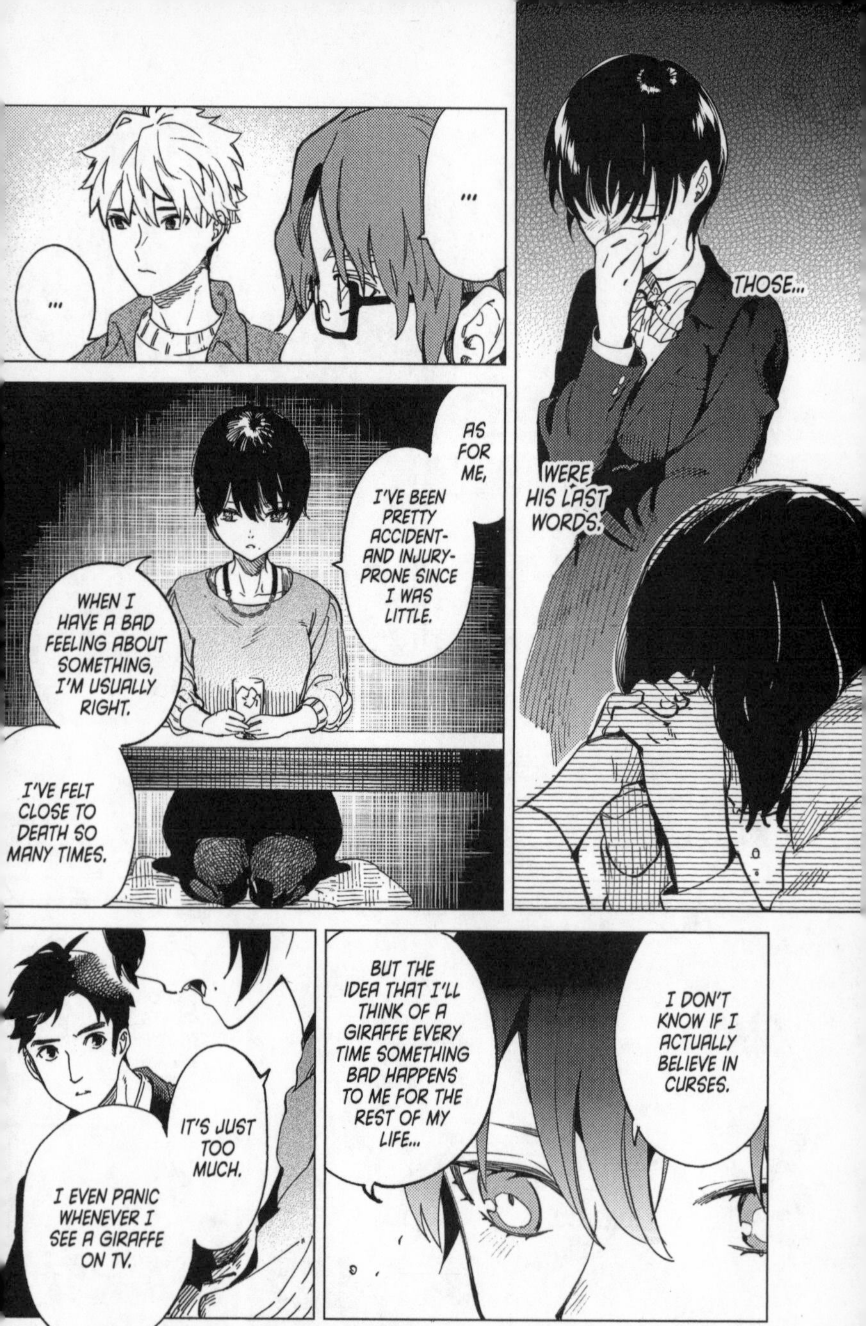
THOSE...
WERE HIS LAST WORDS.
...
...
AS FOR ME,
I'VE BEEN PRETTY ACCIDENT- AND INJURY-PRONE SINCE I WAS LITTLE.
WHEN I HAVE A BAD FEELING ABOUT SOMETHING, I'M USUALLY RIGHT.
I'VE FELT CLOSE TO DEATH SO MANY TIMES.
I DON'T KNOW IF I ACTUALLY BELIEVE IN CURSES.
BUT THE IDEA THAT I'LL THINK OF A GIRAFFE EVERY TIME SOMETHING BAD HAPPENS TO ME FOR THE REST OF MY LIFE...
IT'S JUST TOO MUCH.
I EVEN PANIC WHENEVER I SEE A GIRAFFE ON TV.

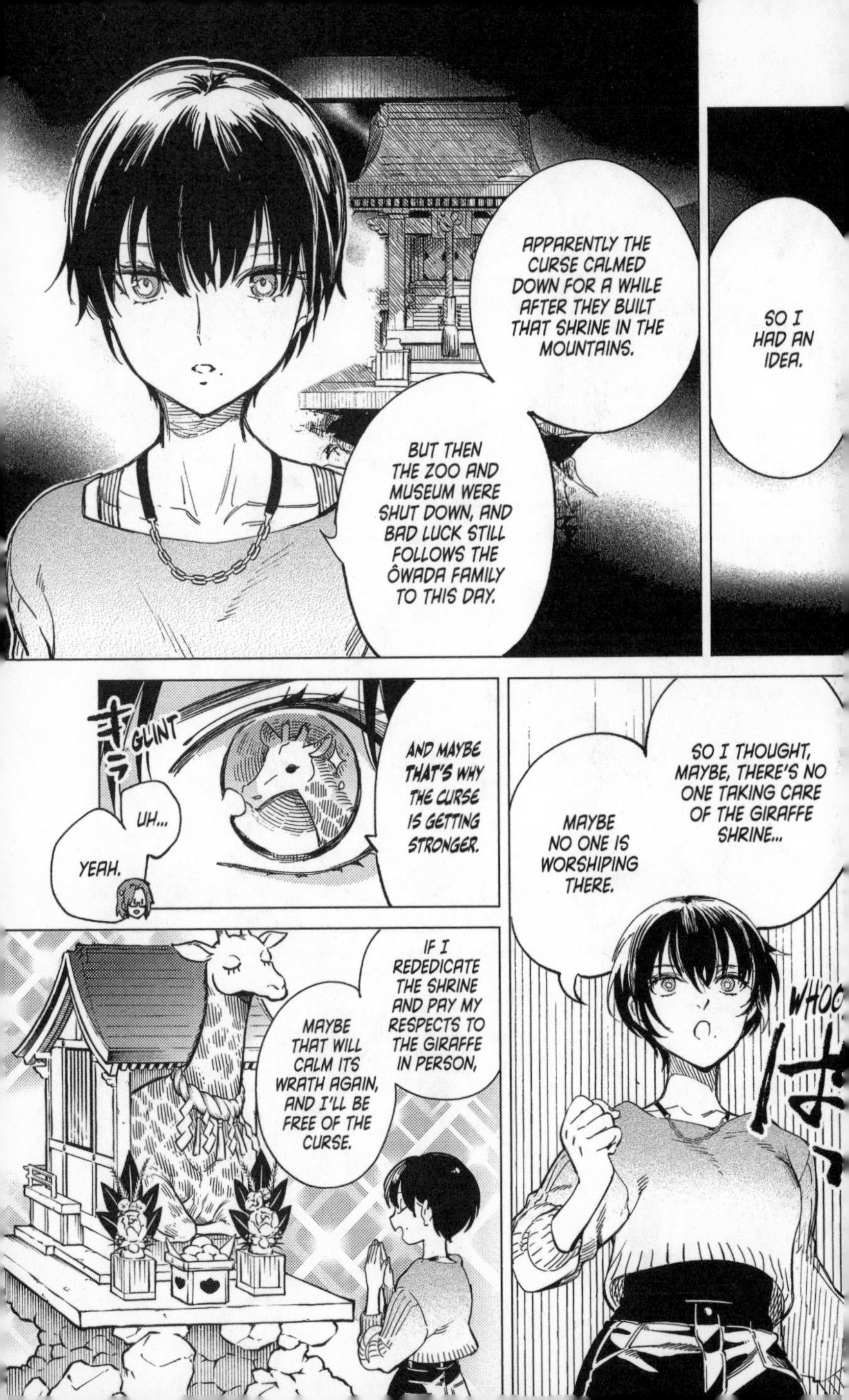
SO I HAD AN IDEA.
APPARENTLY THE CURSE CALMED DOWN FOR A WHILE AFTER THEY BUILT THAT SHRINE IN THE MOUNTAINS.
BUT THEN THE ZOO AND MUSEUM WERE SHUT DOWN, AND BAD LUCK STILL FOLLOWS THE ÔWADA FAMILY TO THIS DAY.
SO I THOUGHT, MAYBE, THERE'S NO ONE TAKING CARE OF THE GIRAFFE SHRINE...
MAYBE NO ONE IS WORSHIPING THERE.
WHOO
AND MAYBE THAT'S WHY THE CURSE IS GETTING STRONGER.
GLINT
UH... YEAH.
IF I REDEDICATE THE SHRINE AND PAY MY RESPECTS TO THE GIRAFFE IN PERSON,
MAYBE THAT WILL CALM ITS WRATH AGAIN, AND I'LL BE FREE OF THE CURSE.

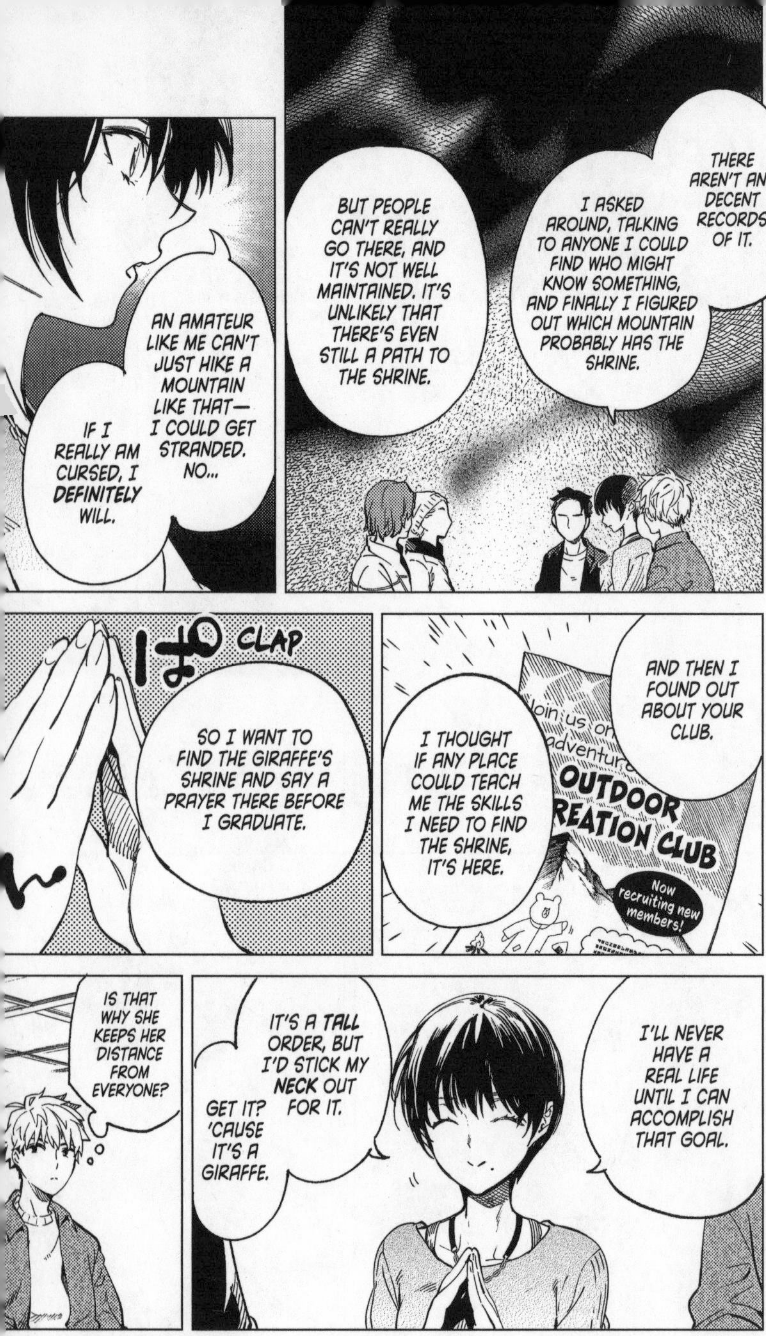
THERE AREN'T ANY DECENT RECORDS OF IT.
I ASKED AROUND, TALKING TO ANYONE I COULD FIND WHO MIGHT KNOW SOMETHING, AND FINALLY I FIGURED OUT WHICH MOUNTAIN PROBABLY HAS THE SHRINE.
BUT PEOPLE CAN'T REALLY GO THERE, AND IT'S NOT WELL MAINTAINED. IT'S UNLIKELY THAT THERE'S EVEN STILL A PATH TO THE SHRINE.
AN AMATEUR LIKE ME CAN'T JUST HIKE A MOUNTAIN LIKE THAT—I COULD GET STRANDED. NO...
IF I REALLY AM CURSED, I DEFINITELY WILL.
AND THEN I FOUND OUT ABOUT YOUR CLUB.
I THOUGHT IF ANY PLACE COULD TEACH ME THE SKILLS I NEED TO FIND THE SHRINE, IT'S HERE.
OUTDOOR
REATION CLUB
Now recruiting new members!
CLAP
SO I WANT TO FIND THE GIRAFFE'S SHRINE AND SAY A PRAYER THERE BEFORE I GRADUATE.
I'LL NEVER HAVE A REAL LIFE UNTIL I CAN ACCOMPLISH THAT GOAL.
IT'S A TALL ORDER, BUT I'D STICK MY NECK OUT FOR IT.
GET IT? 'CAUSE IT'S A GIRAFFE.
IS THAT WHY SHE KEEPS HER DISTANCE FROM EVERYONE?

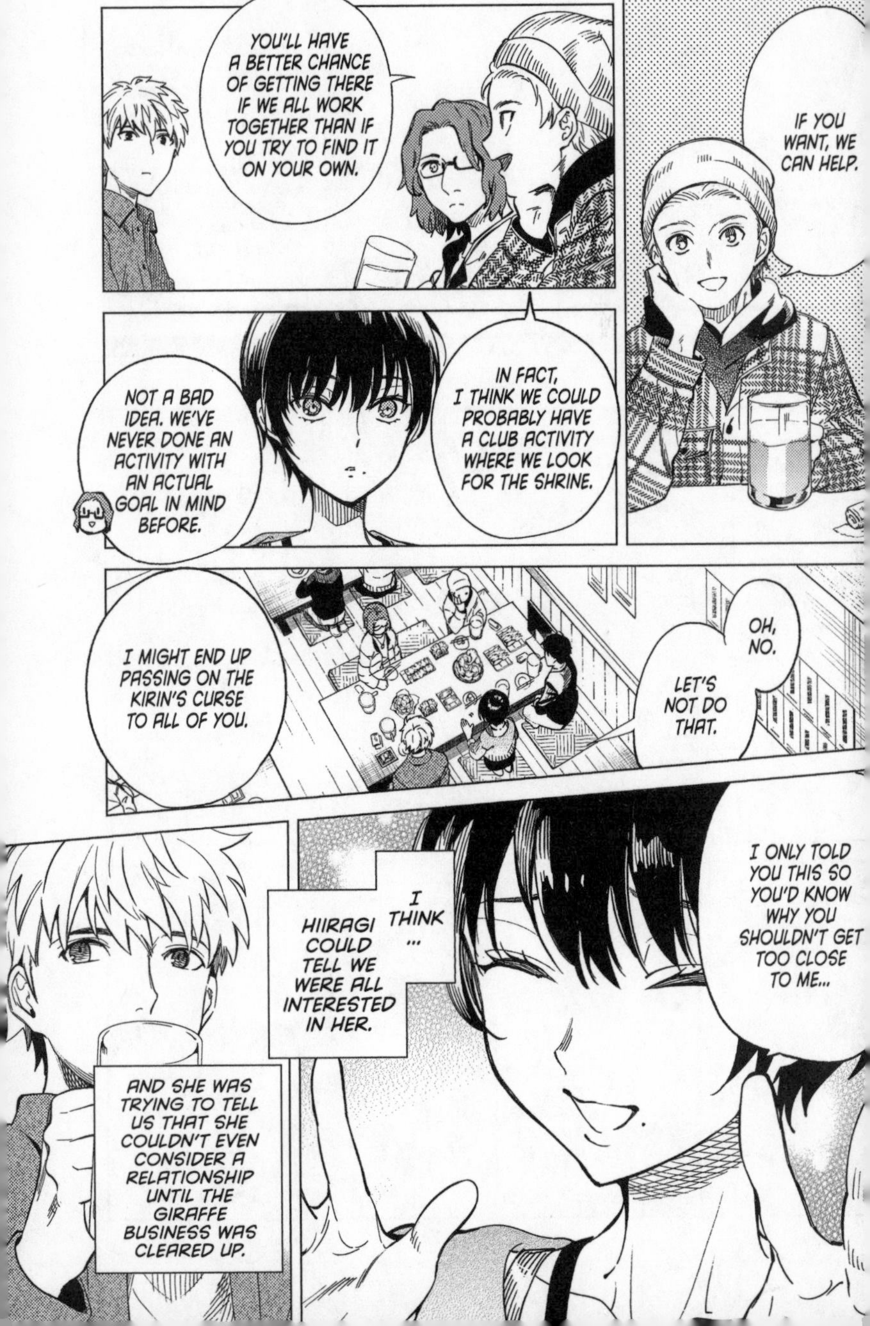
IF YOU WANT, WE CAN HELP.
YOU'LL HAVE A BETTER CHANCE OF GETTING THERE IF WE ALL WORK TOGETHER THAN IF YOU TRY TO FIND IT ON YOUR OWN.
IN FACT, I THINK WE COULD PROBABLY HAVE A CLUB ACTIVITY WHERE WE LOOK FOR THE SHRINE.
NOT A BAD IDEA. WE'VE NEVER DONE AN ACTIVITY WITH AN ACTUAL GOAL IN MIND BEFORE.
OH, NO.
LET'S NOT DO THAT.
I MIGHT END UP PASSING ON THE KIRIN'S CURSE TO ALL OF YOU.
I ONLY TOLD YOU THIS SO YOU'D KNOW WHY YOU SHOULDN'T GET TOO CLOSE TO ME...
I THINK...
HIIRAGI COULD TELL WE WERE ALL INTERESTED IN HER.
AND SHE WAS TRYING TO TELL US THAT SHE COULDN'T EVEN CONSIDER A RELATIONSHIP UNTIL THE GIRAFFE BUSINESS WAS CLEARED UP.

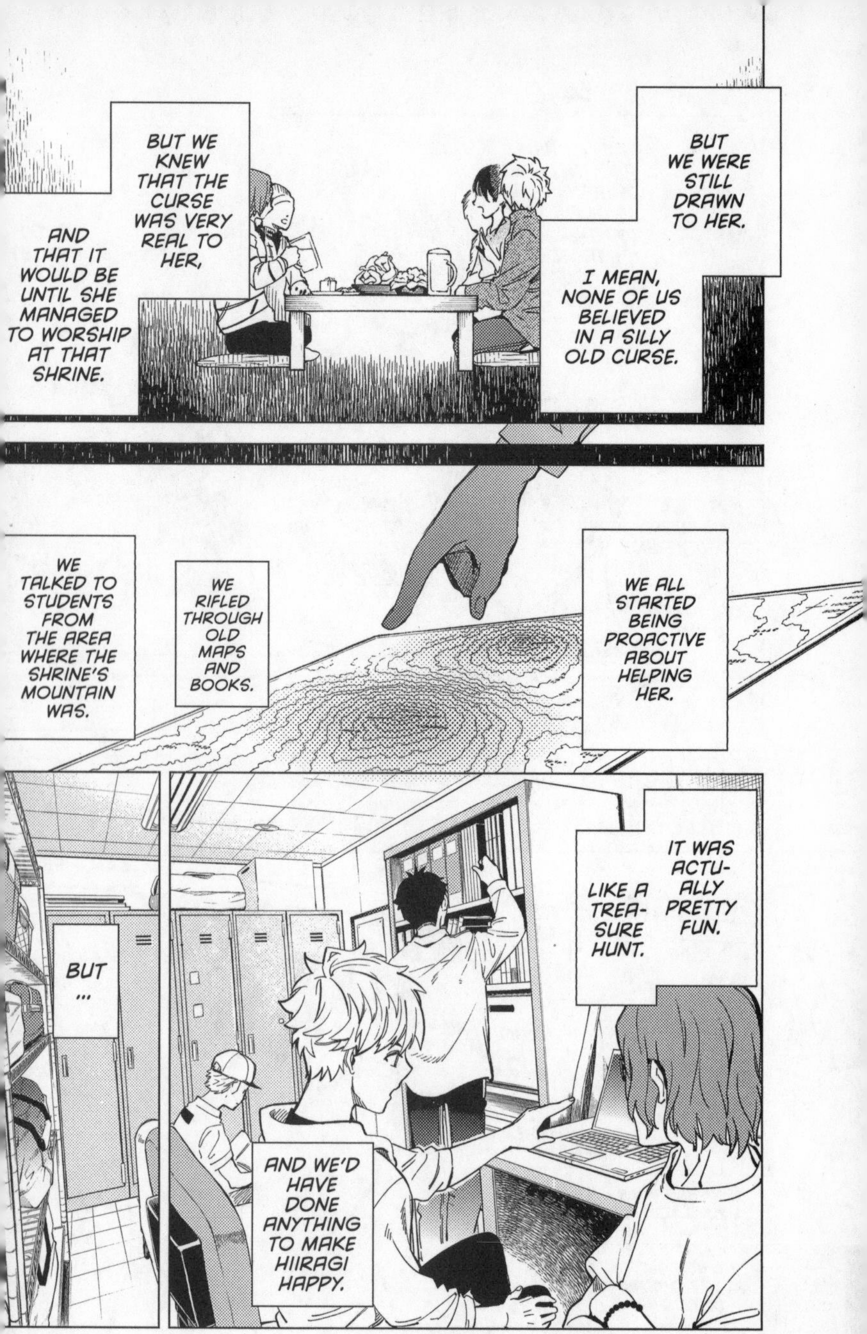
BUT WE WERE STILL DRAWN TO HER.
I MEAN, NONE OF US BELIEVED IN A SILLY OLD CURSE.
BUT WE KNEW THAT THE CURSE WAS VERY REAL TO HER,
AND THAT IT WOULD BE UNTIL SHE MANAGED TO WORSHIP AT THAT SHRINE.
WE ALL STARTED BEING PROACTIVE ABOUT HELPING HER.
WE RIFLED THROUGH OLD MAPS AND BOOKS.
WE TALKED TO STUDENTS FROM THE AREA WHERE THE SHRINE'S MOUNTAIN WAS.
IT WAS ACTU-ALLY PRETTY FUN.
LIKE A TREA-SURE HUNT.
AND WE'D HAVE DONE ANYTHING TO MAKE HIIRAGI HAPPY.
BUT ...

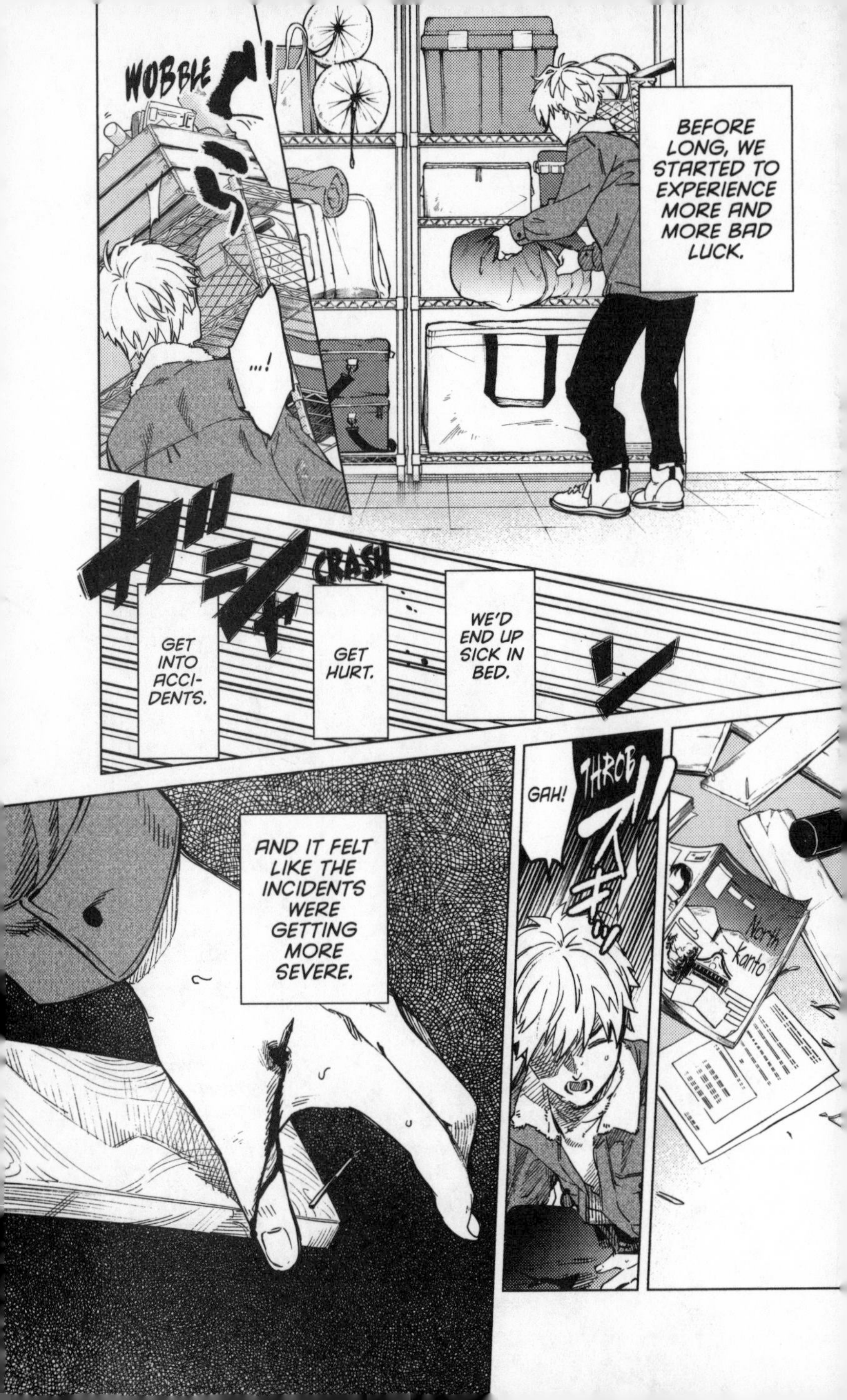
BEFORE LONG, WE STARTED TO EXPERIENCE MORE AND MORE BAD LUCK.
WOBBLE
...!
CRASH
WE'D END UP SICK IN BED.
GET HURT.
GET INTO ACCI-DENTS.
THROB
GAH!
North Kanto
AND IT FELT LIKE THE INCIDENTS WERE GETTING MORE SEVERE.

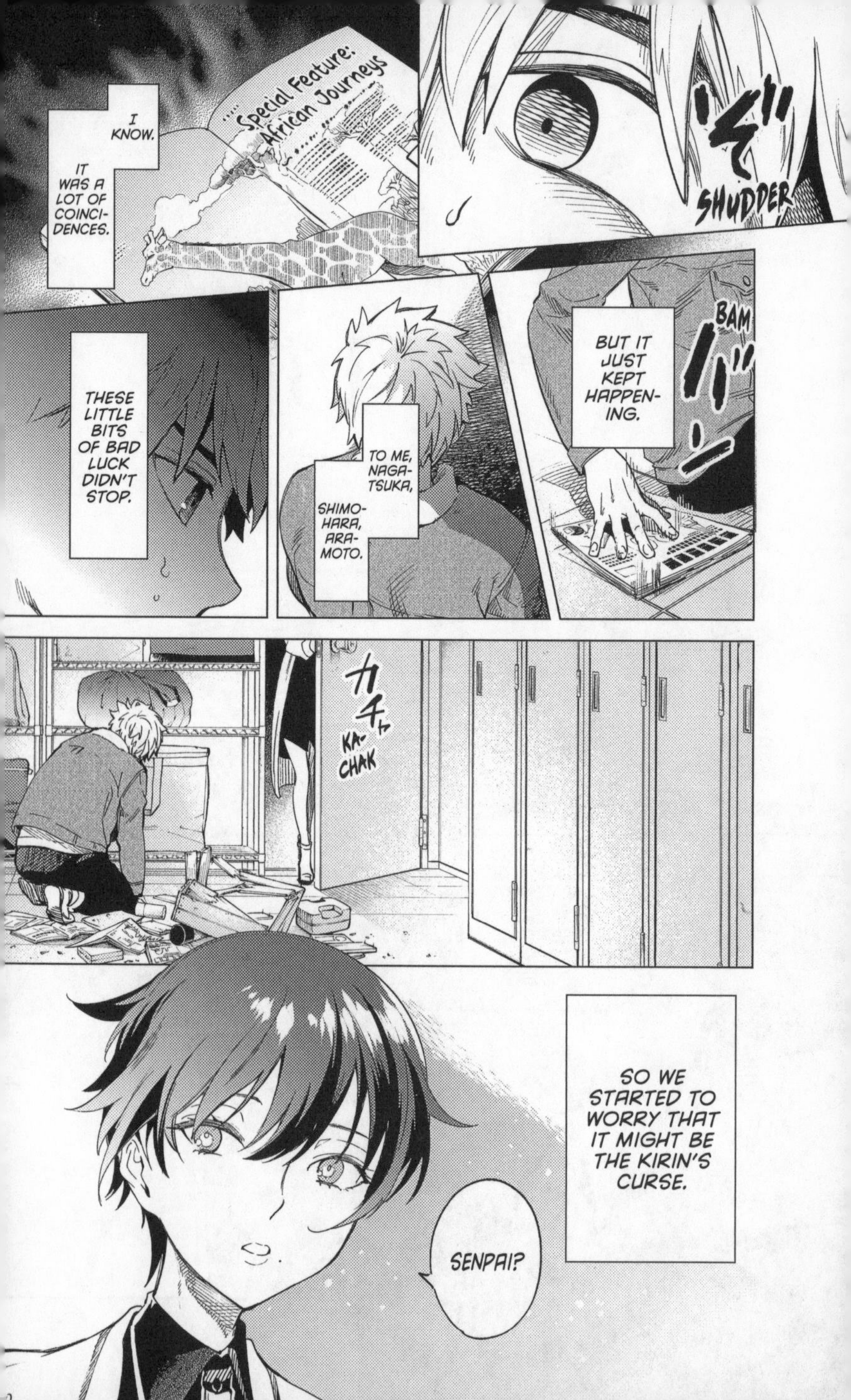
ぞ
SHUDDER
Special Feature: African Journeys
I KNOW.
IT WAS A LOT OF COINCIDENCES.
BAM
BUT IT JUST KEPT HAPPENING.
TO ME, NAGATSUKA, SHIMOHARA, ARAMOTO.
THESE LITTLE BITS OF BAD LUCK DIDN'T STOP.
カチャ
KA-CHAK
SO WE STARTED TO WORRY THAT IT MIGHT BE THE KIRIN'S CURSE.
SENPAI?

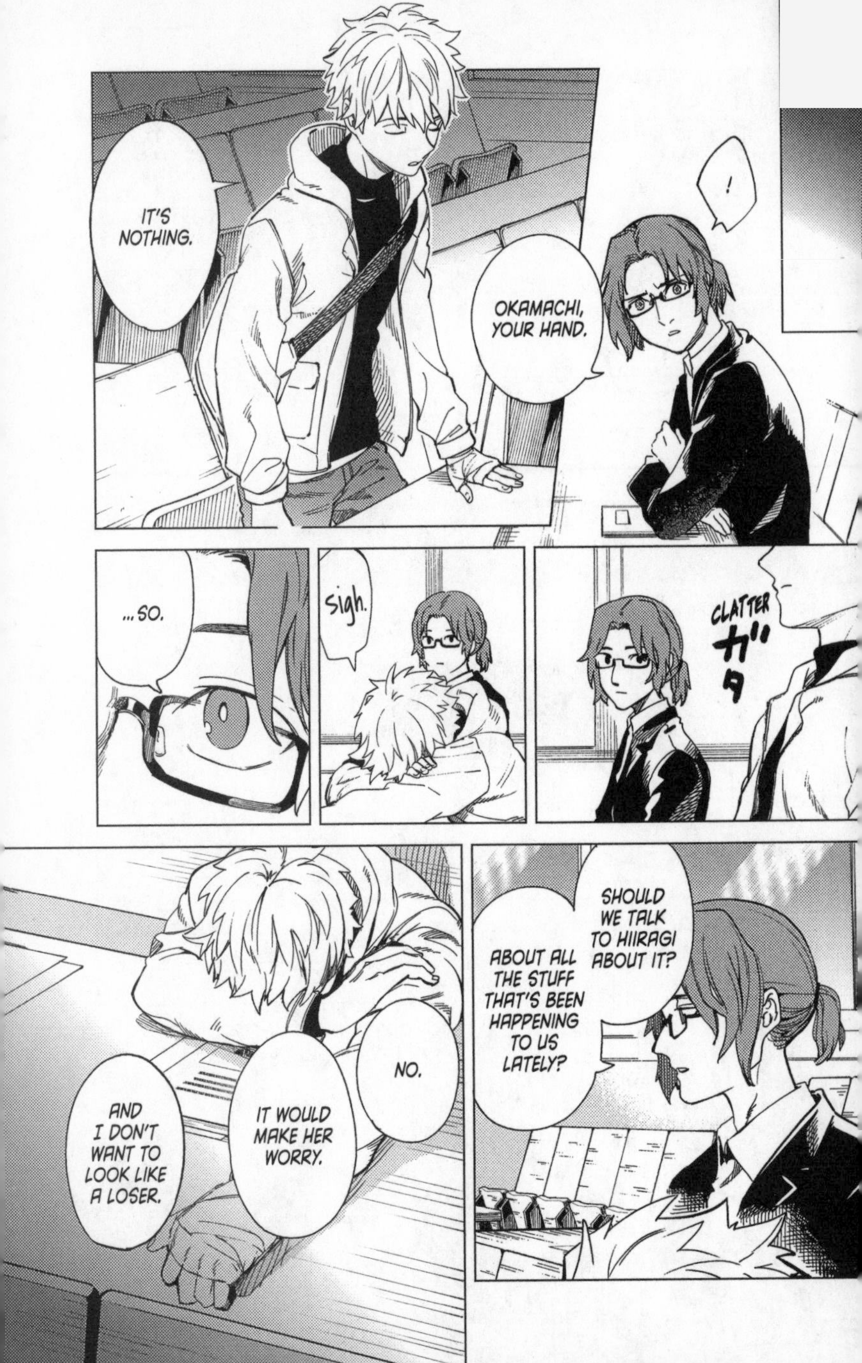
!
OKAMACHI, YOUR HAND.
IT'S NOTHING.
CLATTER
ガタ
Sigh.
...SO.
SHOULD WE TALK TO HIIRAGI ABOUT IT?
ABOUT ALL THE STUFF THAT'S BEEN HAPPENING TO US LATELY?
NO.
IT WOULD MAKE HER WORRY.
AND I DON'T WANT TO LOOK LIKE A LOSER.

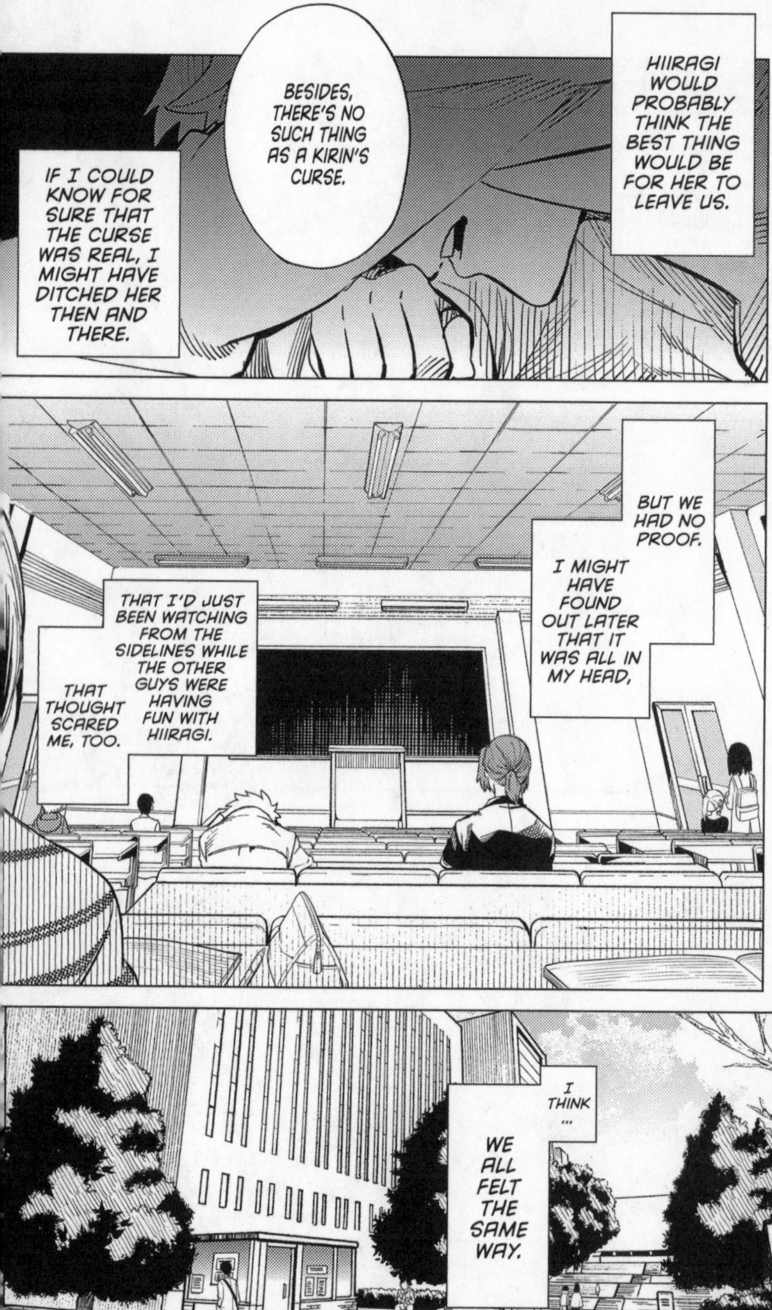
HIIRAGI WOULD PROBABLY THINK THE BEST THING WOULD BE FOR HER TO LEAVE US.
BESIDES, THERE'S NO SUCH THING AS A KIRIN'S CURSE.
IF I COULD KNOW FOR SURE THAT THE CURSE WAS REAL, I MIGHT HAVE DITCHED HER THEN AND THERE.
BUT WE HAD NO PROOF.
I MIGHT HAVE FOUND OUT LATER THAT IT WAS ALL IN MY HEAD,
THAT I'D JUST BEEN WATCHING FROM THE SIDELINES WHILE THE OTHER GUYS WERE HAVING FUN WITH HIIRAGI.
THAT THOUGHT SCARED ME, TOO.
I THINK ...
WE ALL FELT THE SAME WAY.

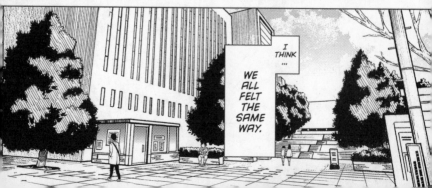

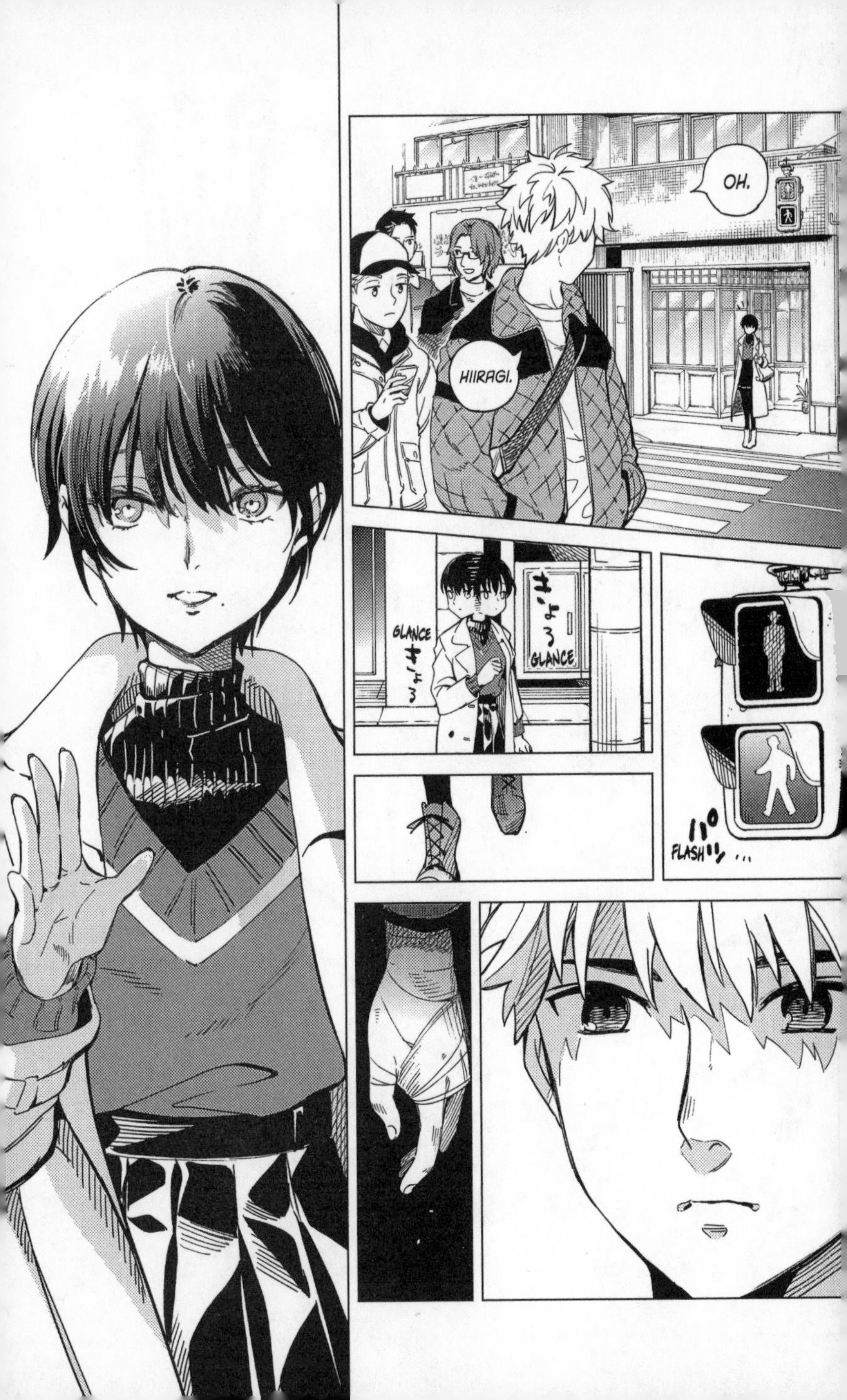
OH.
HIIRAGI.
FLASH
...
きょろ
GLANCE
GLANCE
きょろ

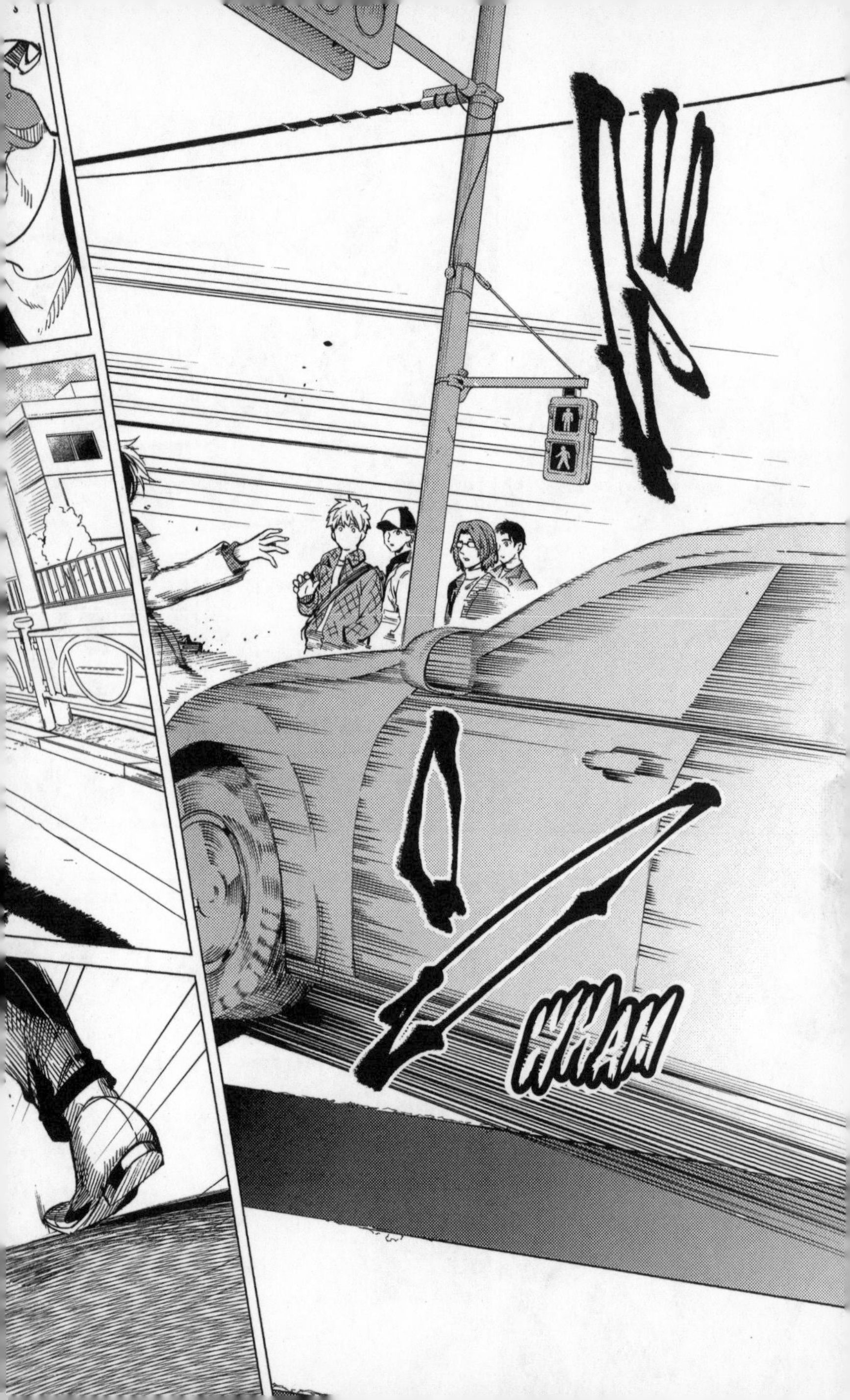
WHAM

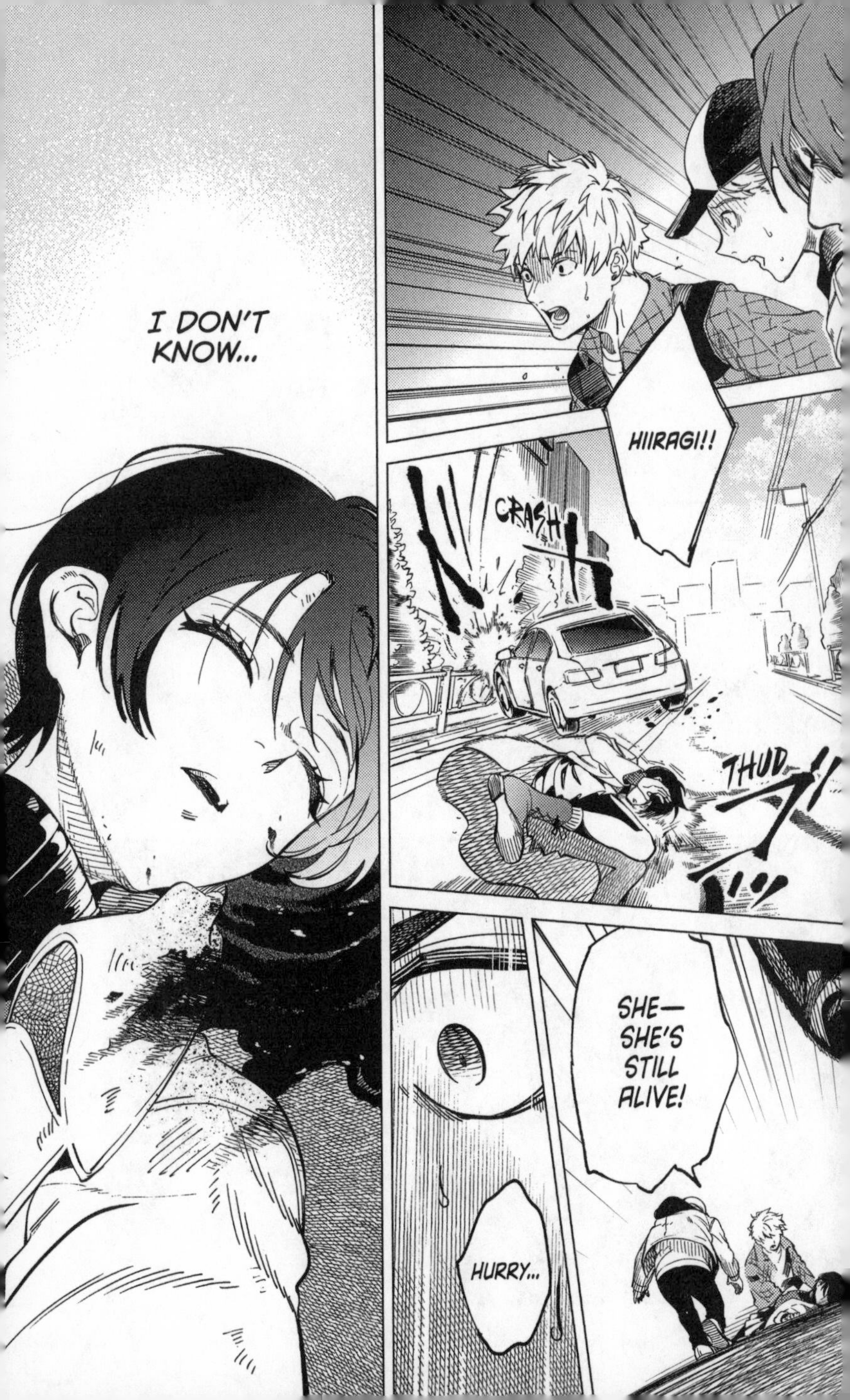
HIIRAGI!!
CRASH
THUD
SHE— SHE'S STILL ALIVE!
HURRY...
I DON'T KNOW...

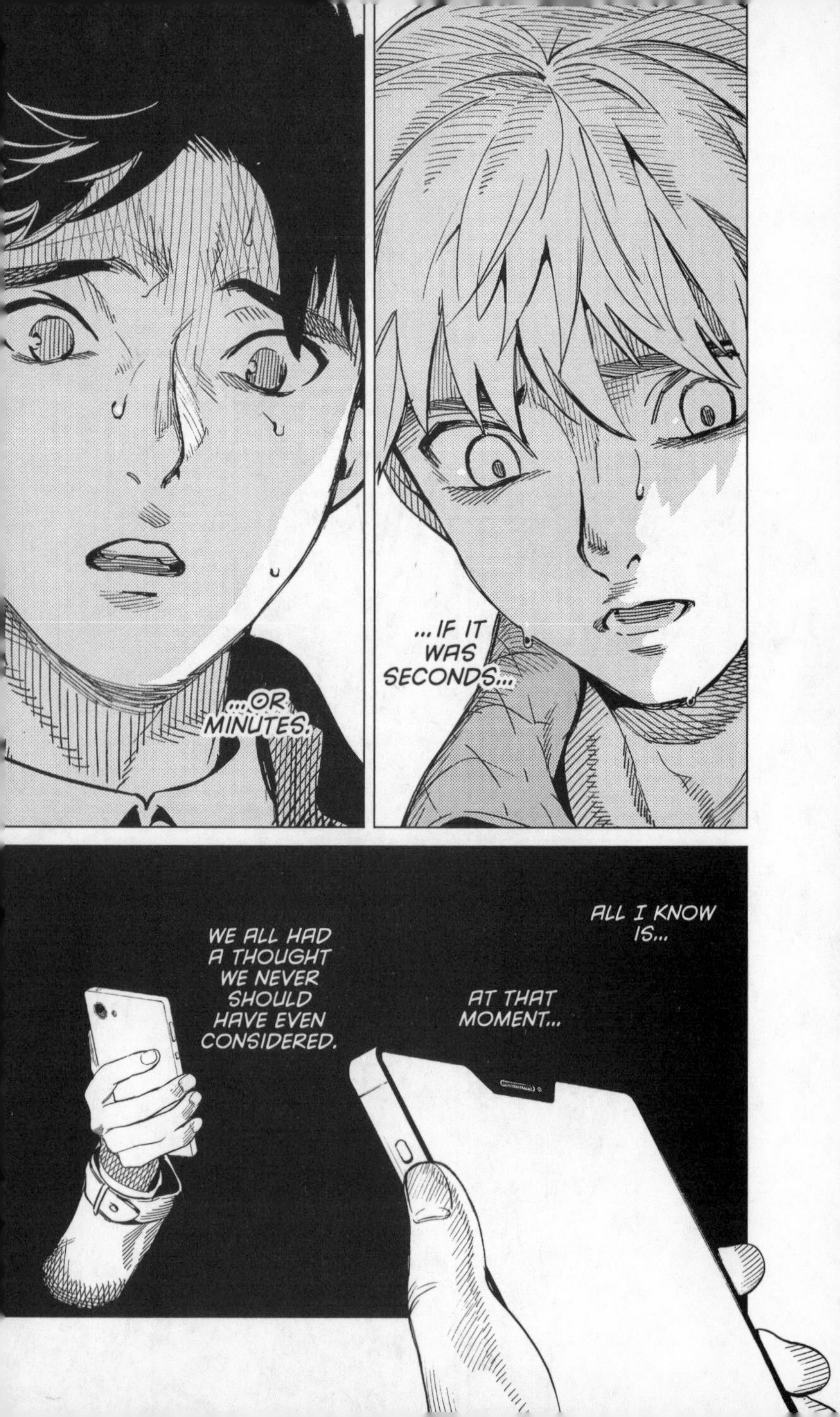
...IF IT WAS SECONDS...
...OR MINUTES.
ALL I KNOW IS...
AT THAT MOMENT...
WE ALL HAD A THOUGHT WE NEVER SHOULD HAVE EVEN CONSIDERED.

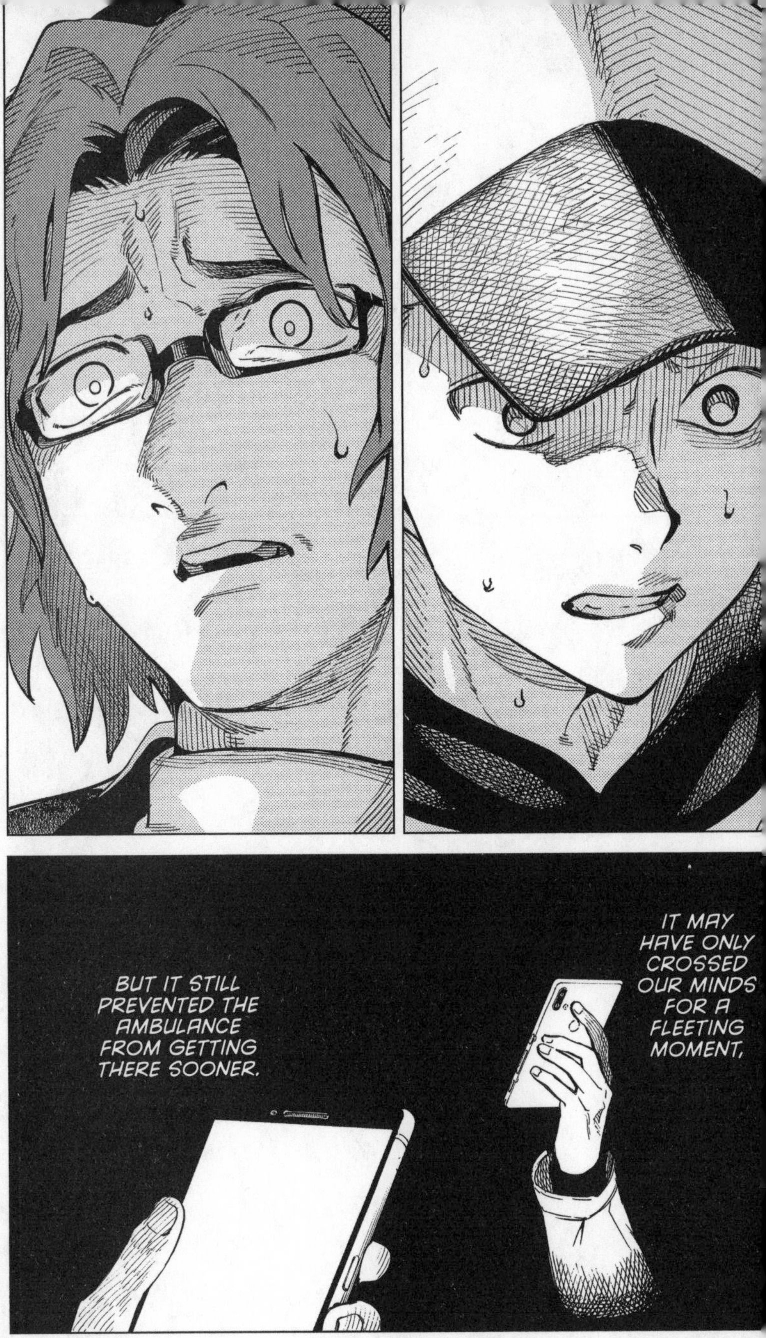
IT MAY HAVE ONLY CROSSED OUR MINDS FOR A FLEETING MOMENT,
BUT IT STILL PREVENTED THE AMBULANCE FROM GETTING THERE SOONER.

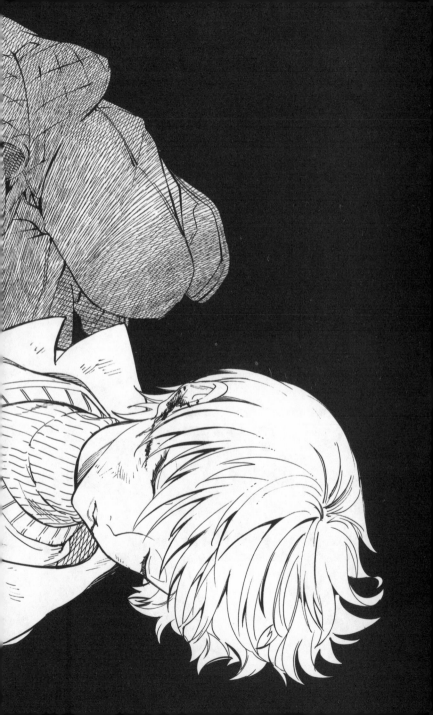

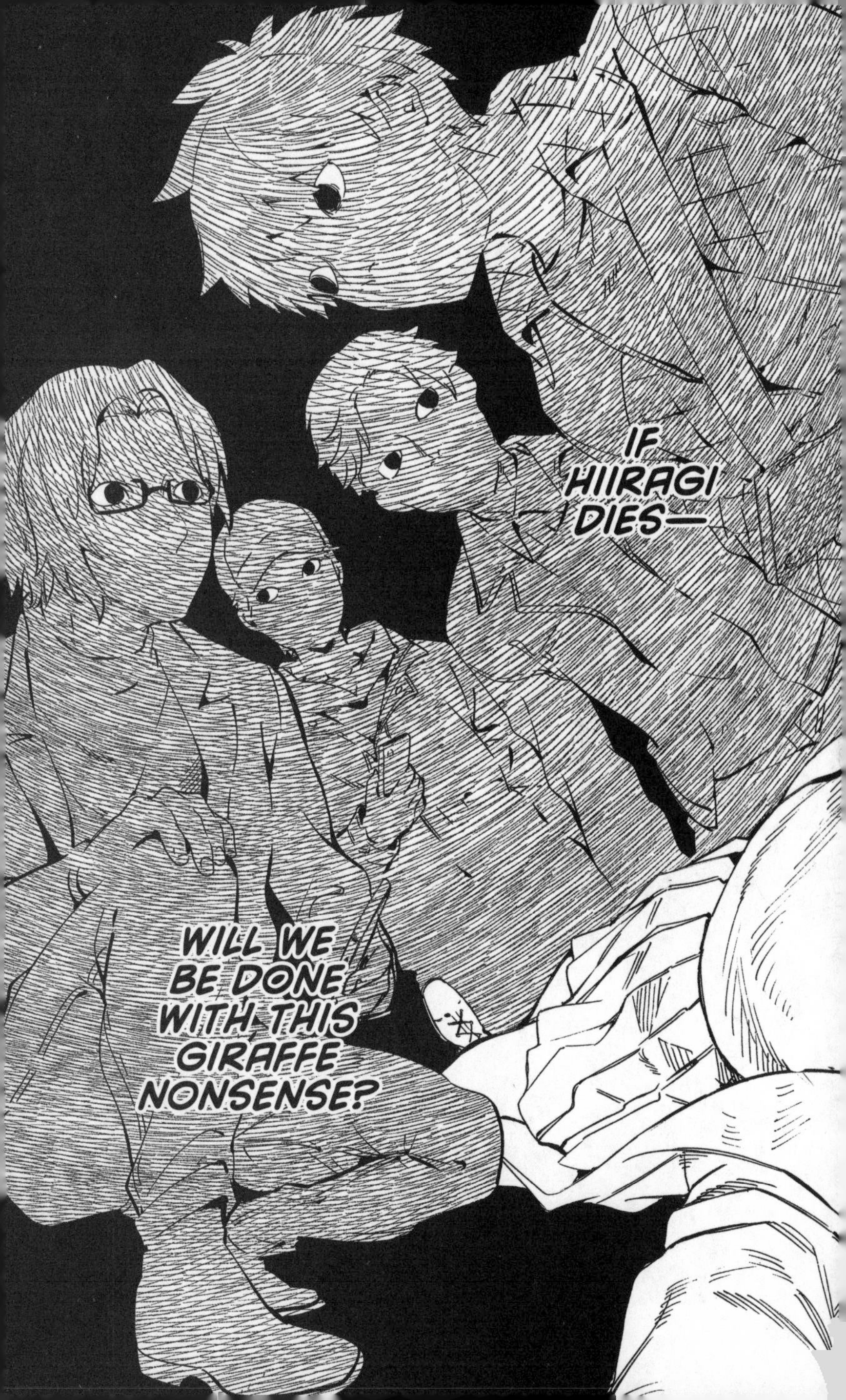
IF HIIRAGI DIES—
WILL WE BE DONE WITH THIS GIRAFFE NONSENSE?

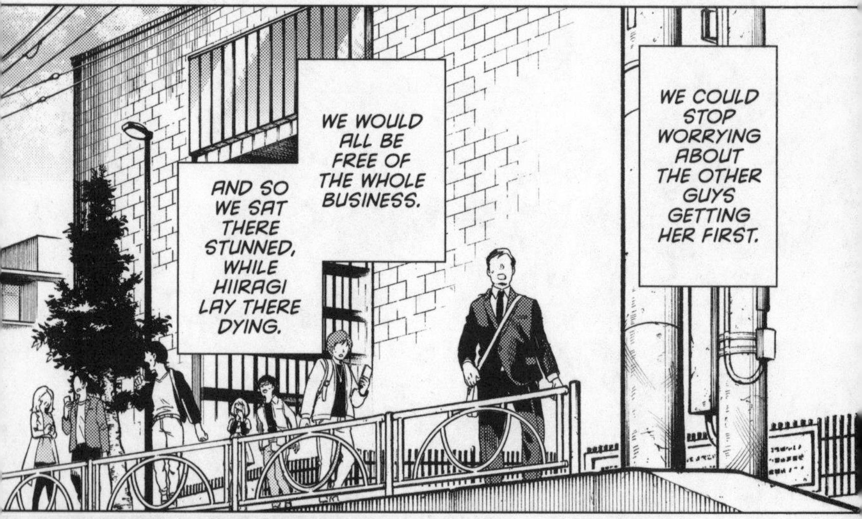
WE COULD STOP WORRYING ABOUT THE OTHER GUYS GETTING HER FIRST.
WE WOULD ALL BE FREE OF THE WHOLE BUSINESS.
AND SO WE SAT THERE STUNNED, WHILE HIIRAGI LAY THERE DYING.

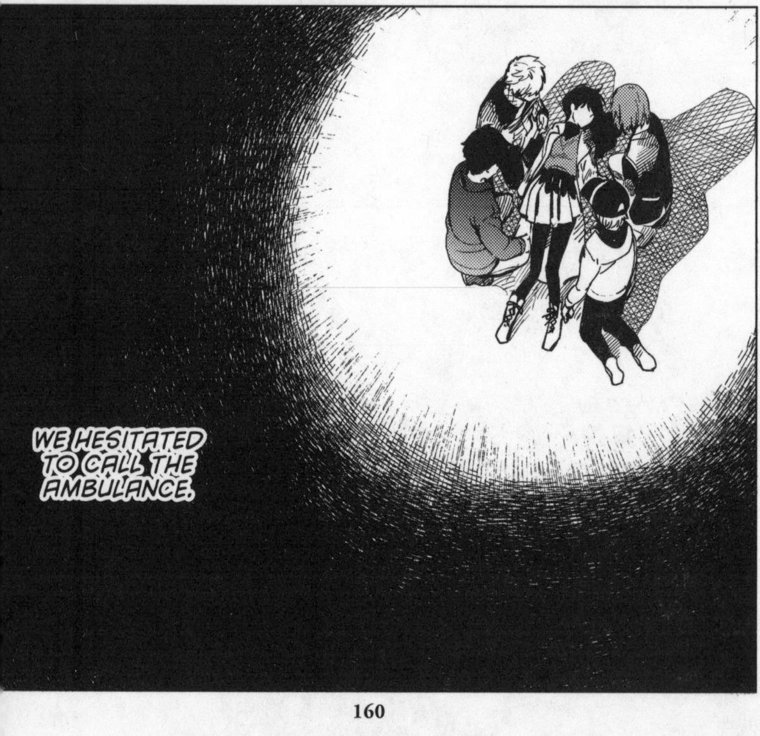
WE HESITATED TO CALL THE AMBULANCE.

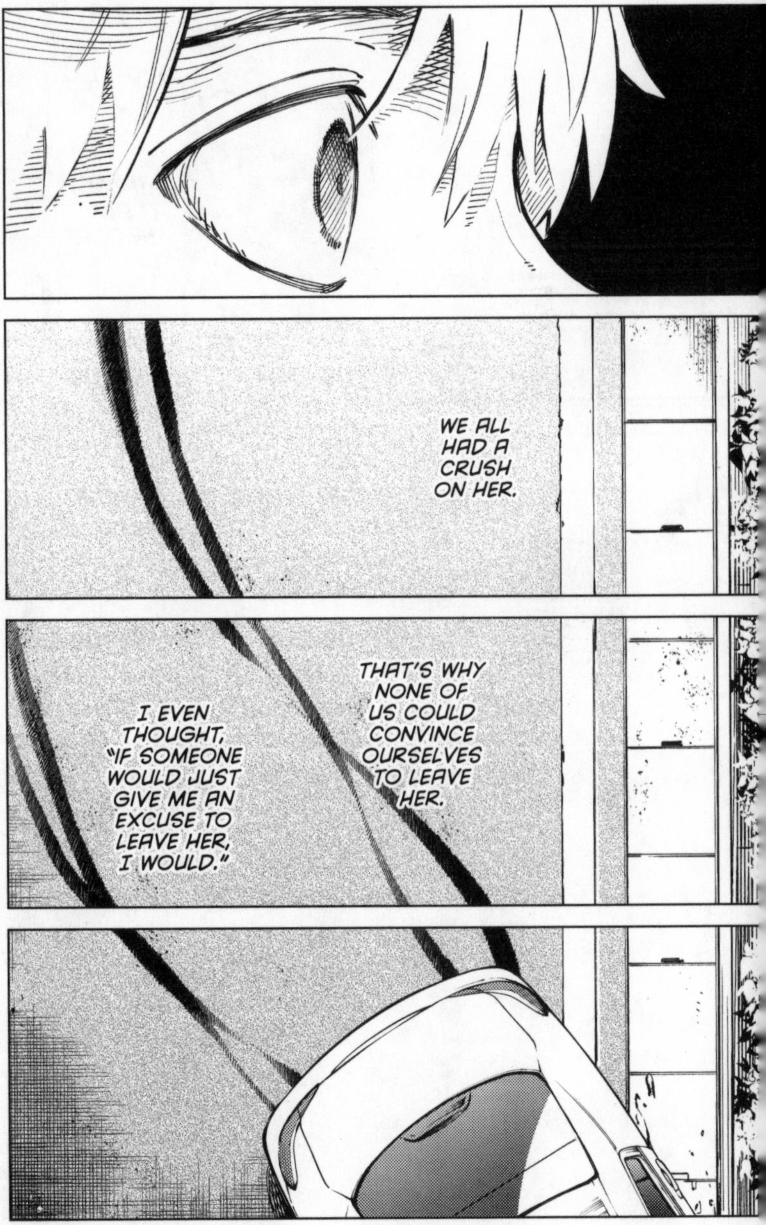
WE ALL HAD A CRUSH ON HER.
THAT'S WHY NONE OF US COULD CONVINCE OURSELVES TO LEAVE HER.
I EVEN THOUGHT, "IF SOMEONE WOULD JUST GIVE ME AN EXCUSE TO LEAVE HER, I WOULD."

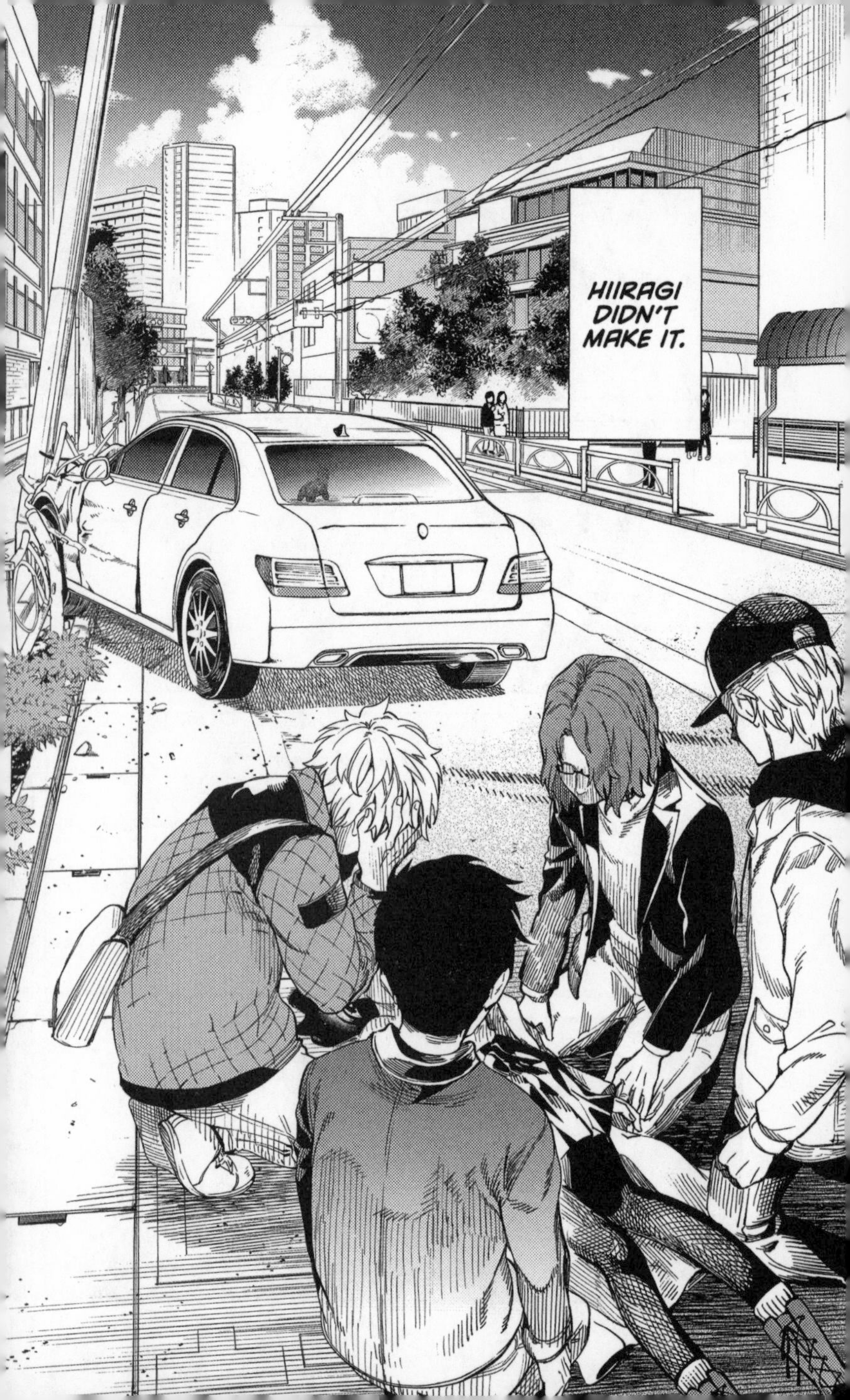
HIIRAGI DIDN'T MAKE IT.

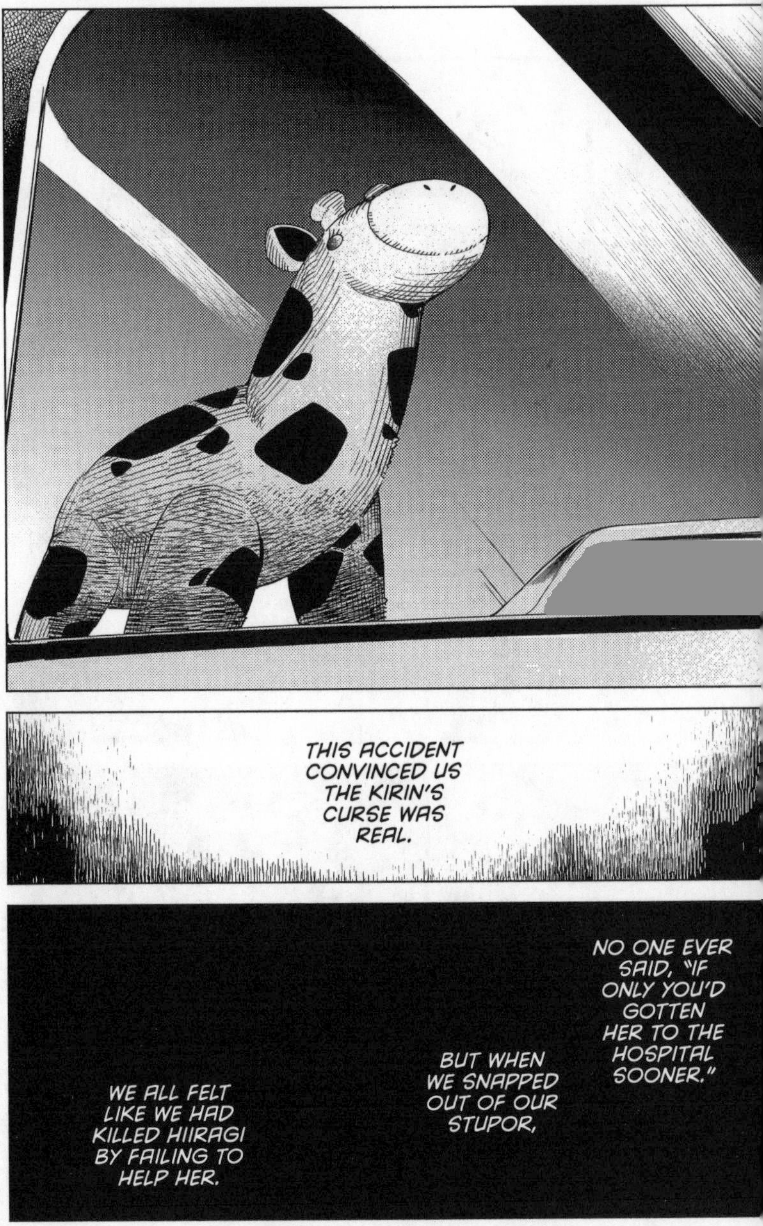
THIS ACCIDENT CONVINCED US THE KIRIN'S CURSE WAS REAL.
NO ONE EVER SAID, "IF ONLY YOU'D GOTTEN HER TO THE HOSPITAL SOONER."
BUT WHEN WE SNAPPED OUT OF OUR STUPOR,
WE ALL FELT LIKE WE HAD KILLED HIIRAGI BY FAILING TO HELP HER.

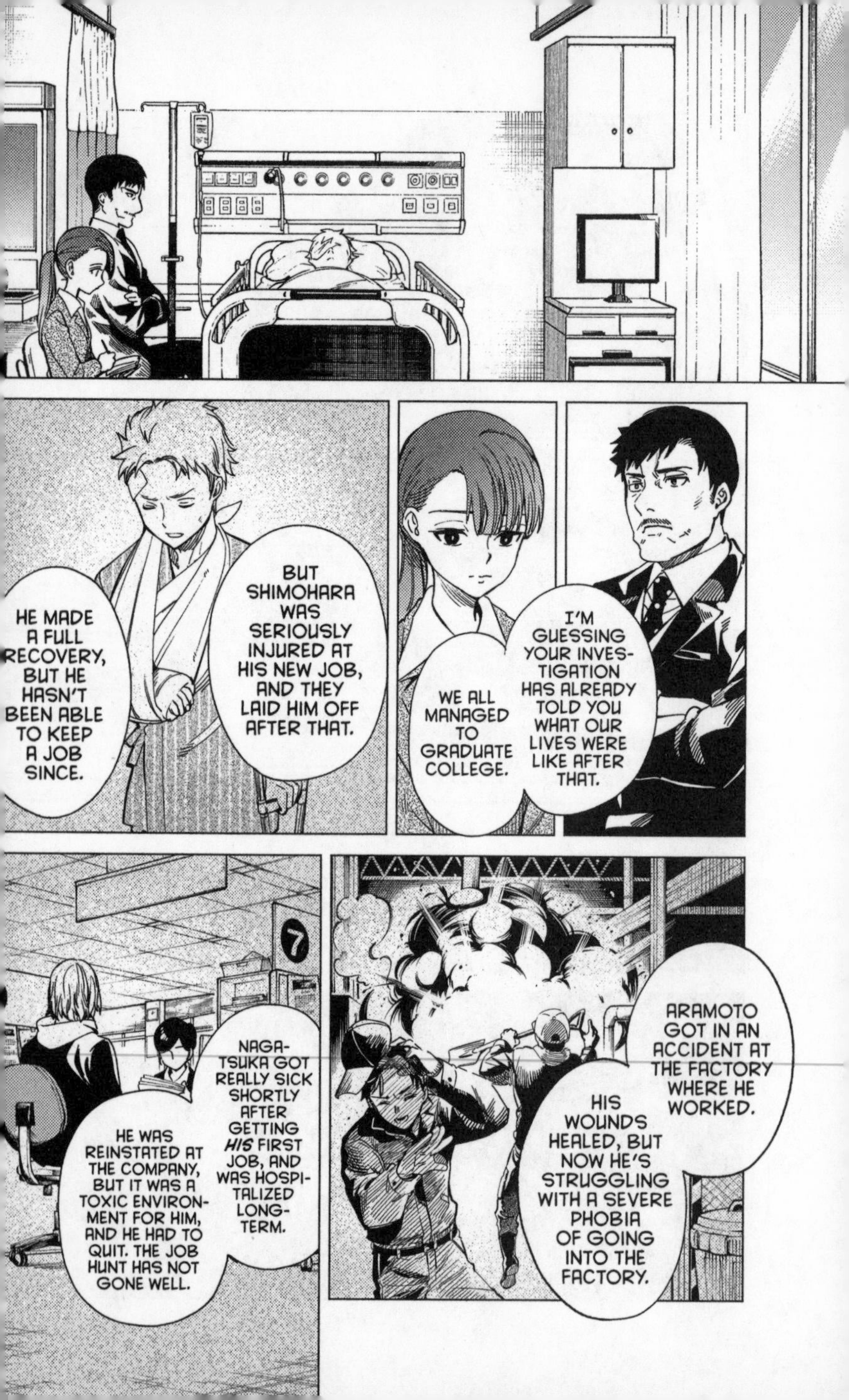
I'M GUESSING YOUR INVESTIGATION HAS ALREADY TOLD YOU WHAT OUR LIVES WERE LIKE AFTER THAT.
WE ALL MANAGED TO GRADUATE COLLEGE.
BUT SHIMOHARA WAS SERIOUSLY INJURED AT HIS NEW JOB, AND THEY LAID HIM OFF AFTER THAT.
HE MADE A FULL RECOVERY, BUT HE HASN'T BEEN ABLE TO KEEP A JOB SINCE.
ARAMOTO GOT IN AN ACCIDENT AT THE FACTORY WHERE HE WORKED.
HIS WOUNDS HEALED, BUT NOW HE'S STRUGGLING WITH A SEVERE PHOBIA OF GOING INTO THE FACTORY.
NAGATSUKA GOT REALLY SICK SHORTLY AFTER GETTING *HIS* FIRST JOB, AND WAS HOSPITALIZED LONG-TERM.
HE WAS REINSTATED AT THE COMPANY, BUT IT WAS A TOXIC ENVIRONMENT FOR HIM, AND HE HAD TO QUIT. THE JOB HUNT HAS NOT GONE WELL.

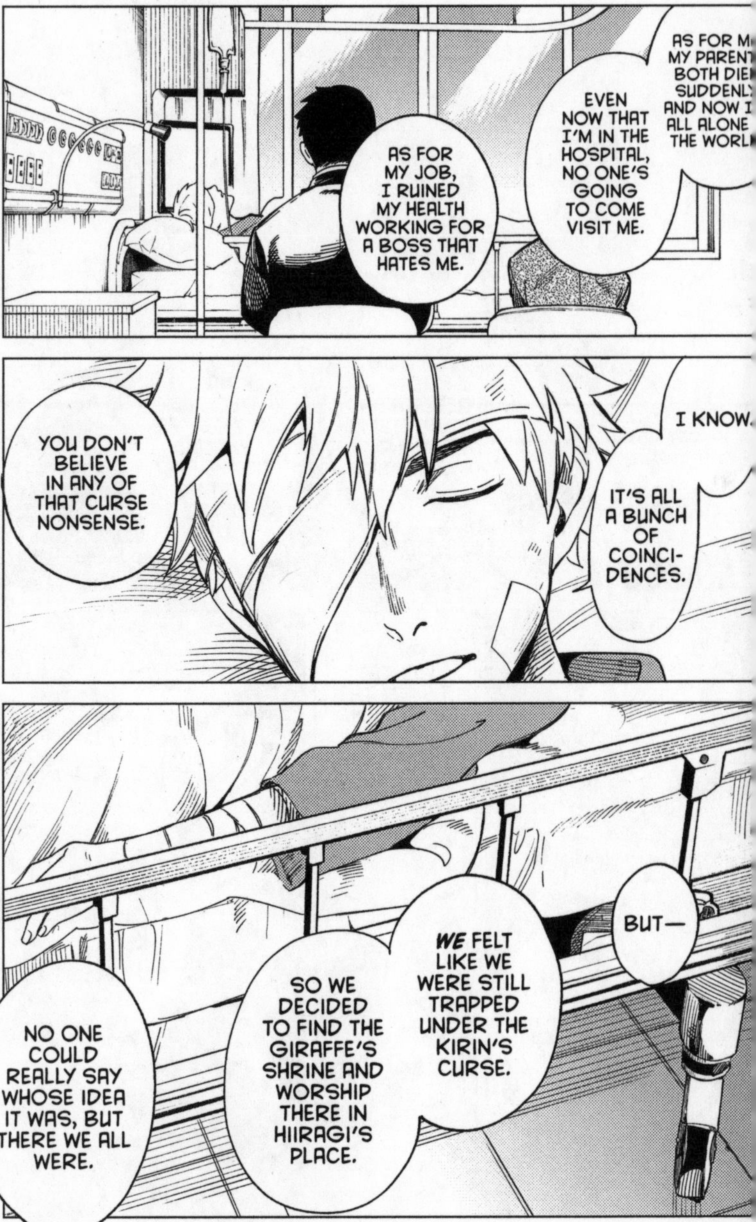
AS FOR M MY PARENT BOTH DIE SUDDENL AND NOW I ALL ALONE THE WORL
EVEN NOW THAT I'M IN THE HOSPITAL, NO ONE'S GOING TO COME VISIT ME.
AS FOR MY JOB, I RUINED MY HEALTH WORKING FOR A BOSS THAT HATES ME.
I KNOW.
IT'S ALL A BUNCH OF COINCI-DENCES.
YOU DON'T BELIEVE IN ANY OF THAT CURSE NONSENSE.
BUT—
*WE* FELT LIKE WE WERE STILL TRAPPED UNDER THE KIRIN'S CURSE.
SO WE DECIDED TO FIND THE GIRAFFE'S SHRINE AND WORSHIP THERE IN HIIRAGI'S PLACE.
NO ONE COULD REALLY SAY WHOSE IDEA IT WAS, BUT THERE WE ALL WERE.

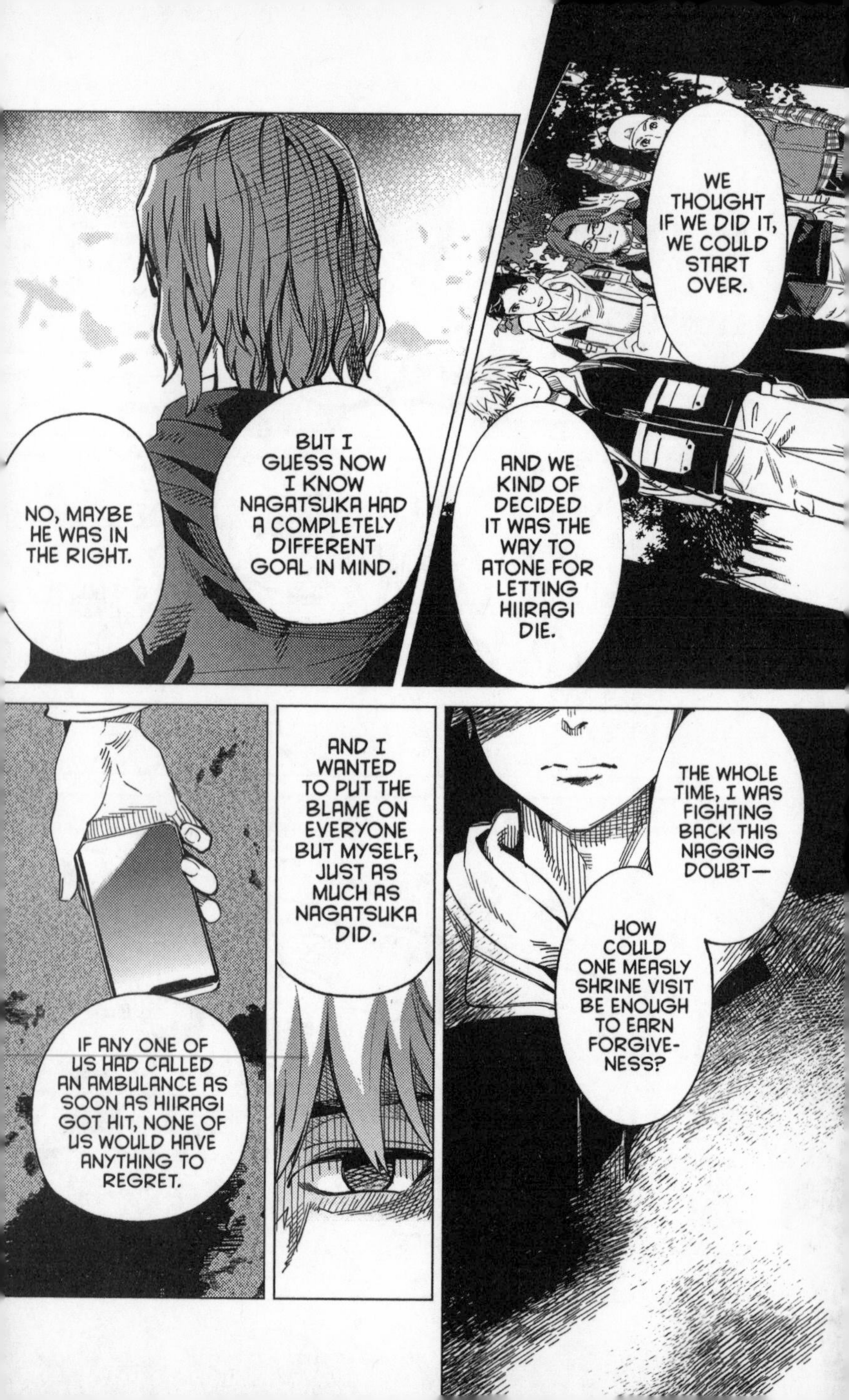
WE THOUGHT IF WE DID IT, WE COULD START OVER.
AND WE KIND OF DECIDED IT WAS THE WAY TO ATONE FOR LETTING HIIRAGI DIE.
BUT I GUESS NOW I KNOW NAGATSUKA HAD A COMPLETELY DIFFERENT GOAL IN MIND.
NO, MAYBE HE WAS IN THE RIGHT.
THE WHOLE TIME, I WAS FIGHTING BACK THIS NAGGING DOUBT—
HOW COULD ONE MEASLY SHRINE VISIT BE ENOUGH TO EARN FORGIVE-NESS?
AND I WANTED TO PUT THE BLAME ON EVERYONE BUT MYSELF, JUST AS MUCH AS NAGATSUKA DID.
IF ANY ONE OF US HAD CALLED AN AMBULANCE AS SOON AS HIIRAGI GOT HIT, NONE OF US WOULD HAVE ANYTHING TO REGRET.

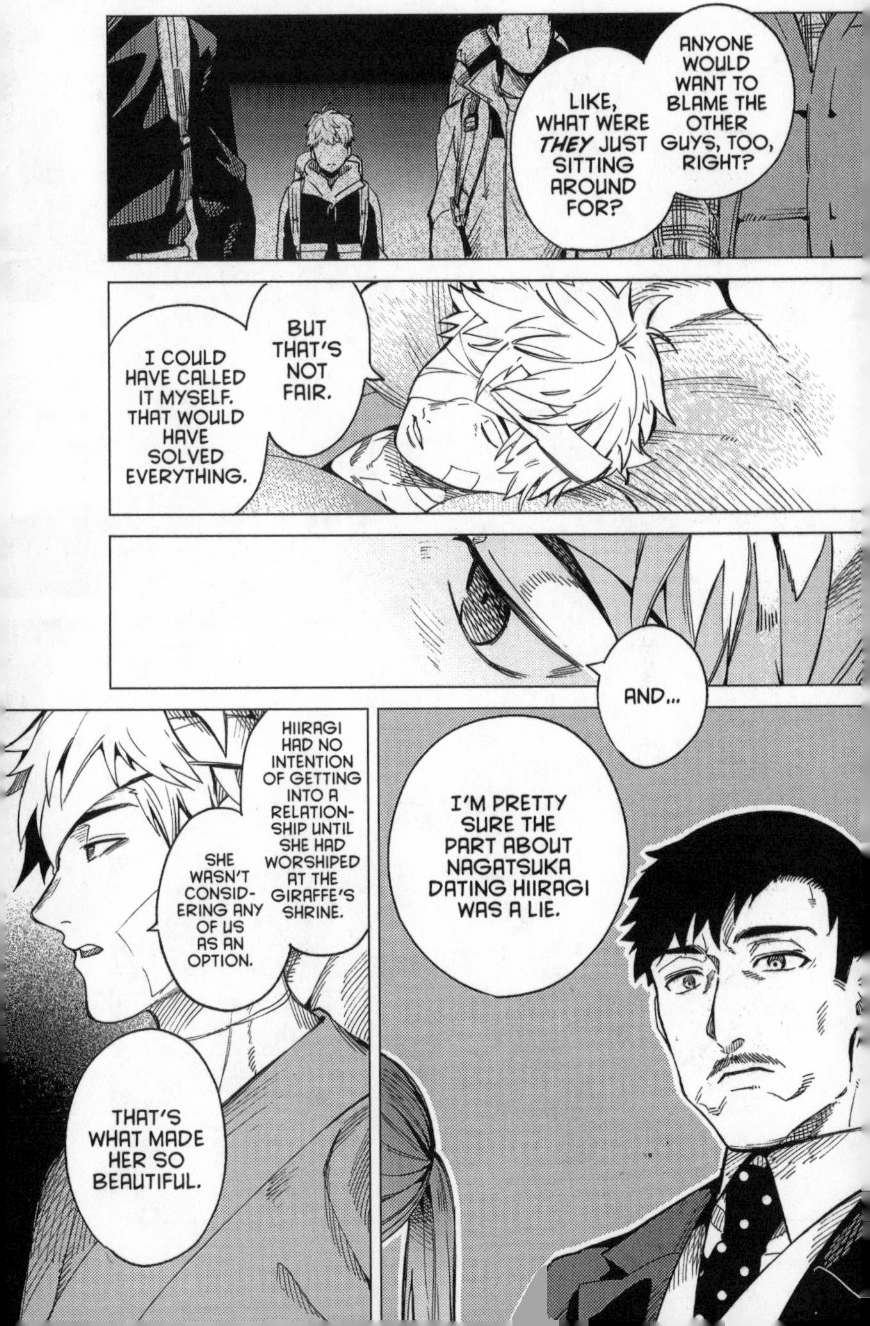
ANYONE WOULD WANT TO BLAME THE OTHER GUYS, TOO, RIGHT?
LIKE, WHAT WERE *THEY* JUST SITTING AROUND FOR?
BUT THAT'S NOT FAIR.
I COULD HAVE CALLED IT MYSELF. THAT WOULD HAVE SOLVED EVERYTHING.
AND...
I'M PRETTY SURE THE PART ABOUT NAGATSUKA DATING HIIRAGI WAS A LIE.
HIIRAGI HAD NO INTENTION OF GETTING INTO A RELATIONSHIP UNTIL SHE HAD WORSHIPED AT THE GIRAFFE'S SHRINE.
SHE WASN'T CONSIDERING ANY OF US AS AN OPTION.
THAT'S WHAT MADE HER SO BEAUTIFUL.

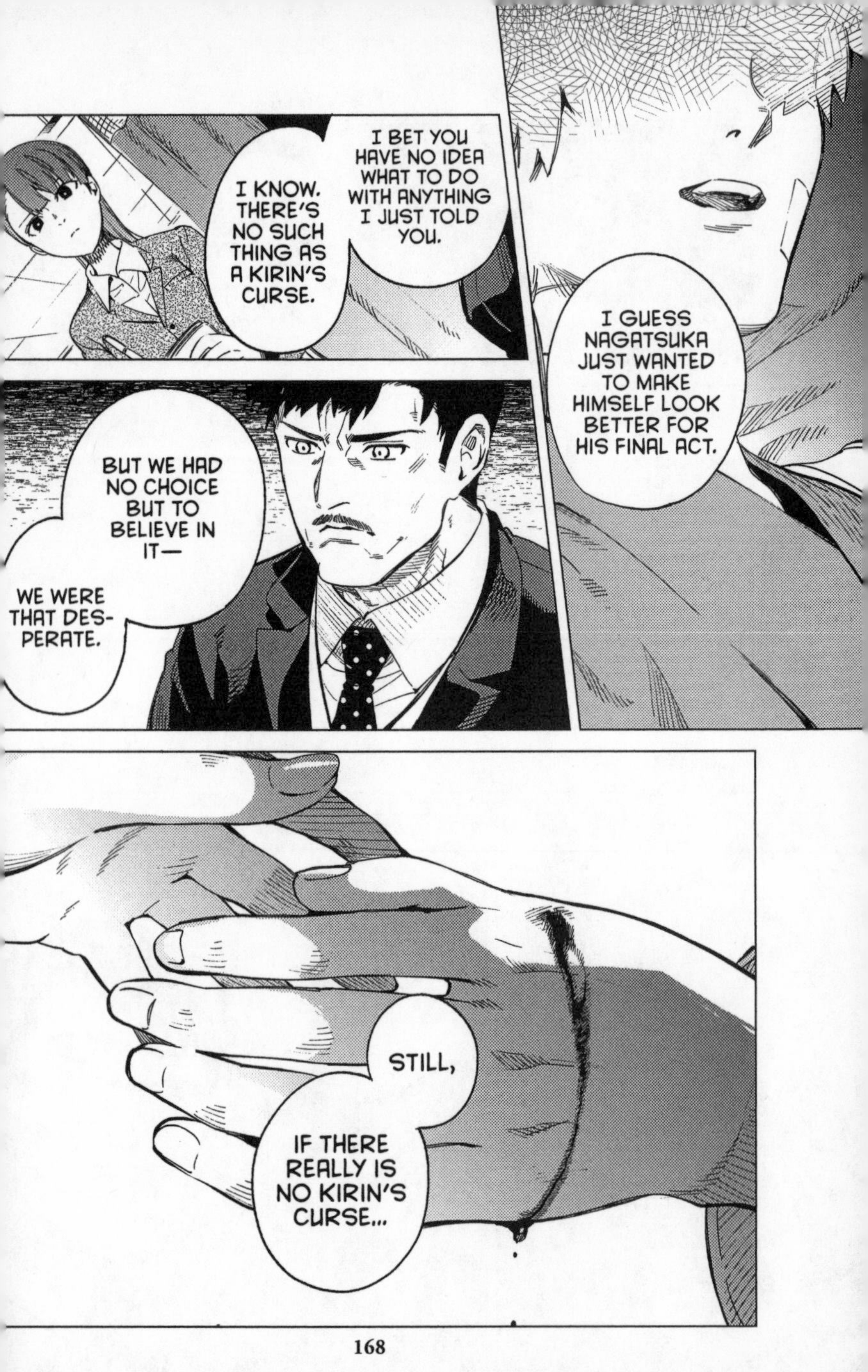
I GUESS NAGATSUKA JUST WANTED TO MAKE HIMSELF LOOK BETTER FOR HIS FINAL ACT.
I BET YOU HAVE NO IDEA WHAT TO DO WITH ANYTHING I JUST TOLD YOU.
I KNOW. THERE'S NO SUCH THING AS A KIRIN'S CURSE.
BUT WE HAD NO CHOICE BUT TO BELIEVE IN IT—
WE WERE THAT DES-PERATE.
STILL,
IF THERE REALLY IS NO KIRIN'S CURSE...

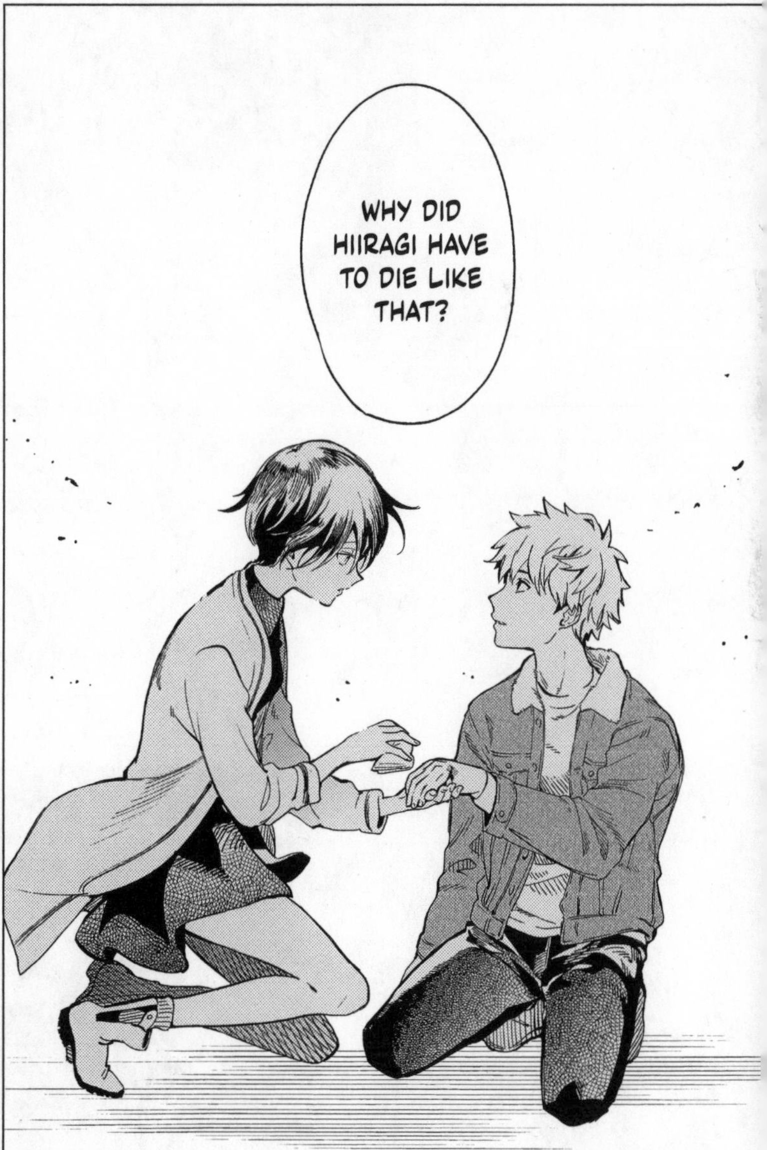
WHY DID HIIRAGI HAVE TO DIE LIKE THAT?

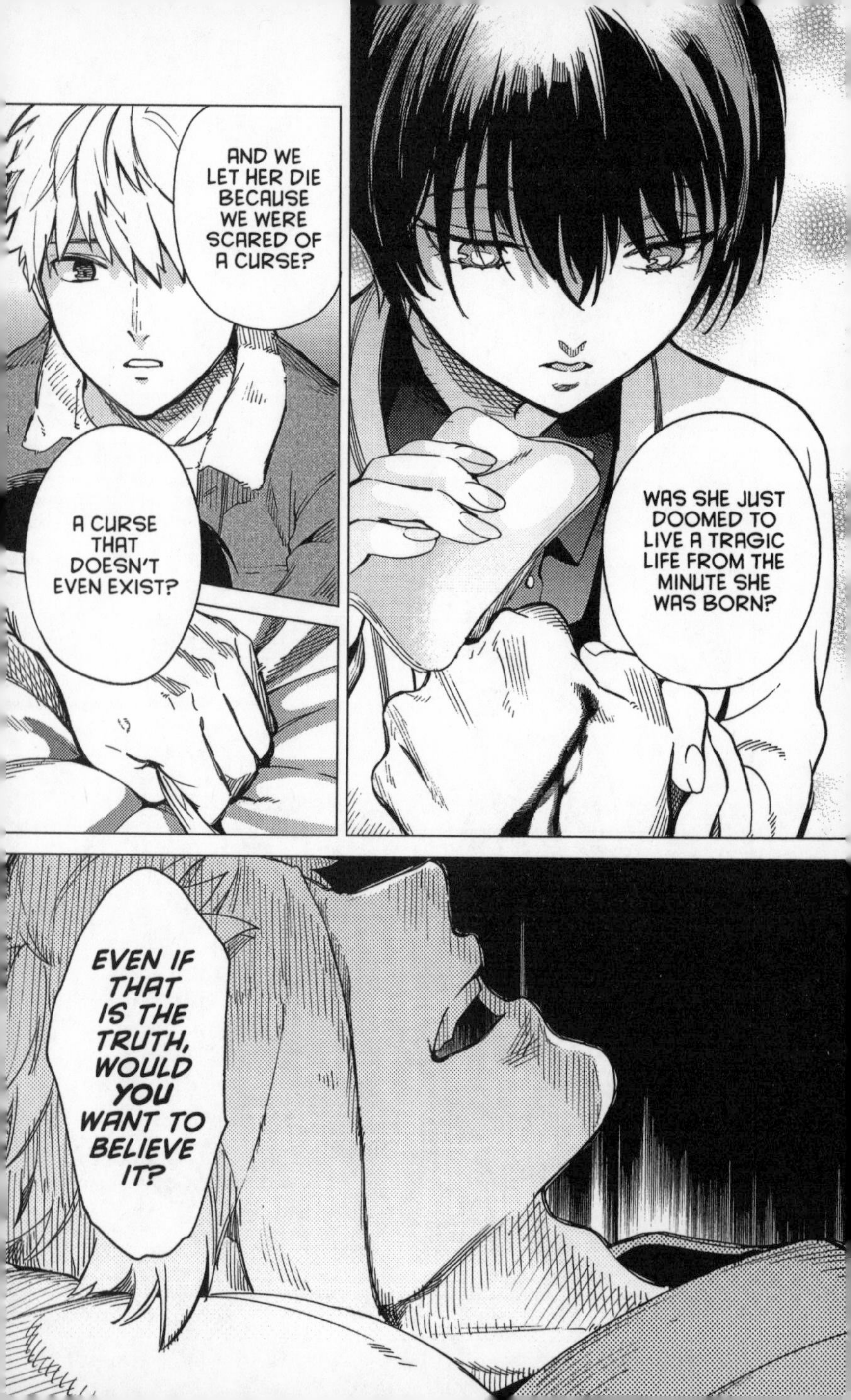
AND WE LET HER DIE BECAUSE WE WERE SCARED OF A CURSE?
WAS SHE JUST DOOMED TO LIVE A TRAGIC LIFE FROM THE MINUTE SHE WAS BORN?
A CURSE THAT DOESN'T EVEN EXIST?
EVEN IF THAT IS THE TRUTH, WOULD YOU WANT TO BELIEVE IT?

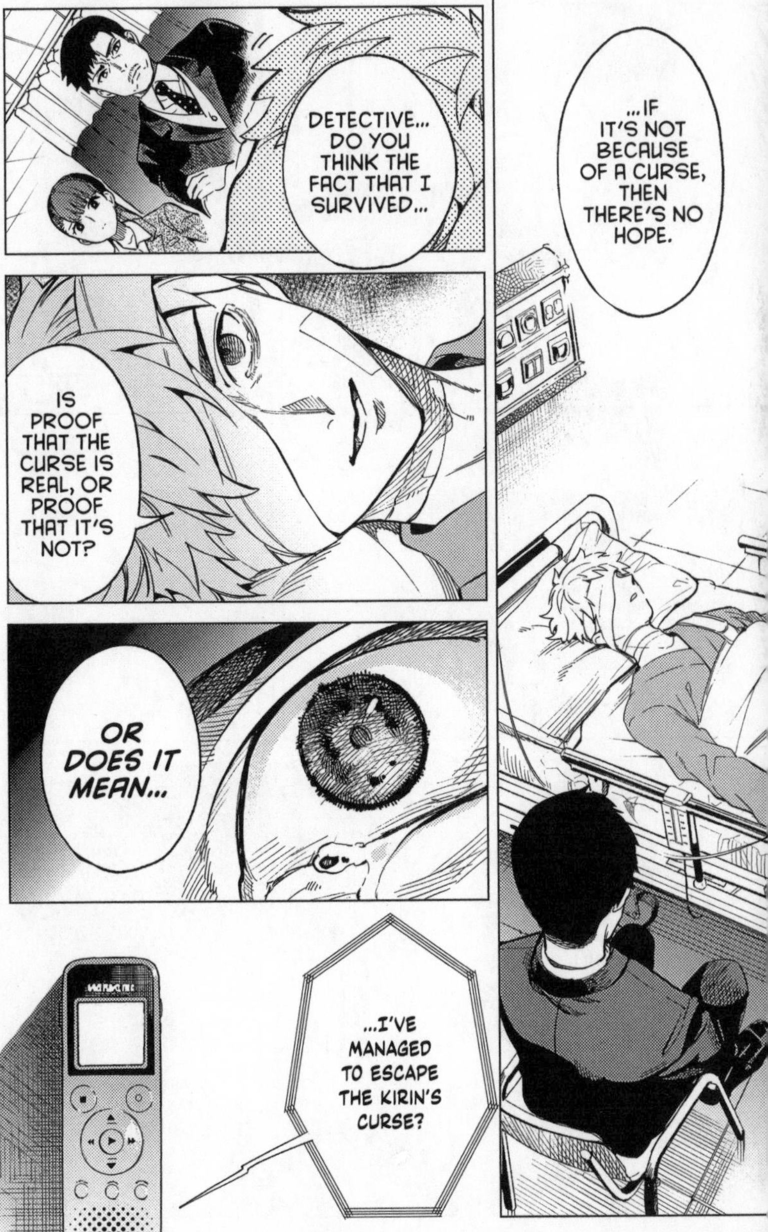
...IF IT'S NOT BECAUSE OF A CURSE, THEN THERE'S NO HOPE.
DETECTIVE... DO YOU THINK THE FACT THAT I SURVIVED...
IS PROOF THAT THE CURSE IS REAL, OR PROOF THAT IT'S NOT?
*OR DOES IT MEAN...*
...I'VE MANAGED TO ESCAPE THE KIRIN'S CURSE?

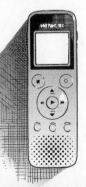

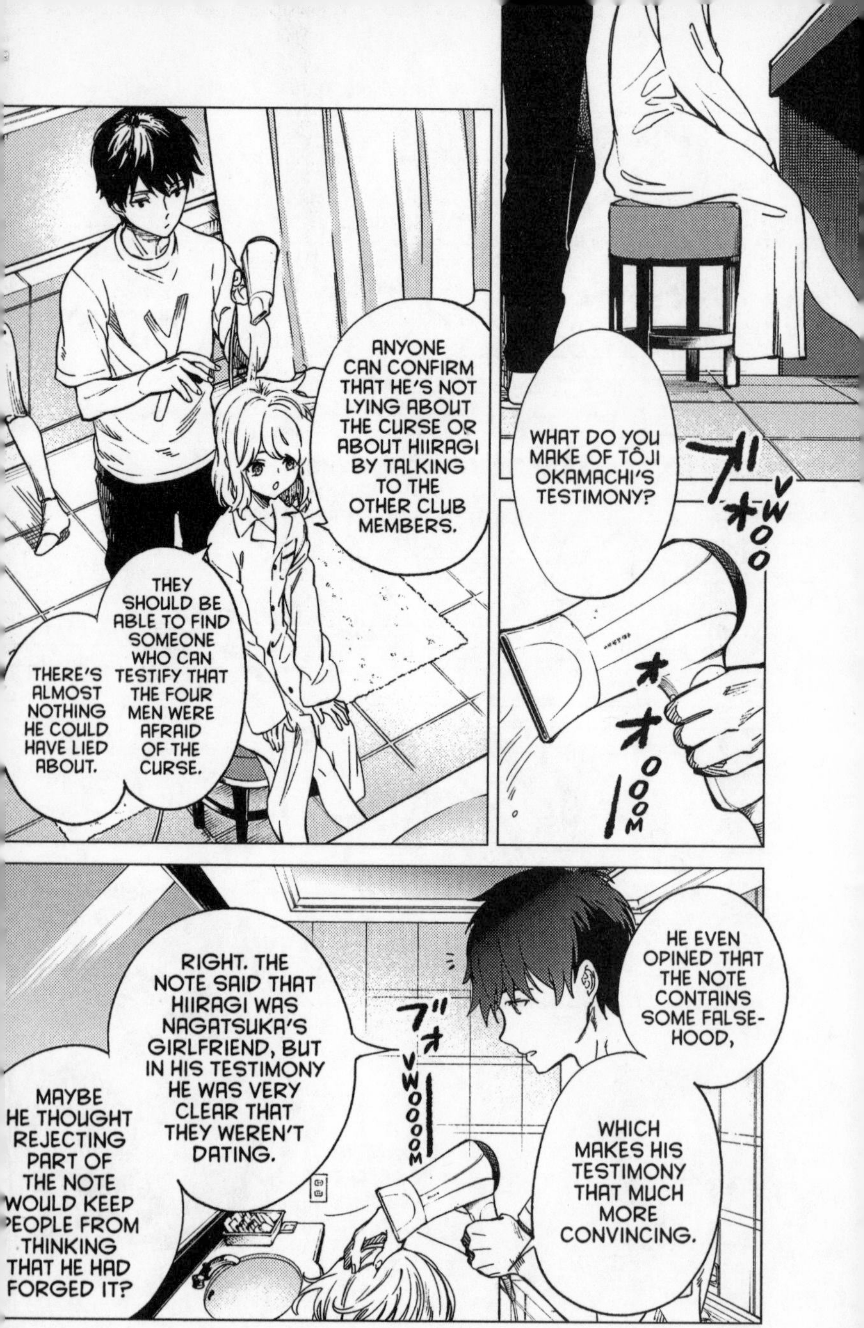
WHAT DO YOU MAKE OF TÔJI OKAMACHI'S TESTIMONY?
VWOOO
OOOM
ANYONE CAN CONFIRM THAT HE'S NOT LYING ABOUT THE CURSE OR ABOUT HIIRAGI BY TALKING TO THE OTHER CLUB MEMBERS.
THEY SHOULD BE ABLE TO FIND SOMEONE WHO CAN TESTIFY THAT THE FOUR MEN WERE AFRAID OF THE CURSE.
THERE'S ALMOST NOTHING HE COULD HAVE LIED ABOUT.
HE EVEN OPINED THAT THE NOTE CONTAINS SOME FALSE-HOOD,
WHICH MAKES HIS TESTIMONY THAT MUCH MORE CONVINCING.
VWOOOOOM
RIGHT. THE NOTE SAID THAT HIIRAGI WAS NAGATSUKA'S GIRLFRIEND, BUT IN HIS TESTIMONY HE WAS VERY CLEAR THAT THEY WEREN'T DATING.
MAYBE HE THOUGHT REJECTING PART OF THE NOTE WOULD KEEP PEOPLE FROM THINKING THAT HE HAD FORGED IT?

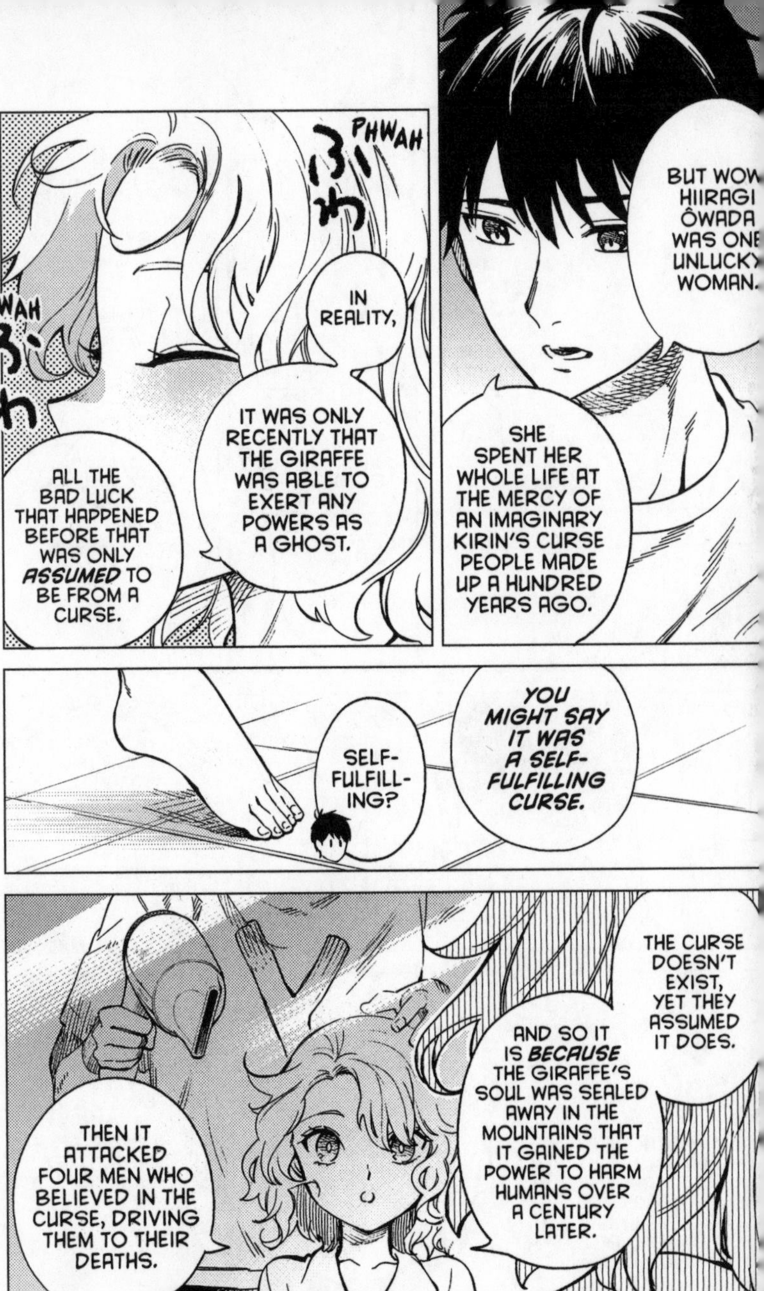
BUT WOW HIIRAGI ÔWADA WAS ONE UNLUCKY WOMAN.
SHE SPENT HER WHOLE LIFE AT THE MERCY OF AN IMAGINARY KIRIN'S CURSE PEOPLE MADE UP A HUNDRED YEARS AGO.
ふわ PHWAH
IN REALITY,
IT WAS ONLY RECENTLY THAT THE GIRAFFE WAS ABLE TO EXERT ANY POWERS AS A GHOST.
ふわ PHWAH
ALL THE BAD LUCK THAT HAPPENED BEFORE THAT WAS ONLY *ASSUMED* TO BE FROM A CURSE.
*YOU MIGHT SAY IT WAS A SELF-FULFILLING CURSE.*
SELF-FULFILLING?
THE CURSE DOESN'T EXIST, YET THEY ASSUMED IT DOES.
AND SO IT IS *BECAUSE* THE GIRAFFE'S SOUL WAS SEALED AWAY IN THE MOUNTAINS THAT IT GAINED THE POWER TO HARM HUMANS OVER A CENTURY LATER.
THEN IT ATTACKED FOUR MEN WHO BELIEVED IN THE CURSE, DRIVING THEM TO THEIR DEATHS.

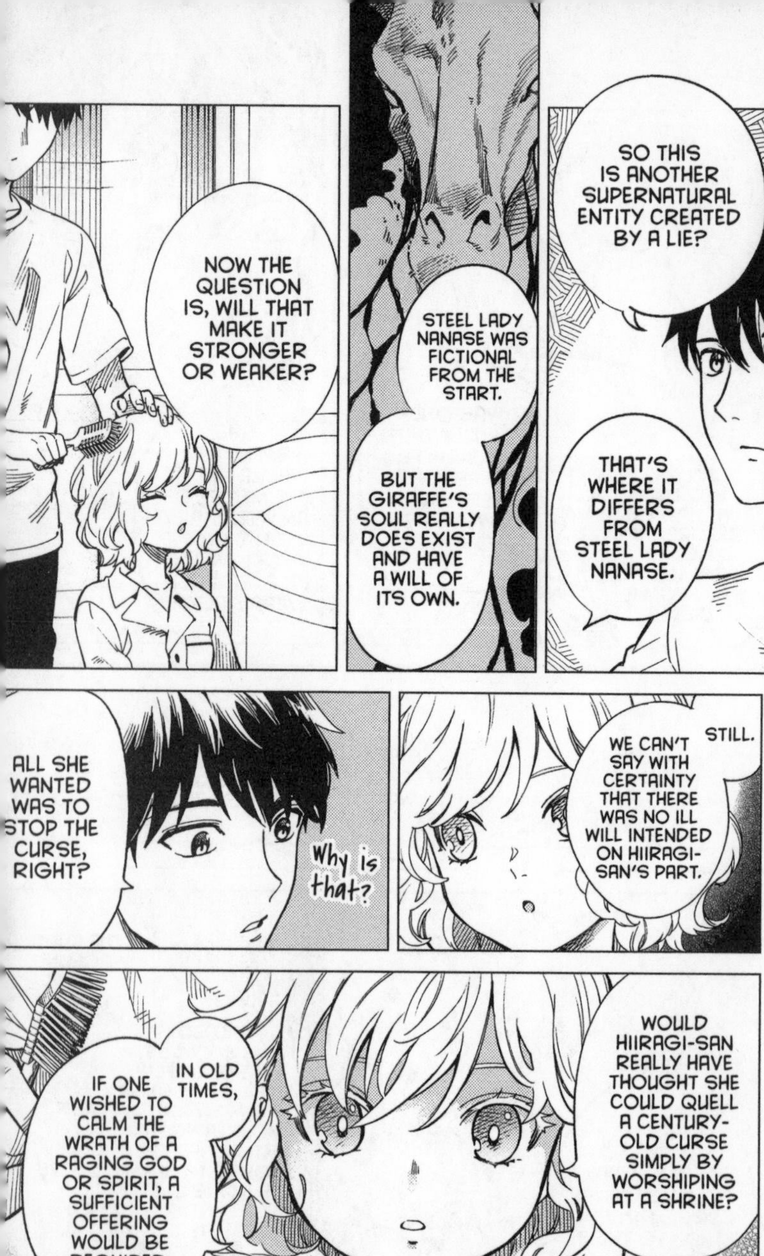
SO THIS IS ANOTHER SUPERNATURAL ENTITY CREATED BY A LIE?
THAT'S WHERE IT DIFFERS FROM STEEL LADY NANASE.
STEEL LADY NANASE WAS FICTIONAL FROM THE START.
BUT THE GIRAFFE'S SOUL REALLY DOES EXIST AND HAVE A WILL OF ITS OWN.
NOW THE QUESTION IS, WILL THAT MAKE IT STRONGER OR WEAKER?
STILL.
WE CAN'T SAY WITH CERTAINTY THAT THERE WAS NO ILL WILL INTENDED ON HIIRAGI-SAN'S PART.
Why is that?
ALL SHE WANTED WAS TO STOP THE CURSE, RIGHT?
WOULD HIIRAGI-SAN REALLY HAVE THOUGHT SHE COULD QUELL A CENTURY-OLD CURSE SIMPLY BY WORSHIPING AT A SHRINE?
IN OLD TIMES,
IF ONE WISHED TO CALM THE WRATH OF A RAGING GOD OR SPIRIT, A SUFFICIENT OFFERING WOULD BE REQUIRED.

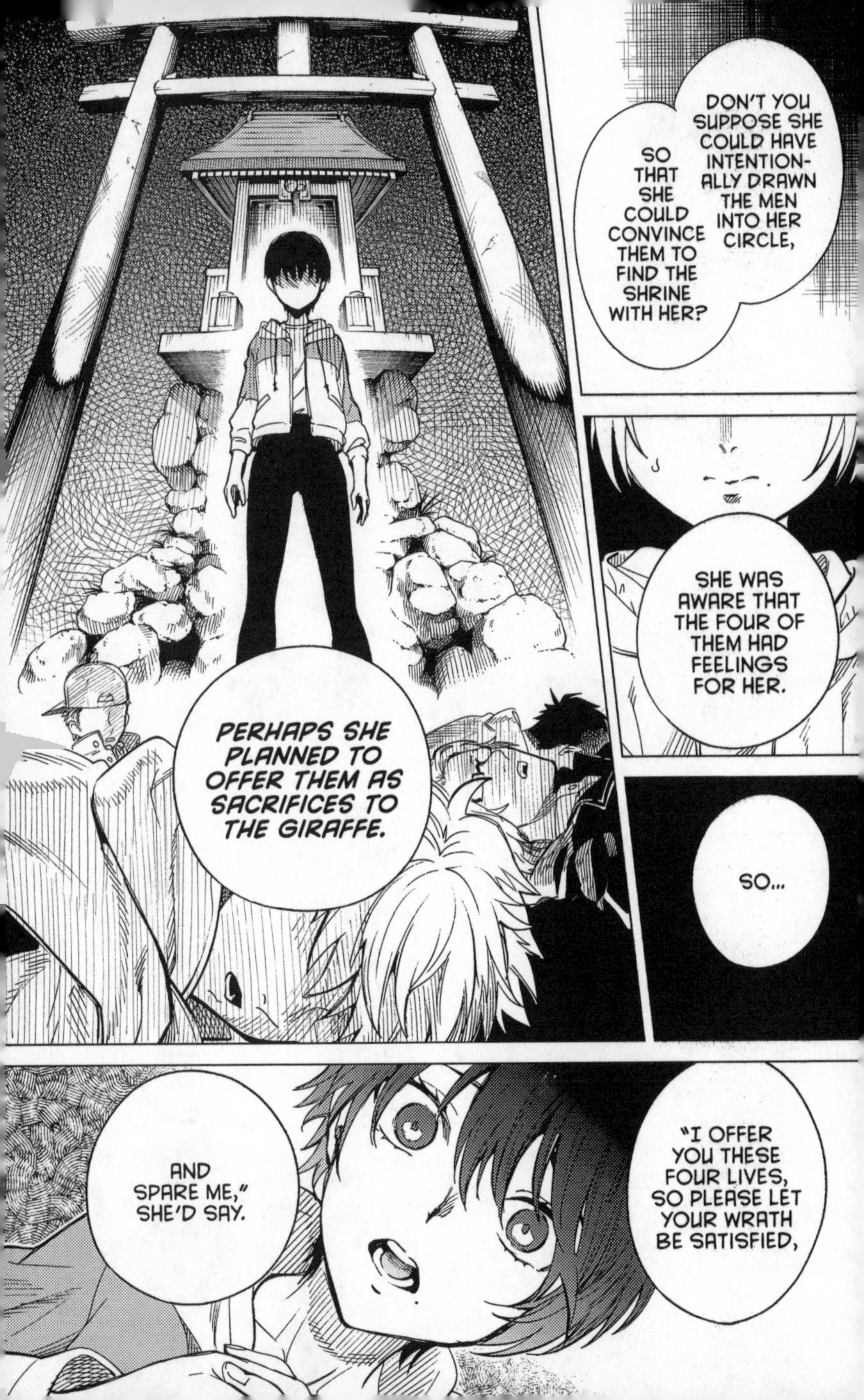
DON'T YOU SUPPOSE SHE COULD HAVE INTENTION-ALLY DRAWN THE MEN INTO HER CIRCLE,
SO THAT SHE COULD CONVINCE THEM TO FIND THE SHRINE WITH HER?
SHE WAS AWARE THAT THE FOUR OF THEM HAD FEELINGS FOR HER.
SO...
*PERHAPS SHE PLANNED TO OFFER THEM AS SACRIFICES TO THE GIRAFFE.*
"I OFFER YOU THESE FOUR LIVES, SO PLEASE LET YOUR WRATH BE SATISFIED,
AND SPARE ME," SHE'D SAY.

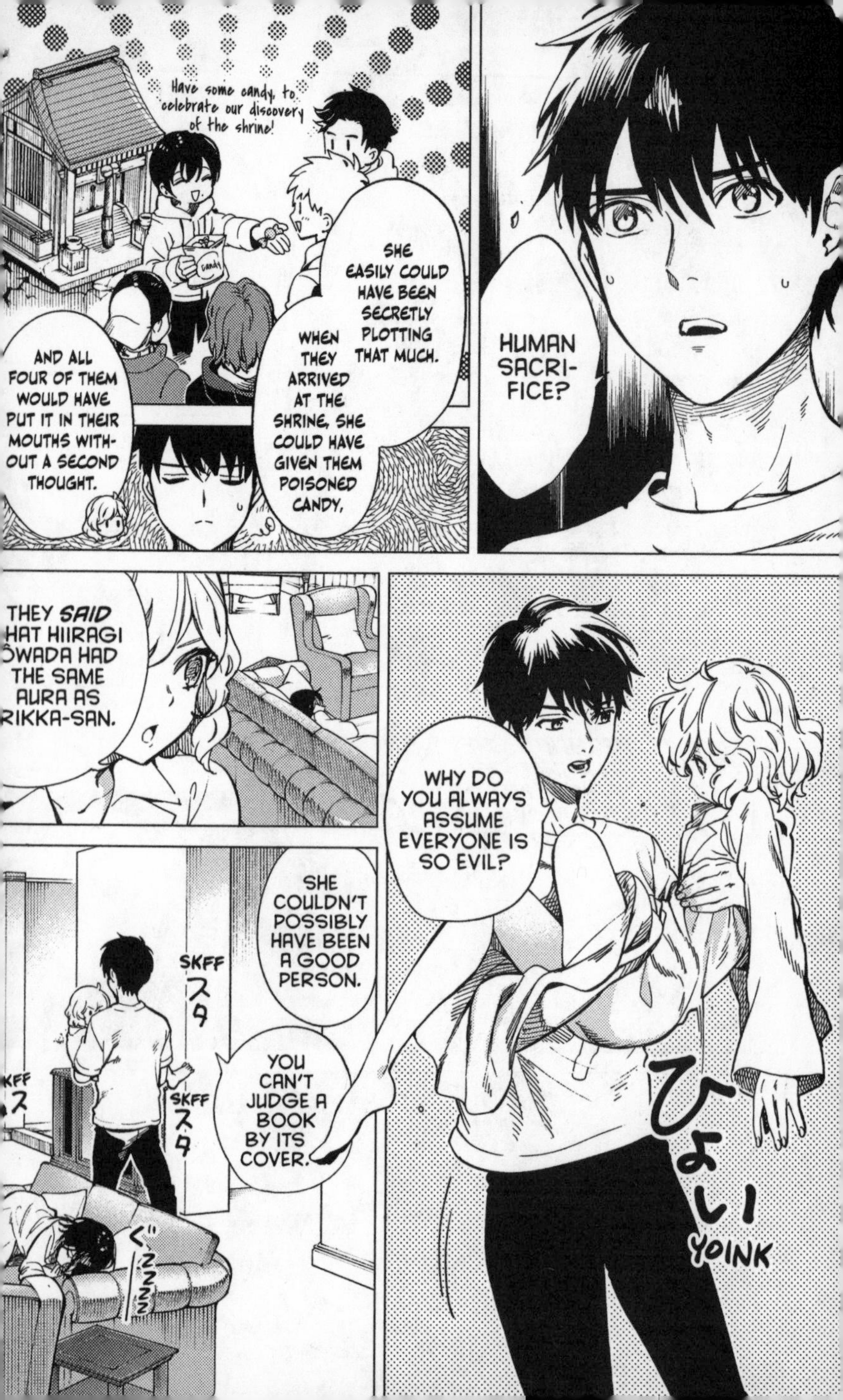
HUMAN SACRIFICE?
Have some candy, to celebrate our discovery of the shrine!
SHE EASILY COULD HAVE BEEN SECRETLY PLOTTING THAT MUCH.
WHEN THEY ARRIVED AT THE SHRINE, SHE COULD HAVE GIVEN THEM POISONED CANDY,
AND ALL FOUR OF THEM WOULD HAVE PUT IT IN THEIR MOUTHS WITHOUT A SECOND THOUGHT.
WHY DO YOU ALWAYS ASSUME EVERYONE IS SO EVIL?
ひょい
YOINK
THEY SAID HAT HIIRAGI ÔWADA HAD THE SAME AURA AS RIKKA-SAN.
SHE COULDN'T POSSIBLY HAVE BEEN A GOOD PERSON.
YOU CAN'T JUDGE A BOOK BY ITS COVER.
SKFF スタ
SKFF スタ
KFF ス
ぐ
ZZZZ

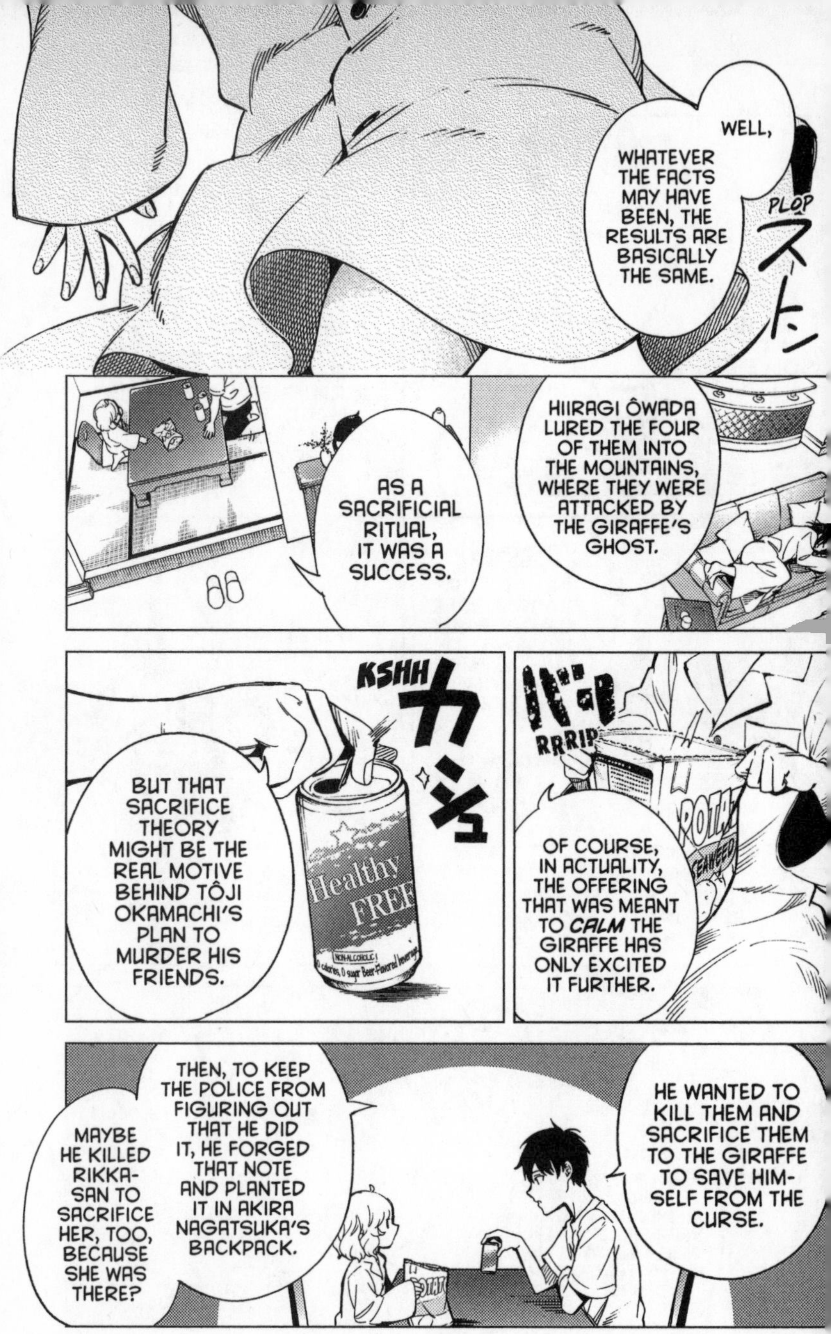
WELL, WHATEVER THE FACTS MAY HAVE BEEN, THE RESULTS ARE BASICALLY THE SAME.
PLOP
ストン
HIIRAGI ÔWADA LURED THE FOUR OF THEM INTO THE MOUNTAINS, WHERE THEY WERE ATTACKED BY THE GIRAFFE'S GHOST.
AS A SACRIFICIAL RITUAL, IT WAS A SUCCESS.
バリ
RRRIP
SEAWEED
OF COURSE, IN ACTUALITY, THE OFFERING THAT WAS MEANT TO *CALM* THE GIRAFFE HAS ONLY EXCITED IT FURTHER.
KSHH
カシュ
Healthy FREE
NON-ALCOHOLIC
0 calories, 0 sugar Beer-Flavored beverage
BUT THAT SACRIFICE THEORY MIGHT BE THE REAL MOTIVE BEHIND TÔJI OKAMACHI'S PLAN TO MURDER HIS FRIENDS.
HE WANTED TO KILL THEM AND SACRIFICE THEM TO THE GIRAFFE TO SAVE HIMSELF FROM THE CURSE.
THEN, TO KEEP THE POLICE FROM FIGURING OUT THAT HE DID IT, HE FORGED THAT NOTE AND PLANTED IT IN AKIRA NAGATSUKA'S BACKPACK.
MAYBE HE KILLED RIKKA-SAN TO SACRIFICE HER, TOO, BECAUSE SHE WAS THERE?

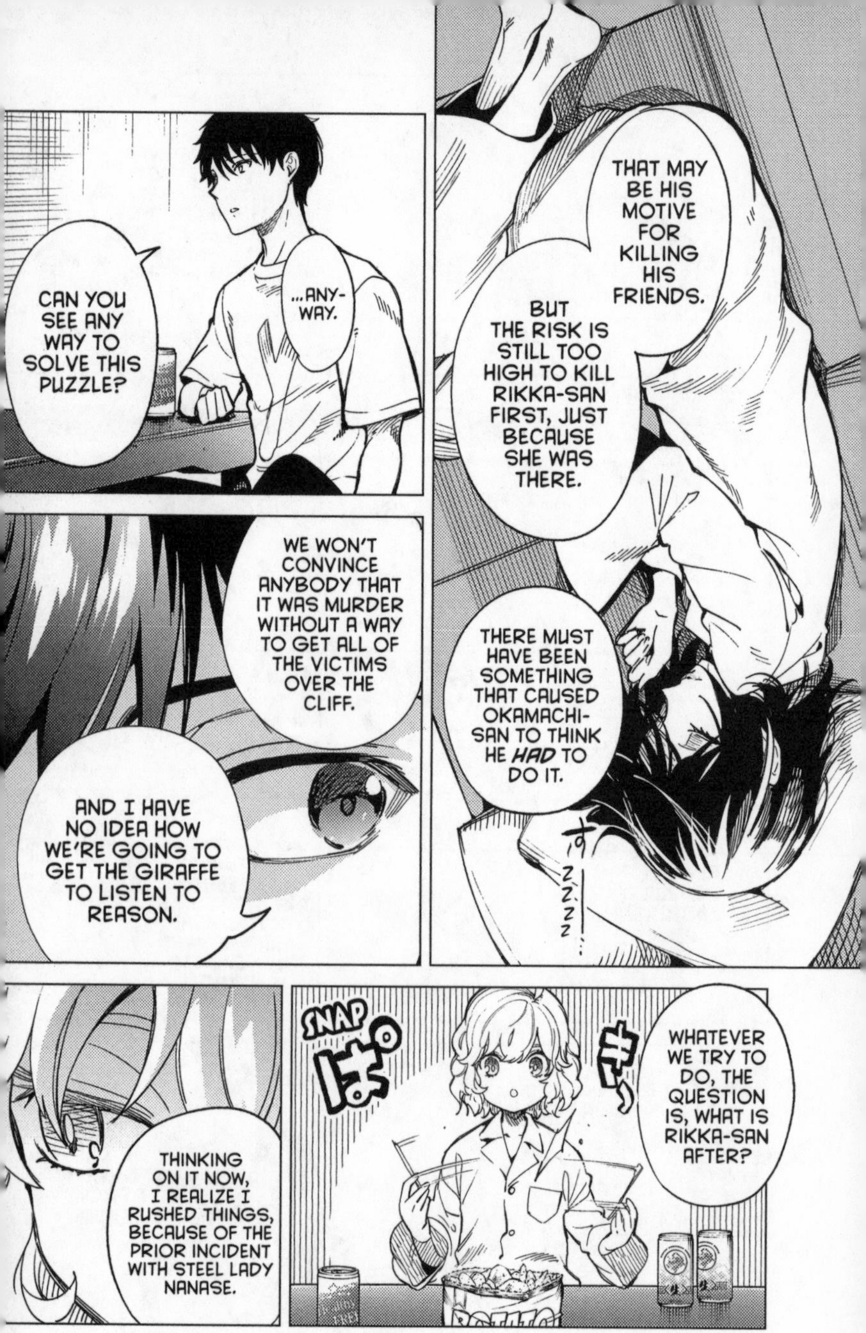
THAT MAY BE HIS MOTIVE FOR KILLING HIS FRIENDS.
BUT THE RISK IS STILL TOO HIGH TO KILL RIKKA-SAN FIRST, JUST BECAUSE SHE WAS THERE.
THERE MUST HAVE BEEN SOMETHING THAT CAUSED OKAMACHI-SAN TO THINK HE *HAD* TO DO IT.
す
ZZZZ...
...ANY-WAY.
CAN YOU SEE ANY WAY TO SOLVE THIS PUZZLE?
WE WON'T CONVINCE ANYBODY THAT IT WAS MURDER WITHOUT A WAY TO GET ALL OF THE VICTIMS OVER THE CLIFF.
AND I HAVE NO IDEA HOW WE'RE GOING TO GET THE GIRAFFE TO LISTEN TO REASON.
WHATEVER WE TRY TO DO, THE QUESTION IS, WHAT IS RIKKA-SAN AFTER?
き
SNAP
ぱ
THINKING ON IT NOW, I REALIZE I RUSHED THINGS, BECAUSE OF THE PRIOR INCIDENT WITH STEEL LADY NANASE.

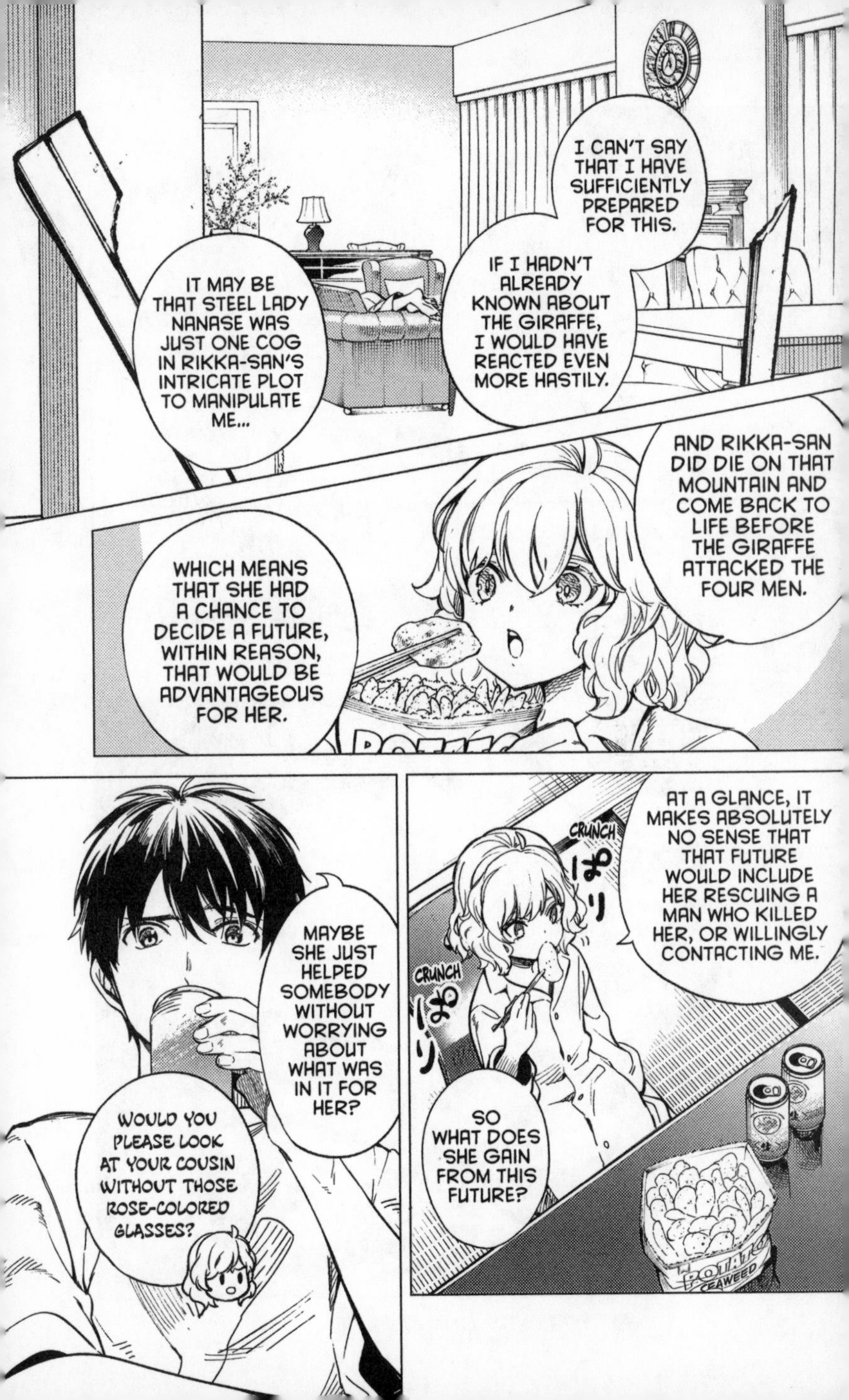

I CAN'T SAY THAT I HAVE SUFFICIENTLY PREPARED FOR THIS.
IF I HADN'T ALREADY KNOWN ABOUT THE GIRAFFE, I WOULD HAVE REACTED EVEN MORE HASTILY.
IT MAY BE THAT STEEL LADY NANASE WAS JUST ONE COG IN RIKKA-SAN'S INTRICATE PLOT TO MANIPULATE ME...
AND RIKKA-SAN DID DIE ON THAT MOUNTAIN AND COME BACK TO LIFE BEFORE THE GIRAFFE ATTACKED THE FOUR MEN.
WHICH MEANS THAT SHE HAD A CHANCE TO DECIDE A FUTURE, WITHIN REASON, THAT WOULD BE ADVANTAGEOUS FOR HER.
AT A GLANCE, IT MAKES ABSOLUTELY NO SENSE THAT THAT FUTURE WOULD INCLUDE HER RESCUING A MAN WHO KILLED HER, OR WILLINGLY CONTACTING ME.
CRUNCH
ぱり
CRUNCH
ぱり
SO WHAT DOES SHE GAIN FROM THIS FUTURE?
POTATO SEAWEED
MAYBE SHE JUST HELPED SOMEBODY WITHOUT WORRYING ABOUT WHAT WAS IN IT FOR HER?
WOULD YOU PLEASE LOOK AT YOUR COUSIN WITHOUT THOSE ROSE-COLORED GLASSES?

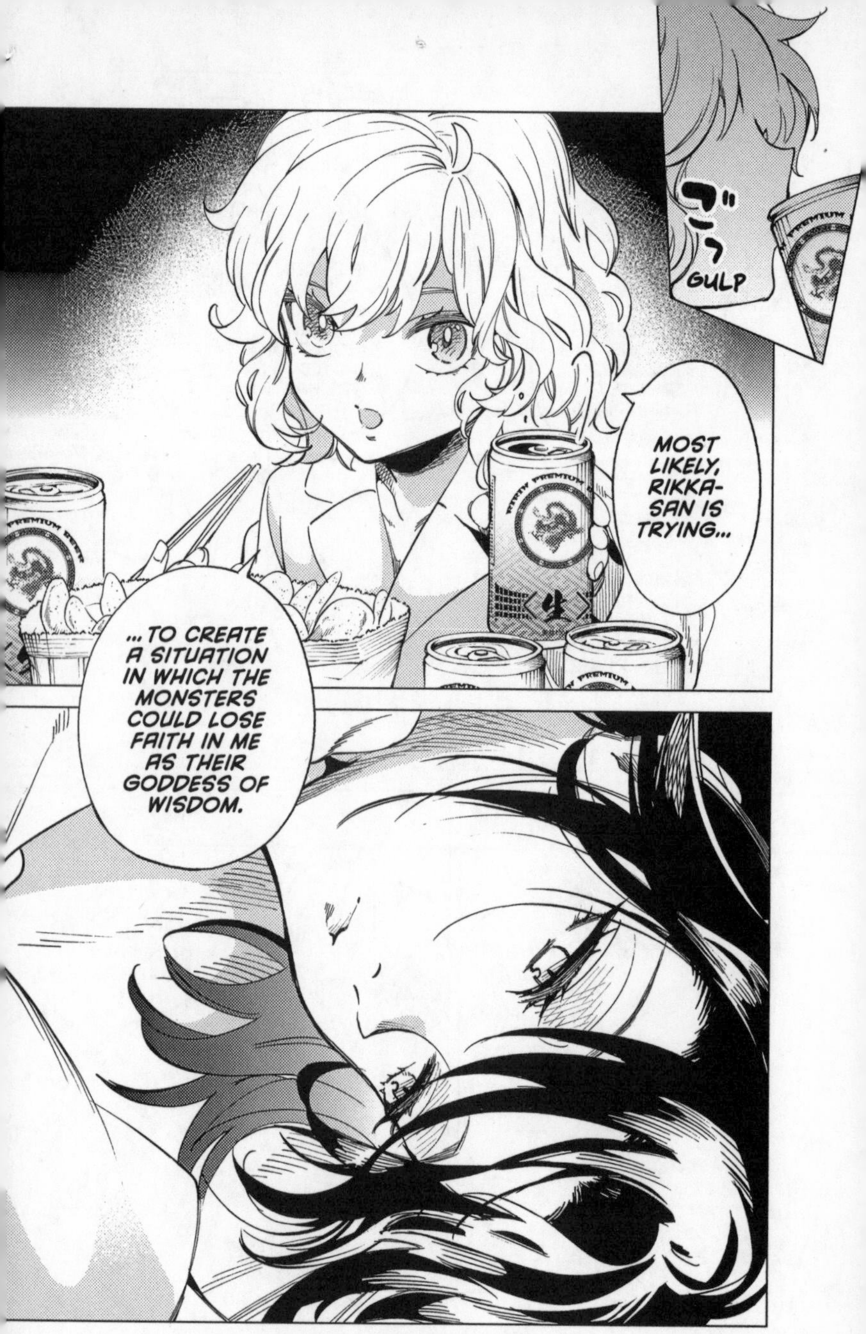
GULP
MOST LIKELY, RIKKA-SAN IS TRYING...
...TO CREATE A SITUATION IN WHICH THE MONSTERS COULD LOSE FAITH IN ME AS THEIR GODDESS OF WISDOM.

TO BE CONTINUED IN VOLUME 16

IN/SPECTRE

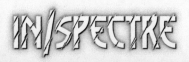

I am the author, Kyo Shirodaira, and this is volume 15. In this volume, we reveal the overall background of the case. The threads connecting the giraffe, the humans, and Rikka and Iwanaga are just so tangled and intricate.

In normal mystery stories, a lot of time is spent gathering information and finding clues, but in this series, the murder victims can come back to life and talk about the crime, and the detective gets ghosts and monsters to collect information for her, so we skip a lot of the actual investigation. But that doesn't make the cases any simpler.

In this particular case, several people, including Rikka-san, are all working to carry out their own plots, so there are many layers, not only of the threads connecting the various parties, but of the deduction and resolution, therefore it gets rather complicated. That may be because this mystery focuses less on who did it and why, and more on what exactly was being plotted that night.

Other authors, like Agatha Christie, have a fair amount of stories where the actual murder was extremely simple, but then characters other than the killer will make matters worse, or tamper with the investigation for their own interests. Then, as the situation becomes more complicated, the solution gets longer to resolve all those details. So this one isn't that exceptional as mystery stories go, but there is a scene where a giraffe ghost slams one of the female leads with its neck, so that claim of it being unexceptional may not hold much water, either.

A giraffe's neck is rather flexible, so it doesn't even need to move its legs to deftly swing its neck around and use its head to hit a target close to the ground with a fair amount of force. If a human were to be attacked in that way, I imagine they would be looking up at the giraffe's head when suddenly it flies at them from the side and crashes into them.

Giraffes are herbivores, so if you run into one in the wild, I doubt you'll be attacked unless you do something really bad, but if it did attack, I get the feeling it would be a very difficult animal to fight off. They're fast, they're big, and their legs are powerful enough to kill a lion with one kick. As stated earlier, an attack that involves swinging the neck would come from a trajectory you basically never see in everyday life, so you would have to be sufficiently wary. If you wanted to attack the giraffe yourself, you wouldn't be able to get close to it without being extremely careful, so it would be hard to reach vital spots like the head or torso.

In terms of how scary they are, carnivores like lions, bears, wolves, etc., may rank higher. Nevertheless, it seems to me that there are still ways to fight off those animals, and I think a giraffe would knock you down before you even knew what was happening, so they induce a different kind of fear.

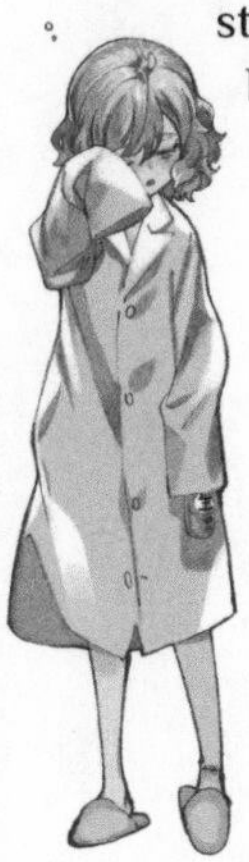

And if you were attacked by a lion or a bear and you won or got away from it, then you could brag about it, but it doesn't seem likely that you'd get a lot of respect if you told people you beat a giraffe. On the contrary, people would probably say, "Those creatures have such gentle eyes. If one attacked you, I think you're the problem." So everyone, let's all live our lives as purely and properly as possible, so we don't get attacked by passing giraffes.

In the next volume we should see Kotoko Iwanaga's retaliation. How will she find the truth in all these various schemes, and bring the case to its solution? And what does the "defeat" in the title mean?

I hope to see you again.

Kyo Shirodaira

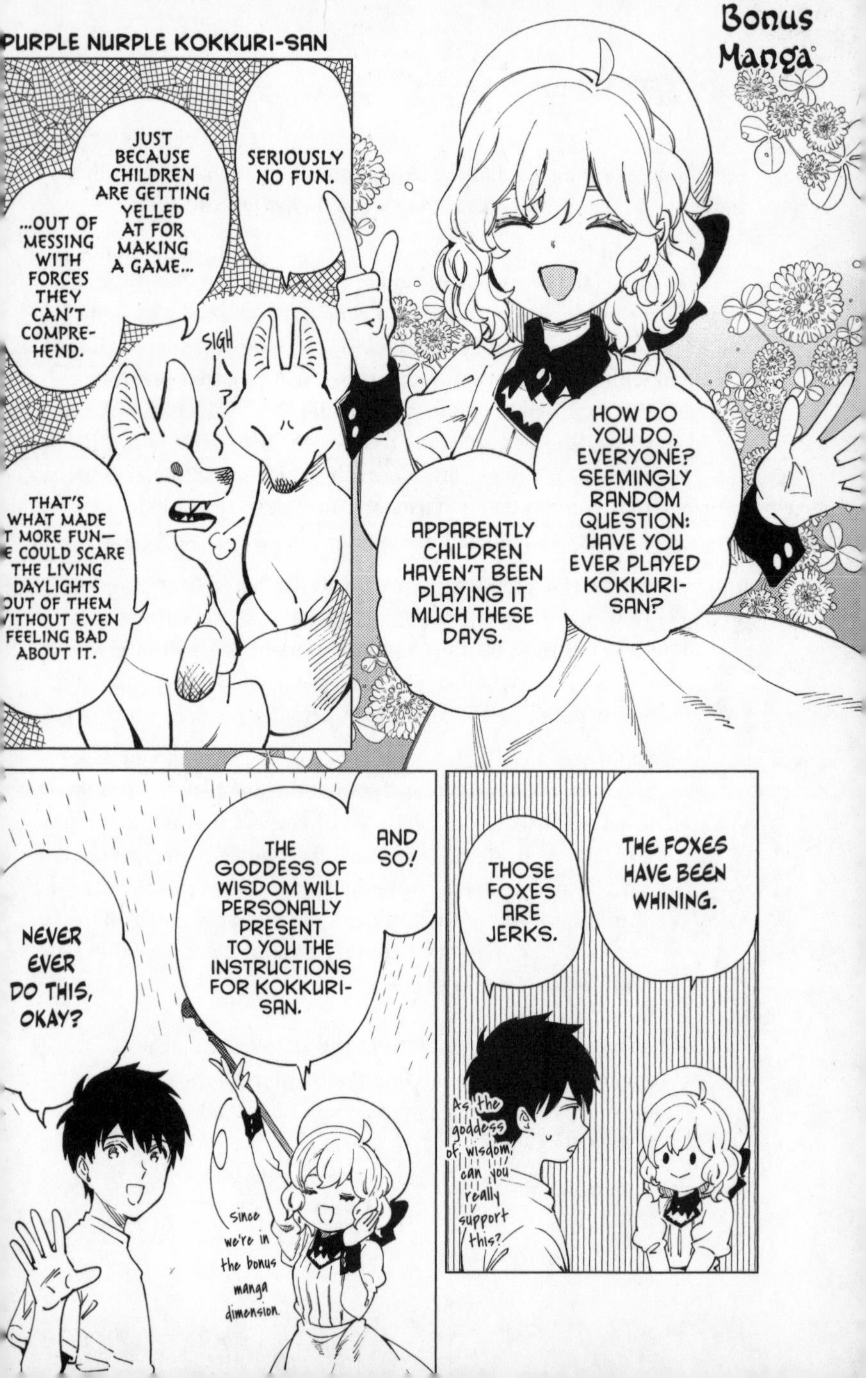

Bonus Manga
PURPLE NURPLE KOKKURI-SAN
HOW DO YOU DO, EVERYONE? SEEMINGLY RANDOM QUESTION: HAVE YOU EVER PLAYED KOKKURI-SAN?
APPARENTLY CHILDREN HAVEN'T BEEN PLAYING IT MUCH THESE DAYS.
SERIOUSLY NO FUN.
JUST BECAUSE CHILDREN ARE GETTING YELLED AT FOR MAKING A GAME...
...OUT OF MESSING WITH FORCES THEY CAN'T COMPRE-HEND.
SIGH
THAT'S WHAT MADE T MORE FUN— E COULD SCARE THE LIVING DAYLIGHTS OUT OF THEM VITHOUT EVEN FEELING BAD ABOUT IT.
THE FOXES HAVE BEEN WHINING.
THOSE FOXES ARE JERKS.
As the goddess of wisdom, can you really support this?
AND SO!
THE GODDESS OF WISDOM WILL PERSONALLY PRESENT TO YOU THE INSTRUCTIONS FOR KOKKURI-SAN.
since we're in the bonus manga dimension.
NEVER EVER DO THIS, OKAY?

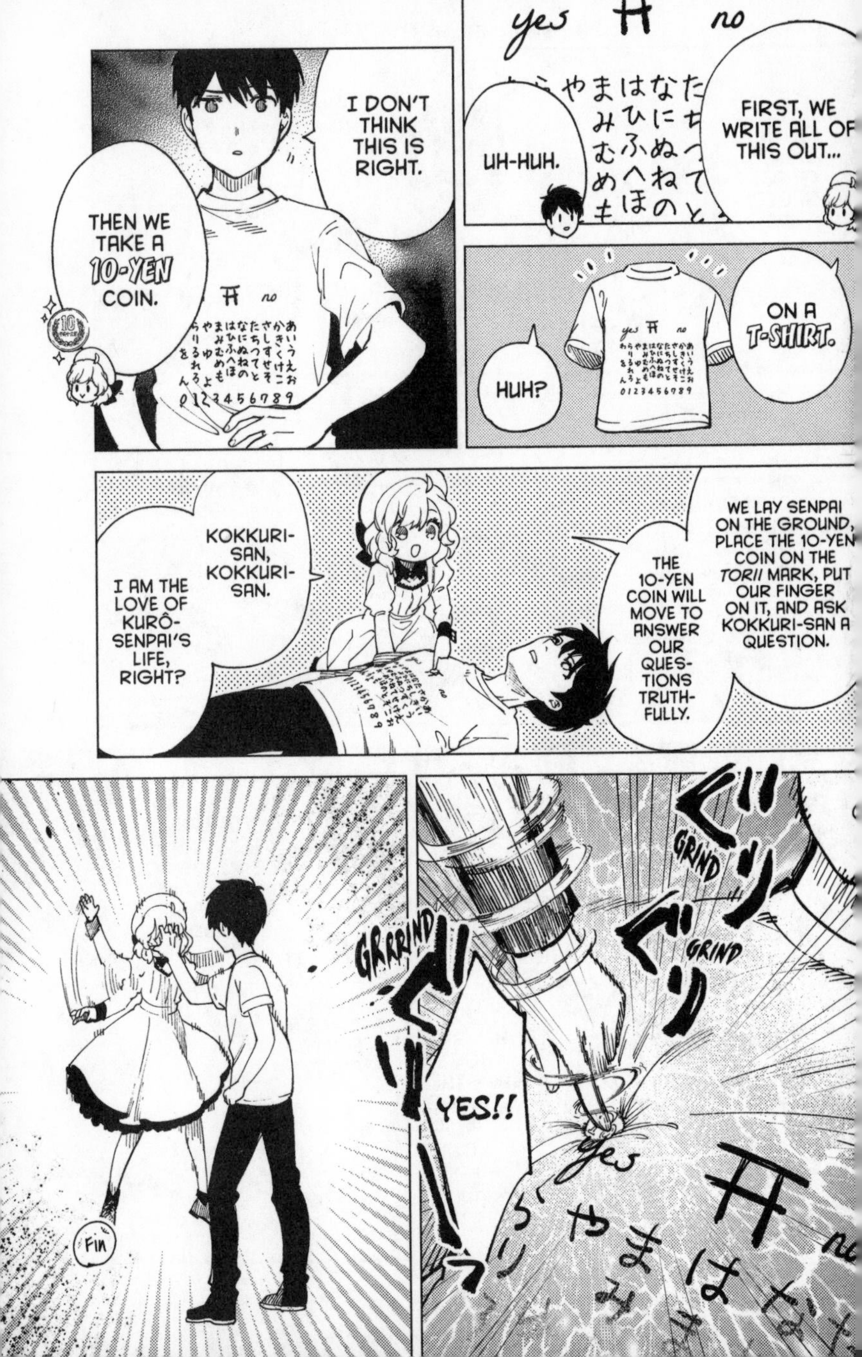
yes
no
FIRST, WE WRITE ALL OF THIS OUT...
UH-HUH.
ON A T-SHIRT.
HUH?
I DON'T THINK THIS IS RIGHT.
THEN WE TAKE A 10-YEN COIN.
WE LAY SENPAI ON THE GROUND, PLACE THE 10-YEN COIN ON THE *TORII* MARK, PUT OUR FINGER ON IT, AND ASK KOKKURI-SAN A QUESTION.
THE 10-YEN COIN WILL MOVE TO ANSWER OUR QUESTIONS TRUTHFULLY.
KOKKURI-SAN, KOKKURI-SAN.
I AM THE LOVE OF KURÔ-SENPAI'S LIFE, RIGHT?
GRIND
GRIND
GRRRIND
YES!!
yes
no
Fin

PARANORMAL ACTIVITY

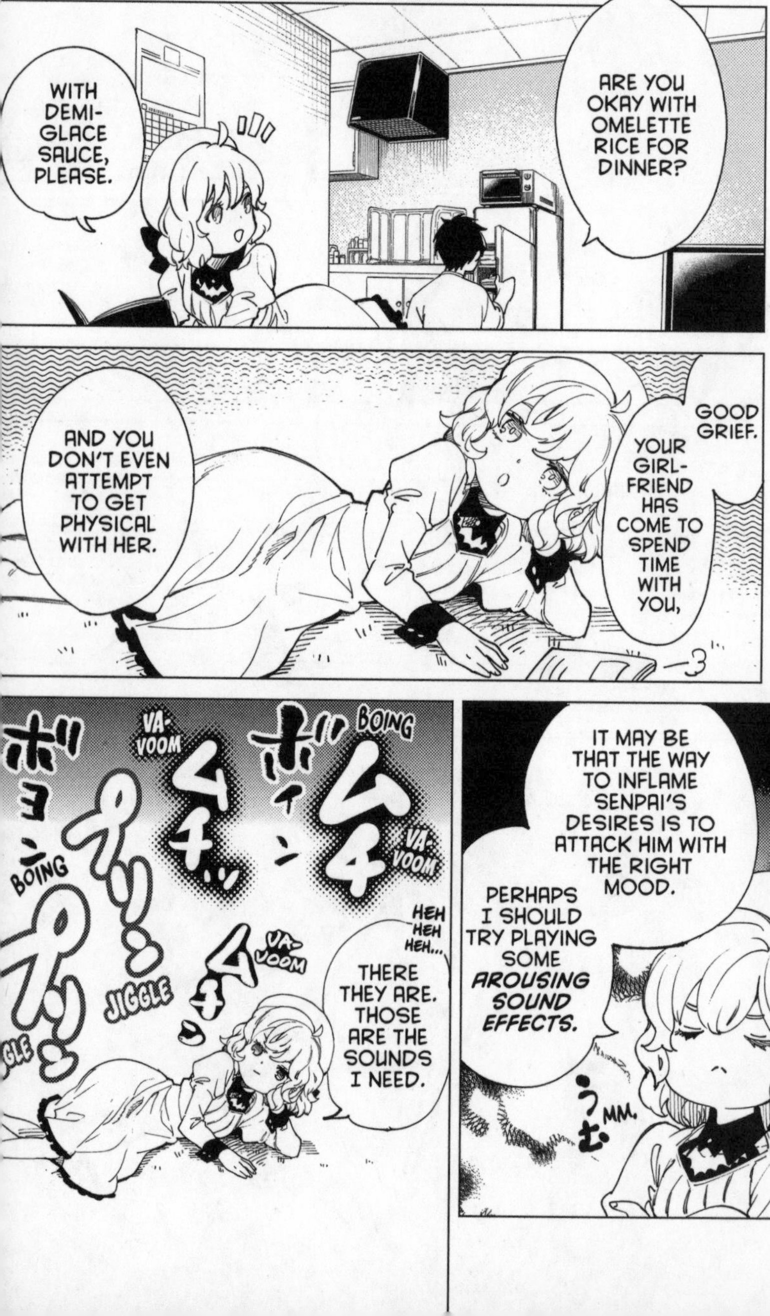
ARE YOU OKAY WITH OMELETTE RICE FOR DINNER?
WITH DEMI-GLACE SAUCE, PLEASE.
GOOD GRIEF.
YOUR GIRLFRIEND HAS COME TO SPEND TIME WITH YOU,
AND YOU DON'T EVEN ATTEMPT TO GET PHYSICAL WITH HER.
IT MAY BE THAT THE WAY TO INFLAME SENPAI'S DESIRES IS TO ATTACK HIM WITH THE RIGHT MOOD.
PERHAPS I SHOULD TRY PLAYING SOME *AROUSING SOUND EFFECTS.*
うむ MM.
BOING
VA-VOOM
VA-VOOM
BOING
VA-VOOM
JIGGLE
HEH HEH HEH...
THERE THEY ARE. THOSE ARE THE SOUNDS I NEED.

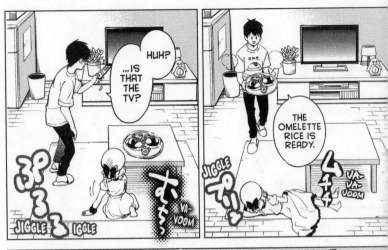

THE OMELETTE RICE IS READY.
JIGGLE
VA-VA-VOOM
HUH?
...IS THAT THE TV?
JIGGLE JIGGLE
VA-VOOM
JIGGLE
JIGGLE
VA-VOOM
VA-VOOM
BOI-OI-OING
TUMBLE
BOING
JIGGLE
VA-VOOM
IWA-NAGA!
JIGGLE
PA-POOF
WE HAVE A POLTER-GEIST!
Is there some really freaky yôkai nearby?!

FIN

Thank you for reading volume 15!
I hope you'll read the next one, too.

Staff
Asai Shimameguri Gomakuro
Nakamura Kujira

Editors
O-kawa T-da
(honorifics exclude

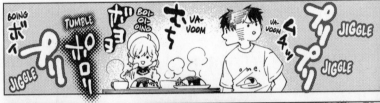

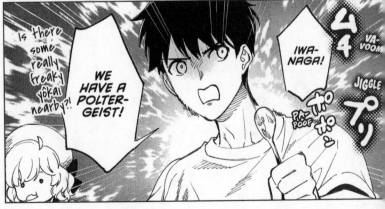

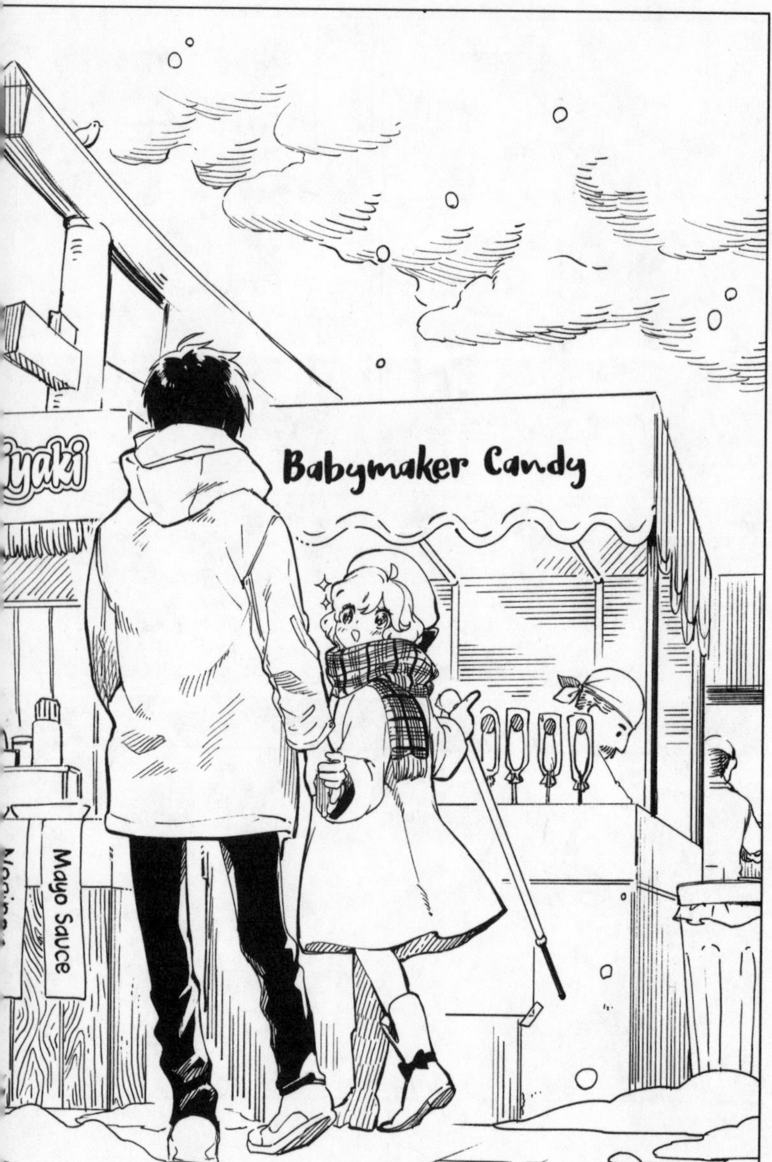
Babymaker Candy
Mayo Sauce

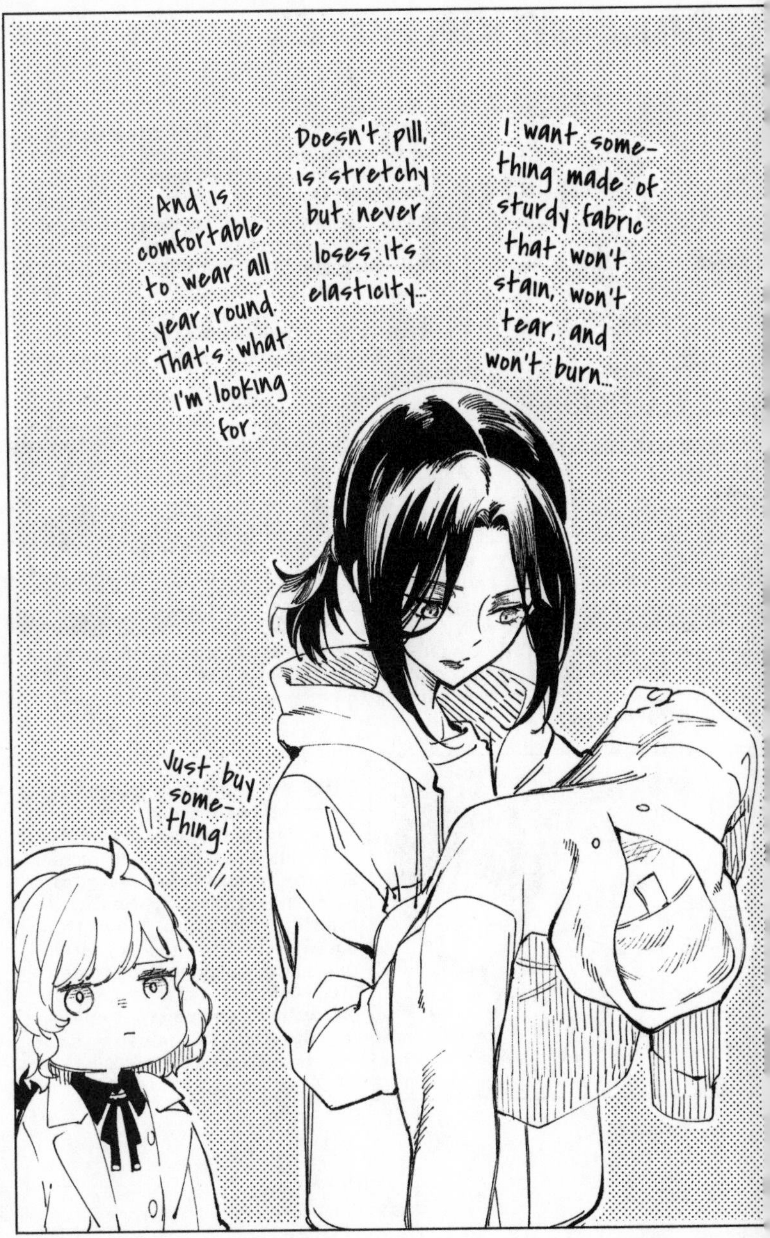
I want some-thing made of sturdy fabric that won't stain, won't tear, and won't burn...
Doesn't pill, is stretchy but never loses its elasticity...
And is comfortable to wear all year round. That's what I'm looking for.
Just buy some-thing!

# TRANSLATION NOTES

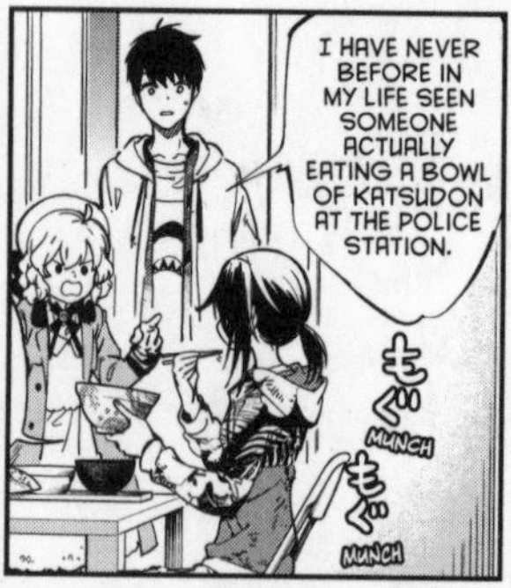
I HAVE NEVER BEFORE IN MY LIFE SEEN SOMEONE ACTUALLY EATING A BOWL OF KATSUDON AT THE POLICE STATION.
もぐ
MUNCH
もぐ
MUNCH

**Katsudon in a police station, page 6**

The common stereotype about police questioning in Japan is that, while being interrogated, the suspect will be given a bowl of katsudon (pork cutlets and egg on rice) to eat. This stereotype comes purely from movies and television, beginning with the 1955 film *Keisatsu Nikki (Policeman's Diary)*, and is not based in reality. In fact, it's not legal in Japan for police to offer any kind of food to their suspects, because it could be seen as trying to bribe a confession out of them.

**I have two legs, page 75**

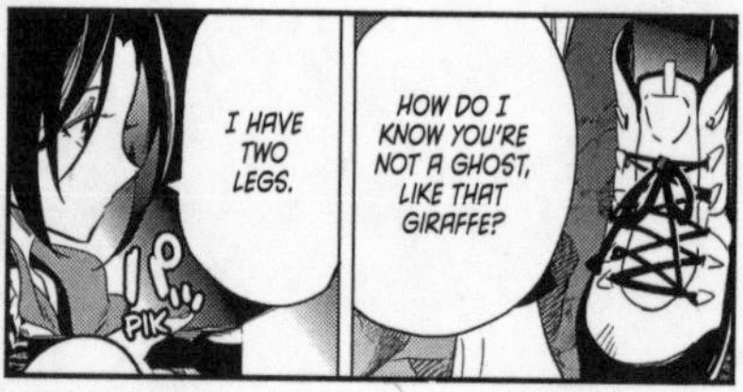
HOW DO I KNOW YOU'RE NOT A GHOST, LIKE THAT GIRAFFE?
I HAVE TWO LEGS.
PIK

Just as ghosts are commonly portrayed in Western media as something resembling a floating sheet, there is a stereotypical way to draw a ghost in Japan. They are more distinctly human than the floating sheets, and are typically wearing a white robe and a headband with a triangle on the forehead called a *tenkan*, which are traditional burial clothes. Furthermore, while the ghost maintains its human shape from the waist up, from the waist down, it fades away into a wispy nothingness. In other words, they have no feet or legs.

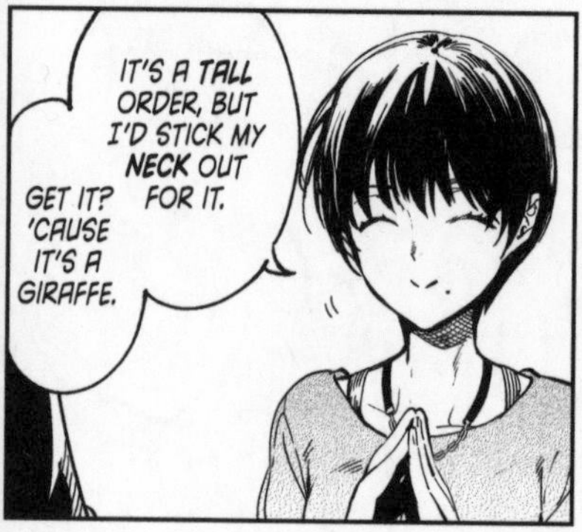
IT'S A TALL ORDER, BUT I'D STICK MY NECK OUT FOR IT.
GET IT? 'CAUSE IT'S A GIRAFFE.

**Stick my neck out, page 146**

A more standard translation of what Hiiragi said in the original Japanese is, "I'm waiting eagerly for that moment." She uses an idiom that means "to wait with eager anticipation" and translates literally to "to wait with out-stretched (lengthened) neck." One possible explanation for the origins of this idiom is that, when one waits for someone or something to arrive from afar, they stretch out their neck to get a better view.

**I don't think this is right, page 185**

As the reader may have gathered from Kotoko's instructions so far, Kokkuri-san is a Japanese version of the Ouija board. As such, it is usually performed on a piece of paper which is placed on a table, not a t-shirt.

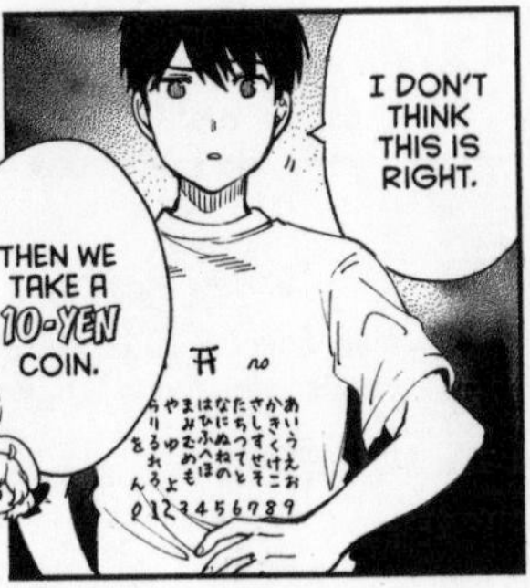
I DON'T THINK THIS IS RIGHT.
THEN WE TAKE A 10-YEN COIN.

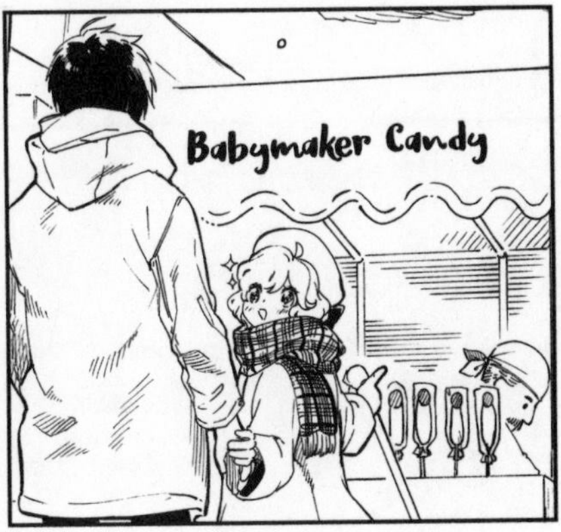
Babymaker Candy

**Babymaker candy, page 188**

This candy, the *kodakara-ame*, translates more literally to "children are a treasure candy." It is candy molded in a very specific shape, to resemble the parts of the human body used to create the treasure that is a child.

A Kodansha Comics Trade Paperback Original

*In/Spectre* 15 copyright © 2021 Kyo Shirodaira/Chashiba Katase
English translation copyright © 2022 Kyo Shirodaira/Chashiba Katase

Published in the United States by Kodansha Comics, an imprint of
Kodansha USA Publishing, LLC, New York.

Publication rights for this English edition arranged through
Kodansha Ltd., Tokyo.

First published in Japan in 2021 by Kodansha Ltd., Tokyo
as *Kyokou Suiri*, volume 15.

ISBN 978-1-64651-423-6

Original cover design by Takashi Shimoyama and Mami Fukunaga (RedRooster)

Printed in the United States of America.

www.kodansha.us

9 8 7 6 5 4 3 2 1
Translation: Alethea Nibley & Athena Nibley
Lettering: Lys Blakeslee
Editing: Cayley Last
Kodansha Comics edition cover design by Phil Balsman

Publisher: Kiichiro Sugawara

Director of publishing services: Ben Applegate
Associate director of publishing operations: Stephen Pakula
Publishing services managing editors: Alanna Ruse, Madison Salters
Production managers: Emi Lotto, Angela Zurlo